COBBLE CIRCLES AND STANDING STONES

COBBLE CIRCLES

AND STANDING STONES

Archaeology at the Rivas Site, Costa Rica

by Jeffrey Quilter

UNIVERSITY OF IOWA PRESS ⨆ IOWA CITY

University of Iowa Press, Iowa City 52242

Copyright © 2004 by the University of Iowa Press

All rights reserved

Printed in the United States of America

Design by April Leidig-Higgins

http://www.uiowa.edu/uiowapress

The publication of this book was generously supported by
the University of Iowa Foundation.

Printed on acid-free paper

Library of Congress Cataloging-in-Publication Data
Quilter, Jeffrey, 1949–   .
Cobble circles and standing stones: archaeology at the
Rivas Site, Costa Rica / by Jeffrey Quilter.
      p.   cm.
Includes bibliographical references and index.
ISBN 0-87745-876-6 (cloth), 0-87745-893-6 (paper)
      1. Rivas Site (Costa Rica).   2. Panteón de La Reina Site
(Costa Rica).   3. Indians of Central America—Costa
Rica—San Isidro de El General Region—Antiquities.
4. Excavations (Archaeology)—Costa Rica—San Isidro
de El General Region.   5. San Isidro de El General
Region (Costa Rica)—Antiquities.   I. Title.
F1545.1.S35Q55   2004
972.86'3—dc22   2003061116

04   05   06   07   08   C   5   4   3   2   1
04   05   06   07   08   P   5   4   3   2   1

For my father,
Thomas Quilter,
1905–1992

CONTENTS

Today, Costa Rica is well known as a peaceful little country, an island of stability in troubled Latin America, with a former president, Oscar Arias, a Nobel Peace Prize recipient. It is a popular destination for tourists seeking pristine beaches, unspoiled tropical forests, and friendly, accommodating people. While the reality of contemporary Costa Rica is more complex than what a sun-seeking tourist on a two-week vacation may see or experience, in many ways this small country does live up to its reputation as a prosperous, peaceful nation. But if modern and "natural" Costa Rica is well known, its native peoples, both past and present, are almost invisible. In the capital of San José, the National Museum, the Gold Museum, and the Jade Museum all have excellent exhibitions and receive substantial numbers of visitors to see prehistoric artifacts. Tourist shops are filled with replicas of ancient ceramics, gold jewelry, and jade pendants that fill the suitcases of returning visitors. But only one archaeological site, Guayabo de Turrialba, is developed for tourism, although many similar sites exist. While some tourists may be interested in Costa Rica's prehistory, no easily accessible book, in English or in Spanish, is available for them to gain basic knowledge of the distant past.

The museum tours and souvenir shops display curiosities of a past long dead and peoples now vanished. There is a disjunction between the prehistoric past as recognized in gold and jade artifacts and a vague awareness of the people who made them. Tourists, guides, and even Costa Rican nationals, or Ticos, as they are called, often treat the prehistoric era as one of mystery and of relatively little importance for the goals and values of a dynamic, modern nation.

This state of affairs is not due to an absence of archaeological research in Costa Rica. The country sustains an active group of hardworking professional archaeologists who often conduct investigations under great difficulties and privations. The reasons for this national prehistorical amnesia are complex, but include the ways in which national identity has been built as well as the vague sense of inferiority when comparing the local antiquities with the pyramids of Mesoamerica to the north or the great constructions of the Andes to the south.

This book does not attempt to provide a comprehensive survey of the peoples and cultures of ancient Costa Rica. But while it concentrates, for the most part, on only two sites, I hope that it will demonstrate that the prehistory of this little country is fascinating and fully deserving of appreciation and study as much as any of the more flamboyant cultures of the New World. In fact, there is plenty of flamboyance in the prehistory of Costa Rica, which is to ancient Mesoamerica as a Japanese tea cup is to a Ming vase. The latter is easily recognized for its beauty, richness, and extravagant decoration. The former requires that the viewer be educated in order to appreciate the thing observed, but once instructed, the trained eye sees marvels.

The sites in question are Rivas and its neighbor, the Panteón de La Reina, high in the General Valley on the Pacific slopes of the Talamanca Mountain range. Once, Rivas was a place renowned throughout a vast region. Now, the great ceremonial center is covered in coffee fields, and cattle graze where crowds of people once danced and sang. In 1992 I came to conduct an archaeological project and hired a few local men and boys to dig. The project grew into a much grander operation than anyone may have conceived when the first shovelful of earth was turned. Other project members and I kept coming back regularly for more work in the succeeding six years.

This book tells what we found at Rivas, how we went about finding it, and what we now think about the site and its builders and users. It is written chronologically, starting with my first trip to Costa Rica and continuing to only a couple of years before publication of this book. I have chosen to write in a narrative voice because I think it is the best way to convey the information I want to present here. Too often, in books such as this, only the results of research are presented, while the ways in which those results were reached are never mentioned. This leads to a style of writing and presentation of material commonly told in the passive voice and the implication that the work was conducted with military precision.

All of my experience suggests that the practice of archaeology and its results are inextricably entwined and that on almost every project lasting for more than a few days, serendipity plays an important role in the work and its results. Perhaps other archaeologists are much more disciplined and organized than I am, though I suspect not many are. In the Rivas project, while we had a definite research goal in mind and a strategy for reaching that goal, the tactics that we took

frequently were shaped by our field experiences. The role of serendipity is not simply the commonly assumed "spectacular" find, stumbled upon in the jungle or unearthed on the last day of fieldwork. That can happen. But one may simply stub a toe on a mundane object and then think about that chance encounter for years afterward before a "eureka" moment occurs. Or it can be a series of unexpected, sometimes disappointing field investigations that gradually lead to a new interpretation of a site. Chance incidents or discoveries or disappointing work only have value when they are reflected upon. I want to convey how that process of discovery and the adjustment of our research program were carried out in our work because they are part of the same process.

There is also the story of the people who worked at Rivas. This tale could be told separately from the account of our research. But that research was lived in the interactions of people: foreigners and locals, archaeologists and farmers. We managed to keep our overall goals in view, but the ways in which various people interacted with one another did have an effect on how the work was done. Furthermore, there are some great stories in this work that I just can't resist telling. They are tales that perhaps may make archaeologists, including myself, look foolish sometimes, but I also hope they show the sincerity, dedication, heartache, and joy with which archaeology is carried out.

I want to keep the personal and professional parts of the story of our project together, and that is why I wrote this book. I hope that it will be of interest to both professionals and a more general audience. A second book is in development that will provide technical information in the somewhat more dry tones of scientific discussion for the specialists who want to know the fine details of our work and its results.

The number of people I have to thank for helping do the work and write this book is huge. I cannot fully express how deeply grateful I am to them for making a significant portion of my life and career not only rewarding but joyous. Although at times it was hot and dusty and at other times soaking wet, Costa Rica is a gorgeous place of stupendous natural beauty, and its people, especially the people of Rivas and San Isidro, are unmatched in their generosity of heart and spirit. Although we had innumerable problems and were scared out of our wits at times, we were welcomed and helped by many. There was danger, high adventure, the thrill of discovery, many good times, some pretty bad ones, and the making of warm and long-lasting friendships. Who could ask for more? I can't thank my Costa Rican hosts and all of the people who worked in and around the Rivas project enough.

Although the number of people to thank is great, there are several who deserve special recognition here. Robert P. Drolet, with his infectious enthusiasm for Costa Rican archaeology, was the chief instigator of my taking the step into the field. Once I was there, John Hoopes warmly welcomed me, introduced me to a host of Costa Rican colleagues, and offered much sound advice. The staff of the San José offices of the Associated Colleges of the Midwest Latin American Program were crucial in helping me with all manner of logistical matters and general support. While a succession of directors of that office were kind and generous in their attentions, Phil Dennis, in particular, was supportive above and beyond the call of duty. Other North American colleagues who offered valuable support included Payson Sheets, Fred Lange, Richard Burger, and Anna Roosevelt.

An archaeological project, like an army, moves on its belly. Funds for beans and rice, shovels and picks, radiocarbon dates, and worker paychecks are essential. The various granting agencies that funded the Rivas project are most gratefully thanked. Those funds might never have been forthcoming, however, if it had not been for the generosity of James Bankard, who at the time was president of the Continental Coffee Corporation. For the most crucial years of the project, he provided generous financial support that was vital for the work itself and for matching funds. The National Endowment for the Humanities provided the greatest sum of money that made this project possible. Additional grants were awarded to the project by the National Geographic Society, the Wenner Gren Foundation, and the Heinz Foundation. Project funds were skillfully managed by Mark Lindquist of Ripon College. Mark went to great lengths to get our money to us in Costa Rica, often entangling himself in complicated reams of red tape but always successfully cutting through it in the end. Special thanks must go to the Floatograph Company, which offered us one of its bal-

loon camera systems at a very low price. This equipment not only produced beautiful pictures but also very valuable ones for our research. The Gold Bug manufacturers also are thanked for the price reduction they offered on their equipment.

For our time in the field, no thanks are enough for the members of the Mora and Mata families. It was their land and their lives upon which we intruded, yet they welcomed us and worked beside us. Our project would never have succeeded, however, without the people who transformed the bits and pieces of other people's garbage into the chapters in this book. My comrades in arms, especially William Doonan, R. Jeffrey Frost, Christopher Raymond, and Lawrence Conyers, have my thanks from the bottom of my heart. Great services also were rendered by Gabriela Castro, Paul Dolata, Andrew Gordon, Bryan Just, Bellina Kweskin, Matthew Reynolds, and James Schumacher. The Rivas research would have been an important project no matter what, but it was a great experience because of the fine people I was able to call colleagues and friends. Jennifer Ringberg came late to the project but proved invaluable in the fine research she conducted and in her beautiful illustrations, many of which grace this book. John Jones and Dolores Piperno analyzed pollen and phytoliths and are gratefully thanked. William Conklin also was most kind in analyzing our one trace of textile from Rivas. A number of visitors also enlivened our times; they are too many to name, but all are thanked.

Aida Blanco's generosity, in so many ways, was the special ingredient in the mix of people and things that was the Rivas project "salsa." All of the North Americans and Costa Ricans involved in the field and laboratory phases of the project owe her a special debt of gratitude. It has been a privilege and pleasure to know Aida and to work with her, and I thank her for all she has done for the project and for me. She was aided by Giselle Mora and other members of the Museo del Sur staff. Edwin Montenegro Cedeno and Olman Vargas Azofeifa were particularly helpful with their extensive labors in the laboratory, and the former did outstanding work in illustrating many sherds. Other Costa Ricans who were kind and generous included Francisco Corrales, Eugenia Ibarra, Carlos Rojas, and Miguel Espinosa.

At Ripon College, my fellow anthropologist Paul

Axelrod was of great help in discussing the site with me, as were Leslie Bessant and Robert Melville. Eugene and Evelyn Kain also were kind and generous in their conversations and enthusiasm for my work.

Most of the field research described in this book took place while I was a professor at Ripon College. But most of this book was written after I moved from central Wisconsin to Garrett Park, Maryland, and began my position as director of Pre-Columbian Studies and curator of the Pre-Columbian Collection at Dumbarton Oaks, in Washington, D.C. At Dumbarton Oaks, I owe special thanks to my colleagues, Loa Traxler, assistant curator; Jennifer Younger, curatorial assistant; and four successive assistants to the director: Janice Williams, Rebecca Willson, Cecilia Montalvo, and Kristy Keyes. I offer a very special thanks to Bridget Gazzo, library specialist for Pre-Columbian Studies, who helped in many bibliographic matters. I also could not ask for a better colleague than Michel Conan, director of Garden and Landscape Studies at Dumbarton Oaks. Michel has been helpful to me in many ways, especially in his encouragement to me as I wrote this book.

Because of my pleasure in working with the staff of the University of Iowa Press when I published my first book, *Life and Death at Paloma: Society and Mortuary Practices in a Preceramic Peruvian Village*, I was pleased when the opportunity to join forces arose again. I offer my very special thanks to Director and Editor in Chief Holly Carver, to Charlotte Wright, and to my copyeditor, Robert Burchfield, for their enthusiasm for this project, their great attention to detail, and their valiant efforts in the task of turning a manuscript into a book, which is no mean task, indeed.

My family—Sarah, my wife, and my children, Susanna and Betsy—were essential in the success of the project. I want to thank them, especially, for their patience while I was away from home and for being "troopers" in coming to participate in the project in 1993. Also, my mother, Joan Quilter, was a supporter and booster of my life and work long before, throughout, and after this project, and I thank her for all of the support through all of the years.

My last meeting with my father, Thomas Quilter, was shortly before I left for the 1992 field season. I regret that he only was able to learn of the very beginnings of this project, but I am thankful that he was pleased to know of my excitement about the site and what it had to offer. His and my mother's enthusiasm for my work and their support of me continues to carry me through good times and bad. I dedicate this book to him.

COBBLE CIRCLES AND STANDING STONES

CHAPTER ONE

GETTING THERE

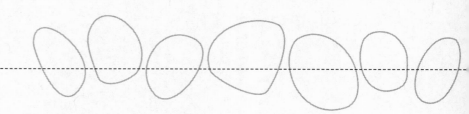

From the Coca Cola to the General

The name of the central bus station in San José is derived from Costa Rica's Coca Cola bottling plant. The "Coca Cola" is not a single building but rather a section of the city streets near the central market. Different bus companies with routes to one part of the country or another are found in separate complexes of large open-air garages, waiting areas, restaurants, shops, and the streets themselves. The place is in a constant state of high energy as everything from modern luxury coaches, as tall as the buildings, to rickety, repainted U.S. school buses arrive and depart in smoke and noise. The exhaust fumes of idling buses mix with the odors of human sweat and dust or, in the rainy season, mildew.

Bus travel is the primary means of transportation for all but the wealthiest Costa Ricans and tourists. The sidewalks are crowded. Pickpockets elbow their way through clumps of prim schoolgirls and grandmothers. Long-haired Californian blonds lug their huge, sheathed surfboards down the streets. Lottery ticket sellers jostle with Canadian ecotourists, European latter-day hippies, American Latter-Day Saints, and, occasionally, archaeologists.

Two bus lines service travel on the Panamerican Highway south to San Isidro de El General, one of the largest cities of the Southern Zone of Costa Rica (fig. 1.1). From there, one can continue on to Buenos Aires, the other main city of the Southern Zone, or to Panama, or stop and take a short ride from San Isidro to smaller, nearby towns, such as Rivas.

From early in the morning to late into the evening, buses leave the Coca Cola for San Isidro. The touring coaches are big, lumbering things. The passengers sit high above the road, perched on top of a spacious luggage compartment. The doors of the luggage compartment are carefully guarded until the last minute by the bus driver's assistant. He shoves taped-up cardboard boxes, stuffed plastic bags, and suitcases into the space with great authority at a frantic pace, like what one might expect of an officer assigning lifeboat seats on the *Titanic*. People line up in the narrow space between the bus and the walls of the garage, piling on a few minutes before departure. Heat, humidity, and

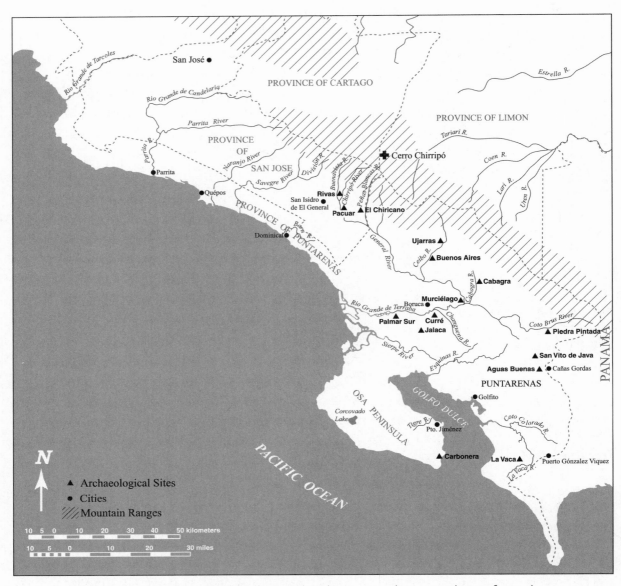

1.1. Southern Pacific Costa Rica with archaeological sites and modern towns and cities. Map by Jennifer Ringberg.

human body odors reach record levels in the bus. Three or four clouds of different perfumes are rising off of young women to waft through the bus like small-scale chemical attacks. Pomade floats around the heads of several men like the halos of saints, though saints they likely are not. Even though seats are assigned when tickets are purchased, there always seems to be much fussing by one person or another in trying to get settled, adding to the discomfort. Babies are wailing, grandmothers are yelling out the window to the families they are leaving. In addition to the driver's radio, another two or three are blasting several different vigorous Latin melodies simultaneously.

There are 12 rows of seats, arranged 2 by 2 on each side of the aisle with 5 seats at the back, totaling 53 altogether. For anyone over five and a half feet in height, there is insufficient legroom, and one must either sit with knees splayed or extended into the aisle. The driver is the last to board. He adjusts his salsa-playing radio and his sunglasses, and the bus roars off, swinging out into the narrow street.

A considerable amount of time is spent winding through the avenues of San José to reach the main highway. Depending on city traffic, about 15 minutes pass before reaching the four-lane highway that heads south. Driving through the Central Valley, after half an hour the bus reaches the outskirts of Cartago. This was the country's old capital, founded in 1563 but rocked by earthquakes and finally abandoned in 1823. Although nearby San José became the new capital, Cartago is still renowned for its famous statuette of the Black Virgin and the rock on which she was found, and it remains a center of pilgrimage for people throughout Costa Rica and beyond.

Just outside Cartago, the bus veers right toward the Talamanca mountain range that is part of the great cordillera stretching from Alaska to Patagonia and which borders the southern and western rim of the Central Valley. Cutting across the Central Valley takes only 15 minutes, and the bus passes the beautiful Hacienda Cartago, with its brilliant green grass fields and prized horses. On the other side of the road are new factories and newer housing developments. Less than an hour into the journey, four lanes become two, and the bus begins to climb the slopes of the mountains. A sign reads 108 kilometers to San Isidro.

Once, at this point in the trip, I decided I would count the number of curves in the mountainous part of the journey. After about half an hour I gave up because the road seemed to consist of nothing but turns in a continuous climb. The quick ascent turns the houses of Cartago in the valley below to a mosaic of white splotches on a green background. The view of the city is brief, however, because once out of the populous valley, tropical forest crowds the road.

The highway straightens somewhat higher up in the journey, though it continues to snake along ridge-tops and around peaks. The bus successively passes through the tropical forest characteristic of the high altitude of the Central Valley, through cloud forest with twisted trees and Spanish moss, to the highest zone with bushy vegetation and areas of short grass known as *páramo*. This is the northernmost extension of the *páramo* environmental zone widely found throughout the northern Andes.

At the apogee of the trip, the air is thin and cool, and bus passengers don sweaters and jackets. They say that you can see both oceans from these heights on a clear day. But clear days are rare, and even in the best weather it is hard to know if the distant shimmer through the clouds is ocean or sky. Depending on the time of year, the mountaintops are shrouded in chilly, damp fog in the rainy season or wrapped in an intense blue sky in dry times. If not completely enshrouded in fog, the mountain ridges afford a spectacular view of clouds rolling far below like tufts of whipped cream. At other times, the clouds form before your eyes, rising out of the forest in long, feathery trails.

The highest part of the road passes by the Cerro de la Muerte, the Mountain of Death, at an altitude of 3,491 meters above sea level. Different versions of how the peak got its name abound. One common story is that horses died from the cold when earlier travelers camped in the heights; some say it was the men. No matter what the specifics, temperatures can hover near freezing at night in these high altitudes, and even today foot travelers say that layers of ice in water buckets are not uncommon in the mornings.

After more than an hour on the ridge, the bus starts its descent. As in the ascent, numerous switchbacks, steep drop-offs, near misses with oncoming vehicles, desperate passings of slower vehicles, and the liberal application of brakes add excitement to the journey. Buses are only occasionally lost. Still, the reroutings of traffic around sections of collapsed and vanished highway, sometimes 20 meters in length or more, are reminders that the region is tectonically active. Sometimes the trip is slowed because an avalanche of unstable earth has completely blocked the highway, and bulldozers must be called in from the nearest big town, either Cartago or San Isidro. If one hasn't been on the bus for a few months, the trip is always interesting because at least some part of the highway is entirely new due to extensive road losses and repairs.

In descent, temperature and humidity increase. Off come the jackets, sweaters, and coats. In the dry season, from December through March, the altitudinal differences in temperature and humidity can be great enough to cause heavy condensation on the bus windshield and foggy areas on the road, adding more excitement to the trip, especially at night.

Despite these various concerns, the journey usually is smooth and easy. Costa Rica maintains its section of the Panamerican Highway in very good condition compared to many countries in Latin America. And so, in slightly less than three hours, the bus groans its way down the Pacific side of the mountains in low gear and lumbers into San Isidro de El General.

In the last half an hour or so of the trip, the bus wends its way along the southern edge of a valley that holds the Quebradas River. This system is part of a number of parallel tributaries of the General River. Slowly descending on the valley edge, the bus passes under a huge white concrete statue of Christ, arms spread wide to bless the valley. Farther down, roadside entrepreneurs sell bags of oranges or avocados, when in season. Finally, the bus stops at the San Isidro bus station—a wide, dusty, gravel driveway running a short city block in length in front of two bus garages—and we have arrived in San Isidro de El General.

The Upper General Valley

I have taken the bus trip to and from San Isidro more than a dozen times in the last decade. Each time it is an adventure, and each time I marvel at Costa Rica's natural wonders. Although Costa Rica is a tiny nation by almost any standard, the Talamanca mountain range divides the land into distinct zones (fig. 1.1). The Central Valley is the smallest of these regions and has prominence mostly because the capital city is located there. It seems to share much with the larger region to the east and north, the Atlantic Watershed. To the west, the mountains effectively cut off the Nicoya Peninsula and the adjacent plains of Guanacaste province into an isolated region. The foothills of the mountains spill down to the Pacific in the middle of the country and join with the Coastal Range. To the south and east lies the Zona Sur (Southern Zone), and San Isidro de El General is at the upper end of the long General Valley that is the main geographic feature of this region. These large geographical regions also serve as references for archaeological zones and are referred to by the same names.

The General River Valley is one of the longest fluvial systems in Lower Central America but only covers about 100 kilometers in stream length (figs. 1.1, 1.2). About two-thirds of the way to the ocean, the General River is joined by the Coto Brus, and the stream turns southwestward, renamed the Térraba River. Passing through a low point in the Coastal Range of hills, the river slows and fans into a broad wetland, known as the Diquís Delta, and melts into the Pacific. In archaeological terms, the Southern Zone, mostly comprising the General–Coto Brus, their tributaries, and the Diquís, is referred to as the Diquís subregion. This sub-

region and areas of adjacent Panama comprise the Greater Chiriquí Region (Drolet 1983, 1984a,b, 1986, 1988).

The traveler stopping in San Isidro can easily take a bus on well-paved roads to destinations farther south or to the nearest coastal town, Dominical, 25 kilometers away. Smaller, less well maintained local roads can take the traveler to a number of pleasant spots in Pérez Zeledón, the district surrounding the city proper, named after a nineteenth-century explorer. This ease of road of travel to San Isidro and neighboring towns is a relatively recent phenomenon. The stretch of the Panamerican Highway that brings the traveler from San José to San Isidro was only completed during World War II, as part of the effort to keep open lines of transportation in the Americas. When the road was first completed, it took eight hours to make the trip by vehicle, and travelers would pack lunches for picnics during rest stops in the heights. In air miles, the distance between the two cities is only 70 kilometers. Thus from about the 1930s through the 1970s the most common way for people who could afford it was to travel by air, a trip of less than an hour in a propeller-driven aircraft. For those without the means to travel high above the terrain, however, the journey was long and arduous. Alexander Skutch (1991), the pioneering naturalist, describes the beauties and the troubles of walking for five days from the upper General Valley to Cartago.

When Skutch and others made their trips by foot, they did not travel through the Quebradas drainage. Rather, they used a valley parallel to it, one that contains the stream that enlarges at lower altitudes to become the General River. This valley is the route taken today by visitors who wish to scale the highest peak in Costa Rica, Cerro Chirripó (3,820 meters). Branching off from the route to Chirripó is a path to the Central Valley that, though arduous, is the best way to walk there. It is likely that this was the ancient route of people from the Pacific slope to the Central Valley and the Atlantic Watershed. This crucial juncture in the upper General Valley system is the same point where two rivers, the Río Buenavista and the Río Chirripó del Pacífico, intersect to form the Río General. Rivers and paths both join immediately below a high, narrow ridge called the Panteón de La Reina, extending out

1.2. The upper General Valley. The Panteón de La Reina is the dark ridge, in the middle distance. The Rivas site is on the other side of the ridge, while the town of Rivas is on the far left.

from the foothills. On one side of the ridge lies the modern town of Rivas and on the other, the archaeological site of the same name (fig. 1.2).

Today, the upper General Valley is south of the chain of active volcanoes that ends in Central America at Mt. Irazú, overlooking San José. But in the Pliocene and Pleistocene epochs, before humans were present, there was a tremendous amount of geological activity throughout the region. Intensive volcanic activity erupted and injected massive amounts of lava onto the landscape. Sometime in the last few hundred thousand years, this area of Costa Rica became volcanically inactive but still tectonically active. Motion of the oceanic plates, offshore in the Pacific, continued, and uplift of the Talamancan cordillera intensified. Coupled with this uplift, rivers flowing from the mountains to the sea intensified their activities, creating periodic floods capable of transporting huge boulders from the highlands down to the General Valley. Periodic down-cutting produced a series of river terraces, each containing river and floodplain sediments, with the higher terraces holding progressively older deposits.

In the last of such erosion and deposition cycles, about 10,000 years ago, a 150-meter layer of sediment in the upper valley was scoured away by a massive flood. One locale where thick deposits remained was the protected area in front of a spur of the Talamanca mountain range. As the young, red sediments of desiccated andesite were washed away in the channels of what became the Ríos Buenavista and Chirripó del Pacífico,

this tongue of soil was shaped and somewhat stabilized into a ridge that is now called the Panteón de La Reina.

Many thousands of years after the volcanic activity, the ridge attracted local peoples as a place to bury their dead. It held several attractions as a cemetery. It was in a beautiful place. Standing on the ridge today, in clear weather and looking downstream, a vista is presented of the valley broadening to the west and swinging southward, while in the far distance lies the Coastal Range, beyond San Isidro, topped by frothy clouds. Another advantage was that the soils were deep and easy to dig, without the shallow topsoil and rocky matrix of many areas in the valley. Finally, this place likely was seen as sacred. In South America, at least, a place where two things come together, a *tinkuy*, in Quechua (Harrison 1989), has a specially charged sacred power, and that concept likely was held by the people of this part of Costa Rica. Rivers in themselves are powerful and carried many symbolic meanings in ancient America, so this ridge almost certainly was believed to be a place of great spiritual power.

Within the forest that today covers the ridge, numerous pavements of cobbles and traces of walls are found. This suggests that the people who used the ridgetop as a cemetery either encountered it clear of trees or, more likely, cleared it themselves. There may have been periods of deforestation in Costa Rica at various times in the past, with the forest returning as populations decreased or moved elsewhere (Hoopes 1996a).

Those people who buried their dead here likely were not newcomers to the region but rather the descendants of folk who had occupied the land for millennia.

Native Peoples of Costa Rica

We have scanty evidence of the earliest human occupants of any part of Central America. Enough information exists to indicate that the first inhabitants likely were in the general vicinity 10,000 years ago, the standard date for the presence of humans in most of the New World. Paleo-Indian artifacts have been found in the Atlantic Watershed zone (Snarskis 1979), so that Pleistocene megafauna—odd varieties of camel-like creatures, giant sloths, and other animals now extinct—may also have been in southern Costa Rica, though whether they were contemporaneous with the first humans is uncertain.

Hundreds of human generations passed, leaving little trace of their presence on the landscape. People were few in number. They gathered and hunted their food from what nature provided and made both the necessities and luxuries of life mostly out of perishable materials that have since disappeared in the tropical environment. Although neighboring Chiriquí province in western Panama has an archaeological record stretching to the Preceramic period, with dates as early as 4600 B.C. for the Talamanca phase (Linares and Ranere 1980: 29), no equivalent dates are known for Costa Rica, mostly due to lack of research.

The evidence for the earliest village life in Costa Rica is much better for Nicoya-Guanacaste (Lange 1993) and central and Atlantic Costa Rica (Snarskis 1992) than it is for the Southern Zone. In Greater Nicoya, stretching from Costa Rica into Nicaragua, the Zoned Bichrome period (1000 B.C.–A.D. 500) was a time of small villages, the inhabitants of which practiced a mixed subsistence strategy of gathering, hunting, collecting, and a little agriculture. They had cemeteries separate from their small communities. As the period name suggests, ceramics were often decorated with two distinct zones of color. Engraving into the soft clay before firing was an additional technique; further elaboration sometimes was done in the form of added clay figures or heads, known as *adornos*, or other techniques.

In Central Costa Rica, the Pavas phase (Aguilar 1975,

1976) and El Bosque phase (Snarskis 1984) are slightly later than Greater Nicoya Zone Bichrome, dating from 300 B.C. to A.D. 500. The lifeways of the people represented by these archaeological culture names were similar to those of their northern contemporaries, although Michael Snarskis (1984: 144) believes that intensive maize agriculture was practiced. Bichrome and engraved ceramics were made with great skill and care. Spectacular "flying panel" metates, intricately carved out of hard volcanic rock, and gorgeous greenstone pendants and other lapidary work are all indications of an exuberant flourishing of crafts and culture.

There has been less research in southern Costa Rica than many places in the New World. Perhaps future work will show the same diversity in crafts and culture as in the country's other zones. Current evidence suggests much lower population densities, however, and less elaboration of stone work and ceramics. In the General River Valley, the Aguas Buenas culture, A.D. 200–600 (Haberland 1955; Drolet 1992; Hoopes 1996b), was contemporary with the later part of Zoned Bichrome to its north, the Bosque and Pavas phases in the Atlantic Watershed, and the Barriles and Bugaba phases to the east and south (Linares 1980). Near Rivas, a variant of Aguas Buenas, known as Quebradas, was identified a few years ago and was first thought to be earlier, though now it seems to be about the same age (Corrales 1986, 2000).

The varying fortunes of the people now abstracted as the Aguas Buenas culture are not well documented. Robert Drolet identified 49 hamlet and cemetery sites in the upper General Valley, suggesting a dense population, but only 5 sites (Las Brisas, Monge, Quebradas, Bolas, and Térraba) have been studied in any detail (Drolet 1992: 210–223). Traces or fragments of the more fancy goods known for Nicoya and across the Talamanca Mountains have been found at some of these sites, but no spectacular discoveries of elite burials or elaborate public architecture have yet been revealed for Aguas Buenas.

For hundreds of years the people of the Aguas Buenas culture lived out their lives in the region, preferring to live in small communities perched on the flanks of hills or tablelands overlooking valleys. They sometimes built small earthen mounds to bury important members of their communities, while lesser-ranking members of society were laid to rest in cemeteries nearby.

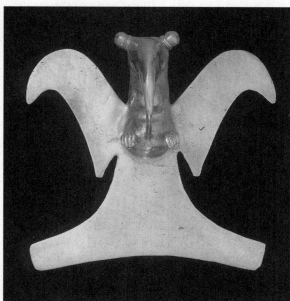

1.3. Jade and similar stones (1) were the first prestige materials used for pendants and other display items in Costa Rica. In many areas, especially the Southern Zone, hard stones later were replaced by gold as valued materials (2). Both objects shown here are from Dumbarton Oaks, Pre-Columbian Collection, Washington, D.C.

Objects of value and beauty included jewelry made of precious green jade or similar materials (fig. 1.3: 1). In this taste for jade, the people of Aguas Buenas were participating in a widespread cultural pattern stretching into Mesoamerica. In fact, most of the Costa Rican

jades appear to have been brought from lands far north of their final resting places (Lange 1993; Jones 1998; cf. Snarskis 2003). Southern Costa Rica is the southern limit of the culture of jade.

Beginning in various places sometime after A.D. 700 or so, new cultural patterns were becoming popular in Costa Rica. While there had been changes in house and ceramic styles in earlier times, large building projects were undertaken and great amounts of prestige goods produced. Though the quality of craftsmanship of some of the stonework and ceramics appears to have decreased, at least from the perspective of a modern viewer, the quantity may have increased. Large cobble mounds, plazas, and other features were entirely new, including long road systems that appear to have joined major sites with secondary centers. One such place was Las Mercedes in the Atlantic Watershed, the first extensively studied archaeological site, investigated by Carl Hartman (1901) at the turn of the nineteenth century. Another large complex was Guayabo de Turrialba, the only archaeological site developed for tourism in the country (Aguilar 1972; Chávez Chavéz 1993; Fonseca 1979).

With large spaces for the gathering of crowds, elevated mounds for pomp and circumstance, and large roadways, these sites were designed to impress the humble with the power and might of the elite and sometimes included stone sculptures of warriors with weapons or trophy heads. The formats of such complexes vary and their numbers are unknown, but there appear to have been many of them. This diversity and quantity suggest that the competition for followers was great and that the strategies for attracting them varied through time and space. Warfare, exchange systems, religious cults, and competitive feasting were probably employed in various combinations as local leaders or communities tried to extend their power and influence beyond the confines of their part of a valley or plain.

In the Southern Zone, culture change beginning around A.D. 700 and accelerating in the next two centuries was highly dramatic in almost a total abandonment of greenstone and the adoption of gold jewelry as prestige material (fig. 1.3: 2). Gold working spread as a technology and a value system from peoples farther south in Central America and, ultimately, from the Andean region (Bray 1981; Snarskis 2003). We have

1.4. The author next to a stone ball at the site of El Silencio in the Diquís Delta. At over 2 meters in diameter, this is one of the largest balls known and apparently has not been moved from its ancient location. The spalling on the ball and its dark color are due to heat generated by the burning of farm fields in its vicinity centuries after it was made.

no evidence nor do we have any reason to believe that new people arrived with the knowledge of gold working. Rather, the technology and the belief system associated with it appear to have moved northward by the spread of new social and ideological systems. In addition to gold jewelry, these new ways of thinking and behaving were expressed in new styles of pottery, stonework, and ceremonial centers, and long-distance trade likely increased.

Although few large-scale sites such as Las Mercedes and Guayabo de Turrialba have been identified in southern Costa Rica, there is ample evidence that ambitious projects were being carried out in stone working. In the southern part of the valley and in the Diquís Delta, great efforts were made to find and carve hard rock into large balls (Stone 1943a,b, 1977) (fig. 1.4). Although this kind of stone working may have begun earlier, it appears to have dramatically increased in popularity by about A.D. 900 or so. There was a complex of large-scale sites throughout the lower portion of the Diquís Delta (Fernández and Quintanilla 2003). Unfortunately, one of the grandest sites, at Palmar Sur,

has been under a banana plantation for more than 40 years and only investigated in small sections (Baudez et al. 1993; Lothrop 1963; Fernández and Quintanilla 2003).

At Palmar Sur, large stone balls were aligned in and around plazas and seem to have served as markers of the burial grounds of people of high social status. At other sites, such as Grijalva II (Fernández and Quintanilla 2003), hectares may have been covered in pavements of river cobbles of uniform size and shape, requiring a tremendous effort to collect and lay them in place. Farther east, near the Panamanian border, in late Aguas Buenas times, statues of what were likely high-ranking men carried on the shoulders of other men suggest that social ranking was developing (Haberland 1968). These things probably were linked to the development of special ranks for high-status people and a ritual and ideological complex that relied upon impressive stone sculptures.

As this process unfolded, the culture in which the people of the General Valley participated began to take on characteristics that today are referred to as an

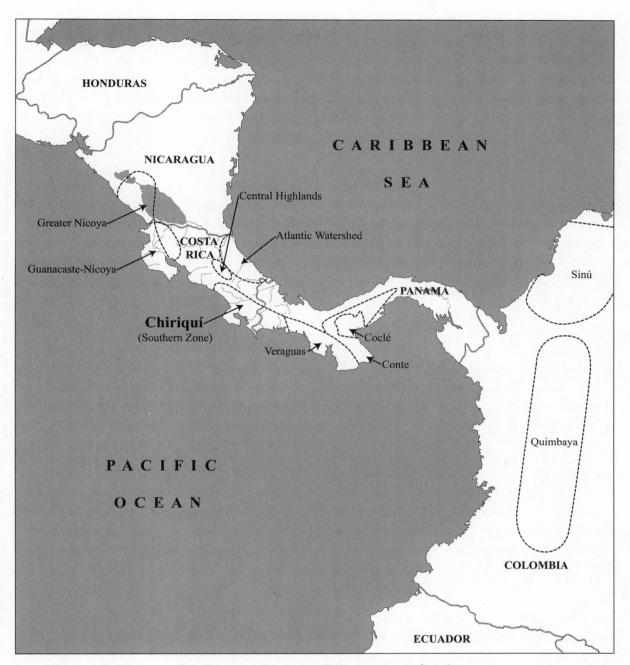

1.5. Archaeological culture areas of southern Central America and adjacent regions of South America. Map by Jennifer Ringberg.

archaeological culture called Chiriquí (fig. 1.5). This archaeological culture is distinct partly because it is in the least-studied region of Costa Rica. It also appears to have been more closely tied to cultural styles in what is now neighboring Panama than with cultures across the Talamanca Mountains or up the coast toward Greater Nicoya.

The Chiriquí archaeological region, in which com-

mon styles of jewelry, ceramics, and other artifacts were shared, stretched from western Panama through southern Costa Rica. Despite shared features, regional differences are in evidence. For example, red and black painted geometric designs on white backgrounds were a common decoration for pottery vessels—a style known as Buenos Aires Polychrome in Costa Rica. In the western part of Chiriquí, these designs tend to emphasize various combinations of triangles. Near the Panamanian border and continuing into that country, however, more curvilinear designs seem to have been preferred. We are not entirely sure if these differences are contemporary preferences of people in different parts of the Chiriquí region, if they are the result of changing tastes throughout the region, or if they are a combination of both of these factors (which is probably the case). Likewise, overall similarities with regional and temporal variations probably also were in effect for gold jewelry and architecture.

Research is only just beginning to tackle these problems, however, and the Rivas project has contributed more, perhaps, in raising many of these issues and only starting to address a few of them. As an archaeological phenomenon, the Chiriquí culture is assumed to have lasted until the arrival of the Spanish. Our investigations have contributed to more precisely defining the end of Chiriquí, at least at the Rivas site, as will be discussed in a later chapter.

Europeans first sailed along the Caribbean shores of southern Central America in the early years of the sixteenth century. On his last voyage to the New World, Columbus named the region the "rich coast" because he found so many people wearing gold ornaments (Morison 1963). He never visited the Pacific side of the isthmus, and although he found the spot where the entry to the Panama Canal is now located, he never traveled the relatively short distance, over land, that it would have taken to add a new ocean to his list of discoveries.

In 1571 the Spanish settlement of Ciudad Nombre de Jesus was established somewhere near the big bend in the General River (Corrales, Quintanilla, and Barrantes 1988). We have little information of how native peoples reacted to the Spanish incursion. Some sites have yielded fragments of Spanish armor and weapons and glass beads. As in many places in the New World, local people appear to have found European material culture attractive. We do not know whether they found the Europeans themselves attractive, however. We do know that the Europeans did not find the area inviting. It became a backwater of the Spanish colonial empire, too far from Guatemala City, from which it was nominally controlled, and off of the major trade route to Panama City, to the south. Although the Spanish were hungry for gold, the conquistadors apparently

missed the ridge-top cemetery of the Panteón de La Reina. The mountains, jungle, and tropical diseases did not make it worth fighting the few indigenous people who inhabited the region. There were easier pickings and more easily exploited land for haciendas elsewhere.

In many parts of the New World, European diseases swept like wildfire through native communities, sometimes killing more than half the population and crippling the rest as economic and social systems collapsed from the onslaught. We do not know the severity of epidemics in southern Costa Rica. Because there was no substantial European settlement, it is likely that survivors in the region readjusted themselves to lives patterned closer to their former ones once the plagues had passed than was the case for other New World peoples. How close new patterns were to older ones we do not know. It is unlikely that large architectural complexes continued to be built. In fact, the age of such constructions might have already passed or at least have been in abeyance a century or more before Europeans were on the scene (cf. Snarskis 1992: 160). A few native people were living in the area by the 1930s, but many appear to have retreated into the Talamanca Mountains (Skutch 1991).

With the arrival of new ways of life, new transportation routes and systems, and new ties to the outside world, the General Valley, especially its upper section, gradually sank into a kind of oblivion as far as the outside world was concerned. The forest grew back on the ridge-top, covering the graves of the ancient dead. By the mid-1800s the center of gravity of the European population of Costa Rica was the Central Valley. By the late nineteenth century, however, a number of explorers began to make the trek across the mountains. They invariably passed by the ridge-top, and we are fortunate to have the comments of some of these people on what they saw there (Pérez Zeledón 1907–08; Pittier 1892).

Unfortunately, the prominence of the ridge made it prey to fortune hunters who looted gold from the site. The explorers were followed by small groups of European farmers who came to live in El General, one of the first places where settlers staked claims after crossing the Talamancas. Before the boom in coffee and bananas, there were few sources of wealth to be converted to cash for farmers in any region of Costa Rica. To add to a basic subsistence gained from farm work, a gold item or two from a cemetery could do wonders. It became clear that a fortune was waiting to be had by digging on the ridge-top. That promontory came to be called the Huaca of the Queen, some say it was once the Huaca of the King and Queen. *Huaca* is a Quechua word, originating in Peru, to refer to any kind of sacred object (Rowe 1946: 295–297). Lower Central America is the northernmost extent of the region in which the term is used, though in Costa Rica and Nicaragua "*huaca*" only refers to an ancient cemetery. Also, the Spanish term "*panteón*" is used to refer to any cemetery, ancient or modern, and although we may wonder what happened to the king, the ridge today is known as the Panteón de La Reina.

Immigrants continued to settle the region. The name of the area, El General, eventually was restricted to the town of General Viejo, while a somewhat newer settlement was named Rivas. Rivas was the name of the town in Nicaragua where a combined Central American force defeated the "filibusters" under William Walker, attempting to establish an Anglo-American empire in Central America in 1857. In the 1940s a number of families moved from an area known as Los Santos, on the Pacific side of the rim of the Central Valley, to stake claims to farms in the upper General Valley. These are among the most important and widespread families in the Rivas area today.

Finally, with the need for open terrain for an airport and, eventually, the route of the Panamerican Highway, the main population center of the region shifted from Rivas and General Viejo to the town of San Isidro, 8 kilometers downriver. The city saluted tradition, however, incorporating "El General" into its name, though who this general was, no one knows.

Why Costa Rica?

In 1985 I was a young assistant professor at Ripon College in Ripon, Wisconsin. Ripon was and is a small college with an average of about 800 students and about 70 faculty members. My research interests were in Peru, where I had done my doctoral dissertation research in 1976 and two projects afterward (Quilter 1985, 1989). I knew little about the prehistory of Costa Rica. No one had ever taught me anything about it, nor had I bothered to learn. Professors had skipped lightly over the sections usually labeled "Lower Cen-

tral America" in textbooks in order to discuss the Maya, the Aztecs, or the Inca in more detail. I knew that in the late 1950s the northwestern part of the country Calude Baudez and Michael Coe (1962) had shown that there were some Mesoamerican influences in the ceramics, but I didn't know much else about the prehistory of the place. About all I knew was that ancient Costa Rica was a place where "chiefdoms" were prevalent by the time the Spanish arrived and that in one place or another, down there, the natives had made unusual large stone carvings in the shape of big balls.

Ripon College was part of a consortium, the Associated Colleges of the Midwest (ACM), consisting of 13 colleges (now 14) that pooled their resources to sponsor overseas and other programs difficult to maintain by any one institution. The only ACM Latin American overseas program was in Costa Rica. It so happened that Alexander Hooker, who had taught Spanish at Ripon College for many years and had helped establish the Costa Rica program, was about to retire and asked me if I would succeed him as ACM's campus representative. Looking toward my review for tenure in the following year and with at least a mild interest in Central America, I agreed, presuming I would have to do little more than push papers and sign application forms. The head office of the ACM, in Chicago, had other plans, however. The officers there said that if I was to represent the program, I should know something about it, and so they offered me a free week-long trip to Costa Rica for such an education. A free trip sounded good to me and fit conveniently in the time period of the upcoming fall break.

So, the next thing I knew I was in San José, Costa Rica. It wasn't exactly a free trip, as they worked me very hard. I spent every day touring different sites where students were working on projects, meeting staff members at the ACM office, and otherwise keeping very busy. Most of this occurred in San José and vicinity, and most of the students I met were involved with sociology, urban planning, and political science projects. I attended classes; I saw students working in the poor districts of town; I visited the campus of the University of Costa Rica; I met all of the faculty and support staff at the ACM headquarters; and otherwise I was kept very busy indeed. As a reward for my service, I was told that my last full day in Costa Rica would be spent at the beach. Since the country is so small, I could board a bus in San José in the morning and could return late in the evening in time to catch my flight the next day. The opportunity to spend a day at a tropical beach in mid-October sounded most appealing.

About halfway through my visit, amid another day of meeting students and staff, a tall, lanky gringo walked into the ACM office. He had a laptop computer slung in a carrying case over his shoulder and a cigarette hanging from his lips. He looked like he had spent a lot of time in the sun, with a dark tan and a squint that could not hide sparkling blue eyes. His name was Bob Drolet, and he worked at the National Museum as an archaeologist while also serving as the part-time instructor in anthropology and archaeology, for ACM students interested in those subjects. He had an easy, soft-spoken, almost shy manner, but we soon started talking archaeology, and I could sense great competence and enthusiasm in his voice and manner as he started to discuss the work he had been doing in the General Valley in southern Costa Rica.

After we had been talking for a while, Bob started to say what a shame it was that I didn't have time to come and see some of the sites he had been studying. I mentioned that I had a pretty busy schedule but that there were plans to send me to the beach on Friday. Bob said something like, "Well, hell, you don't want to go to the beach, do you? Don't you want to come and see some sites?" And I said, "Absolutely!" That was the first step in how this book came to be written.

We took the bus across the Talamanca Mountains and had a whirlwind tour of San Isidro, the big town of the Southern Zone, and vicinity. I stayed to the last minute and rushed to catch my plane. But what a time I had. San José has certain attractions, but it would be a stretch to call it charming. Now I was seeing the real Costa Rica, found in the beauty of its countryside and the charm of its people. Bob took me around as best he could in the short time we had. I was exposed to a beautiful tropical landscape, friendly people, fascinating archaeological collections, excellent steaks, and many beers. By the time I left, I realized that Costa Rica had an extremely rich archaeological heritage of which I really knew very little and that there were potentials for interesting work there.

We only had time to see a couple of sites. We drove down the General Valley to Murciélago, where Bob had conducted extensive excavations (Drolet 1983, 1984a,b). We went across the river by ferry and saw another site, Limón. The sites were not impressive at first glance, although cobble pavements were visible in some areas. What was impressive was the extent of the sites as indicated by Bob; they stretched over many hectares. Even more impressive was the beautiful setting in which the sites were located, with vistas out over the valley, palm trees swaying, and the landscape bathed in the golden light of late afternoon. And even more impressive still was Bob's enthusiasm for the archaeology of the Southern Zone.

Bob suggested that I should consider conducting an archaeological project in Costa Rica. Even though I had been entranced by my brief exposure to the land, the people, and the past, I told him that I simply had too many commitments in Peru, where I was still planning to do more fieldwork. Bob said we should keep in touch and if I ever wanted to do something in Costa Rica, to just ask.

I went back to Ripon and made a much better ACM campus representative than I would have if I had not made the trip. Within a few months, however, I was back involved with plans to do research in Peru, though I did take the trouble to do a little reading on some Costa Rican prehistory. A number of factors began to come into play. Although I had experienced some initial success in getting grant money for my research in Peru, winning the big grants I wanted in order to do excavations the way I had hoped proved difficult. In addition, Peru was becoming dangerous as the Sendero Luminoso, the Shining Path guerrilla movement, increased the level of violence and fear in the country. Although they had not attacked foreign archaeologists, I didn't want to be around the day after a policy change was made. Costa Rica, famous for its peaceable nature, seemed like it might have something to offer.

Why the Rivas Site?

Picking up on Bob's suggestion, I called him and said I'd like to come down to Costa Rica. So, in 1989 my nine-year-old daughter, Susanna, and I went to Costa Rica, this time to spend over a week, mostly with Bob and his young son, Adam.

The four of us had a great time. It was January up north, but the weather was gorgeous in Costa Rica. Rattling around in Bob's old Land Rover, we went to hot springs, ate great food, and had various adventures while at the same time touring a number of sites that Bob had investigated. We played Roy Orbison tapes as we climbed above coffee fields and the tropical forest. "Pretty Woman" and "Only the Lonely" wailed across the valley as we rumbled along precipices overlooking rushing mountain streams.

On my earlier, first visit to Costa Rica, my trip to the south with Bob had been so overwhelming that much of it was a blur in my memory. I had only been in the country for a week, and my time in the General Valley had been little more than a day. This time, I had the leisure to savor the place and its people with more attention. It was spectacular, filled with lush vegetation in more shades of green than I had ever seen. Exotic birds in bright colors sang in the mornings; iguanas flitted across the roads in the hotter, lower regions of the valley at mid-day; and in the evenings, by the pool at the Hotel del Sur, huge toads lumbered about. Peru had been wonderful in a grand, vast way with immense deserts and towering mountains. This place, though, offered very different charms, ones much more tuned to my boyhood fantasies of archaeology in the jungle. I encountered the tropical forest with an intensity that I had never felt before. It was magical.

The archaeology was as fascinating as the environment. My research interests in Peru had focused on a number of issues but had become increasingly centered on questions concerning how people related to one another and organized themselves before societies with distinct social classes—states—came into being. Mostly, I had concentrated on very early periods of prehistory. In Costa Rica, similar issues of social complexity in nonstate societies were available for study. Since it was assumed that states never existed in Costa Rica, any period of the prehistoric past was a potential topic for investigation.

Bob showed us many sites, including a huge boulder about 3 meters high, with petroglyphs carved all over it. We saw maize fields with dense scatters of pottery sherds, and again my head started to swim with all the places we visited in just a few days. Like many other U.S. archaeologists, I had never studied the pre-

history of Costa Rica in any detail and knew very little about it. What struck me was the density of habitation in the region; there seemed to be sites everywhere. The pottery was interesting and abundant, and the cobble pavements I saw in the dust of farms and pastures were impressive. I began to be fascinated with thoughts of this beautiful landscape packed with people and structures in ancient times.

Through Bob's eyes, the artifacts I had seen in museums started to come to life. I could picture a landscape filled with villages and fields of maize and beans. From a distance, the ancient communities would have appeared as collections of tipilike structures with thatch roofs. Some of these villages may have had 50 houses or more. The scraping of grinding stones could be heard as women ground meal while dogs barked and children laughed and played. The men would have been working in the fields, too, or perhaps painting their bodies for a festival and checking their costumes. There would have been craft specialists, producing axes, fancy ceramics, and other goods for trade with distant communities. Others might have specialized in carving stone statues or making gold jewelry. The landscape may have looked different, with the forests reduced to make way for maize fields or perhaps cut down for firewood, over generations. On feast days, villagers would have gathered to carry out rituals that honored their gods or their ancestors. Such ceremonies probably ended with feasting, drinking, and dancing in the tropical night.

As the past started to come alive as we toured the Southern Zone, I realized that Bob and his Costa Rican colleagues had done a lot to flesh out the living past from the stones and broken artifacts that made up archaeological sites in the region. I also realized that there were a lot of unanswered questions, too. What were those stone balls all about, and what was going on at those big sites with them, down in the Diquís Delta? What about the petroglyphs, often of spirals or circles connected by long lines, found on dozens of rocks, clustered in some areas but not others? Were there other ceremonial sites besides those with the stone balls? Was warfare common or rare? What were relations like between different parts of the Chiriquí region, between villages within it, between people living in those villages? If these were "chiefdoms," then how did these societies actually operate in terms of who got to be a chief and who didn't? There were lots of other questions that popped into my head and which seemed like they could be addressed with some work.

One of our last stops was at a bend in the road in a valley near San Isidro. The late afternoon sun cast the valley bottom in shadow but lit up the forest on the heights of the mountains and a long, fingerlike ridge projecting out from them. Two rushing rivers were on each side of the ridge and apparently joined somewhere below it, underneath the tree canopy. Bob said there wasn't enough time to visit the site because it was getting late. "That site is called Rivas, after the town," he said. "There are some very interesting things there, and it's too bad we don't have time to visit."

Bob had come to Costa Rica ten years earlier at the invitation of Michael Snarskis, then at the National Museum, in order to conduct a survey and emergency excavation of sites to be drowned by the construction of a dam on the Térraba River. The dam construction was canceled the day Bob and his wife, Patti, arrived from Panama, but Mike was able to find money for Bob to conduct the survey anyway.

Over the next decade, Bob added to the basic framework of prehistory first sketched by William Henry Holmes (1888) and George MacCurdy (1911) through study of artifact collections and later worked out in the field by Wolfgang Haberland (1959a,b, 1976). Bob had discovered both Chiriquí sites and earlier ones of the Aguas Buenas culture (Drolet 1983, 1984a,b, 1986, 1988). Traces of even more ancient cultures also were present, but the best known were the two later, major ones (fig. 1.6).

The biggest sites were Chiriquí. There was the well-known huge archaeological complex of Chiriquí sites in extensive banana plantations in the Diquís Delta, near the town of Palmar Sur (Stone 1943a,b; Lothrop 1963). In addition, however, Bob (Drolet 1992) had identified or reconfirmed the presence of 14 other Chiriquí sites strung like pearls on a string along the river valley. He also had conducted extensive excavations at Murciélago.

There is a premium in archaeology for working on the "earliest" anything, whether the earliest plant or animal domesticates, ceramics, or metallurgy. But if we were interested in questions about nonstate com-

plex societies, it seemed to make sense first to get the best idea of what those societies were like at the end of prehistory: you can't study the "origins" of something unless you know what that something is. By developing an understanding of the latest societies in the region, we would contribute to future work to investigate the processes by which such societies transformed from their earlier forms.

The sites in the Palmar Sur area were big, complicated, and under hectares of banana plants, and Costa Rican (Fernández and Quintanilla 2003) and French archaeologists (Baudez et al. 1993) were conducting work there. Bob had already excavated Murciélago. It seemed worthwhile to consider working at a site in the upper reaches of the valley system. This would allow us to develop a comparison of human habitation at sites in different valley sectors and environmental zones. We could examine the degree to which sites shared common styles of artifacts, architecture, mortuary practices, and other traits; how their inhabitants organized themselves; and how they did or did not interact with one another. All of this would be done in a region thought to be a place where exemplars of chiefdom societies existed.

Why Chiefdoms?

A number of serendipitous events had led me to the Rivas site, but the decision to commit my time and energy to a project there was not due solely to an opportunistic chance to dig a big site in a pretty place. Rivas would allow me to continue my interest in investigating nonstate societies. My work in Peru had been mostly devoted to examining how early people, from 5000 to 1500 B.C., had been able to prosper in the transition period from reliance on gathered resources to increasing dependence on plant cultivars. On the coast of Peru, large-scale public constructions of temples and similar facilities occurred in this early Preceramic period without a maize-based subsistence economy. Based upon and linked to the work of other scholars, my investigations also suggested that the grand building projects were feats of cooperative labor made by people who apparently had not been organized in a highly stratified social system (Quilter and Stocker 1985; Quilter et al. 1991). There may have been little in the way of permanent "leadership" in the form of a rul-

Date	Periods[a]	Periods[b]	Diquís	Chiriquí	Bocas	Rivas
1500	VI	Contact	Coto Chiriquí•	Urraca/Chiriqui Chiriquí•	Cerabaro Bocas•	
1000		III Precontact				▮
	V		?	San Lorenzo•	Aguacate	
600				Boruca		
400			Aguas Buenas			
200	III	II Formative		Bugaba•		
B.C./A.D.				Concepción		
200				Barriles•		
500			Quebradas•	Aguacate•		
2000	II	I Preceramic				
5000				Talamanca•		

[a]After Snarskis 1982   [b]After Drolet 1992   • Associated with uncorrected radiocarbon dates
Black bar in "Rivas" indicates range of (uncorrected) RC dates

1.6. Culture periods and chronological chart for southern Costa Rica.

ing class or king, as might be expected for such works to be built.

My Peruvian research had been stimulated by a fundamental question in archaeology, anthropology, and social science in general: What are the causes of social inequality? When, how, and why did societies change from more or less egalitarian ones in the Paleolithic and early Neolithic periods (to use Old World terms) of human history to those of later times in which there were distinct classes of rulers and ruled? These are grand questions that have been discussed for centuries. In anthropology and archaeology, there have been two major schools of thought regarding the matter. One, typified by Lewis Henry Morgan (1877) and later Elman Service (1962, 1993), Morton Fried (1967), Robert Carneiro (1967, 1970, 1981, 1998), and others, searches for patterns and universal characteristics of human societies. They have tended to be scientific in their methodologies and emphasize common patterns, paying less attention to differences. The other group, including such scholars as Franz Boas (1982) and Clifford Geertz (1980, 1988), has tended to approach the study of societies from a more humanistic perspective, emphasizing the differences between cultures, their unique characteristics, and the role of chance and specific historical circumstances in the origins of cultural traits and patterns. Although the situation is more complicated and many scholars, even ones mentioned, cannot easily be characterized as in one camp or another for all of their careers, this binary division of investigators has generally been in operation.

In Europe, archaeologists are commonly thought to investigate the past of nation states (see Patterson 1994). "France," "Germany," and other such entities only were created in the last few centuries. But today, archaeologists are seen as excavating ancient French or Germans, even though the Neolithic, Bronze Age, and later peoples who lived in the areas now comprising these states never thought of themselves in terms of those nationalist categories. In the Americas, however, archaeology mostly has been done by people of European heritage who see themselves as investigating "other" people in a kind of anthropological laboratory. For a variety of reasons, including the notion that peoples of America represented "earlier" stages of cultural development that were long passed in Europe by the time of the discovery of the New World, there has been a strong emphasis on testing anthropological theory in regards to cultural evolution. Theories of cultural evolution have been most vigorously developed by the "scientific" variety of archaeologist.

The basic framework of cultural evolution has been a ladder of increasing cultural complexity from band to tribe to chiefdom to state. In the nineteenth century, anthropologists such as Edward B. Tylor and Lewis Henry Morgan believed that all humans had or would climb this ladder in the same way, eventually developing societies that would be just like those in which these proper bourgeois British and American gentlemen lived. In the century and a half since they wrote, however, scholars interested in evolution have revised their views, seeing many pathways to complexity and many subcategories of these four major cultural steps.

Recently, trends in anthropology, subsequently influencing archaeology, have given rise to a group of scholars who strongly disavow any attempts to study humans scientifically. The most extreme version of this position sees little value in any kind of generalizations about human societies, even questioning the use of such terms as "society" or "culture." From this perspective, archaeology, relying upon material remains from long ago, can say very little about the past. At best, anthropology is interpretive, and what we seek is a convincing or compelling interpretation, not some absolute "truth." This is as about as far away from searching for scientific facts as one can get.

While much debate has occurred about whether such concepts as band and tribe are appropriate, no one doubts that states are distinct political and economic phenomena that only came into existence tens of thousands of years or more after the first Homo sapiens walked the earth. Chiefdoms are viewed by some as societies in the process of becoming states. The archaeology of Lower Central America has received less attention than that of Mesoamerica or the Andes, partly because chiefdoms there at the time of the Spanish arrival are viewed as having failed in not evolving into states: they didn't become "civilizations" erecting large stone buildings and other impressive public works. Neither did they make art suited to the tastes of twentieth-century citizens of nation states strongly influenced by European culture. These ideas are part of a view of cultural evolution in which it is assumed that there is an inevitable growth from simple societies to more complex ones (e.g., Fried 1967).

Throughout my archaeological career I have been intrigued and vexed by the debate about cultural evolution and, particularly, about "chiefdoms." In short, I think it is a worthwhile pursuit to search for human universals and for those characteristics that reflect common humanity and common patterns of social development, despite apparent differences. But placing different societies into categories such as "chiefdoms" has its disadvantages: the trend is either to make the categories so extremely broad and general that they do not serve as much more than handy terms for discussion. Or the chiefdom "type" is divided into so many subcategories that the overall term, again, has little more than heuristic value (see Feinman and Neitzel 1984). Nevertheless, there will always be people who want to find general patterns while others prefer to look at individual uniqueness. Thus working in an area where chiefdoms once existed inevitably draws one into such debates. Whether one favors evolutionary categories perhaps depends on one's theoretical interests. The issue is hotly debated.

I have tried to pick projects in which I could clearly add to basic knowledge about what happened in the past—research that can contribute to building or clarifying cultural chronologies and to delineating regional culture history. But I also have tried to do research that can contribute to larger theoretical questions, too. I didn't go to Rivas to prove that it was a chiefdom or to disprove it. I went to try and answer basic questions, such as when and for how long the site was occupied and what kind of activities took place there. After that, I was interested in how Rivas could be placed within a fairly specific, though vaguely known, framework of what happened in Costa Rica, especially southern Costa Rica and neighboring Panama, in the ancient past. Then, if some of these questions could be answered to some degree of satisfaction, issues of how all of this information might link to issues of chiefdoms might be considered.

Among those scholars who wish to generalize there are also two main schools of thought regarding the origins of social inequality. In one model, inequality comes about when individuals or communities sacrifice their autonomy for a greater good. The classic example is irrigation agriculture. Since water flows downhill, people living higher in a fluvial system can control the amount of water received by those downstream. Karl Wittfogel (1957) suggested that the state came into being to manage such irrigation systems, since how water is allocated needs centralized decision making. It now appears that canals and similar works were in operation long before centralized authority in most parts of the world (see Geertz 1980), but the idea that people give up some sovereignty in order to have better lives is still a powerful theory.

The other approach to the origins of inequality argues that it comes about when one group dominates another (Carneiro 1970, 1981, 1998). This could occur when a group conquers another, producing rulers/ conquerors and subjects/conquered social strata. It

also can come about when individuals use special knowledge or skills to make others do their bidding, such as religious specialists or military men. The ancient Romans honored Cincinnatus in the days of the early Republic because he led the army against Rome's enemies but resumed his role as a citizen after the battle was won. Too many times in the imperial age, Roman generals seized power when they returned home from foreign campaigns or civil wars in front of a victorious army that maintained its leader in power.

Many variations of the two models for social change just discussed have been proposed by various scholars. Once the state comes into existence in any region, however, pressure mounts on outlying peoples to develop similar institutions, perhaps even to become secondary states themselves, to safeguard against the powerful force over the horizon that may conquer them. Therefore, scholars are interested most in the origins of pristine states—ones that arise without the influence of other states.

As far as we can tell, no locally developed states existed in Costa Rica in prehistoric times. Nevertheless, there are good indications that societies in the region became more unequal through time and that the greatest inequalities likely existed sometime in the three or four centuries prior to the arrival of Europeans. By examining the way in which these inequalities were structured, we can contribute to knowledge of the diversity of human existence in the past and begin to explore how social inequalities in ancient Costa Rica may have come about. What makes the Costa Rican case particularly interesting is that Costa Rica is a land in which food and other essential resources are fairly well distributed. This is quite different than places such as Mesopotamia, Egypt, China, highland Mesoamerica, and the coast of Peru, where resources were restricted in narrow river valleys. The origins of social inequality in tropical forests has not been much explored.

An issue to keep in mind is that we know very little about the basic cultural chronology of southern Pacific Costa Rica. As noted above, we only have a skeleton outline of the succession of archaeological cultures, mostly in late prehistory, and little understanding of how these cultures were organized on family, community, or regional levels. Since at least some information was known about the sites of the lower valley, around Palmar Sur, and since Bob Drolet had excavated at

Murciélago, working at Rivas, up-valley, could contribute to understanding how a particular community was constituted and organized. By comparing our findings at Rivas with information from the mid and lower valley sites, we could help to start to develop an understanding of how the regional system worked in Chiriquí times.

Rivas was an attractive site to work at for this goal. Bob had conducted a preliminary study there and established that it had a Chiriquí occupation. The landowners were willing to let us work in their coffee fields and pastures, and the site was adjacent to the small town of Rivas and only a twenty-minute drive away from the regional center, San Isidro de El General. Of all the prehistoric population centers stretched along the river, Rivas was the farthest up-valley. Hemmed in by the foothills of the Talamanca Mountains, the inhabitants of the site may not have had as much farmland compared to those living farther downstream. They would have had access to a more diverse set of resources, however, because of the range of environmental zones in the heights nearby. They also had easy access to routes across the mountains to the Central Valley and Atlantic slopes, providing possibilities for the long-distance exchange of goods. Throughout the Americas, high mountains have religious significance as the places of gods or ancestors, so the Rivas population might have specialized in religious practices. All of these possibilities attracted me to work there. Investigations at Rivas would clearly enlarge knowledge of variability between settlements in a late period prehistoric chiefdom system in southern Costa Rica. Now that Bob and I had clear research goals and a site in which to investigate them, all that we needed was the money to support the project.

Of course, I had never actually been to the site; I had only seen it from a distance, late in my final day in the region. But Bob had been there and had even conducted some test excavations. Together, we made a good team. Bob had plenty of experience working in the area, and I had experience applying for grants back in the United States.

Funding the Project

We had grand ambitions and needed the funds to match them. We would need to excavate extensively in order to have an adequate comparative sample of artifacts and other data to compare Rivas with Murciélago. Archaeology, especially overseas, is expensive. It requires money for food, housing, excavation equipment, a vehicle and its gas and maintenance costs, payment for radiocarbon dating and other tests, expenses for bags and storage equipment of artifacts, wages for excavators, air fares for foreign specialists, and a wealth of other expenditures great and small. The research required a survey of the property, mapping of observed features, test excavations, and, eventually, full-scale excavations. We expected that it would take us at least two field seasons at Rivas to do all of this, with year-round lab work and another year devoted exclusively to laboratory analyses and writing after the fieldwork was completed.

Our first plans included not only Rivas but also at least one more site lower in the valley in order to have a greater diversity of data to compare. The only granting agency that funded large projects such as we envisioned was the National Science Foundation (NSF). The NSF had received no significant increases in its budget for anthropology and archaeology for years, making winning a grant extremely difficult. Generally, a proposal does not have a chance of serious competition for funds unless the investigators have already done preliminary work on the topic in question. It is also advantageous to apply for as little money as possible, in the hopes that in parceling out its limited resources, the NSF might take a chance on many economical projects instead of a few big ones.

The NSF stated that it gave grants strictly on the basis of scientific merit, however, and no other criteria. We thought that we should have as good a chance as anyone. We had clear-cut research goals that could be investigated with the kinds of data we would recover. Differences in village plans, ceramic styles, mortuary practices, craft and economic specialization, and the like could be gauged by comparing the kinds of data recovered from the different sites. Bob had extensive experience working in the area, including full excavation at Murciélago and test excavations at the other sites. We thus felt optimistic that we had a reasonable chance to be funded.

Despite such optimism, I cautioned Bob that we had to try and keep our expectations low. With limited funds, the NSF can't fund all the good project proposals it receives. It is common for a first-time proposal not to be granted, requiring a second or even a third application before winning a grant, if at all. Since it takes months to write or even revise a proposal and months to review it, the process of applying for funds can stretch over years.

Then, complications were added to the plot. Patti, Bob's wife, worked with refugees for the United Nations. Her tour of duty in Central America was about to end, and she would be reassigned to a new country. Thus, although the Drolets had spent ten years in Costa Rica, Bob and his family faced the likelihood that they would be moving somewhere else. Bob was concerned that he wouldn't be able to do the project with me. I told him that if I could be based in the United States and work in Costa Rica, there was no reason why he couldn't do it from abroad, too, especially if Patti were to be posted to Switzerland as they hoped. Still, it made things complicated.

And it turned out that we did not win the grant. Both Bob and I were disappointed, but I thought it was worth reapplying. But things were moving fast, and Patti was assigned to Palawan, one of the outer islands of the Philippines where she would work with Vietnamese refugees. I suggested that we diversify our strategy. The Fulbright Program mostly funds scholars to teach in other countries, but it also had a research fellowship program. Perhaps I could apply for one of those grants. It wouldn't provide the kinds of funds for a multiyear project at two or more sites, but it might provide enough support to work at Rivas. I would have to be the sole applicant for the grant, but Bob and I could work together at the site and begin our project. We could still try and get a big NSF grant, but at least the Fulbright would get us moving in the direction in which we wanted to go.

I applied for and won the Fulbright Fellowship. By the time it came through, though, Bob and his family had moved to Palawan. He had helped to establish the Museo Regional del Sur in San Isidro before he left, and a Costa Rican colleague, Aida Blanco, was to be in charge of it. In addition to this new responsibility, Aida taught at the branch campus of the National University of Costa Rica. Bob decided to make a clean break of things and generously suggested that I should work with Aida. He would be too far away, had family responsibilities, and needed to start afresh, across the

Pacific. So he wished me well and suggested that I team up with Aida.

I hadn't met Aida, and I hadn't been to the site. I had relied upon Bob and his experience to complement my position as a newcomer to Costa Rican archaeology. I had the Fulbright, but I was now in a position in which I felt lost and uncertain as to how I could proceed without the guidance of the person who had first introduced me to the archaeology of the region and whose enthusiasm for the project had energized me. So, as there were several months between the time I received notice that I had been awarded the Fulbright and when work was to commence, I made another trip to Costa Rica, using my own funds, to meet Aida to see if we could work together and to do a preliminary scouting of the site. I went to Costa Rica for a brief visit of one week in 1991. Aida was kind and generous with her time and advice. She had a good sense of humor and clearly was a fine archaeologist. She was enthusiastic about the project, and it seemed as if we could indeed work together.

At this point, I wish to make a parenthetical remark about research grants and scholarship. The reader may note that although I had a "free ride," thanks to the ACM, for my first trip to Costa Rica, I personally paid for two additional trips before my grant covered my costs. This is not uncommon in archaeology, geology, biology, and many other research fields that require travel away from home. Researchers gladly pay these expenses because they love what they do. Sometimes their costs are partly covered by grants from their colleges or universities if they are well endowed. More often, the money comes out of the scholars' own pockets, with varying and not always sufficient opportunities to recoup the costs through tax deductions. Anyone who thinks that scholars who dedicate their lives to research are unfairly using taxpayer dollars is mistaken; the researchers often give more than they get, not only in cash but also in sweat and sometimes in blood.

Aida and I went to visit the site and the farm families who lived on the land. They, too, were generous and hospitable. On a misty, rainy, cool day, I was welcomed into the house of the senior member of the Mora family. Don Leobihildo Mora and his wife served Aida and me rich tasting *café con leche* and fresh, home-baked sweet rolls while a cat curled itself around the base of a blazing cast-iron stove as rain pounded on the tin roof above us. They were willing to let us come and do the project, although they seemed slightly puzzled as to why we wanted to dig up the broken pots they commonly came across in their coffee fields.

Things finally began to fall in place for our first field season. I delayed my Fulbright Fellowship until January 1992. Although I could have taken double the amount of time, my family decided it was too difficult to join me, so I planned for a minimum stay of three months, still plenty of time for an archaeological field season. I got a leave of absence from Ripon College in order to take the Fulbright. The ACM personnel in San José offered help in many ways to facilitate all of the details needed to make the project operative, and we planned to have some ACM students working with us. A proposal was submitted to the Comisión Nacional de Arqueología of Costa Rica, and a permit was granted for the work. Now all that was left was to go and do it.

Artifactual Expectations

In addition to reading articles and books on theories on chiefdoms, I familiarized myself with the kinds of artifacts and other remains I expected to find during excavations. Bob Drolet helped a lot by simply showing me collections of materials he had made during his work in the region. Trips to the major museums in San José—the National Museum, the Jade Museum, and the Gold Museum—also helped in my education. I looked through books with lots of illustrations, such as the catalog for the exhibition *Between Continents/Between Seas* (Benson 1981), Luis Ferrero's (1987) *Costa Rica Precolombina,* earlier works by William Henry Holmes (1888) and Grant MacCurdy (1911), and other things I could find (Hartman 1907; Lange and Stone 1984; Linares de Sapir 1968; Linares and Ranere 1980; Lothrop 1926, 1963, 1966; Stone 1972, 1977, 1986). Many illustrated books concentrated on jade or gold jewelry or on elaborately carved, large stone metates and statuary. The majority of these things came from the activities of looters, sold on the international art market. While I would have welcomed finding any of these fancy goods, I expected to find more mundane items and to find them in fragments. Broken everyday dish-

ware and discarded stone tools and fragments of them are what archaeologists usually encounter and what they have to use to make their interpretations of the past.

I learned that there were five common ceramic styles representative of Chiriquí material culture: Buenos Aires Polychrome, Papayal Engraved, Ceiba Red-Brown, Sangria Fine Red, and Turucaca White-on-Red. These mostly were defined by the way in which vessels were decorated and, secondarily, by the predominance of different vessel forms, though the styles shared many forms. Although the names have changed, the basic categories were first recognized more than a century ago by Holmes (fig. 1.7). In an ironical twist of archaeological history, the massive looting of sites for gold in what is now western Panama yielded abundant ceramics for study, even though little was known about the sites from which they came.

Simple vessels used for everyday activities were not decorated at all or minimally treated by being covered in a thin paint known as a "slip," usually red or brown in color. Decorated varieties consist of two main types. One type was decorated by incising the vessel with lines or punctates (fig. 1.7: 1–3). In the upper General Valley, where Rivas is located, the most common version of this kind is known as Papayal Engraved (fig. 1.7: 2, 3). The second decorative method was to paint the pot. One of the hallmarks of Chiriquí ceramics is the use of three colors—a white-slipped background on which decorations were made in red and black. Such designs include animal figures or triangle motifs. Holmes and MacCurdy thought that all designs referred to alligators and therefore called the style Alligator Ware (fig. 1.7: 5, 6).

In early days, the naming of pottery types was somewhat whimsical and inconsistent. Black Ware (fig. 1.7: 1) included a range of colors from black to dark brown (fig. 1.7: 2). In the case of Alligator Ware, the inferred symbolism of a ceramic design was used to name an entire type. A beautiful ware with thin walls and often highly polished had unadorned surfaces but sometimes was decorated with tiny sculptures (*adornos*) of animals, the armadillo being a favored subject. Thus this became Armadillo Ware. Many decorative types shared common forms, such as open bowls on tripod legs. Tripod Ware was a category based on form shared by other "wares," and therefore the categories were inconsistent. One type with legs represented as fishes was singled out to be called Fish Ware (fig. 1.7: 4). This rather haphazard nomenclature was partly rectified by Wolfgang Haberland (1959a,b, 1961a,b). In particular, he renamed Alligator Ware as Buenos Aires Polychrome and Armadillo Ware as Tarragó Biscuit. Pottery similar to Fish Ware was distinguished as a general category by use of two colors and became known as Ceiba Red-Brown. Further refinements were made by Calude Baudez (Baudez et al. 1993) and his associates. For our purposes, it is important to note that they identified a distinctive pottery style consisting of a dark red, polished slip as Sangria Red Fine and a similar pottery with the addition of white paint as Turucaca White-on-Red (see Corrales 2000). By examining the collections Bob Drolet had made at the site in his earlier work, it became clear to us that the decorated pottery we were most likely to find at the site consisted of Buenos Aires Polychrome, Papayal Engraved, and Ceiba Red-Brown. There seemed to be few examples of Tarragó Biscuit.

The other major category of artifact we expected to find in our excavations was stonework. There are three types of stone artifacts likely to be found: lapidary work in semiprecious stone for items of jewelry; ground and polished stone tools and weapons; and chipped stone tools. Remnants of the production processes of the last two, such as flakes and cores of tools being worked into shape, also should be at the site.

Stone jewelry was an important high-status item in early times, but we did not expect to find many examples at this later Chiriquí site. Ground and polished stone tools were assumed to be present, though. Ground and polished stone axes are known in almost all early agricultural societies and are commonly called adzes and celts.

Another important category of ground stone tools consists of the two implements used to grind foodstuffs—in the New World, commonly maize. The simplest of these tools is a loaf-shaped cobble mano used to grind on top of the passive metate, commonly a large, heavy stone with a flat surface. But Costa Rica is famous for elaborately carved manos and metates. The "flying panel" metates, best known in the Atlantic Watershed and Central Valley regions, were carved out of very large solid blocks to produce three-dimensionally complex sculptures. Frequently, manos also were made with great care and elaborate decorations.

As for chipped stone tools, sometimes called "lithics," little seemed to be known about them. In many tropical regions where good chipping stone is rare, cutting instruments are often made of hard woods, such as the heart of the peach palm. These hard wood tools rarely are preserved in the archaeological record, however. We welcomed the opportunity to find out if chipped stone tools would be found in any numbers at the Rivas site.

These, then, were the artifacts we expected to find. We also hoped to encounter petroglyphs, perhaps carbonized plant remains, and archaeological features such as hearths, storage pits, cobble pavements, house rings, and other nonmovable constructions.

Beginning Work

A few days after Christmas 1991, my family and I flew to Costa Rica. My wife and children had come for the winter vacation. We would see some of Costa Rica and then they would return home, leaving me to do the project. We arrived in San José on New Year's Eve day, expecting to join the celebrations in the capital city. It was oddly still and vacant, with nary a person on the street and 1992 quietly creeping in at midnight. Only later did we learn that the holiday was celebrated by Costa Ricans at the beaches, which were jam-packed with revelers, leaving the capital deserted.

We eventually made it to Jaco Beach in a car I had bought from Phil Dennis, director of the ACM program. After a few days at the beach, we drove from Jaco down one of the worst roads in the Americas, traveling on a gravel road through mile after mile of palm oil plantations in dust and over potholes. The air was hot, heavy, and humid, and the perfect rows of palms were surreal—neither fully "natural" nor fully "cultural"—stretching into infinity on either side of the road. At one point, the choking dust stopped as we entered a long stretch of road that had recently been sprayed with a thick, black oil, probably used engine oil, of some sort. The undercarriage of the car was completely covered in oil after a few miles, with considerable black splotches on the white upper side of

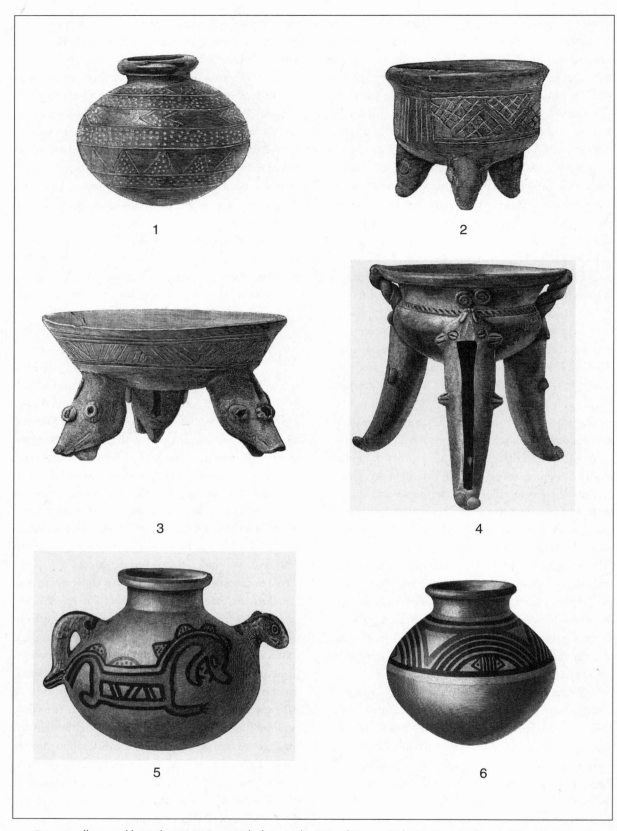

1.7. Ceramics illustrated by Holmes (1888). 1–3: Black Incised; 4: Tripod Group (Fish Ware); 5–6: Alligator Ware. Not to scale. From Holmes 1888, figs. 113–115, 143, 202, 195.

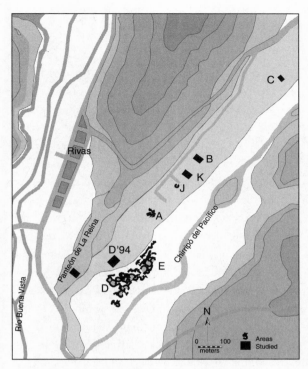

1.8. Map of the upper General Valley with significant work areas at the Rivas site noted. Operations indicated by letters.

the vehicle as well. We must have looked a sorry sight as we trundled along: some kind of Lost Gringo Family. Much later, two different car wash companies in San José pointedly refused to clean my car. I had to get street urchins to do a preliminary cleaning before a professional company would accept my vehicle for a full scrub-down.

We made a left turn at the beach town of Dominical, passed through the Coastal Range of mountains, and entered the upper end of the General Valley. Our first order of business was to visit Aida and see the site. Although I had visited earlier, it was still new to me.

To get to Rivas, one heads south out of San Isidro on the Panamerican Highway and turns left, driving through the outskirts of San Isidro, past the branch of the National University named after Pérez Zeledón. The road is on the ridge bordering the northwestern side of the valley, eventually dropping down to Rivas, 8 kilometers from the main highway. Driving through Rivas, the road changes from blacktop to gravel as one climbs a ridge, the Panteón de La Reina, which separates the town from the farms where the site is located. These stretch from Rivas proper to the small community of Guadalupe de Rivas farther up the road.

If one continues on the road, as most people do, it leads to the Chirripó National Park ranger station at San Gerardo, only a few kilometers more, where information may be had on climbing Mount Chirripó, the tallest peak in Costa Rica. But to visit the site one turns right after leveling off from coming down the Panteón, onto a street, with a small sign labeled Calle Mora, which swings to the right again, down-valley (fig. 1.8). The houses of many Mora family members occupy plots along the first hundred meters of dirt road. Although houses continue, scattered along the way, they decrease in frequency as coffee fields, interspersed with pastures or overgrown areas known as *monte*, become more common. The regularity of the rows of coffee plants is broken by the occasional banana plant, orange or avocado tree, or other useful vegetation. It is only 10 meters or so, on the right-hand side, to the foot of the steep slope of the Panteón de La Reina, with most of the fields on the left. After about 800 meters, the road takes a short left turn and ends in front of a large pasture cordoned off with barbed wire.

Conversations with Mora family members as well as Bob Drolet's research indicated that artifacts were to be found throughout the fields bordering the entire Calle Mora. Pottery sherds or other remains were not readily visible on the ground surface, however. Most of the earth had been tamped down or was covered by leaf fall from coffee plants and other vegetation. At the far, southern end of the pasture, however, a grove of small guava trees shaded part of an exposed circular ring of river cobbles that outlined the remains of a prehistoric structure. I showed my family this feature since it was one of the few visible signs that there really was a site on the Mora farm. As we were heading back to the car, my wife, Sarah, pointed southward, into the thick vegetation beyond the ring of stones and said, "The big stuff is down there," and smiled. It seemed an odd thing to say since she had never been to where she pointed. I assured her that we would look down there, eventually, although my mind was preoccupied with exactly what I was going to do in general. It is one thing to have plans on how to excavate a site, writing merrily in the comfort of one's own office; it is another to finally be faced with figuring out how one is going to actually carry out those schemes when confronted with the realities of field conditions.

Developing and Implementing a Research Strategy

I was challenged with the problem of trying to make sense of a big site with relatively little time and few resources available to me. The ideal archaeological project is designed to follow a series of stages in which the steps move from recovering general information to investigating more specific questions. Bob Drolet had already completed the first two steps by conducting surveys to identify sites in the valley and by following with test excavations at many of them. He had continued with mapping, testing, and eventually excavating the Murciélago site. If I were to conduct the Rivas research "by the book," I should begin by doing a reconnaissance of the site, map all archaeological features I found, and then, since it was hard to detect remains from the surface, conduct a shovel test pit survey. Only then might I consider excavations of structures and other features.

The ideal program of field research as presented in class lectures or research grant proposals often stumbles upon the harsh realities of conditions in the field. Any schemes I had to follow the rules met with an obstacle right from the start: lack of workers. I had planned on the large male population of the Mora family to provide me with workers after the coffee harvest was over. But families often own coffee fields a day or more distant that are ready for picking later than those near home, or they have relatives who need help with their harvests. Most of the Mora men were out elsewhere picking coffee, so we could only assemble a crew of six workers to begin the project, including an elderly gentleman from town and a couple of young teenage boys.

How was I going to possibly get any control over a site spread out over a kilometer or more, apparently hidden under coffee plants, pasture, or *monte* with six untrained workers? One option was to begin by making a detailed map. Mapping doesn't necessarily need a lot of workers, but if I returned home with a nice map showing the distribution of pot sherds in shovel test pits over hill and dale, what might my chances be of getting funding to return to do extensive excavations? In Peru, I once had gotten a relatively small grant to do work at a large site but never received the funding to go back and clear buildings and open big excavation units to better understand the site. I didn't want history to repeat itself.

The circle of stones in the southern end of the pasture at the bottom of the Calle Mora that my family and I had seen at least offered the opportunity to excavate a Rivas house, and the artifacts found there might serve as a starting point for more work. I thus decided to begin there; there seemed to be other structures in the field that also might be excavated or at least mapped. With the guarantee that I would have some architectural remains and artifacts to study by working in this location, I could have results right away and then, gaining more familiarity with the site, work outward, mapping, identifying other areas of habitation, and building the project from a "sure thing."

Any spatially distinct area in which Bob Drolet conducted excavations was referred to by him as an "operation," and he numbered them sequentially. I decided to give my operations letter designations, to avoid confusion with Bob's work and collections. Thus the fieldwork conducted in the pasture at the end of the road was called Operation A. It included not only excavations of the structures at its southern end but also all other work in the area bounded by the barbed wire fence on three sides and by the drop off of the terrace on the side closest to the river. This was the uppermost terrace of the site, formed thousands of years ago when the ancient river gouged out the landscape. A good portion of the site was on this uppermost terrace, although significant remains were found on the terrace below it.

While I was not going to begin the project by trying to map the entire site, I still needed to map the portion where I planned to work. For convenience, I made the corner of the field fence near the Calle Mora the datum —the 0/0 point—for a grid system that could be extended to map the entire site.

The upper portion of the valley in which we worked ran from the northeast to the southwest. It was confusing, however, to be referring constantly to the upstream direction as "northeast" and the downstream direction as "southwest," and orienting our excavation grids to true magnetic north and south was awkward since the grid system would run diagonally to the main axis of the valley. This could become extremely difficult to manage if we wished to expand our grid system over the entire kilometer or more of the site. In order to simplify matters, then, I arbitrarily established a compass bearing more or less following the axis of the terrace and valley and called the upriver direction Grid North and the downriver direction Grid South. All references to directions at the site in this book are to the artificial grid directions and not the "true" cardinal points, unless otherwise stated.

Although I wanted more workers, at least I had enough to begin work. Aida had been of tremendous help in getting these people to work for us and in assisting in many other ways. We had one or more houses identified, and all of our permits and finances were in order. We had a grid and mapping system set up. We had all of our equipment ready, too. Now, seven years since I first stepped foot in Costa Rica and three years since Bob and I had started talking seriously about working together, I was about to turn my first shovelful of earth to investigate the prehistory of Costa Rica.

I followed a custom from Peru. I made a *pago*—a "payment"—giving the Earth Mother, Pachamama, a sacrifice. To do it properly one needs alcohol, coca leaves, and *spondylus* shells. I had to improvise and use the local hard liquor that all of our workers drank, *guaro*, for the alcohol. I smoked a cigarette and blew it in the cardinal directions and down to the earth and up to the sky, asking for forgiveness for breaking into Mother Earth and for good fortune in our investigations. Considering how the project developed, it seemed to work.

CHAPTER TWO

THE 1992 FIELD SEASON

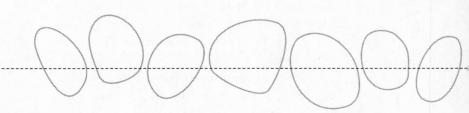

Operation A

The Operation A field at the end of the Calle Mora, on the uppermost terrace of the valley, was bounded by barbed wire except for the eastern side, at the terrace edge. This was close to where my family and I had stopped the car on our visit, though it did not seem to hold the significance that my wife had implied in her advice on where to dig. Most of the field was in short grass, cropped by grazing cattle. At the southern end of the field there was a grove of guava trees. Their thin, spindly trunks were irregularly spaced, and their leaves offered a modicum of shade. In the southwestern corner of both field and grove, cobbles laid in a circular ring protruded above the ground. Less complete stone circles also were visible elsewhere in the field (fig. 2.1).

The cobble rings resembled those reported by Bob Drolet (1986) for the Murciélago site. These are the remains of house foundations or walkways and sitting areas. At Murciélago, most circles measured about 10 meters in interior diameter, with some significantly larger ones that may have been for high-ranking indi-

viduals or community activities. Some of the rings had expanded sections, which likely provided relatively dry places to sit outside in the rainy season. Before we even began excavations, surface indications suggested a similar situation at Rivas. It thus seemed that work in this area would be useful as a means to collect data for comparison with Murciélago, as part of our developing a record of late period chiefdoms in the Southern Zone.

Although we could pinpoint any find to less than a millimeter on the grid system, we usually worked in excavation units measured in meters. To more efficiently identify any unit, we followed a convention of referring to it by its southwestern corner. Thus a 1 x 1 meter size unit that had coordinates at S1/E9, S0/E9, S0/E10, and S1/E10 would be known as S1/E9. A 2 x 2 meter unit would have a designation such as S0–1/E9–10, and so on. We always referenced the numbers in relation to movement away from the southwest corner of the pit, however. For example, pits larger than 1 x 1 meter that were north of the datum would be designated such as N4–5, but a pit the same distance south of the datum would be written S5–4.

The same system held for east and west coordinates (E4–5 and W5–4). In 1992 each operation had its own grid system, starting at a local 0/0 point. This was because we did not have the time to link the local grid into a master system. As already noted, theoretically, our 1992 grid, with its 0/0 point in Operation A, could have been extended over the entire site. Starting in 1993, however, we decided to shift the master datum point of the site, and so a new grid that did cover all of the site was established then.

Since we could see cobbles rising out of the ground as part of what appeared to be a circular structure, we started work by clearing this feature. We began by using hand tools to remove a few centimeters of soil from above those stones still covered by earth. This allowed us to better determine the pattern of the architecture and to plan our excavations. Clearing the cobbles became a standard practice in the rest of our work when rings and lines of stones were present. This upper soil was often rich in artifacts.

As we worked, it became apparent that the cobbles indeed formed a circle, and we named it Structure 1 (figs. 2.1, 2.2). Two lines of stones projected outward from the southwestern side of the structure and were buried much deeper than the circle. Excavations in this area revealed that the cobbles formed the outer edges of a quadrangle that may have served as a patio and perhaps also was the entry area. Since the ring of stones was unbroken, there was no clear indication of an entryway free of stones, however.

Our work in the quadrangular patio area was conducted mostly using 1 x 1 meter excavation units. It became extremely difficult to work in this manner, however, because each unit required a separate designation in notes and on artifact bags. It also took much more supervision of the workers when they were each excavating in a very small unit. We soon abandoned excavating in such small units except for situations that clearly warranted tight control. All indications suggested that we were digging in refuse, outside of the walls of the circular structure, with few artifacts located inside it.

We did find a lot of artifacts, however. The majority of these were sherds—broken pottery. We also found fragments of stone tools, mostly large, sharp-edged flakes knocked off larger chunks known as cores. Less frequent were teardrop-shaped stone adzes and other

ground stone objects, fragments of little ceramic whistles and figurines, and rare, one-of-a-kind objects.

In one of our southernmost pits in the Operation A excavations, S75/E14, we found a small carved stone miniature object shaped like a barrel. Large carved stone barrels are distinctive works of public art found farther south. They were first identified in Panama and later found in southern Costa Rica (Haberland 1968; Balser 1971). They also are believed to be relatively early in the monumental stone-working traditions of the region, later succeeded by the famous stone balls, also found farther south than Rivas (Fernández and Quintanilla in press). The presence of this miniature barrel in Operation A suggested that the Rivas site was occupied relatively early in the Chiriquí phase and that the barrel tradition had not completely died out in the greater region or that it had been kept as an heirloom, perhaps, from earlier times. Since no large stone barrels are known for the upper General Valley, the miniature suggests some kind of contact with people farther south. Perhaps someone from Rivas brought one back from a visit or carved a miniature once home, in commemoration of the trip.

We also placed excavation units in rows to create trenches running across the structure. These and other excavations consistently revealed similar patterns in the distribution of artifacts, with many found in the soil on the stones and immediately outside the structure and very few artifacts inside. It was impossible, however, to find evidence of floors inside structures. Since dense amounts of materials were found outside, it is likely that these were places where people carried out the activities of everyday life, leaving such refuse. The lack of refuse in the interiors suggests that these structures were kept clean and perhaps used mostly for sleeping or residence on the rainiest of days.

The great amounts of sherds and other refuse found outside structures might be explained by cleaning activities in which residue was deposited outside the dwelling, but this does not fully explain the absence of floors inside the structures. In many societies in which houses have earthen floors, there is an accretion of floor layers throughout time. This occurs when new earth is brought into a dwelling and tamped down or otherwise sealed over the old floor. Perhaps due to the moist climate of Costa Rica, the local preference may

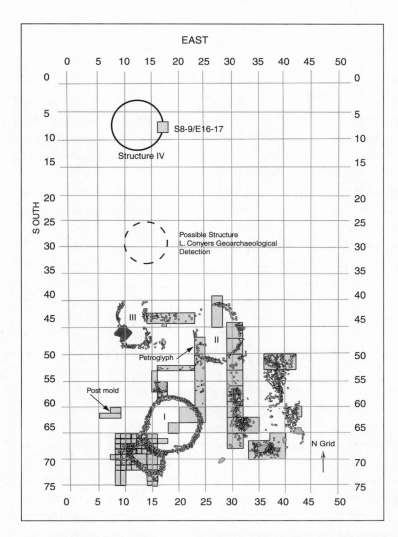

EAST

2.1. Excavations in Operation A, 1992. Map by R. J. Frost and J. Quilter.

2.2. Excavations in Operation A. View of Structure I from Grid NE looking in the direction of Grid SW.

have been to clean floors by sweeping out accumulated rubbish and the layer of soil in which it was embedded. If so, over time, the floor levels of houses might have sunk below the ground surface outside.

There also was no evidence of post molds in Structure 1. Aida had been away from the digging for a while when I told her one day that I was frustrated because, try as we might, I couldn't find any post molds. She started laughing. She said that it was very uncommon to find post molds in Costa Rica. We excavated in the interior of the structure near and just north of the possible entryway connected to the patio at its southwest corner, where the remains of a post might be expected to be located. We also placed a 3 x 5 meter pit that traversed the wall of the structure at its northeast side. In neither location were post molds found.

It may be that the nature of the soils at the site does not preserve disturbances such as rotted wood that would discolor the soil, gradually filling in the space as the post rotted away. The soil at Rivas is composed of weathered andesite, a close relative of granite. It compacts in such a way that little trace is left of prior disturbance, unlike soils in more temperate regions. This is due to intense bioturbation by roots and animals as well as intense leaching by rainwater percolation. Only in areas where there had been extensive deposition of household trash and similar organic materials was there a buildup of dark soils. Since there was some discoloration of the soil due to decomposition of organic materials, it was curious that there were no post molds. Large post molds should have left traces if they had disintegrated in place. If several to a score of posts were necessary to support a roof over a structure 10 meters in diameter, at least some traces of old posts should be found when many structures are excavated.

A single post mold was found in Operation A, but it was not found where it would have served to support the roof of the structure. We had placed a 2 x 4 meter trench west of Structure 1 to see if there was substantial overburden from erosion off of the Panteón de La Reina. We did not find signs of erosion in this trench, but we did find a very clear post mold with a pointed end, suggesting that the post had been sharpened to drive it into the ground. Despite the enlargement of the trench, we found no additional post molds. Perhaps the post served to hold a standard or a trophy skull. Or it may have been part of a small structure for

storage or cooking, and the other posts did not leave a trace because they were pulled out for reuse or fuel and thus did not rot in place.

The lack of post molds may be related to another aspect of the site. In Operation A and throughout Rivas, we found very little evidence of disintegrated adobe or wall plaster. Throughout the world, people who build houses with vertical walls made of twigs, saplings, or posts often coat them with a mixture of mud and other materials to insulate them. In Latin America, this material is called *bajareque*. When the site is abandoned, the *bajareque* crumbles, leaving soil of different color or texture around structure foundations. Sometimes due to high heat, through a house fire, for example, the *bajareque* is hardened, preserved in large fragments that may exhibit negative impressions of the canes or posts against which it was plastered. We found only one clear example of *bajareque* at Rivas, in Operation D, an area in which we worked after Operation A.

Lack of post molds and *bajareque* suggests that we might reconsider how Rivas structures were roofed. Instead of vertical, mud-plastered walls supporting conical roofs, the roofs may have been completely conical, like tipis, with the butts of sloped posts supported at the inner edge of the ring of stones or even placed within or on it for support. A photograph (fig. 2.3) of the "last *cacique*" (chief) of the Talamancas, taken around the turn of the nineteenth century, shows Antonio Saldaña and his family in front of just such a structure. The butts of the posts even appear to be resting on cobbles to the right of the figure at the extreme right. In addition, the roof over the entryway is quadrangular in shape, similar in form to the cobble patio in front of Structure 1 at Rivas.

Near the center of Structure 1, we found a large stone, 44 centimeters high and with an angled face 47 centimeters wide. On this broad face there were three ridged, parallel grooves with other, shallower ones to each side. The widths of these three grooves (5, 5.5, and 7 centimeters) fit the working ends of adzes commonly found at the site, and so it is likely that this artifact was a whetstone for such tools. It seems unlikely that this stone has stayed at the center of the house, in an original location, for a thousand years, uncovered by soil processes. While it may not have been where it was last used, it is likely that this stone hasn't been moved very far over the years, suggesting that the man-

2.3. Photograph of the "last *cacique*" (chief) of the Talamancas, Antonio Saldaña. The butts of house posts can be seen resting on the ground and perhaps behind a stone at the entry. Note the gold "eagles" worn by Saldaña at far left. Photo by Luis Ferrero.

ufacture or maintenance of wood-working or agricultural tools was one of the activities carried out in or near this structure.

We located the remains of two other cobble circles near Structure 1. The northwestern side of Structure 2 and the northern edge of Structure 3, both outside the guava grove, had been disturbed by recent agricultural activity. We placed a long 2 x 13 meter trench running from the northeast side of Structure 1 to intersect with the southwest area of Structure 2. We also placed a 2 x 6 meter trench overlapping the northern edge of Structure 2 and a 2 x 9 meter trench running from the western edge of Structure 3 to the eastern edge of Structure 2. These trenches were excavated to retrieve samples of artifacts from outside structure walls and to examine possible activities in the areas between the structures. We recovered great amounts of ceramics and other materials in these excavations. Elsewhere, the first evidence of maize consumption at the site was found immediately outside of Structure 3 (S44–43/E15–17) in the form of carbonized kernels.

One of our most interesting finds was in the area where the long trench intersected the cobble ring of Structure 2. One of the dish-size cobbles forming the ring had a petroglyph carved on it (fig. 2.4). The style of carving is distinctive of the numerous petroglyphs that can be found throughout the region (Zilberg 1986). It is possible that the petroglyph had been carved on the cobble in earlier times and later reused in the pavement of the structure. We do not have enough information on Chiriquí houses to know if the incorporation of a cobble with a petroglyph on it in a structure pavement is common or rare. The fact that the cobble was placed with the petroglyph side up, however, suggests that the design was appreciated. Since other petroglyphs are found at the site, it is likely that the design was indeed part of the stylistic and ideological world of the Chiriquí inhabitants of Rivas.

There was a very large boulder only a meter north of the Structure 1 house ring. We excavated around the boulder, finding dense deposits of artifacts, including a fragment of a Buenos Aires Polychrome figurine.

2.4. Petroglyph on a cobble forming the stone ring of Structure II. Looking to Grid S, along the trench. The petroglyph has been chalked to highlight its design.

We extended our excavations at this boulder northward a distance of 2 meters and then made a 7-meter-long trench, connecting it to our long north-south trench to check if a structure was in the area. No such structure was found.

The work around the boulder uncovered concentrations of small cobbles in addition to artifacts, mostly on top of them. There was another large boulder located at S68/E36, with large spall fragments around it and cobbles densely packed around the larger stones. Because they were located in the southeastern portion of our work area, we referred to this concentration for a long period of time as Piedras SE. We opened up a series of pits around this concentration of cobbles and boulders and found great amounts of artifacts. The cobbles were so neatly arranged that we wondered whether a burial lay beneath them, but excavations revealed that this was not so. In later work, in Operation E, we found a large, isolated stone with a ring of cob-

bles placed around its base. Standing stones have received veneration throughout the world. Perhaps this large, pillarlike stone in Operation A was of some special significance to the people who lived in this area of the site.

The Piedras SE feature was close to the edge of the terrace. To the north, there were two concentrations of cobbles resembling irregularly formed pavements, running north-south (fig. 2.1). One line ran close to the north-south 30-meter line of our coordinates and was higher in elevation than the second concentration. The second concentration was less linear and more spread out than the upper one. A few small excavation units in these cobble concentrations yielded dense quantities of sherds. We decided to place a very large set of 3 x 3 meter excavation units running like a trench along the upper concentration and to continue them through the southeastern section of Structure 2.

The lower concentration of cobbles was even richer in ceramics, lithics, and carbon than the upper one. We scraped off the soil from the cobbles and then placed a large north-south-running trench in it. Deep excavations revealed masses of cobbles probably left by ancient floodwaters before the site was occupied. We found the majority of remains in the upper layers, between 10 and 30 centimeters, with other artifacts among the cobbles immediately below as the soil decreased and cobbles increased.

When we began work on these cobble concentrations, we weren't sure what they were. We thought that they might be parts of structures. Our work, however, indicated that they were simply accumulations of cobbles but that some had been deliberately placed in position by humans. It seems as if this was an area of naturally occurring concentrations of rocks augmented by additions of pavementlike areas. This pattern of using natural landscape forms, sometimes slightly modified and then added to with deliberate construction, was one we were to find repeatedly at the site.

Artifact concentrations were very dense among these rocks, particularly in the more eastern areas. We found lots of spindle whorls (weights to aid in spinning thread) and ceramic disks, whistle and ocarina fragments, and the usual dense concentrations of stone tool remains and ceramics. These cobble concentrations may have been a combination of work areas and refuse dumps. They would have afforded a fine place to sit, on the terrace edge, looking out over the valley, and prevailing winds would have blown the smoke of fires near the structures away from anyone sitting in the area. The cobbles would have created a relatively dry surface, or at least a quick-draining one, as a place to spin thread and work on other tasks while conversing. The lower, more eastern cobble concentration would have been less ideal, and the higher concentration of artifacts there may signal that it was used more for disposing trash than the upper cobbles. Over time, however, both areas may have been used to dispose of refuse, resulting in the gradual buildup of materials.

While we were working in Operation A, the coffee plants bloomed. Although workers were still picking coffee elsewhere in the region, the local fields had been picked early and were flowering again. The shimmering, dark green of the coffee plants was now dotted with white blossoms. The perfume was rich, with a scent resembling vanilla but deeper, like roses. The scent would roll in waves in a slight breeze, and it was wonderful. Later, as the blossoms dropped, a surreal appearance of snow drifts could be seen in patches underneath the tropical sun and sky. Back home in Wisconsin, my poor wife and kids were suffering through one of the worst winters on record, with snow piling up by the inch. Here, under the hot tropical sun, the breezes blew the coffee blossom petals in swirls around our feet.

Continuing Work in Operation A

The three structures we found appeared to have been part of a complex, perhaps representing the compound of an extended family in which the head of the household lived in Structure 1. Structures 2 and 3 might have been occupied by the families of two adult children of the senior family in Structure 1. Another possibility might be that the smaller structures each had been occupied by a wife of a senior man residing in Structure 1. Even though Structure 3 had been damaged by recent farm activities, it appeared to have been rather poorly made, so another possibility was that it was some kind of outbuilding, such as a cookhouse for families living in one of the other structures. In many societies it is common to cook in a structure away from the main house to reduce risk of fire. Even at George Washington's Mount Vernon in Virginia, the kitchen was in a separate building away from the residence. Only when hard-to-control open fires ceased to be the chief heat source for cooking were kitchens commonly integrated with residences.

An obstacle to determining the relations among the people who built, used, and may have lived in the area is that we were uncertain of exactly how the three structures related. Because we had excavated them as a group, we came to think of them as a group. In reality, however, they could be three separate dwellings, or Structures 2 and 3 may have been secondary buildings related to some other structure. There could be other structures to the north, west, or east of Structures 2 and 3 to which they were related.

To the south lay an overgrown banana field. To the north, the guava grove in which we worked ended near the northern sides of Structures 2 and 3. The likelihood of finding additional structures to the west seemed low, because the Panteón slope began only a few meters distant, and the coffee in it precluded work there. The terrace edge to the east limited the chances of discovering structures there.

The southern tip of the Structure 1 patio crossed a fence line into an adjacent field with banana plants in it, somewhat overgrown in high grass. The earth seemed to rise in this field, and we suspected that there might be another structure there. We were working to maximum capacity in terms of our workers, but I spared two laborers, and we placed a 1.5 x 1.5 meter test pit in this area at S91.6/E20.6. The soil here was very dark, unlike the paler, more orange soils in most of the site, and there were dense concentrations of artifacts between about 13 and 33 centimeters. Although we could not work more in this place due to the lack of a sufficient workforce and our need to examine other areas, the organically darkened soil and dense artifacts suggest that this area received the remains of intense activities nearby. There likely are more structures similar to Structure 1 and its neighbors in this area.

To the north, there was clear evidence of a circular ring of stones at the far end of the field demarcated by a barbed wire fence separating pasture from the road where we parked the car. We exposed this ring of stones, calling it Structure 4. It was rather deep, below ground, but we did get a sample of sherds during our exposure of the ring. In addition, a Ripon student, JoEllen Ross, who was in the ACM Costa Rica program, excavated a pit crossing the ring of stones of Structure 4. The

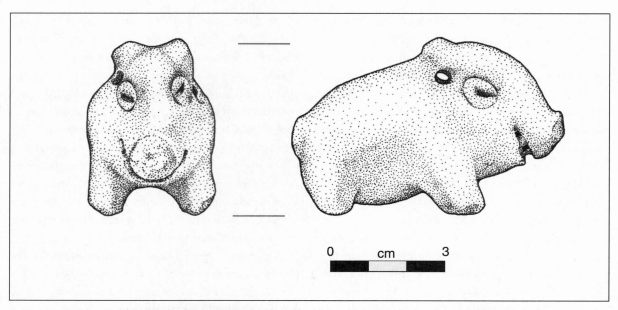

2.5. Peccary figurine from Operation A shovel test pit survey. Length: 7.6 cm. Illustration by Jennifer Ringberg.

materials she recovered were similar to those we found in the structures in the guava grove at the southern end of the field. The presence of this structure at the north end of the field with artifacts similar to the ones we had found suggested that there may have been others between it and the ones we excavated to the south. For example, another low mound that seemed unnatural was located on the eastern side of the area and about midway between the three structures and the northern fence.

Another ACM student, Lenorha Pohlman, did a shovel test pit survey of the field. She dug small holes, the width of a shovel, about 15 cenitmeters square and 40 cenitmeters deep, every 10 meters, in a grid pattern across the field. She found an abundance of sherds throughout the field, suggesting that this area saw intensive use in the past. Finding evidence of a house ring by this method is difficult, given the narrowness of the cobble pavement, but nonetheless she did encounter a segment of a pavement at 30–35 centimeters in a hole that was enlarged slightly for a better view (S20.5–20/E30–30.5). We never found the time or resources to expand excavations in this area, but we had uncovered enough evidence to suggest strongly that this upper terrace of the site likely had been covered by many circular structures similar to the ones we had already excavated. Among the artifacts recovered in the shovel test pit work was one of the "cutest" of the

site: a small figurine of a baby tapir or collared peccary (fig. 2.5).

Six years later, in 1998, we returned to Operation A to further investigate the question of additional structures in the field. Project geologist Larry Conyers used two different kinds of electromagnetic conductivity meters in an attempt to detect subsurface features. This work gave more evidence that there are buried stone structures in the field, and a subsequent excavation guided by the maps produced by Larry's high-tech machines confirmed that a structure probably exists north of the area of our work.

Beyond the Operation A area, so intensively studied over the years, it is likely that additional residences stretch for a considerable distance northward on this same high terrace. A much larger shovel test pit survey was conducted in 1994. In addition, 135 meters north of Operation A is Operation J (see chapter 5). This consists mostly of a very large circular structure just south of a prehistoric cemetery, Operation K. The Operation J structure appears to mark the northernmost limit of the occupation area on the terrace, as there is a cemetery to its north and no evidence of structures beyond it.

To the south of Operation A, the same 1994 shovel test pit survey revealed no clear evidence of structures. This area was filled with overgrown and cultivated fields. The only field in which we could work to the south with some ease was 100 meters distant (Shovel Test Pit Operation 10). There, the shovel test pit survey identified another cobble pavement near the terrace edge. Unlike the two found in the eastern part of the main Operation A area, this cobble platform appeared to be constructed by humans, or at least it was not as jumbled as the other pavements. We did not find evidence of structures in this area, however. While it is possible that our shovel test pit survey simply missed detecting evidence of structures, it appears that an occupation area with structures similar to the three we excavated may stretch a distance close to 250 meters along the terrace edge.

Interpretations

Our work in Operation A at the close of the 1992 field season had been quite satisfactory. We had defined and excavated three structures, identified cobble work areas, and discovered a number of interesting features and artifacts. At the time we finished our work in Operation A, we were under the impression that the Rivas site was a lot like Murciélago, as we had expected, consisting of the remains of round structures 10 meters in diameter.

During the five weeks we worked in the area, we accomplished enough to believe that we had a fairly good understanding of what had happened in the Operation A area in ancient times. We had excavated intensively and extensively around a single structure and a considerable amount around two additional structures, and we had a substantial collection of artifacts. But we had not had a chance to examine the artifacts carefully. After excavation, they were washed and rebagged to wait for future analysis. Our general impression was that the kinds of materials we had found were what one might expect in a suite of domestic structures. I had seen some of the artifacts when unusual ones had been found by workers and brought to me. I also had briefly reviewed artifacts as they were being washed and sorted. As this was my first excavation in Costa Rica, my understanding of what we were finding was based upon only what I had read and seen illustrated in books and what I had seen in museums.

All of the observations we made while excavating and our limited understanding of recovered artifacts suggested that we had a representative sample from a household of one of the groups of a community that had stretched along the terrace below the Panteón de La Reina. We knew that there was more to the site than this one area of Operation A, however, and that if we were to understand the site as a whole we should investigate other areas in it. It was thus time to excavate elsewhere in order to have a better understanding of the Rivas site and its ancient inhabitants.

Operation B, Work around a Petroglyph

While I had decided that I did not want to spend a lot of time making a detailed site map, I did want to try and get as much information on different areas of the site as possible. Demonstrating that there are signs of intensive occupations widely spaced along the upper terraces of the site would be sufficient proof that Rivas was a large and important place in prehistory. This would be valuable in itself, useful for comparisons with other sites and helpful in securing more funds from granting agencies for more work in the future.

Three hundred meters north of Structure 1 in Operation A there was a large boulder with a carving on it (fig. 2.6). The area around this petroglyph seemed like a good place to work, and so we called it Operation B. It was quite a distance away from Operation A, about 300 meters, and since it had a petroglyph, the area offered a different set of materials and problems to investigate. Operation B is on the uppermost terrace of the site (fig. 1.8), as is Operation A. We worked there to determine if other petroglyphs were present and to examine the nature and quantity of prehistoric refuse as indicators of the kinds of activities that may have taken place near petroglyphs. I also had an intuition that this petroglyph was at the northern end of the occupation area represented by Operation A, although at the time we began work in this area this was only a guess. Our later investigations supported the view that Operation B may have been some upper limit to the site.

In the Operation B area, the terrace is distinct and relatively narrow. The Panteón de La Reina ridge rises steeply 100 meters to the west, and the terrace is only 127 meters wide. The petroglyph boulder was at the eastern end of a field of tall grass, about 19 meters from the terrace edge (fig. 2.7). Fifteen meters to the west was a pile of big boulders, some the size of small

2.6. The petroglyph on the Operation B boulder. Traces of what was once a more elaborate design have been highlighted with chalk. Folding rule for scale.

cars. The grassy area was only a little more than 10 meters in width, bounded on the north by a barbed wire fence and foot path with coffee fields beyond and on the south by dense *monte*. The *monte* immediately around the petroglyph was like similar areas around the site. These often were old fields allowed to become overgrown. Much of the vegetation in or immediately surrounding the clearing consisted of useful trees such as lemon and *achiote* (*Bixea orellana*).

There is very little evidence of human occupation to the west of the Calle Mora in this area of the site and northward. Gilbert Mora, one of the older men and a valued worker, stated that he had helped build the road and that the work crew rarely encountered much in the way of artifacts during their construction efforts. It may be that continuing erosion of the hill slope, with resulting redeposition of materials along its base, has covered remains that now lie deep beneath the surface, or perhaps the area was avoided for settlement for fear of landslides of the unstable material from the Panteón de La Reina. We never con-

ducted detailed study of this area to the west of the road. Over the years, however, there have been a number of disturbances there either due to house construction or agriculture. We consistently checked any trenches or other cuts into the soil in this area and never found artifacts or signs of occupation.

Work in Operation B

I had first seen the petroglyph (figs. 2.6–2.8) in 1991 (Quilter and Blanco 1995: 208), at which time it was in high, thick brush. The design was carved on a large boulder, slightly more than 3 meters long, about 1.5 meters maximum width, about as high as it was wide, and roughly teardrop in shape on its upper, slightly rounded surface. Some time ago, a large section of the boulder had broken off of the bulbous end, and there was clear evidence that another piece also recently had separated from the parent boulder on the same end.

At the time of my 1991 examination, enough of the original petroglyph remained that I recorded a

1-meter-long section of the design. It also was clear that the design originally had been more complex but had eroded from the surface of the stone over time. Sufficient detail remained to infer that the design of the engraving followed the general pattern of rock art for the region, consisting of undulating lines, connecting circles, and probably spirals.

The tall grass surrounding the boulder likely had slowed erosion, but we cut it down in order to view the petroglyph. When we returned in 1992, it appeared that our advice to cover the remaining carving had not been followed, and most of the design we had observed in the previous year had vanished. Such rapid rates of weathering made us wonder how many other boulders at the site may once have had engravings that can no longer be seen.

After preliminary clearing, work began on February 13, 1992. We spent the shortest amount of time in Operation B in comparison to work in all other locales at Rivas given a formal operation letter designation. We were finished with excavations there by the 24th of the month.

As our purpose was to try and investigate the kinds of activities that took place next to and near the petroglyph, we began by placing a 2 x 2 meter pit on the west side of the boulder. Two more 2 x 2s were added on the south and east sides, respectively, and, as work continued, excavation units were gradually expanded and added, all dug in 10-centimeter levels, as no natural stratigraphy could be observed (fig. 2.8). The final excavation here was 32 square meters in area.

In addition to the work around the petroglyph, pits were placed on the edge of the boulder concentration on the western section of the cleared area, eventually expanding to cover another 32 square meters. We were interested in the other boulder concentration because we wanted to see if any petroglyphs might be found on rock surfaces below ground level. We also wanted to study the relative intensity of activities, as determined by artifact densities, in this area in comparison to the area around the petroglyph. In addition, we excavated a 2 x 2 meter pit in an open area with no visible concentrations of boulders to see if we might encounter evidence of a structure and to try to judge how activities away from boulders may or may not have been different from areas closer to them.

Compared to other sectors of the Rivas site, the density of artifacts throughout Operation B was relatively low. Most units were dug no deeper than 40 centimeters, and quite often less than that, because we found so few artifacts. As is common in archaeology, we often dug an extra 10 or 20 centimeters below the level of artifacts to be sure we had reached sterile soil. Only occasionally did we dig deeper pits, usually to better understand the patterning of boulders and cobbles rather than to investigate an abundance of sherds. So, too, our later 1994 shovel test pit survey confirmed that this area had few traces of ancient debris.

We found a possible activity area in pit S6–5/E6–7. This consisted of materials associated with stone tool production (debitage) in a space that could have surrounded or been within reach of a single worker, all on the same level. Stone tool fragments were arranged as if they were left in place after work was finished or as if someone was in the middle of working when he or she got up and did not come back. The patterning of the artifacts had not been strong, however, although their location at the same depth suggested that they were contemporaneous.

In pit N0–1/E14–15, we found a concentration of cobbles about 1 meter in width. This looked like a possible path, perhaps leading toward the petroglyph or some other feature; another pit, N0–1/E17–18, also seemed to contain some kind of pavement near the petroglyph. In the latter pit, we encountered cobbles at a depth of about 30 centimeters clustered together, and they appeared to be oriented in a northeast-southwest direction, diagonal to our grid system. The single row of cobbles in N0–1/E14–15 had the same orientation. Aida Blanco believed that none of these cobbles constituted a path or pavement, while I thought they might, though I wasn't strongly committed to the idea.

Expansion of excavation units to follow these possible paths and pavements may have clarified the matter, but it also might have remained ambiguous. We had not found artifacts directly resting on the pavement in N0–1/E17–18, but that, by itself, did not necessarily rule out the possibility that these cobbles had been deliberately aligned by humans. Both in Operation A and in later work we frequently confronted the problem of finding lots of buried cobbles, some of which appeared to be ordered and some of which did not. Like taking a Rorschach test, our minds may

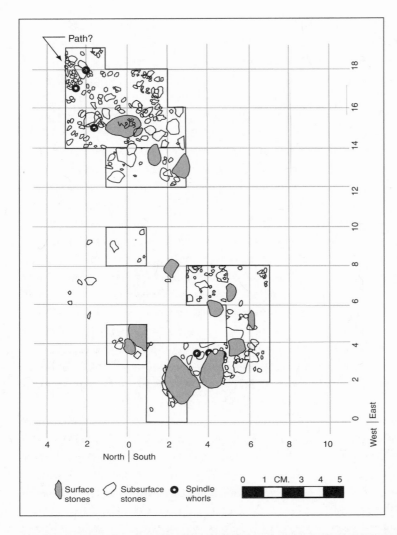

Path?

18

16

14

12

10

8

6

4

2

0

West | East

4   2   0   2   4   6   8   10

North | South

Surface stones   Subsurface stones   Spindle whorls

0   1 CM.   3   4   5

2.7. Map of the excavations in Operation B. Note that Grid N is to the left. Map by R. J. Frost and J. Quilter.

2.8. Work around the Operation B petroglyph at an early stage of excavations. View to Grid SW.

have been imposing order on a randomly created pattern. Later, we found cobbles clearly arranged around a natural boulder far from the site, the Piedra del Indio (see chapter 7). By the time this issue became clear, we had begun to work in another area of the Rivas site, the Operation C cemetery, where we were much more certain about what we were finding. So rather than pursuing an uncertainty that might never be resolved, we let the matter rest for Operation B.

In the *monte*, slightly more than 20 meters south of our main work area, we did some clearing to examine the ground surface. We discovered a low but distinct mound of stones mixed with earth, 2 to 3 meters in width, running in a north-south direction, rising gently above the ground surface to a maximum height of about 10 centimeters. We thought that this might be some kind of structure, so we set up a series of excavation units, which eventually expanded to two 2 x 2 meter units placed catercorner. Our work in this locale uncovered dense accumulations of stones. Unit S24–23/ E12–13 had so many rocks in it that there was little soil to excavate. It soon became clear to us, however, that this pile of rocks and artifacts was not part of a house or an activity area of the kind found in Operation A. The stones were all jumbled and not laid flat so as to provide a surface on which to sit or walk.

In pits in this southern area that had less dense accumulations of cobbles, we found great numbers of artifacts. Such was the case in an additional excavation unit opened on the mound, a 3 x 3 meter unit, S34–32/ E13–15. The soil in this pit was very dark, organic, and powdery. These pits yielded not only great amounts of ceramic sherds but also such things as the broken leg of a fancy metate and a finely made mano. Most of the pits in these rich deposits were empty of artifacts or nearly so by 30 or 40 centimeters depth and were closed accordingly.

Even though there appeared to be a dense deposit of artifacts in the mound south of the petroglyph, subsequent analysis suggested a relative paucity of remains useful for study. When all of the materials were cleaned and processed, there were only eight rim fragments large enough to reconstruct vessel mouth diameters of the original vessels. We did not find any "special" ceramic items, such as ocarinas, whistles, or figurines, with the exception of six complete or partial spindle whorls. As for stone tool remains, again there was little of special note. We only encountered typical stone cores and flakes removed from them or ones like them, as well as a couple of polishing stones and mano fragments.

Interpretations

Our excavations in the Operation B area do not provide clear-cut answers to the question of what kinds of activities took place near the petroglyph in the past, but then again, few excavations ever provide clear answers. Furthermore, it is by now an archaeological truism that excavations or the artifacts recovered from them never provide any answers per se. Rather, it is the interpretations made from study and analyses of the site, excavations, and recovered materials that contribute to potential answers. So, what kinds of inferences might be drawn from the data retrieved and the information drawn from them?

From a behavioral point of view, petroglyph sites have many characteristics that suggest they were sacred places. Carving a design on a rock was a deliberate effort that, at least from our perspective, was beyond the activities that maintained life or supplied the basic needs of individuals or society. Was this then some kind of religious activity, perhaps induced by dreams or visions, or maybe part of some obligation of people following a particular set of rituals associated with their beliefs? We don't know for sure. The repetition of similar sets of designs and the fact that petroglyphs are commonly found among groups of rocks in some boulder fields but not others hint that rock carving was a special activity that occurred in special places.

If making a petroglyph had some special significance, then we might expect that such significance would also be marked by giving the places surrounding rock art special status. For example, sacred spaces are almost always kept immaculately clean. This is true not only in the buildings of contemporary Western religions but also holds, for example, for temples and similar structures in prehistoric Peru and Mesoamerica. Using this logic, if rock art was carved as a sacred activity, then we would expect the spaces around petroglyphs to have been swept and kept clean.

If the Rivas site was occupied for several generations, the light density of artifacts in the Operation B area might be explained as the gradual accumulation of very few deposits of refuse piled together over the centuries. In other words, the area was kept clean, but after so many hundreds of years some buildup of deposits did occur, resulting in the archaeological deposits into which we excavated. Furthermore, if this area of the site was abandoned or fell into disuse, or if the ideological values associated with petroglyphs waned while there was still occupation nearby, then perhaps the sparse amount of materials that did accumulate was during times of inattentiveness in keeping the area clean.

The presence of some ceramic remains in the Operation B area does suggest that few activities occurred near the petroglyph. These remains were mostly large-mouthed vessels, indicating that these were used for carrying, serving, or consuming food and drinks. Feasting is a common activity in public spaces associated with "ceremonial" or "religious" activities in the New World and elsewhere, so this hints that the petroglyph area may have been a place where such things occurred after all.

The issue is not quite as clear as this, however, because we have at least one example of a rather mundane activity, stone tool manufacture or repair, not too far from the petroglyph. Perhaps the activity was just far enough outside of the sacred zone surrounding the petroglyph. Perhaps the person making the tools was a member of a special kin group responsible for the maintenance and protection of the rock art. Members of that group might have had a special relation to it that other people didn't, allowing that person to sit nearby and work on stone tools while other members of society couldn't come near the rock. Perhaps the sharpening of tools was related to the carving of the petroglyph.

We also found six spindle whorl fragments, three near the petroglyph and three near the western cluster of rocks. In many Native American societies, women spin constantly as they walk from place to place, sit and talk, and so forth, any time they have their hands free. This is thus a very mundane activity. The spindle whorl fragments don't necessarily mean that spinning occurred where they were found, since they may have ended up there through sweeping or some other activity that moved them from their original places of discard.

Even playing with these possibilities still leaves one uneasy, however, because the density of artifacts around the petroglyph intuitively seems just high enough to suggest that some people, over the centuries, prepared or consumed food and did other mundane things nearby. The general kinds of artifacts found do not seem to differ significantly from those found elsewhere at the site either.

The final point to consider is that we found a petroglyph on a cobble that was part of the ring wall of a domestic structure in Operation A, as mentioned earlier in this chapter. Of course, this might have been some special religious structure, but there is no reason to think this necessarily. It may have had some special occupant or status, though, but the only thing to indicate this is the petroglyph itself; we have no corroborating evidence.

We are left with the following facts as derived from our investigations. The petroglyph was in an area with no houses near it for several meters and probably more. The area immediately around the petroglyph did not accumulate much trash, but there was a slight buildup of deposits over the years of the occupation of the site. The materials that did accumulate consist of broken ceramic vessels, stone tool fragments, and spindle whorls, and there were no "fancy" materials. Operation A has many more figurines, whistles, and other such materials. A cobble path may have been made near the petroglyph, and perhaps a small pavement was constructed close to it. If so, however, these features were not made with enough care and attention to detail that future archaeologists could be sure of the ancient peoples' behavior and intentions.

About 20 meters south of the petroglyph, a long, low mound contained accumulations of trash, including some fancy materials such as carved stone metate legs. This mound is puzzling. Perhaps it is analogous to the two stone piles found in Operation A, and the unevenness of the cobbles is simply due to minor perturbation of the soil in this locale or some other, unknown factors. If this were the case, then, using Operation A as a model, we would expect houses to be present about 10 meters or so from the deposit, perhaps to the west or farther south. Alternatively, the trash could be a deliberate deposit made after clean-up operations around the petroglyph, explaining why the area is relatively free of artifacts. The few sherds and other materials that we did recover immediately around the petroglyph may simply be the results of less than perfect sweeping of the area.

Another point to consider is that the petroglyph seems to be on the northern end of the Rivas occupation centered in Operation A. True, we later found a cemetery (Operation K) bordering the northern end of the area of houses, but perhaps houses continued northward, beyond the cemetery. Nevertheless, the number of sherds recovered in the general area, including south of the petroglyph, was not great, suggesting that activities decreased somewhere south of this location.

Finally, it is worth considering that our ideas of sacred and profane spaces are set up as binary categories, but in reality there is a gray area between them. There are many spaces in contemporary Western culture that are not as holy as a church or as mundane as a house. For example, public parks, such as the National Mall in Washington, D.C., are respected as places generally to be kept clean and to have nothing more than temporary structures put on them, such as tents for celebrations on national holidays. Over the years, however, trash accumulates in the grass around picnic areas, trash bins, and so forth. Loose change is dropped when buying a hot dog, toys are accidentally broken after leaving a museum and pieces scattered or discarded on the Mall itself. With enough time, certain areas may have higher concentrations of the residues of human activities than others. Formal ceremonies are held on the Mall, but people also relax with family and friends. Other examples of spaces like the Mall can be found in cities throughout the world.

People respect these spaces as having symbolic meanings in the histories of their countries, counties, or towns. The range of behaviors carried out in them is different than what people might do in their own backyards, yet both sets of behaviors overlap to a considerable degree. While they respect these places as special and are prohibited or inclined not to do certain things there that they might do elsewhere, people are not inhibited from doing many other activities. They might eat a hot dog and drink a soda, losing change, key rings, and other small items from their pockets while purchasing these items or while sitting on a bench or the grass. Even a stray small plastic catsup or mustard package might get buried in the grass. But

people wouldn't cook hot dogs on the National Mall (it's against the law, anyhow). So the various small items associated with barbecuing (the caps on lighter fluid cans, bits of charcoal briquettes) would not enter the archaeological record there. There would be an overlap of items associated with festival foods (hot dogs and hamburgers) but some distinctions. Those small plastic packages of catsup and mustard are mostly used by people eating purchased foods, while at home they tend to use larger, plastic or glass containers for those condiments.

Perhaps the petroglyph in Operation B marked a place similar to the ones described: a special place but not a highly sacred one. We need more excavations around the many petroglyph sites in southern Costa Rica to test these ideas there as well as comparative research throughout the globe. This example also shows how hard it can be to interpret an archaeological site where the evidence does exhibit behavior that has clear analogies to our own ways of doing things.

As we were puzzling on the ambiguities of the petroglyph area, Gilbert Mora told us of a cemetery located behind the cluster of houses at the northern end of the Calle Mora. We decide to move on from an ambiguous situation to one that we hoped would be more clear-cut, the excavation of a cemetery associated with the Rivas site not located on the Panteón de La Reina.

Operation C

The cemetery that Gilbert Mora had mentioned was located behind the house of Don Leobihildo Mora, known affectionately as Don Bildo, one of the two senior Mora men. The younger Mora said that as a child he and his brothers had dug in the area and found pots and other things. We asked permission from Don Bildo to work on his land, and he granted it.

The cemetery was on the edge of a terrace remnant perhaps two or three levels lower than the terrace on which Operations A and B were located (fig. 1.8). The cemetery also was partly separated from the other terraces by a gully. Running off of the Panteón de La Reina, small streams such as this which thread through the site may have served as handy water sources for site residents.

The area was flat and mostly in tall grass and weeds. There were some smaller boulders around, but most of the cemetery had few stones on it. The total area in this condition was about 200 square meters. In a number of places in this field, there were disturbed areas that had been looted, as revealed by partly filled holes in the ground. To the south, on the other side of a barbed wire fence, the cemetery continued. Good-quality, thick grass was in this field, and the owner did not want it disturbed. The cemetery may have stretched into this field, covering an additional 200 square meters or so, but we could not investigate this possibility.

We called this entire area Operation C and began by clearing near one of the looter holes. The grass was removed and the shallow roots scraped off to expose the first layer of soil, as was the procedure in every other area in which we worked. There was no ready place on which to establish a local datum, so we put a nail in the stump of a very large burned tree to serve as the 0/0 point for our map. We laid out a north-south running line and an east-west one.

We began by placing our transit to lay out excavation units at the S10/W7 point of our grid, slightly west of one of the looter holes. As we removed the grass layer, we found a cluster of stones at S4.4/W4.9. It soon became clear that this was a pavement of the kind that covers graves, so we named it Burial 1. As the clearing continued, we found several clusters of these cobbles. We began excavation, and by the time we were finished we had concentrated work on seven numbered burials in an area slightly larger than about 40 square meters (figs. 2.9, 2.10).

The total area that was scraped clear was slightly less than 200 square meters. In the area, outside of where we concentrated our work, we found more cobble concentrations. These appeared to have been badly disturbed because there was no pattern to them except for a few lines of stones, here and there, yet there was no sign that these areas had been looted. Cobbles were not strewn about but rather badly jumbled, as if they had been moved back and forth but never taken out of the ground. It is likely that the disturbance is due to relatively recent agricultural activities, in the last forty years or so. There was a large concentration of rocks and boulders in the northwestern corner of our work area. Most of these seemed to be in situ as the result of natural processes, although a few may have been moved there if the cemetery had been cleared of miscellaneous stones in antiquity.

Near the concentration of rocks there was a straight line of cobbles, with each placed on edge, rather than lying flat, and buried halfway into the ground. If the line had once continued in antiquity, none of it was preserved for us to find. It seems likely that this line formed a border to the cemetery area, enclosing the burial area.

The standard way to excavate burials is to scrape the earth until the outline of the grave can be seen, usually as an oval or a rectangle. This establishes the ancient ground surface from which the pit was dug. Then excavation usually proceeds by removing the earth within the boundaries of the pit, eventually reaching human remains and any artifacts buried with them. If the skeleton is preserved, all of the earth around it is removed to expose the entire burial assemblage for illustration, photography, and subsequent removal of all or some of the artifacts and human remains. Once the contents are removed, excavation continues to fully determine and document the shape of the ancient grave. Unfortunately, this procedure could not be followed at Operation C.

As discussed in reference to post molds, the soil at Rivas is a fine, powdery, weathered andesite, the same stone that forms the boulders and cobbles that abound in the region. It feels like sand to the touch, and, like sand, when it is poured back into a hole no traces remain of the excavation. We therefore usually were not able to determine the outlines of burial pits. Our excavation strategy had to try and find a way to excavate burials efficiently. We had removed the grass roots from a large area and had found several distinct cobble pavements of the kind known to cap graves, so we decided to open up a large area around them. Using our grid system, we carefully mapped the pavements and then continued to scrape down the area until we encountered artifacts. These artifacts were the only clear remains of the burials, due to tropical leaching and acidic soil, except for occasional black stains.

When we were certain that artifacts were directly under a cobble pavement, the artifacts were given numbers based on the number of the pavement, designated as a burial. In some areas, where two cobble pavements joined or where isolated finds were encountered, it was less clear which artifacts belonged to which pavement, so the grid coordinates of the artifacts were used to designate artifacts there. Some of the areas of

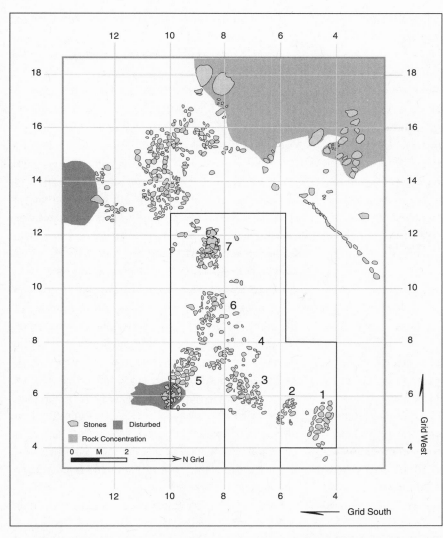

2.9. The Operation C study area. Burials are numbered. Note Grid N is to the right. Map by R. J. Frost and J. Quilter.

2.10. Cobble pavements in the Operation C cemetery. Burial 1 is in the foreground. Disturbed pavements of Burials 2 and 3 are in the middle and rear.

disturbed cobbles appear to have originally been wide pavements that possibly covered group burials rather than individual graves.

The pavements were made of carefully selected cobbles (fig. 2.10). The ideal cobble seems to have been almost circular, though oval ones are more common. Three rows of cobbles, laid flat and running the long axis of the burial, are the norm, with an additional perimeter of cobbles placed on edge and buried half way in the ground around the pavement. Given that the outer perimeter of the cemetery appears to have been defined by cobbles placed on their edges and that the burial pavements also were defined with cobbles placed the same way, it seems reasonable to suggest that cobbles-on-edge were used to define boundaries.

The burials excavated varied in the number of artifacts found in them (figs. 2.11, 2.12). With usually no evidence of bodies, it often was very frustrating to try and determine exactly how a group of offerings was related to pavements previously excavated above them, even with coordinates of both features carefully monitored. In excavations at the La Pista Cemetery, associated with the Murciélago site, Ursula Iwaniec (1986: 3) noted the same phenomenon. In her excavation of 16 graves, there consistently was no clear correlation between surface cobble pavements and the graves themselves. Perhaps this was deliberately done to foil ancient tomb robbers. More likely, it may be that the pavements were used as places on which to perform ceremonies after burial rather than to mark graves per se. Perhaps the pavements were made sometime after the actual burial in a ritual performed to commemorate the deceased.

In some cases we could make out faint, dark soil stains —traces of human remains that we called "shadow corpses." It was fairly clear that the grave offerings had been placed at the head and feet of the deceased or slightly to the sides of these areas. Ceramic vessels also may have been laid over the body or other remains. In one grave, Burial 7, large slabs of stones, called *lajas*, appear to have been placed over the dead, a burial practice that Doris Stone (1962: 339) stated was common to the Atlantic Watershed region of Costa Rica. We found it in only a few cases during our work at Rivas. In many places in the ancient world, stones or other heavy objects were placed on top of corpses, perhaps to keep them from rising from the grave. Cases similar to this are found in Preceramic Peruvian burials, for example (Quilter 1989).

Another strange occurrence in graves was the presence of circular stains, about 2 centimeters in diameter and of different color than the surrounding earth. These tended to occur immediately above the level of grave offerings—about 30 centimeters or so—and continued to about 10 or 20 centimeters below the level of the offerings. When we first encountered these stains we thought that they might be the filled-in remains of some kind of burrowing animal, perhaps an insect that fed on carcasses as is common at many archaeological sites. We cross-sectioned some of these stains, however, and found that they generally were straight in length and ended in a point, suggesting they are traces of sharpened canes or sticks. There were sometimes scores of these stains in burial areas. Perhaps they are the remains of some kind of stakes, flags, or other pointed sticks used in burial rituals. They are occasionally found in other areas of the site but rarely so. Perhaps the stakes or flags were placed around the dead as the grave was filled with earth and left in place for a while. If so, it would have been impossible to place a stone pavement directly over the grave pit. The pit would have to have been constructed on the side of the actual pit. This might explain why pavements are not aligned directly over graves.

Burial 1 had only a single artifact (fig. 2.11: 1). In the general area, however, we did encounter a small ceramic vessel buried, right side up, just below the ground surface. This pattern of small vessels near the surface was found elsewhere at the site as well. Most of the grave goods occurred at about 1.5 meters to 2 meters in depth. Due to soil conditions, we only found fire-hardened ceramics and stones in graves. Most of the burials had between two and four pots. Large tripod bowls were often inverted, legs pointing up, sometimes over another vessel (fig. 2.13). Sometimes bowls were stacked inside one another or piled in groups. In one case, in Burial 3, we found a small bowl with three miniatures of different forms and decorations inside it, all placed in another bowl (fig. 2.11: T3, 1–5). There is no evidence that vessels were ritually "killed" by breaking them. All breaks appear to have occurred during the use life of the object, through the pressure of earth, or from accidents of excavation by our crew.

Burial 5 had the greatest number of grave goods

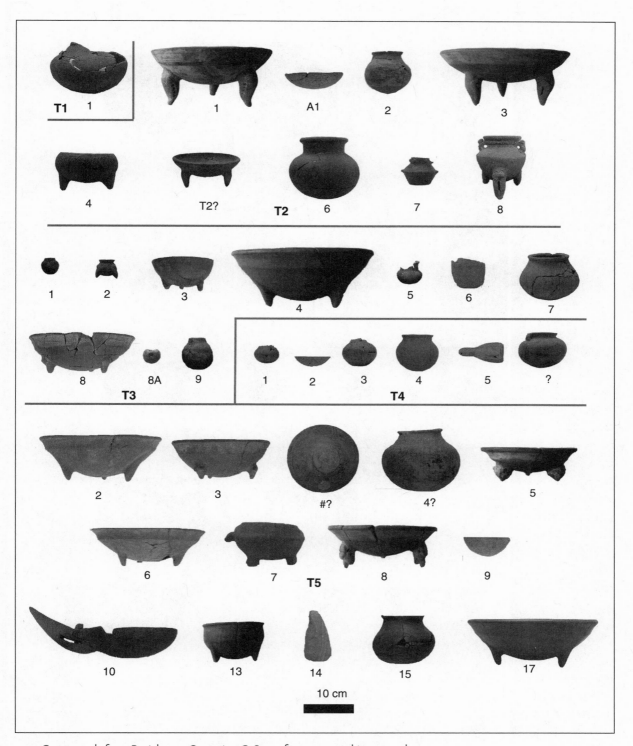

2.11. Grave goods from Burials 1–5, Operation C. Some fragmentary objects not shown.

with a total of 24 objects (figs. 2.11 and 2.12: T5). These included two stone adzes, a small jar, three simple jars, a small simple open bowl, two small pedestal bowls, six tripod open bowls, what may have been a small open pedestal bowl with the pedestal broken off, an elaborate tripod jar, three large jars, and a "frying pan censer," in Spanish called a *sartén*. The quality of manufacture of these objects, to modern eyes, varied widely. Two tripod open bowls (fig. 2.11: T5, 5, 8) were among the finest ever seen by project members and

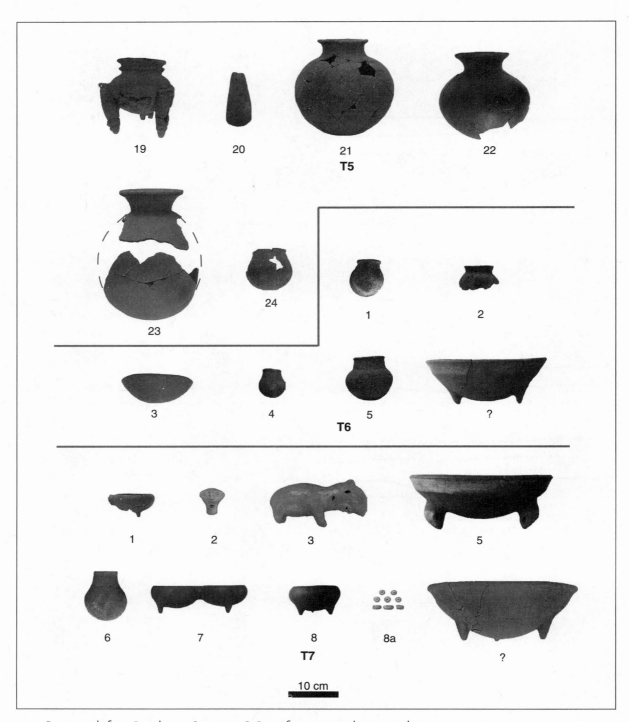

2.12. Grave goods from Burials 5–7, Operation C. Some fragmentary objects not shown.

had elaborate legs in the form of animal heads. The other large bowls, however, were not as well made or elaborately decorated. The tripod jar (fig. 2.11: 5) had poorly made legs, was not symmetrical, and was made of a poor-quality clay, and the vessel appears to have been overfired.

Burials 2 and 3 were similar in that they both contained two large tripod open bowls accompanied by additional small bowls and jars. Burial 2 had a very handsome tripod jar in Ceiba Red-Brown style (fig. 2.12: T5, 19). It was a better example of the poor-quality Ceiba tripod found in Burial 5. Burial 3 is notable in that it

2.13. An inverted tripod bowl from Burial 3 in the foreground and two jars from Burial 5 at the rear. Operation C.

first person to sound a note on this instrument in a thousand years or more.

Evidence from the seven excavated burials suggests that these were the graves of people of middle to low status. This interpretation is based on the simple fact that there were no gold ornaments in the graves, nor were there fancy carved stone metates or other objects that would indicate high status. Since we lack human remains, we cannot develop theories about different grave goods for men or women, young or old. Poor preservation conditions leave open the question of perishable goods that probably were included with ceramics and stone tools. If (and only if) stone adzes were men's tools and if grave goods were once owned by the grave occupant, then Burial 5 was the final resting place of a man. It is usually assumed that the number of grave goods is positively correlated with the rank of the individual. Using only this criterion and assuming that the number of perishable grave goods was proportional to ceramics and stone tools (which may not have been so), Burial 5 was of much higher rank and Burial 1 much lower than any of the dead in the other graves we excavated. It also seems that two tripod open bowls and two or more smaller jars or bowls were a kind of minimal ceramic grave good set for some of the dead. This may reflect some kind of basic dinner service, too, perhaps a large bowl for a main course with a second one, in reserve, and smaller bowls to hold condiments or savory dishes to add flavor to the starch (maize?) that likely was the foundation of most meals. Some vessels may not have been used for food or drink at all, however, such as the small jar placed in Burial 7 in which the beads were kept.

The Operation C ceramic assemblage is dominated by the ceramic types known as Turucaca White-on-Red and Sangria Fine Red. All tripod open bowls are in these styles except for one Buenos Aires Polychrome example in Burial 2 (fig. 2.11: T2, 1). The only other Buenos Aires Polychrome style ceramics are the tapir figurine and human head whistle from Burial 7. The quality and light color of the fired clay of a tortoise effigy bowl (fig. 2.11: T5, 7) suggest that it may have been Buenos Aires Polychrome, but the entire surface treatment has been worn away over time. Ceiba Red-Brown is represented by a variety of vessels such as the single, poorly preserved jar in Burial 1 (fig. 2.11: T1, 1). There are only two examples of Papayal Engraved.

was the grave in which the two stacked bowls with miniatures were found. It also contained a clay spindle whorl or ornament with incised decoration (figs. 2.11: T3, 8A; 2.14), which may have been broken in antiquity. Burial 4 had no open bowls but did contain a clay rattle (fig. 2.11: 25). Burial 6 also had two tripod open bowls, a number of small jars, and two very large jars. Burial 7 had a single tripod open bowl, a small tripod bowl, and two small jars. In one of these jars eight clay beads had been stored (fig. 2.12: 8, 8A). A conjoined bowl also was found in this grave, as was the broken half of another. We also found a ceramic tapir figurine (fig. 2.15) and a small ocarina in the shape of a human head (fig. 2.16). There was a suspension loop on the back of the ocarina so, when worn on a string, it would have hung upside-down like a trophy head. It was a thrill to play a little tune and realize that I was the

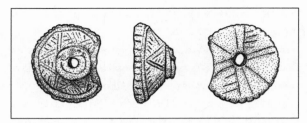

2.14. A decorated spindle whorl from Operation C. Diameter: 3.3 cm. Illustration by Jennifer Ringberg.

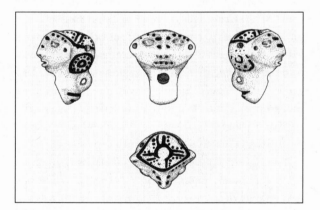

2.15. The ceramic tapir figurine (Burial 7, Artifact 3) from Operation C. Length: 14 cm. Illustration by Jennifer Ringberg.

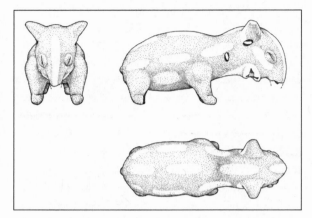

2.16. Human head ocarina (Burial 7, Artifact 1), Operation C. Height: 5.2 cm. Illustration by Jennifer Ringberg.

They are similar small tripod bowls found in Burials 2 and 7 (figs. 2.11: T4, 4; 2.12: T7, 8).

Since we had recovered relatively great amounts of Buenos Aires Polychrome and Papayal Engraved in Operations A and B, we were struck by the apparent underrepresentation of these types in the Operation C burials. We had not had enough time in the laboratory,

however, to develop a sense of the degree to which the predominance of Red Wares—Sangria Fine Red and Turucaca White-on-Red—in the cemetery collection differed from the proportions of ceramic types in domestic areas of the site.

Excavations in Operation C were complicated by the fact that work was starting in another of the site, Operation D, located a kilometer away. It was difficult trying to supervise these two areas simultaneously. To add to the complications, I had to go to San José for three work days in order to get more money to pay workers and to attend a reception for Fulbright scholars. Due to these difficulties, some of the recording of grave goods in Operation C was confused during my absence, although we have worked out most of the associations of ceramics with burials in the laboratory.

Our project geologist, Larry Conyers, made an interesting observation. It was obvious, once he said it, but that is often why we pay experts to point out things. He noted that the soil in Operation C was clear of boulders and very deep and thus the perfect locale for a cemetery. It was true; many areas of the Rivas site have very shallow soils above dense gravel deposits or large boulders. The people who inhabited the site had searched to find places where there were deep deposits of earth so that they could use them for the resting places of their dead. Presumably, some people were not allowed to bury their dead on Panteón de La Reina, where soils are deep. This meant that they had to seek out other places to serve as cemeteries. But where were the houses of the people who buried their dead in Operation C? This question was pursued later in the project.

Our work in Operation C was exciting and rewarding. We had found a Chiriquí cemetery that was not on the Panteón de La Reina and that did not have gold. The fact that the ceramics were of types found in other parts of the site indicated contemporaneity, but the preponderance of Turucaca and Sangria (Red Wares) in the grave assemblage was worth consideration. We had started to look at the ceramics more closely. While Red Wares were present in our collections from Operations A and B, they were in the minority compared to Buenos Aires Polychrome and Papayal Engraved. The fact that Red Wares were in the majority for the Operation C cemetery could be interpreted in a number of ways. Since the popularity of ceramic styles shifts through time, the greater proportion of Red Wares in Operation C might be an indicator that the graveyard was in use slightly later or earlier than the occupations of Operations A and B. We could not tell whether the date was earlier or later until we did more research, either through developing a seriation of artifacts or getting radiocarbon dates. The other explanation could be cultural. Perhaps the people buried in Operation C were part of a social group of some sort that favored Red Wares, while other, contemporaneous folk used the other pot styles. Or perhaps Red Wares were preferred as grave goods, possibly because they were more valued than the other wares.

We had only found one decent-size sample of carbon to date for the Operation C cemetery. We had to wait until we returned to the United States to send it to a lab for a date. Meanwhile, we were left frustrated by our inability to be more precise but excited that we may have had evidence of two different sectors or classes of Rivas society, one that had the right to gold and burial on the Panteón de La Reina and another that did not. This could have great implications for understanding chiefdom societies in ancient Lower Central America. We might be looking at classes, at something more like a stratified society resembling a state in its political structure.

Operation D

We had been excavating for six weeks and had begun work in Operation C when Aida was asked to take a tour of interesting local sites by a man in charge of local sanitation who had grown up in the area. They had gone off in the morning, and it wasn't until nearly the end of the work day that Aida returned. I asked her if she had seen anything interesting, and she replied in a voice filled with wonder, "I have seen something that our grandchildren will be excavating!"

We got in the little white Datsun I had bought as a project vehicle and drove down the Mora Road to its end. On foot, we crossed the Operation A field, heading south and passing our back-filled excavations. At the end of another pasture we negotiated a barbed wire fence and passed through more coffee fields. We were no longer on Mora family property but on that of the Matas, who mostly lived along the road leading from Rivas to General Viejo. Breaking through the coffee

plants but still on the same terrace as Operation A, we came into a clearing of grass cropped short by cattle grazing. Below us, on the next terrace, a huge ring of stones was clearly visible (fig. 2.17).

While the Operation A structures had maximum diameters of slightly over 10 meters, this circle was double them in size. Furthermore, some of the stones that made up its ring were not the usual dinner-plate-size cobbles but huge boulders 50 centimeters to 1 meter across. Descending to the lower terrace, we found more wonders. There were other circles of giant size and clear alignments of stones connecting many of them. They seemed to comprise a large complex of interconnecting structures and low cobble walls. Many of the circular structures appeared to have one or more extensions on them, similar to the quadrangular patio on Structure 1 in Operation A. Some of this architecture was quite visible in the pasture. Elsewhere, there were small plots in cultivation that hid some of the structures stretching off as far as we could see. There was a fairly small cane field, another plot with maize in it, and coffee fields extending to the south, but everywhere there were lines, rings, and other formations of big boulders (fig. 2.18).

A mystery was solved and another begun. In Bob Drolet's report on the site, he stated that there was evidence of quadrangular structures at Rivas. This was a mystery because quadrangular structures had not been previously reported for southern Costa Rica. We had not yet searched for these in our work, although we had planned to look for them. We had been too busy in our various operations, but here was an apparent quadrangular structure. Projecting out from a coffee field was a line of stones, most of which were more than 50 centimeters in maximum length and often as wide. The wall ran for about 15 meters and then made a sharp turn, running for another 10 meters or so before disappearing into another part of the cane field. It seemed likely that this quadrangular corner was the one to which Bob had referred. But why hadn't he mentioned the big circular structures and other features that we saw throughout the area?

When Bob had done his studies at Rivas, he had limited resources and time. Furthermore, this field had been in tall grass, but he saw this sharply angled corner and mapped the stone alignments. Apparently, since Bob had been here, tall grass had been replaced by

2.17. Complex II in Operation D as first viewed from the upper terrace in 1992. View to Grid E.

pasture, revealing the structures. When we visited this area in 1992, we could see stone alignments that had not been visible to Bob. Still, there were many areas in dense vegetation, but we could see enough to know that this was a very important part of the site that deserved our attention.

The other mystery made my hair rise. In looking at this collection of impressive remains, I remembered Sarah's prediction: "The big stuff is down there." We hadn't bothered to check before, but here we were at the big stuff.

Time was running short. We only had about three weeks left for the project, we were in the middle of excavating Operation C, and, as noted earlier, I had to go to San José to get money and attend the Fulbright events. As soon as I was back from San José, I left the continuation of the excavation of the burials to a crew chief and began to do a sketch map of what we called Operation D. Mapping is best done with a minimum of two people. I took Jeff Frost, an undergraduate from Ripon College, with me.

As we mapped, we began to better understand the organization of the large architecture in Operation D. East of the first large circle we had found was an even

larger one with what appeared to be two or more circular additions attached to it. We called this area Complex I. It appeared to be located at a lower elevation than the first circle, to its west, which we called Complex II. We named the large quadrangular-looking structure Complex III.

East of the coffee field into which the wall of Complex III disappeared and south of Complex I there was a large pasture. The grass in this area was higher than elsewhere, as it was fenced off from cattle. On the north side of the barbed wire fence, however, cobble pavements and alignments of stones were clearly in evidence, appearing to continue into the grassy field. The field itself was quite large, about 4 hectares in area. On its western side, there was a long, high mound running north-south and, to the east, a somewhat less pronounced height. In between them was a sunken, relatively flat area, as best we could tell. We called this area Complex IV, but we also often referred to it as "the plaza" because that is what it appeared to be. It is dangerous to give these kinds of nicknames to areas of sites because doing so often predisposes archaeologists to confirm that, in this case, the place actually had been a plaza. All we had done was to give it a

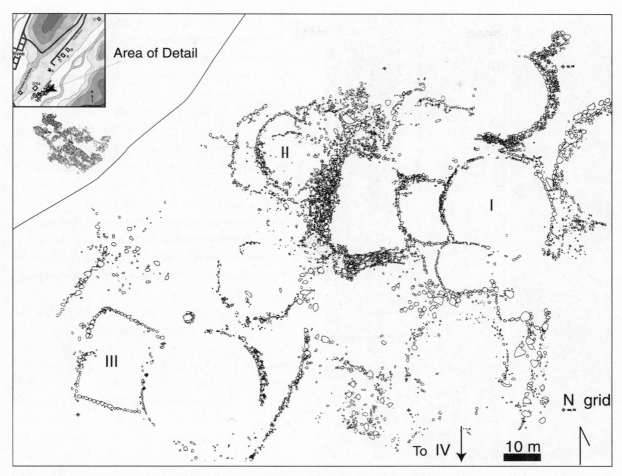

2.18. Operation D. Complexes marked with Roman numerals. Complex IV is off of the map, to the south. In 1992 Complex III was thought to consist only of the rectangular patio. Many of the other features also were mapped much later in the project. Map by R. J. Frost and J. Quilter.

name based on a first impression, though that impression could turn out to be wrong. But many archaeologists do things like use nicknames, and so did we.

Our sketch map was extremely crude. We didn't have time to map individual stones, so we just tried to get a general sense of where the lines of stones ran and the correct distances between them. We used a combination of a theodolite and tapes and hand-held compasses. I realized, though, that at least some excavation was necessary. There was no certainty that I would ever get the funds to come back and do more work. At least a sample of materials from this part of the site was essential for our research. Of course, I wasn't even entirely sure that this was part of the Rivas site as I had understood it up to this time. It was quite possible that there was an empty space in the presumed spread of architecture from Operation A, on a higher terrace

and more than 200 meters away, and that Operation D was occupied earlier or later than the other area. Digging might help address these questions as well as why there was such a difference in the scale of structures in each place.

The excavation of Operation D seemed a straightforward matter to me. We would simply place a large trench directly across the eastern edge of the largest circle, the one in Complex I. We established a local datum point and then laid out a trench area 2 meters wide and running east-west across the large circle. We began by excavating segments of the trench, but eventually it ran a length of 15 meters (W2–E13/N50–51) (fig. 2.19).

Although this circle was much bigger than those we had excavated in Operation A, it revealed the same general characteristics in having dense accumulations of

2.19. Excavating around Complex I, east side, Operation D.

artifacts on the cobbles that formed its circumference and immediately outside of it, with relatively few artifacts inside. In fact, inside the circle we found some sherds for the first 10 centimeters but then almost immediately encountered a dense layer of gravel made of stones ranging from the size of chickpeas to large potatoes. Outside, however, there were dense artifact deposits. In the easternmost section of the trench, excavations went below a meter in black, rich soil with many artifacts. At the bottom there was a concentration of cobbles that appeared to be deliberately arranged. Even though the area of the trench here was 2 x 5 meters, the great depths prohibited us from being certain that this was part of a circle. In addition, unless we ripped up the cobbles, which was extremely difficult to do given their size and the narrow working space, we could not go much deeper because they blocked our access to lower levels. We did excavate in the corner of the trench for a few levels more, however.

On the north side of Complex I the cobble ring

widened. The cobbles in this pavement were small for Operation D—dinner-plate size—and apparently they had been carefully selected, as they were of a uniform oval shape. The pavement also was interesting because it appeared to slope toward its middle. We couldn't tell what was on the north side of this pavement because it disappeared into the slightly elevated ground surface of the neighboring coffee field. Given the slope of the pavement, however, it appeared that it had been built to funnel rainwater away from the Complex I structure. We therefore nicknamed this area "the drain." The middle section was covered with silt. We excavated down to the cobbles but left them in place. There were a considerable number of sherds in the fill that had accumulated in soil on top of the drain, probably washed there in rains.

In addition to the excavations in the drain and the long trench, we placed three 2 x 3 meter conjoined pits in the southern interior of the circle. As in the other interior excavations, some sherds were encountered, but we quickly reached the gravel layer.

One of the most interesting areas of Operation D was in a sugarcane field. It was in the area between the large circle of Complex I and the eastern edge of the terrace on which Complex II was located (N35–40/ W30–45). When cane is ready to be harvested, the field is burned and then cut, and this is what the Mata family planned to do. Although an archaeologist might cringe at the thought of burning material above archaeological remains, potentially contaminating radiocarbon samples, it did offer an opportunity not to be missed. We didn't know if we would ever have access to this area of the site again. Furthermore, the burning and cutting would be done rapidly and would leave only charred stubble that could be quickly cleared, revealing the stone alignments below.

As soon as the farm work was done, we started scraping away the ash and the still-smoldering stalks of the cut cane. We worked in an area of about 200 square meters. Running out of time, we couldn't afford to dig deeply. But scraping, clearing, and mapping would help us to produce a good map and help us understand this part of the site. Scraping revealed clear architectural features in some areas, but in others, where soil had accumulated, it was harder to understand what was going on, architecturally, without excavating.

This scraping revealed what appeared to be a cob-

2.20. The causeway in Operation D, looking to Grid E, toward Complex I.

ble causeway (fig. 2.20), elevated about 1 meter above the ground, 3 to 5 meters wide, and 15 meters long, although where the causeway began was hard to determine. The eastern end of this cobble causeway was hard to pinpoint because it intersected one of the smaller, outer circles of Complex I. In order to better determine how the various architectural sections interrelated, we placed pits in an area that appeared to be an intersection of lines of cobbles.

We placed large pits in a line with unexcavated spaces between them. We then expanded the pits in the area closest to what we thought would be the location of the intersection of the causeway and the smaller circle, eventually creating an irregularly shaped unit. We also opened two more units, one just inside the circular unit of Complex I and the other one on the edge of the northern side of the causeway. We didn't find the place where the causeway and circle met—it may have been a few meters north—but we did find something

very interesting. We dug down about 20 centimeters, finding sherds as usual. We then came upon a sterile layer of orange soil, contrasting with the darker material above it (fig. 2.21). As is standard procedure in archaeology, we excavated into this sterile layer in a corner of the pit to be sure that there wasn't another artifact-bearing layer below it. But there was indeed another artifact layer below it, beginning at about 30 centimeters below ground surface. This layer was dark like the upper layer and contained what appeared to be similar Chiriquí phase sherds. The layer cake thus had an upper layer, between 30 and 40 centimeters thick, of dark, artifact-bearing soil; then the sterile orange layer, which varied in thickness but averaged about 30 centimeters; and then another dark artifact layer about 20 centimeters thick.

In addition to the layer cake–like stratigraphy we had discovered, we also confirmed that there was a lower and earlier construction phase in Operation D. In the largest pit in this area, we found a single line of cobbles in an arc through the pit. Apparently, it was a circular part of a structure. This suggested that the wide cobble arrangement found in the eastern end of the large trench crossing the wall of Complex I was indeed a deeply buried earlier ring of stones, similar to the one above it.

We thus had two independent confirmations that the Operation D area contained two distinct building phases. The early construction phase may also have consisted of fairly large structures, although this was hard to tell with certainty because the later architecture was above it. We didn't have the time or resources, nor were we eager to destroy the upper architecture, to better see the lower level. Nevertheless, it was clear that, after a period of use, the site made up of the lower, earlier structures either was abandoned or deliberately covered with orange soil. This sterile soil is the same as that found on the slopes of the Panteón de La Reina. The earth appears to have been deliberately transported when the area was remodeled as earlier architecture was covered up and replaced with newer structures. Activities in the remodeled and new constructed complex could have quickly caused the accumulation of the organically rich, upper dark soil layer.

In both Mesoamerica and the Andes, the "burying" of temples was a common practice in antiquity. In the lands of the Maya and Aztecs, temples were renewed

2.21. View of the profile of an excavation pit on the eastern end of the causeway. 1: upper soil horizon; 2: sterile Piedra Muerta Fill; and 3: lower soil horizon. Note the layer of construction cobbles resting on the lower soil horizon, below the fill, on the right.

by adding a new layer of architecture on top of older pyramids and other structures, effectively burying them and creating a bigger structure encasing the older one. In the Andes, similar practices occurred, and sometimes huge amounts of sandy soil were deliberately transported and poured into the halls and plazas of temples no longer to be used. A similar practice of site "burial" may have occurred at Rivas. Although some soils may have washed into the area, the Panteón slopes are too far away to expect erosional processes to have filled in the interior of circles so precisely. Desiccated powdery rock is called *piedra muerta*—dead rock—by local people, so we called this material Piedra Muerta Fill, or PMF for short. The discovery of two layers of architectural construction was exciting and encouraged us to come back to the site for more work.

Our Perspective of the Site at the End of the 1992 Field Season

Our time was up. The discovery of the spectacular architecture in Operation D and our attempt to conduct enough work to gain an understanding of it had been

successful, but it had also raised more questions. We knew that Rivas was not simply a carbon copy of Murciélago. The site had many more diverse kinds of architecture than Murciélago. Many of the structures in the large-scale architecture replicated the form of the smaller houses we had excavated in Operation A but on a grander scale. We thought that these structures might represent very large households, perhaps those of chiefs. Furthermore, some of the architecture was not strictly for domestic use. The large structures with their multiple additions and great spaces suggested that they may have been public areas, perhaps for gatherings and ceremonies, and not merely dwellings.

As for the questions, there were many. How extensive was the large-scale architecture in Operation D? How did it relate to the smaller structures of Operation A or, for that matter, to the petroglyph in Operation B and the cemetery of Operation C? What was the relationship of the large-scale architecture and the activities carried out in those structures to the Panteón de La Reina? What was the significance of the two phases of architectural construction in the large architecture—why was the earlier architecture buried?

There were other mysteries, too. Bob Drolet had reported that there were abundant remains of manos and metates at Murciélago, but we had found few of either at Rivas. The few metates we did find were almost always broken and incorporated into cobble rings, often turned upside down. If the inhabitants of Rivas had processed maize and other plants, they apparently had not done so using standard equipment such as found at Murciélago and to be expected at similar sites, or perhaps they weren't doing these activities at all.

And there were discoveries that simply didn't seem to make any sense. On days when work was proceeding with no new discoveries and no major decisions to be made, I often took walks away from the excavations. I did this to try to get a better sense of the larger context of the area in which we were working. Since we had not had the opportunity to get to know the site in the way that a thorough mapping and survey project would provide, these walks helped me to better understand where we were in terms of the terraces and other natural and cultural features of the site.

One day while we were working in Operation A, I took a path that descended the face of the terrace and headed toward a grove of tall guava trees. The shade was welcome, and although there was a fair amount of leaf litter on the ground, I noticed a single, straight line of cobbles running in a north-south direction not very far at all from the bottom of the terrace (fig. 2.22). We put a couple of workers on the job of cleaning the stones for a better view of them and investigating if the line widened into a pavement or continued into a structure. It did neither. Instead, it continued as a single line of stones in not quite a straight line for about 50 meters. This was most strange, and we referred to this feature for some time as the "line of stones," since we had no other idea of what it could be.

Running southward, the line of stones seemed to end just at the point where a barbed wire fence ran perpendicular to it. Beyond, there was a plot of ground with extremely dense *monte*. It was unpleasant to walk in, with thorns, stinging nettles and vines, and the threat of snakes, so for some time we did not venture into it.

While working in Operation D, we took walks northward into the coffee field on the other side of the fence that bordered the drain. Knowing that the prehistoric cultural landscape had not respected modern-

2.22. The line of stones. The photograph was taken at about N40, with 30 m of the line behind the photographer. About 15 to 20 m are seen here. To the south, in the clearing, are the stairs that ascend the terrace. Christopher Raymond is shown at left.

day fence lines, we assumed and were proved right that the architecture we had been excavating continued into the coffee field. It was extremely difficult to make out the features of cobbles in the coffee field, however, because of many seasons' accumulations of leaf fall. There was no time to do any work in the coffee field, and we were already busy in Operation D. We asked the owner if we could have permission to excavate in the coffee field in the future season, but he didn't want his plants disturbed.

We went back to the line of stones and braved entering the *monte*. The overgrown field was only 30 meters wide. Its southern side bordered the northern edge of the coffee field that we had been entering on its other side in Operation D. Even though the *monte* was thick, there were some areas where the vegetation was not as dense as in others. In these places, we found lines of huge stones resembling the large-scale architecture in Operation D. The *monte* was not valuable and could be cleared easily. Our next work area, Operation E, would lead us to better understand what the remains of these large structures were all about.

The Party

It had been quite a time. I had arrived at the site uncertain of what I was getting myself into. Even though I had gotten a prestigious Fulbright Research Fellowship, I had wondered if I was doing the right thing. While Peru was a hard place in which to work due to terrorism, there were other opportunities, in Chile, Bolivia, or Ecuador. I had stumbled into working in Costa Rica, and doors had seemed to open for me that had been closed when I had tried to get funds, permits, and projects going in other places, at other times. Here, everything had worked.

I had really enjoyed the first few weeks of investigations, in Operation A. It was great to be in the field and working with new tactical problems of how to excavate in the tropics. Still, during my low points, I thought all I was going to find were a bunch of cobble circles and some pot sherds. But gradually the place began to seduce me. Finding the petroglyph on a cobble in a house ring had made me believe I was going to be able to contribute something to the study of prehistory, if only a little note, somewhere. Although Operation B had yielded few artifacts, again I thought I was contributing to a better understanding of the archaeology of Costa Rica and Central America. By the time we were working in Operation C, however, finding burials where we had not expected there to be any, my interest grew exponentially. It exploded on finding the large-scale architecture in Operation D. By the time the 1992 field season had ended, I was convinced we were engaged in an exciting project that would make a very important contribution to understanding how chiefdom societies were organized.

I was very grateful to my Costa Rican hosts. I decided to throw a big party in thanks. The Mora and Mata families were happy to pitch in. I bought great quantities of food and drink. The Mora and Mata women cooked up huge tubs of beans and rice, and the men grilled meat in quantity. We hauled in kegs of beer. On a gorgeous sunny afternoon, we set up the tables in a large open space in front of the house where one of our best workers, Gilbert Mora, lived. In addition to the food and drink, I had arranged to have T-shirts made up with the name of the project and the design from the Operation A petroglyph silk-screened onto it. I invited people from the ACM, the National Museum, and the U.S. embassy. Fred Lange, noted Central Americanist, came down with the embassy staff. They quickly snatched up the T-shirts and had some of my crew and me pose for a photo with us all wearing project shirts. It later appeared in a Fulbright newsletter. Even John Hoopes and his students showed up. John had been running a field school for the University of Kansas in Golfito, and Larry Conyers and I had visited them, briefly, in the middle of our field season. They were working in hot, humid, and difficult conditions, much tougher than our experience at Rivas. When I invited them to come up and join the party, he and his students were only too happy to accept.

With palm trees waving around us, we piled our plates with refried beans, fried bananas, barbequed meat, and salad. Cases of beer and bottles of *guaro* were drunk in quantity. There were more than a hundred people gathered, including two groups of gringo archaeologists, most of the Mora and Mata families, the embassy staffers, and miscellaneous folks we had met during our stay. As the day quickly slipped into dusk, the salsa music started to throb from huge speakers on the bed of a pickup truck. We ate, drank, and danced late into the night on grounds where others had done the same a millennium ago.

CHAPTER THREE

FIELDWORK IN OPERATION E, 1993

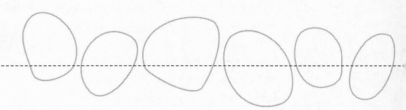

Where We Came From and Where We Wanted to Go

Our three months of fieldwork at the Rivas site in 1992 had been quite successful. We had sampled a variety of different locales: a set of domestic structures, the area around a petroglyph, and a cemetery. We also had discovered some very impressive architecture not known for the area before. Now we had to determine what to do next. It seemed reasonable to try and explore the large-scale architecture more thoroughly since we were rushed during the final weeks of the 1992 field season.

I spent the months immediately after the excavations in a variety of activities related to Rivas. I went over the field notes, got film developed and the resulting slides labeled and sorted, wrote and submitted a report of my work to the Comisión Nacional de Arqueología in San José, and sent radiocarbon samples off to be analyzed. When the results came back, they were a little surprising (see appendix). Bob Drolet and I had hoped and expected that Rivas would date to just

before the Conquest. Sites in the region, especially near Murciélago, often yielded pieces of Spanish armor or trade beads. We had not found any of those materials in our work at Rivas, but a cluster of dates between A.D. 900 and 1300 was still somewhat surprising. They suggested that Rivas was contemporary with the well-known site of Guayabo de Turrialba on the Atlantic Watershed side of Costa Rica. It also appeared that, like Guayabo and other large complexes in Atlantic Costa Rica, Rivas had been abandoned two centuries before any Spaniard got lost in the tropical forests of southern Pacific Costa Rica.

The dates were nicely clustered around this general time period. There also was one that was slightly later than the rest, the single carbon sample we retrieved from Operation C. Its age range did overlap the others within the second standard deviation, a statistical range that is the acceptable time span most archaeologists rely upon for dating. Part of the problem was that carbon or other suitable dating material was very hard to obtain at the site, especially from the cemeteries. The tropical climate and soils were hard even on charcoal.

Absence of charcoal in the cemetery area itself probably was due to the fact that the kinds of activities that would produce it, such as food preparation, didn't occur there. We thus had found only one sample of carbon in the cemetery that was large enough to assay for a date. It is possible that the charcoal had entered into the soils of the cemetery at some time quite different than when graves were made there. A few extra dates might at least offer a range of possibilities as to when the graveyard was in use. But we had to rely on a single date since it was all we had, and we thus could not take that date too seriously. This lack of dating caused some problems of interpretation: simply put, we are still uncertain as to whether the cemetery was in use before, during, or after the time when the areas to its south were occupied.

The major problem facing the project was finding the funds to work again at the site. Deadlines for grant applications are usually in the late autumn or early winter, at least to get the funds in time to dig again in the following summer. Since I returned home in March, at least I had the spring and summer to work on the proposals. This is where the hardest work in archaeology takes place—spending days writing proposals to convince agencies to fund your project with little chance of getting funding because the number of projects proposed is always much greater than the amount of money available to fund them. I was lucky, though, and the project was awarded a grant from the National Endowment for the Humanities, with matching funds from a number of other institutions.

The monies from the grants were substantial enough that we could plan the project in stages for future years. We decided that we should maintain our course in excavating the large-scale architecture, in the section we called Operation E, for the next year, 1993. We weren't sure if the field we had seen at the end of the 1992 excavation season would be available to us for very long. Like farmers everywhere, when prices for their crops fall, farmers in Costa Rica tend to plant more, hoping that they can make up in volume what they lose in the price per bushel of coffee. Because Colombia and Brazil are the world's largest producers of coffee, what happens to their crops affects smaller producers, such as Costa Rica. Environmental conditions and the vagaries of the commodities market make it very hard to predict what even the near future will

bring. Thus the forces of world market systems could impinge upon the plans of archaeologists in unforeseen ways. We wanted to dig in Operation E before we were told we couldn't because it had been planted in coffee while we were away.

As for the longer-term future of the project, we realized that a survey should be done to better understand how the different parts of the site fit together. The survey also would allow us to discover interesting areas that we might have missed through our casual and not always organized ramblings across the pastures and through the coffee fields of Rivas. We planned to conduct the survey after we worked in Operation E. We wanted to return to Operation D to better understand some of the structures there, particularly Complexes II, III, and IV, as well as some unusual features we had discovered that did not appear to be architecture as we had come to know and identify it at the site. We also hoped to excavate another cemetery at the Rivas site, to have material to compare with Operation C. Finally, we hoped that we might eventually be able to work on the Panteón de La Reina. Although it had been very badly looted since the beginning of the twentieth century, we believed that work there could help answer many questions about the Rivas site. We also wanted to remain flexible. As work continued we would have new questions to ask that would make us change our plans and do things differently. We would have to wait and see; we had a lot of work ahead of us.

Devising Strategies to Investigate Large-Scale Architecture

In approaching the 1993 field season, we had to take several new factors into consideration. In 1992 I had worked on an ad hoc basis, taking advantage of whatever came my way in many aspects of the project. Aida Blanco had kindly put me up in her house. The small car I had bought from my friend Phil Dennis in San José was adequate to take Aida, a couple of workers, and me out to the site and back every day. Jeff Frost had lived with one of the Mora families, and we had stored our equipment with them. We also had employed a few of the older children and women to wash sherds for us and do other chores. As for workers, we had started out with only half a dozen or so, because most of the able-bodied men in the area were out picking coffee in fields more than a day away from their homes.

I had done the best I could with what I had. The size of the field crew had grown as men came back from their distant coffee picking to find I was paying good money to do this strange work called "*arqueología*." Jeff had been a tremendous help in mapping and other activities. We had gotten help from two Costa Rican students, Miguel Espinosa and Carlos Rojas, and by the time we were a few weeks into the project we had a crew that could get the job done.

Now, however, I was responsible for a relatively large grant, and I had to deliver the goods. I wanted to hit the ground running as best as possible, especially because my field season had much more sharply defined limits. My teaching duties at Ripon College ended in mid-May but began again in mid-August. I couldn't get any more time off to work in the dry season, from January through March, as I had done in 1992, so we would have to work in the middle of the summer rainy season. I was worried that rain would delay our excavations. In addition, I couldn't rely on my little white car to serve as a field vehicle for much longer, and we would need to find places to stay other than Aida's small house. I also needed to assemble a crew, and I had to have personnel who would be able to direct them.

Successful archaeology in foreign lands depends on planning and a good deal of luck. I initially went to Costa Rica with two weeks of preparation time before the commencement of excavations. In retrospect, this was too short a time, but luck was with me. I had sent in my proposal for continued work at Rivas with plenty of time for it to be approved by the Comisión Nacional de Arqueología, so at least that potential obstacle was overcome. We were able to negotiate with some of the Mora family members to rent a large house that was not currently occupied. It was painted a rather bright green and quickly became known as the Casa Verde by everyone on the crew.

That left purchasing a vehicle as the only problem to solve. I didn't have funds to buy a brand new four-wheel drive, but I needed something serviceable. I spent quite a lot of time driving around the greater San José area with Pepe Zeledón, the reliable and generous jack-of-all-trades of the ACM program, looking at various possibilities. None of the vehicles we inspected seemed quite what I wanted given what I could afford. It was getting so late that I had to abandon the search in San José and get to Rivas to begin the project.

I was explaining my problem of searching for a vehicle to some of the locals in Rivas when they all recommended that I talk to an old gentleman who lived up the street. I went to see him and there, parked under the protective roof of a *ramada*, was what appeared to be an almost mint-condition 1972 Land Rover. He was the original owner of the vehicle and had only used it to drive into town once or twice a week. It was like one of those jokes about a used-car salesman who says that a car was owned by a little old lady who only had used it to drive to and from church! We quickly struck a deal, and I drove away in my handsome and quite serviceable vehicle. It not only had its beautiful Indiana Jones–like green paint intact, but it even had a cassette tape player that worked.

In the ten years since the Land Rover was purchased, it has aged rapidly. We have put it through some tough times, but it still rolls along, having been given the equivalent of numerous injections of monkey glands, electroshock therapies, total blood replacement, and heart transplants.

I decided, as a backup, to keep the white car at least through the 1993 field season. As the project was developing and growing in size, I realized that two vehicles might come in handy. As for the crew, word had spread through the area that the gringo was back and would pay well. We made an agreement with the Mora and Mata families that if they would give us permission to work on their lands, in return we would hire only members of their families to work for us. Although there had been some very good workers and definitely some entertaining ones in the previous field season whom I regretted not being able to rehire, I made the deal. I needed all the help I could get, planning to put as many as 30 workers in the field. That meant I also needed help in supervising them.

For the big project I was planning, I needed supervisors who could direct the workers. I had two readily available who had worked for me in 1992. R. Jeffrey Frost had not been an outstanding student of mine at Ripon College, but in the middle of his junior year he started to show signs of great creativity and dedication to his schoolwork and in his senior year did high-quality original scholarship in both an independent study and his senior thesis. It was in that early junior year, however, that he heard I was planning to dig in Costa Rica. He came to my office and asked me if he could come along. I said something such as, "Come back in a couple of months; I haven't worked out my plans for the project." I thought maybe he'd forget about it, but sure enough he asked again, two months later. I kept on trying to stall him, but he kept on coming back. Finally, I told him that I was somewhat leery of taking him not because I thought he wouldn't do a good job but simply because this was going to be a first-time experience for me. I wasn't quite sure what I was getting into in terms of the work, living conditions, and so forth. All of this was true. He said it didn't matter; he would pay for his own flight, room and board, and so forth. Between his persistence and his willingness to pay for his expenses, it was hard for me to say no.

Jeff came to Costa Rica a couple of weeks after we started, and I quickly realized he was extremely gifted in this work. Through the years of the project he went from being my assistant to being completely in charge of mapping to being the acting field director many times when I wasn't able to be in Costa Rica for the entire field season. He also went from being my student to being my colleague and friend.

Miguel Espinosa was a Tico who had heard about the project while we were digging Operation A and asked if I could take him on as a crew chief. I welcomed him. He was a small, skinny guy with a thin mustache, a damaged leg from a motorcycle accident, and one of the most winning smiles in all of Central America. He was a great digger and a great crew chief, especially in his ability to get along with our crew members. As a native Spanish speaker, he helped explain to the diggers why we were doing what we were doing. He also helped me to increase my Spanish vocabulary tremendously, and I learned a range of words never taught in Spanish classes, here or there, but sometimes quite useful, especially when under stress.

Another Tico who had worked with us in 1992 was Carlos Rojas. Unfortunately, Carlos had other commitments and couldn't join us for the second field season. I still needed more supervisors, though. In 1992 I had taken a long weekend visiting the project of John Hoopes of the University of Kansas, based in the town of Golfito. John had taken on a Tulane graduate student, Bill Doonan, to serve as a field director

for his project. The Golfito project was done, and I asked Bill if he would be interested in working at Rivas with me. He was happy to do so. In addition, a student with crew chief experience, Chris Raymond, also signed up for Rivas. Bill and Chris quickly became core project members.

Bill had spent part of his childhood in Puerto Rico, so his Spanish was excellent. He knew Latin American culture well. In addition to Puerto Rico, he had dug at Copán, Honduras, with the Tulane University project there. Wearing a wide-brimmed hat, long-legged trousers, and dark sunglasses to protect his fair skin and eyes, Bill always presented the impression of the "cool" field director, totally in control. His image was enhanced by one of the driest and sharpest senses of humor I have ever encountered. With just a few words, in Spanish or English, Bill could perceptively skewer just about anyone.

Chris Raymond also spoke excellent Spanish, including Ticoisms so obscure (and sometimes so salacious) that the workers would ask him to repeat them so they could memorize them. Whereas Bill was Mr. Cool, Chris was the project Tigger, bouncing around the site and region. He got into bar fights, affairs, and wild schemes. One field season, he raised a chicken, as a pet, in the house we rented, totally mystifying our neighbors. He was sometimes found in the middle of a distant field, sitting cross-legged on a rock and meditating to the absolute astonishment of the local residents. At other times he could be found running through cane fields in a driving rain, like some latter-day Walt Whitman, in the exhilaration of being totally alive. With his nose ring, tattoos, and boundless energy, he was the talk of the project and town.

We also expected a visit from Larry Conyers, our project geologist, at that time a graduate student at the University of Colorado, Boulder. Tall and lean, with a Groucho Marx mustache, Larry became a local legend. His first day on the site he walked the legs off of a local Tico by climbing up several hills to get good views of the site. Through the years he brought several different kinds of detection devices—ground penetrating radar, magnetometers, electromagnetic resistivity and conductivity meters—and walked over the site like a space-age dowser. In addition to his relish of physical hardship, Larry's geophysical machines gave him the status of some kind of magician. I called those boxes and rods and such his "gizmos," and it became a standing joke between us, as he would yell in (I think) mock anger, "Stop calling them gizmos!"

Adding to the mix was an advanced undergraduate student from Yale, Bryan Just. My wife, Sarah, and my daughters, Susanna, 13, and Betsy, 6, also would be coming to Costa Rica. In addition, we had short-term volunteers in the form of Paul Dolata, a friend from Ripon; Bill Doonan's dad; and Gabriela Castro, a Costa Rican who had been a Spanish assistant at Ripon College. Sarah's cousin Mary Jane showed up with a Jesuit friend, Francis Xavier, but better known as "F.X." Steve Blau, professor of physics at Ripon College, and his wife, Lynette, appeared briefly as volunteers. Some of these people worked for a few days, some for many. They all added interest to our project. I sometimes felt like the master of a three-ring circus, though, in trying to juggle work, family, visitors, and all the other matters that make up a busy field season.

All in all, the 1993 Rivas field season was taking on a very different character than the 1992 work. A year earlier, despite previous trips to visit the site and people, I felt as if I had been plunked down in the middle of a coffee field with a razor, a string, and a compass and told to figure out how to survive. Now I was running a major project with sometimes as many as 50 people involved in the work. I had a big grant and big plans. I had the money, the vehicles, the housing, the crew, and the supervisory personnel, and it was time to get to work.

The overgrown field we had stumbled into at the end of the 1992 field season was where we would concentrate our efforts, calling it Operation E (figs. 3.1, 3.2). The field was quadrangular in shape, bounded on its north and south sides by barbed wire fences. A coffee field was to the south, and in the western area of its northern boundary there was a guava grove with somewhat less overgrown pasture in the rest of that side. The eastern boundary of the field was the terrace edge with a rather sheer drop of about 5 meters to the next terrace. On its western side rose the terrace on which Operation A was located, or at least at about the same height as it, farther north. The slope up to the terrace was more gradual here than in other areas, partly because boulders and earth had tumbled and eroded the terrace face. This western side was in thick *monte* like the rest of the field but was even more diffi-cult to walk through because of the rocks and slope of the earth there. In all, Operation E as it was first defined covered about 5,000 square meters.

The grass, shrubs, trees, and vines were so thick that the visibility was a meter or less. The first thing to do, then, was to clear enough of the vegetation so that we could work comfortably and see what we were doing. We hired about 15 workers and told them to clear the field. We then left for about five hours to take care of various matters regarding our equipment, lodging, and other logistical issues. We were surprised when we returned to find a field stripped bare. We could now stand at one end of the field and have a clear line of vision 70 meters to the far terrace edge to the east.

In addition to stripping the field, the workers also killed two fer-de-lances. They were little snakes, supposedly the most dangerous. I now was doubly glad that we had plenty of clear space in which to work. Almost every time we cleared a fairly large field we found snakes. Although we walked through thick brush and forest, luckily no one ever was bit, though we likely often had many a close call without even realizing it.

We hadn't necessarily expected that our workers would be so efficient, removing all of the vegetation in the field so rapidly. Having done so, however, we decided to take advantage of the clearing to expose and map as much of the architecture in Operation E as possible. As work continued, this strategy came to make more and more sense. Since we were working in the rainy season, any attempt to dig deep excavations would be frustrated by the rains that constantly filled our pits, making them look like a series of miniature swimming pools of odd dimensions. We were able to do some relatively deep excavations, but most of our work was designed to laterally expose architecture and avoid the problem of pit flooding that would prevent work from proceeding.

The rain was not as big a problem as I had feared. The mornings usually were fresh, clear, and sunny. We began work at 7:00, had lunch at about 10:00, and planned to work until 2:00. Sometimes we could work that late, but often the rain would come at about 1:00, sometimes as early as 12:30, but rarely earlier. Working conditions were actually more pleasant than in the dry season since the humidity was not overpowering but rather added softness to the air. We also had the pleasure of watching the weather change daily.

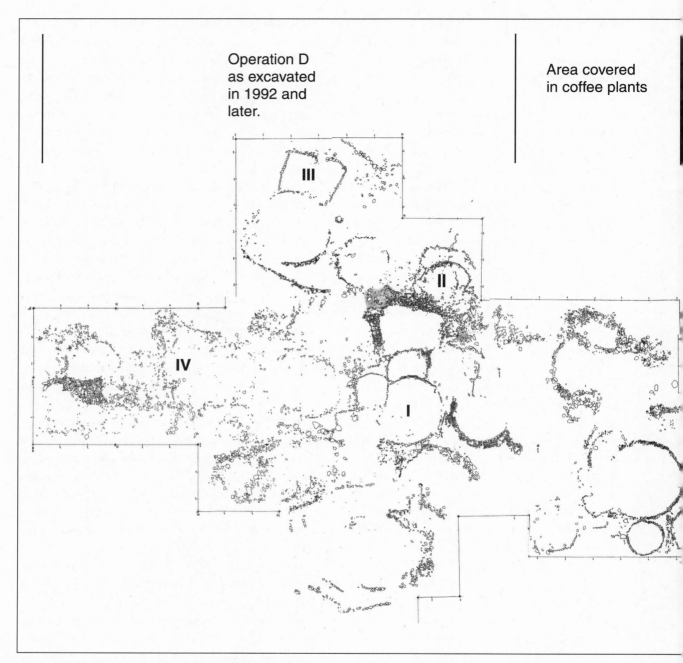

Operation D as excavated in 1992 and later.

Area covered in coffee plants

3.1. Operations D and E. Complexes indicated by Roman numerals. Map by R. J. Frost and J. Quilter.

The mornings were often clear and bright, though sometimes at dawn a thin wisp of long clouds would stretch out from behind the Talamancas. Gradually, through the morning, clouds would slide over the mountains like soapy foam in slow motion. If we were lucky, the cloud cover would reach us by about 11:00, offering welcome shade, and then spread farther, down toward the Pacific coast. But the rain didn't come from the mountains, the north. Rather, almost like clock-

work, sometime between around 12:30 and 1:00 we would see a gray wall gradually working its way up the valley from the direction of San Isidro. Sometimes, when it moved slowly, we could look down toward the south end of a long field and watch our colleagues react to getting soaked for several seconds, though it seemed longer, before the rains reached us farther up-valley.

These afternoon rains would last sometimes only an

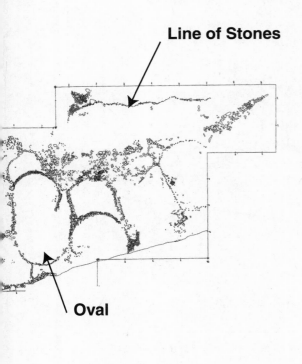

Area of 1993
excavations in
Operation E

Line of Stones

Oval

wanted to have a few daylight hours to themselves to do essential tasks in their fields or complete other chores.

Working in the Oval

With the vegetation cut down, we could see the outlines of what appeared to be a large, roughly oval structure dominating the field. Measuring about 20 meters in width and about 30 meters long, it was the largest architectural feature we had seen at the site. We decided that we would begin our work by more clearly delineating the shape and nature of this feature and then work outward from it, attempting to connect it to other architectural features. Deep excavations, where possible, would help us determine if there was more than one architectural phase, as we had noted at the end of the 1992 field season, as well as allow us to retrieve samples of ceramics and other artifacts.

We established a datum just south of a large boulder that was part of a semicircular extension west of the oval. Whereas in the previous field season we had used separate data points for each operation, continued work at the site required a master datum point, and we made this one, in Operation E, as that point. All of the coordinates for every square millimeter of excavations at the site were tied to this o/o point, except for the work done in 1992. As in the previous work, however, our designations for the cardinal directions referred to the grid system, not to true or magnetic north. For the master grid, the main north-south line was at a bearing of 43 degrees east of north, while our east-west line was at a bearing of 133 degrees east of magnetic north.

As we were setting up the grid system, workers were busy removing the soil immediately above the most easily followed lines of stones. As elsewhere, this work yielded considerable numbers of artifacts. With just a little clearing, the oval revealed itself. On its western end, it had a wide band made up of four lines of cobbles all carefully selected for uniform size and shape (fig. 3.3). The northern end of this arc seemed to be under a jumble of rocks that rose more than a meter above the surface of the center of the arc. It is likely that these boulders fell onto this section of the arc, perhaps during an earth tremor. The southern end of this feature appeared to stop with a gap of no stones slightly less than 2 meters in length, followed by an

hour, sometimes less or more. They usually stopped by sunset, at 6:00, but it might shower, on and off, during the evening. The afternoon showers usually ended our fieldwork, however. We lost some excavation time, unlike working in the dry season, but not much. In completely dry conditions, we would still only work as late as 2:00 P.M. because by then it was too hot to continue. Also, by beginning at 7:00 A.M. we already had completed a full day of work by 2:00 P.M., and our workers

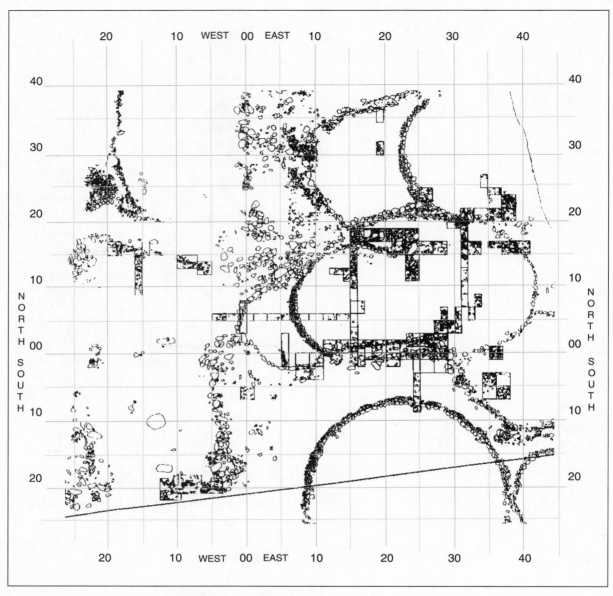

3.2. Operation E, central sector, 1993. The diagonal line near the bottom is a fence. The coffee field is to the south of this fence. Map by R. J. Frost and J. Quilter.

east-west line of boulders and cobbles running for about another 15 meters.

We cleared and excavated in the area of the gap. Before excavating, we often used a *sonda*. This is a straight metal rod with a sharpened end. Some *sondas* are longer than others, but ours was a little over a meter in length with a T-shaped handle. *Sondas* are used by looters to search for graves. We used ours to determine if there were stones beneath the surface, and they came in very handy. By using the *sonda* as a probe, we could rapidly determine the extent of a cobble pavement or

a line of stones underground and thus focus our research efforts directly in places that would reveal more architecture.

As we cleared more of the structure, it became evident that the oval did not maintain a uniform construction pattern. It was not even a perfect or near-perfect oval shape; it was more like two parallel walls with arcs on each end. Not only did the arc of four stones swing around into the interior of the space, but each of the four sides was constructed differently. On the west, there was the arc of four lines of cobbles.

3.3. The arc of four lines of stones at the western end of the oval in Operation E. View toward Grid E.

On the south, there was a very straight wall made of large boulders. The eastern arc consisted of a single line of cobbles rather thinly spread out, not tightly fitted like the arc of four cobbles on the western end. On the north, there was a thick wall made of large and irregular stone blocks mixed with cobbles. As work continued, it became clear that this northern wall was as much the southern edge of a large patio-like structure attached to a circle of cobbles northeast of the oval as it was part of the oval proper (fig. 3.1). This pattern of a line of stones simultaneously serving as part of the boundary of two different structures was common throughout the site, as we later discovered.

We worked in three main areas. The first was a group of pits near the circle that joined the oval at its northeastern side. If this circle had once been complete, its eastern side would have run off the present-day edge of the terrace. This suggests that some erosion has worn away the eastern edge of this area of the site, unless incomplete circles were deliberately constructed. We worked in an area where we thought we might get a better understanding of the relation between the two

structures. There was evidence of arranged cobbles in these pits but also many jumbled ones, but the work did clarify the fact that the two structures of oval and circle shared common cobble lines.

A second area in which we concentrated work was farther to the west, immediately below the odd-angled northern wall of the oval. The maps in this book show all of the work, complete, after many weeks of excavation in any particular area. When we began this work, however, it was unclear that the northern wall of the oval was part of the large patio to the north. In fact, as figure. 3.1 shows, the patio is larger than many circles at the site. It was only after much more excavation and mapping that these relations between structures became clear.

We excavated a number of other trenches. Some excavations were inside the oval to search for internal features. Two long trenches extended north-south across the oval (fig. 3.4). The first ran from the western end of the work we were doing in the northern part of the circle and eventually extended all the way to the trenches on the southern wall. The second long trench stretched from the work in the northeast area to our pits on the southern wall of the oval. The excavations in the space between the arcs did not provide conclusive evidence of internal features, such as patios or walls. There were dense accumulations of cobbles and boulders relatively close to the surface, but the varying sizes of these stones, from huge boulders to fist-size cobbles, suggested natural formations. These layers of cobbles are known locally as *rípio* and probably are part of the cobble deposits washed in during massive floods thousands of years ago, before human habitation. Although naturally occurring, these cobbles certainly comprised an ancient living surface nonetheless.

We placed another long trench running 40 meters east-west. This trench went from outside the entire architectural complex over the wall of the first arc and then over the second, four-cobble-row arc into the oval, connecting with one of our long trenches. There was a cluster of stones in the western end of this trench. This feature may have been part of a structure or other activity from an earlier phase of occupation. Other than this cluster and a few smaller ones, the trench mostly encountered soils. Thus, up to this point, we had cleared cobbles to reveal that they defined an oval space with little inside it other than soil.

Never Mix Business with Pleasure

We had begun work in early June, and by the end of the month we were well on our way to clearing the architecture in Operation E. I decided to try and mix business with pleasure. July 4th was coming, and while this date is not a holiday in Costa Rica, I thought we should do something special for the occasion. Although attitudes in Costa Rica are somewhat more relaxed than in the rest of Latin America, many of my South American colleagues express shock that U.S. attitudes toward our own Independence Day are so relatively casual compared to the fervor with which national days are celebrated in their own countries. Thus,

3.4. Operation E from the air. The coffee field at upper right separates Operation E from Operation D. The western end of the oval is near the bottom. The line at the right is one of the cords attached to the balloon. Long trenches cutting across the oval and its walls, as well as extensive excavations on the southern wall, can be seen.

when I have been abroad, I have always tried to do something to at least recognize the day, trying not to injure any local sensibilities but nevertheless marking the day in some special way.

During the time between the last field season and this one, I had tried to get a couple of private companies interested in the project. The Gold Bug Company, which makes metal detectors, had given us a very good price on a gold detection device that we hoped to use one day, although not in the 1993 field season. The Floatograph Company had been especially generous in offering one of their rigs at a very low price, and the large area excavations we had done in Operation E were perfect for using the Floatograph to take aerial photos.

The Floatograph system uses a weather balloon inflated with helium to carry a camera aloft. The camera is suspended on a platform, below the balloon, with a motor attachment and cables extending to the ground. One cable attaches to a box that allows the person on the ground to rotate the camera by use of a toggle switch. The other is a fiber optic cable, attached to the camera eyepiece on one end and to a small television screen on a control box on the ground. The operator can thus look through the lens of the camera, adjust the view by rotating the camera, and snap a photograph. This is a fine system to take aerial photographs to reveal large-scale architecture such as we were uncovering.

We ordered a tank of helium from the gas depot in San Isidro. We did a dry run of setting up the Floatograph in our house, making sure that all of the equipment worked but without an inflated balloon. Then I got the workers to make the site immaculate. Since we would be photographing a huge area from above, any miscellaneous trash had to be removed, pit walls straightened, and so forth. We even took down some barbed wire fences so that the pictures would look better. I bought some hot dogs and buns for the traditional feast after the "shoot." I even went to great trouble to find charcoal so that we could barbecue the frankfurters in traditional style. Since the site area would be clean, the workers could have most of the day off, and they were invited to come with their families and watch us use the Floatograph. It would be a great way to have a festive, holiday spirit, while at the same time getting some work done at the site.

Then the big day came, July 4th. We drove to the far side of San Isidro and picked up the helium cylinder. It was heavy and awkward to carry. We had to have workers straddle it in the back of the Land Rover for fear that it would slam into the thin aluminum walls of the cab. The ride back was a little tense, with thoughts of us creating our own massive fireworks somewhere on the road back to Rivas if that tank should somehow suddenly explode. But we got to the site with no trouble, though we were relieved when we didn't have to worry about that heavy tank banging up the car or blowing up.

The closest we could get to Operation E was the end of the Mora Road. The workers had to haul the cylinder a distance of 50 meters to the far end of the field where the limp red and white balloon waited. Expectations were high, and so was the temperature by now, as it had taken us longer to get the tank than we had expected. We had fun taking turns sucking helium and talking like cartoon characters. The Costa Rican workers were completely unfamiliar with the effect of helium that constricts the windpipe and makes everyone sound like Mickey Mouse, and they had a ball. We gringos laughed doubly hard to hear not only our own voices sound like Loony Toons but to hear the local Spanish dialect in the same high pitch; the Ticos probably thought the same in reverse—Mickey speaking bad Spanish.

We filled the balloon. By this time it was blazing hot. The orb rose slowly to just above the tree line. This seemed sufficient for us to maneuver it down to Operation E. It was another 75 meters to the oval, and getting the balloon there wasn't an easy job. At about a meter in diameter, the balloon was large enough that a height of 15 meters above the ground made it sensitive to the slightest breeze, even though it was roasting hot on the ground. We had to gently guide the balloon above the trees and avoid getting the cables tangled in lower branches. Any slight gust would make the balloon lurch and us scramble over rocks, through brambles, and around fence posts in desperation to avoid entanglements. We got the cords tangled in tree branches —we were tugging one way and the balloon was going in the other direction more than once. We were scratched and slapped in the face by branches and bruised from stumbling on boulders along the entire route to Operation E.

3.5. The attempted launch of the Floatograph balloon in Operation E, July 4, 1993. View toward Grid NE from south of the oval.

By the time we got the balloon to Operation E, I was already exhausted (fig. 3.5). There, we lowered the balloon, attached the camera to the platform, and released the assembly for its flight. The balloon rose about 3 meters above the ground, not much higher than we could get standing on a large rock with the camera held in our hands above our head. The weight of the camera and its rig were apparently enough to counterbalance the balloon's capacity to rise. I tried coaxing the balloon aloft, but it only bobbed sadly back down, now only 2 meters high. Apparently, there was not enough helium in the balloon to give it the lift we needed.

While all of this was going on, the workers who had cleaned Operation E so neatly had taken seats or laid in the shade, joined by wives, girlfriends, drinking buddies, and children. I could hear the guffaws and the chortles. Even many of the gringos were laughing.

I was not in a good mood. Gone were the expectations of a big red and white balloon, soaring high above the site and snapping gorgeous photos. We floated our pathetic balloon around the excavations, taking overhead shots of some of our more interesting pits. By now the sky was overcast, and rain was coming with its usual clockwork precision. We soon called it a day and put all of the equipment away.

I certainly was not in the mood to hold a cookout but felt obliged to go ahead with the plans. When we got back to the Casa Verde, however, we found some of our sherd-washer women chomping on uncooked hot dogs; they were mostly all gone. Then it started to

rain, making the day a total washout by anyone's account. Someone had rented a video player, so we drank many beers and watched a sci-fi movie, *Freejack*, with Mick Jagger, which, like our balloon, never rose above a mediocre level. Evening descended, obliterating a miserable day.

The sorry start to aerial photography at the Rivas site was fortunately followed by success. Before the field season was over, we had a good launch taking some spectacular pictures of Operation E (figs. 3.4, 3.6). We even successfully attached our video camera. Although we had other frustrations—once a cylinder of helium was underfilled—we put the Floatograph to good use in many of the field seasons that followed. All of these efforts did not just produce pretty pictures. The bird's-eye views of the large-scale architecture permitted us to improve our maps and to better understand how different sectors of the site related to one another in the past.

Some Interesting Discoveries

Our studies of the southern boundary of the oval comprised some of the most interesting work we ever did at Rivas. After our initial scraping and clearing, we uncovered an unusual feature in the area where the arc of four stones terminated. Here, the two inner lines of stones ended while the two outer lines curved outward to form a circular end to the arc. There was no evidence that this circular form held a post or some other special feature, although as previously noted, soils

3.6. The Operation E oval and structures in the northern sector of Operation E, from the air. 1: the oval; 2: large circle; 3: possible drain at the terrace edge (see fig. 3.11); 4: terrace edge; 5: cleared area for test pits heading northward.

throughout the Rivas site often do not preserve evidence of previous disturbance. While there were a few small cobbles scattered about, there seemed to be a clear break in the stone features: there was about a 3-meter gap between the circular end to the arc and the place where the line of stones that formed the

southern side of the oval began. Perhaps this gap in the architecture may have been an entry into the oval since the absence of stones would have made it easier to enter and leave the area.

A little north of the possible entry, our *sonda* detected a stone that was part of a line of buried boul-

3.7. View of the double wall on the southern side of Operation E. One of the broken ceramic vessels can be seen in front of the inner wall, at center left. View toward Grid ENE.

ders and cobbles north and parallel to the one that we had just cleared (fig. 3.7). We began excavations in this area (No–1/E11–14). As work continued, a large trench, 3 meters wide on average, was created running eastward from this point. It soon became clear that the buried line of boulders was an earlier construction. It was neatly made and formed by a line of large boulders, often a meter or more in maximum dimension, bordered by a smaller line of cobbles that presumably had been on the exterior of the earlier feature. The year before, we had observed this same pattern of a line of smaller cobbles paralleling a line of large ones on the northern side of Complex I in Operation D. More important, however, we had once again found evidence of an earlier, buried building phase. The earlier lower wall was inside the more recent one. When the area was remodeled, it was made larger, expanding outward.

We observed something else that this area shared in common with Operation D. A layer of orange soil, PMF, was sandwiched between two darker layers, just as in the stratigraphy seen in Operation D in 1992. The buried line of cobbles was lying in the orange layer, and most of the cobbles were clearly resting on the interface between the orange layer, between about 20 and 40 centimeters, and the bottom dark layer that eventually blended with *rípio* (fig. 3.8). The lower dark layer was a former living surface, built up and darkened through the decay of organic material, probably food remains and other detrius such as decaying roof thatch. The red-orange layer in the middle of the "sandwich" was identical to the material we saw in road cuts and other exposures. It had been laid down and had never been subject to processes that would have darkened it. There were no artifacts in this layer, unlike the upper and lower dark strata. The upper dark layer had been a living surface, however, during a second occupation of the area and then, after the site was abandoned, to the present day. Thus there was little doubt that there had been two major building and occupation phases in the large-scale architecture at the site.

At the eastern end of trench, we found that a pavement of cobbles expanded southward, away from the wall, and was underneath the outer, upper line of boulders. It was very neatly made. Unfortunately, after two days of clearing this feature, we returned one morning to find that someone had vandalized the pavement. The damage may have been done by local teenagers who had been out to cause trouble, or perhaps some irate former worker took out his anger because we hadn't hired him. We were upset at the destruction, especially because we had not had been able to map this feature before the vandalism had occurred. We were very worried that this might be the first of more trouble. Foreign archaeologists who bring jobs and money into an area can sometimes cause resentments. Often, if the outsiders are isolated from the locals, resentments breed without the diggers knowing what is occurring among the workers or their friends or families. Then, suddenly, trouble seems to come from nowhere and can get very serious very quickly. Luckily, we had good rapport with people in the farms and town. We went to the local bars, danced in the local dance halls, and tried to be as considerate of other people's needs and concerns as much as possible. Although we never

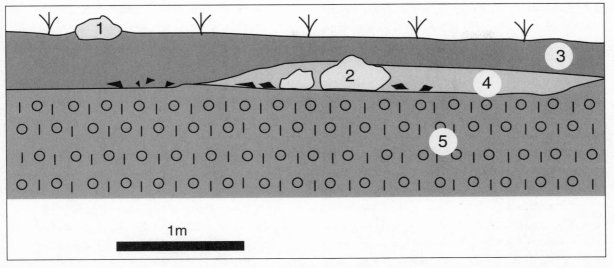

3.8. Diagram of the layers of soil in Operation E. North is to the right. 1: outer ring of stones; 2: inner, buried ring of stones; 3: topsoil; 4: Piedra Muerta Fill and spillage outside of oval (to left); 5: subsoil.

3.9. Two smashed bowls outside the buried, interior wall on the south side of the Operation E oval.

found out who had done the damage, this event was the only one of its kind during the six years of field seasons we spent at the Rivas site.

Our interest in the buried wall and pavement increased even more when we discovered a number of very large, almost complete ceramic vessels outside the wall (fig. 3.9). Two of these were on the exterior of the inner wall, while three others were farther away beyond the outer, more recent wall but at the same depth as the others. These appeared to have been whole vessels that were smashed, either dropped or placed on the ground and then deliberately crushed. The most interesting vessel consisted of a bowl that had supports in the form of small atlantean figures (see fig. 7.4: 3). These appear to be female, judging by the buttons of clay that served for breasts, and they seem to be wearing masks that resemble frog faces. This bowl was done in a style resembling the local type Papayal Engraved, in terms of the decoration on the sides of the bowl that the frog-masked women figures support. But the overall style of the vessel resembles ceramics from the Atlantic Watershed and Central Valley regions. Other ceramics seem to have been direct imports from those places. Additional research in the laboratory revealed a great number of sherds from distant regions. Many of these also likely represented complete vessels. Before our research, not a single sherd from regions across the Talamanca Mountains was known for the region.

Now we had found many. Obviously, this suggests that long-distance contacts were maintained by the people of Rivas or that the site attracted people from afar.

The large oval may have been some sort of ceremonial precinct, using the term loosely. It seems much too big to ever have been roofed. The cobble rings served to delimit spaces used for special purposes. Given the size of the space, at approximately 2,000 square meters in area, it could have held large gatherings. Perhaps it was used for dances. Throughout most of Latin America, ancient peoples combined the consumption of large amounts of alcohol with ritual practices. The smashed vessels just outside the pavement of the oval may have been dedicatory offerings, or they may have been the remains of vessels that had been part of feasting and drinking activities.

The oval is also interesting because a close examination seems to reveal remodeling activities in the last occupation in addition to those seen in the buried features. The upper part of the western end of the oval arcs so far into the space that it suggests that it once was a complete circle (fig. 3.6). The eastern end may have been a separate circle, though it may have been built to complete an oval space. No matter what the precise sequence of construction, it seems quite likely that the oval as we see it today was due to the modification of earlier structures. This suggests a very active program of modifying the site even in its later phase of use, as represented by the upper dark layer and the construction phase associated with it.

Outside the Oval

Beyond the oval, we placed a number of pits to examine other aspects of Operation E. To the southeast of the oval, we placed two pits in an irregularly shaped structure that shared an edge with the limits of the terrace. In this location there was no "sandwich" of soils. Instead, we encountered *rípio* immediately below a thin surface layer. Without the stratigraphy, there was no way to know if this structure dated to the earlier construction phase or to the later one. If the people of Rivas preferred to make their structures in circular shapes, then the fact that this structure is irregular may be an indication that it was made before the late-phase circle on the eastern end of the oval. This is just a supposition, of course, but it seems to be a reasonable one.

If this is the case, then we can argue that this structure is earlier than the structure to its northwest and much earlier than the oval. Nevertheless, we cannot say if the original structure was contemporary or later than the lower level of architecture beneath the oval. When working with ancient architecture in which walls and other structural elements were reused while others were destroyed, this kind of interpretation is standard practice. The Rivas site is simple compared to some of the very complex remodeling that occurs in adobe or masonary structures.

Sometimes what one finds in excavations seems to make no sense at all. Between 20 and 30 meters west of the northern rim of the oval, in the vicinity of N1–17/W20–17, we noticed a few stones protruding above the surface. This area seemed to be generally free of cobbles, so the few that appeared to be in a rough line running southwest-northeast had drawn our attention. We placed several pits in the area and, to our surprise, found that there was a clear line of stones running in the direction that was suggested by the few we could see from the surface. This was near to our enigmatic line of stones that we had found in the previous field season. But that line of stones had run north-south. We couldn't work anymore in the area because other issues were more pressing. We stopped then, presuming that this line of stones was either the edge of a structure or perhaps a path running from the oval and other architecture, to the east, toward the terrace. It was only in the 1994 field season, when we had time to come back to this area, that we finally made sense of this and the other line of stones.

All of the circles and other architecture in the Operation E area seemed to be bounded by boulders and cobbles running in a north-south direction. From the northwestern edge of the oval, going north, these stones lay on top of a *ballena*, a long hillock of stone in the shape of a rising whale from which this geological feature derives its name. The *ballenas* at the site were formed when water rushed down the terraces in ancient times, similar to the way in which the Panteón de La Reina was formed. We had placed a few pits on the *ballena*, and it appeared that many of the cobbles and rocks on top of it were in the places where natural processes had brought and left them. In some areas, however, there were clear signs of human arrangement of cobbles, although it was quite confusing to deter-

3.10. Excavations in the southwestern area of Operation E. A large boulder, in the foreground, lies on top of a cobble path.

faces all facing up, as if they formed a cobble walkway. A huge boulder lay directly on top of this walkway, and a smaller one was nearby (fig. 3.10). These boulders would have blocked anyone walking along the path. There was no earth between the boulders and the cobbles, which suggests that the boulders had arrived at this spot at a time when the path could still have been used. This must have been during the occupation of the site or very shortly after it; otherwise, soils would have developed, and there would have been a layer between the boulder and the path. We do not know if the boulders were moved to this location by humans or rolled there due to one or more earthquakes, but they certainly blocked any further use of the cobbles if they had indeed formed a walkway.

We had begun fieldwork at the beginning of June. By the beginning of July we had excavated enough pits and trenches in the oval and nearby that we had a fairly good idea of the organization and history of this part of the site. We had enough resources and time that we could consider expanding our work elsewhere. The field to the north of the oval clearly had architecture in it, and it was in short grass. We decided to expand work in this direction. There was not enough time to work in as detailed a way as in the oval, and, furthermore, the owner of the field was worried about us destroying the grass he needed for his cattle. With these two factors in mind, we struck upon a compromise plan of work. We would only scrape the topsoil to expose architecture for mapping, leaving the grass roots to sprout again. We would put selected excavations in limited areas to retrieve artifact samples. To get some idea of subsurface features, we would place 1 x 2 meter pits along a line extending northward. This combined clearing and excavation strategy revealed that large-scale architecture stretched northward from the northern border of the oval for a distance of another 50 meters, at least. We never were able to define the northern limit of this part of the site because we ran out of time and also because the short grass field ended and *monte* and trees began, making work difficult.

The work in this northern sector of the large-scale architecture revealed several interesting patterns (see fig. 3.6). First, on the northern end of the circle that intersected the oval, we found a segment of another well-made structure (fig. 3.11). There was a pavement of cobbles between the two ends of the circles, similar

mine patterns of construction in most of these places. The *ballena* ends exactly at the point where it intersects the Operation E oval, and it appears that the ancient builders utilized the feature as part of the overall plan of this area of the site.

On the outer semicircle attached to the oval, a wide set of cobbles runs for 20 meters southward and then swings to the west. Lacking the height offered by the *ballena*, this cobble alignment appears to have served the same purpose of providing a boundary for the architectural complex to its east. We chose the southernmost area of this line of cobbles in which to work, just to the north of a barbed wire fence that separated Operation E from the coffee field to the south. This was a low-lying area that retained rainwater, making excavations difficult.

We encountered neatly laid lines of cobbles in two parallel lines, with other areas widening to three lines. Unlike many other cobble constructions at the site, these stones were arranged with their smoothest sur-

3.11. A drainlike cobble pavement at the intersection (N45/E35) of two structures in the northern area of Operation E, at the terrace edge. Looking north.

to the "drain" found the year before in Operation D (fig. 3.6: 3). When we used the *sonda* to try and trace the path of the arc of this next circle of stones, however, we could not detect cobbles. We then placed pits in this area to be sure that the arc was incomplete, and these excavations confirmed that this was so. This is most curious. It seems odd to imagine that such care would have been taken to build a short segment of arc and a drain without completing the rest of the circle or arc. This could be the case, or it could be that the rest of the structure was made of perishable materials, and, for some reason, no cobble ring was required. A third possibility is that there had been a ring in this locale but that the stones that formed it had been removed for new construction elsewhere at the site. Perhaps this last end of the arc and the drain were not disturbed because they were useful in channeling rainwater off of the terrace edge. Or it may be that the ring was never completed.

The issue of the terrace edge itself is another curiosity. It seems odd that the semicircle just discussed is cut off by the terrace edge. Thirty meters farther south, cobbles and boulders are carefully aligned on the edge of the terrace (see fig. 3.1). It seems quite likely that the terrace edge near the drain and to the north and south of it may have eroded away, tumbling large boulders that once defined the eastern edge of the architecture there onto the terrace below.

The terrace to the east and below the one on which the large-scale architecture was located was examined to see if more remains of human presence could be detected. But no architecture or artifacts were found. There is a small stream on this terrace, and it is likely that if it was there when the site was occupied, it may have been the chief source of drinking water for the inhabitants of the site. Larry Conyers supervised the excavation of a pit at the base of the terrace on which Operations D and E were located. He found no evidence of occupation, but he did find indications that the stream once flowed directly next to the bottom of the terrace, though whether it was during the occupation of the site was hard to determine.

To the west of the drain there was a huge patio-like area, defined by two straight parallel walls with an arc connecting them, to the west, and running into the *ballena*. The northern edge of this patio formed the southern boundary of another space with a parallel wall made of a single line of cobbles 20 meters to the north. A small oval structure was part of the western boundary of this space, although the cobbles that made up this structure were mixed into the apparently random stones on the *ballena*. From the single line of cobbles and close to the northern end of the oval, another arc of single cobbles trailed off into the *monte* at one of the farthest reaches of our investigation area.

It is worth noting that the architecture in this far northern part of the site is made of single cobbles of stones. Perhaps less energy was invested in making constructions here than in Operation D or in the western and southern sections of Operation E. The spaces defined by the cobble lines in the far northern area of the site are as big and sometimes bigger than the more elaborate architecture farther south. If the bounded spaces were associated with groups of people, then the groups were of fairly equal size throughout the site, but some had simple structures to define the spaces that they occupied or in which they carried out activities, and others had more elaborate spaces.

The other work in the far northern end of Operation E showed a continuation of boulders and stones along the *ballena*. The western side of the *ballena* descended into the guava grove on the west side of which was the mysterious line of stones from 1992. On this western edge of the *ballena* we found a series of very large boulders carefully arranged, giving the impression that they delimited the edge of the large-scale architecture. Some of these were massive, 1.5 meters in maximum length and almost a meter wide (see fig. 4.2).

Although we were blocked from working farther northward by dense vegetation, our forays by foot showed no signs of architecture there. If there were more features, they probably were built to the less elaborate standards of structures we had found to the south. It may also be that pavements and patios are hidden by modern vegetation and might be found if more time were devoted to their discovery.

Our work was almost done for the field season. There remained the issue of the coffee field that separated Operations D and E. From observations made by walking (and sometimes crawling) through it, we knew that there were very significant features there. The large, 30 meters in diameter, beautifully made circle that extended into Operation E (see fig. 3.2) continued into this coffee field, and on the other side in Operation D, the cobble "drain" was associated with another large circle that entered the coffee field. We asked the landowners if there was any chance we could work extensively in the coffee field in the following year. Our plan was to cut a 5-meter-wide swath through the coffee plants and, at a minimum, scrape the soil to find and map a continuous stretch of architecture between Operations D and E. We offered to reimburse the owners for coffee plants that we wished to remove in order to do this. The owners were willing for us to tramp around and map and even put small excavations between the plants, but they valued their coffee too highly to sacrifice it to archaeology, even

with the prospect of reimbursement. While we were disappointed, we realized there was still plenty to do, even if we did not excavate in the coffee field.

What We Learned in 1993

The 1993 work did not present us with surprises the way the discovery of the large-scale architecture did in 1992. Nevertheless, the work was productive and informative. We confirmed that there were two phases of building big constructions at the site, as indicated by two layers of stone features. The orange layer of soil was identified as separating the lower, earlier architecture that was covered by it and the upper, later constructions. We found evidence of exotic ceramics on the southern edge of the large oval, and we inferred, through this evidence, that feasting may have taken place there. We were able to examine some details of construction, such as the boulders on the eastern edge of the Operation E terrace.

It also became clear that our common confusion in not always being able to distinguish between lines and other arrangements of cobbles and boulders made by humans and those made by nature was due to the fact that distinctions between the two sometimes were simply not that clear-cut. The work on the *ballena* and vicinity showed that while sometimes the Rivas inhabitants went to great trouble to move big stones into position, at other times they used naturally occurring formations of rocks to serve human purposes. The *ballena* boulders were a naturally formed boundary to the zone of large architecture. A few boulders, such as those where the western edge of the *ballena* and the guava grove met, likely were moved into place, but other formations, such as on the *ballena* itself, probably were moved slightly or not at all.

The architecture was so large and complex that some questions could not be addressed but instead merely raised. The cobble path with the big boulder on top of it in the southwest corner of the operation is but one example. We didn't know where that path came from or where it went, and we never found time to explore the matter fully. Why did some circles have *rípio* close to their surfaces while others had layers of orange soil? Was the presence of orange soil due to natural erosion processes, or was it fill, deliberately transported for the renovation of the large-scale architecture? The latter explanation seems most likely. The soils in most of the site area are rarely bright orange. Such soil is found only on the slopes and top of the Panteón de La Reina and immediately at its base. The orange soils in Operations D and E must have been deliberately carried from the base of the Panteón to serve as fill in the second-phase building project.

The people of Rivas seemed to share the practice of "temple reburial," widespread in ancient America, and probably the ideological concepts tied to it. Ancestral architecture was treated with respect and its spiritual power utilized by burying it, perhaps to continue to radiate its power outward, while at the same time incorporating it as the foundation for later construction. But not all of the older architecture was deliberately buried. Why this is so is uncertain. Perhaps only areas that were deemed to be of special significance were filled with orange soil. Alternatively, it may be that those areas that were filled simply were ones that were part of the redesign plan. That might explain why some cobbles may have been robbed from the missing circle associated with the drain in the northern area of Operation D, at the terrace edge.

Another example of leaving an earlier construction without filling it in can be seen at the northern end of the arc of four stones that forms the western boundary of the oval in Operation E (see fig 3.6). Existing structures appear to have been modified to produce the oval form. It is quite likely that the western end of the oval was a former circle that had been robbed of cobbles on its eastern side for use elsewhere during the remodeling. This might explain why no trace exists of the circle beyond the arc, swinging into the plaza of the oval. Perhaps enough cobbles had been taken that the builders didn't bother to remove the rest of the stones, creating this arc that extends past the join line between the oval and the terrace edge. The less than perfect connection between the southern end of the arc of four stones and the lower boundary of the oval may be the result of similar manipulations.

Another possible earlier structure that may have been modified in the later building phase is the large patio on the southeastern end of the oval. This feature is unusual for several reasons. First, most patios are found on the western sides of circles, often oriented slightly southwest. This patio, however, is on the opposite side of most of the others. Considering the ac-

curacy with which many of the other circles were built, this one seems notably lopsided, being neither a circle nor a quadrilateral patio. One explanation for the odd location and shape of this structure is that it was a circle modified in the building program that had created the oval to its northwest. The small circle to its south also seems oddly placed.

Of course, it is quite likely that during the two or three centuries of occupation of the site there were a number of building phases. People frequently remodel houses, churches, and other structures, even today, to suit new needs and desires. We may not be always able to distinguish one phase from the next. Perhaps some of the incomplete circles were made that way for other reasons, such as continuing walls with perishable construction. There seems little to indicate that the orange earth covering the lower structures in Operations D and E was the result of natural processes. The soil is too evenly spread over cobbles, and there is just enough to cover them before the higher, darker layer of earth begins with new construction on top of it. This suggests that the orange soil was carried to these locations to cover the old structures so that new ones could be built.

Not all of the old architecture was unserviceable for the new purposes that required remodeling. Some structures may have stayed in use, while others were modified. For these earlier structures we were only able to excavate 10 or 20 centimeters, and sometimes a lot less, before we hit the hard, densely packed layer of *rípio* gravel. Complex I in Operation D is one example of this. Elsewhere, including only a few meters east of the Complex I ring of stones, the soil was deep. It is often in these deep layers of soil where the earlier architecture is found, below the level of the later structures. But only in those cases where we have one layer of architecture superimposed above another can we be certain of the relative age of one structure to another, based on whether one is below (earlier) or above (later) the other. The only exception to this rule is the rare case where the evidence suggests that a former structure was mostly dismantled so that its cobbles could be used in new construction. Such a case is the circle that has left only a small section of arc next to the northern drain in the northern area of Operation E. Otherwise, the location of a circle in *rípio* is no clear indication that it was earlier or later than any other one.

When major remodeling of temple structures was undertaken in Mesoamerica, it was often due to the accession of a new ruler. But we had no evidence that the people of Rivas had been under the rule of a monarch or paramount chief. There was no structure so different from the others in size, quality of construction, or distinctiveness of features and with evidence of habitation that might suggest it was a palace of a ruler. Might there be some other explanation as to why the inhabitants of the site undertook the task of drastically changing the structures there? Going through our notes after the 1993 field season, we didn't have an answer to such a question. In fact, the question was far from our minds, as we were simply trying to make sense of what we had found, of the very fact that there was extensive rebuilding at the site. We did notice some odd things about the last phase of architecture, but we weren't certain about them. Indeed, the pieces of this puzzle didn't fully come together until I was writing this very chapter, more than six years after the 1993 field season.

As the 1993 field season ended, we thought we had a pretty good understanding of the site and what had happened there. We were mostly drawn to the sharp contrasts between the small-scale architecture in Operation A and the large-scale architecture on the terrace below. We thought that these differences were indicative of a society of two ranks: high-status people who lived in the big houses in Operations D and E and commoners who lived in the small houses on the upper terrace. This theory fit well with our discovery of apparent low-status cemeteries on the Rivas terraces, such as Operation C. The low-status people who lived in small structures had no gold and were buried in nearby cemeteries. The rich folks, who lived in Operations D and E, were of higher status, lived in bigger houses, and were buried on the Panteón de La Reina. It all seemed to be working out quite well.

I was glowing with self-satisfaction. We would be able to present a new model of chiefdom society in the region. This model was based not on the idea of complex clans arranged in some kind of pyramidal structure but rather on a system resembling classes of rich and poor. Morton Fried (1967) had discussed the idea of a stratified society that was not a state, and it appeared that Rivas might be just such a society. Perhaps it was an "almost state" that had never reached the level of power resting firmly in the hands of a single family to produce a ruling lineage. If we could convincingly demonstrate that this was the case, it might be of considerable interest to other archaeologists and anthropologists concerned with issues of the development of complex societies. As we planned for the 1994 field season, I thought that we mostly needed to refine this understanding and to fill in some gaps in our information, such as the development of a better map and site plan. I didn't realize that, as our work continued, we would find evidence to significantly alter our view of the Rivas site and the people who made and used its structures a thousand years ago.

CHAPTER FOUR

EXPANDING OUR UNDERSTANDING OF THE SITE, 1994

Wrapping Up and Moving Forward

For the 1994 field season, we had three things we wished to accomplish. First, there were a few loose ends to tie up in Operation E. Second, we wanted to dig in an area that might yield some spectacular burials in Operation D. Depending on the outcome of that work, our third goal was to do a shovel test pit survey of the entire area that we knew was part of the site, from Operation D all the way to Operation C.

We arrived in Costa Rica in mid-January. I had a sabbatical, so I could be in the field through most of February although, due to family obligations, I couldn't stay longer. The excavation of the suspected cemetery in Operation D would take a lot of planning, and the shovel test pit work would take a long time. Our plan, then, was to begin with the more straightforward work in Operation E while we figured out the details of how to do the Operation D work. Then we would dig the burials in Operation D, to be followed by the shovel test pit survey.

Starting Off with a Bang

Jeff Frost, Chris Raymond, and I all arrived in Costa Rica within a few days of one another. I had some business to do in San José, to get our excavation permits in order, so we all met there and went down south together, on the bus, over the mountains, to San Isidro.

Aida Blanco kindly offered us space in her home in San Isidro while we looked for a house to rent in Rivas. We never stayed in the same house twice, but there was always some place to rent since one family or another was away picking coffee, staying with relatives elsewhere in Costa Rica, or living in New Jersey, making money by working at jobs such as busboys or kitchen assistants in restaurants. But who was away at any particular time varied, and this time it seemed as if everybody was staying in Rivas. The three of us spread out on Aida's couch and floor. After a week we still hadn't found a place to rent, and we were feeling uncomfortable imposing on Aida for so long, although she never complained.

One Sunday night, Jeff and Chris said they were going to a dance farther up the valley from Rivas at a place called San Gerardo. I told them to try and be back at least by midnight as we had work to do in the morning. They took off in the Land Rover.

I stayed up late, reading. They weren't back by 11:00, and I dozed off with the lights on. I woke at 2:00 and they still hadn't returned. I began to worry and drifted fitfully between sleep and wakefulness for the following hours. Finally, at 5:00 A.M. I heard the sound of the Rover coming up the silent street.

Jeff and Chris burst in. They had been driving back from San Gerardo fairly early when they rounded a corner near Rivas to find a car wreck. It must have just happened. A jeep had overturned after a collision with an avocado tree. It lay on its side with pools of gasoline around it. Nine people were lying all over the road, groaning, some with twisted limbs and others with head injuries, a broken leg, and a broken pelvis. Despite the quantities of alcohol they had consumed at the dance, they were in a lot of pain. Chris attended to the injured as best he could while Jeff used a chain hitched to the Rover to drag the jeep to one side to clear the road. The gasoline pools made the operation particularly dicey, as it was a rocky road and a spark easily could have set off a blaze and explosion.

The injured were piled into the Rover, and the two gringos drove them to the nearest hospital, in San Isidro. Jeff and Chris waited until the doctors had fixed up the walking wounded and then drove them back to their homes. Jeff and Chris became local heroes for a while, treated to many drinks at bars. For several weeks we drove around with a single cowboy boot in the back of the Rover, left by one of the injured. Eventually, the owner started complaining that we had stolen his boot. We told him to come and get it and he did. Heroism doesn't last long, anywhere, but the good deed may have been recognized somewhere since soon after this incident we found a small house available for rent in Rivas.

It wasn't much of a house, even by local standards. Like most places, the structure was set on a larger poured cement slab creating a walkway running around the house perimeter similar in function to the cobble rings at the archaeological site. The structure itself was made of unpainted ½ x 3 inch (or thereabouts) wooden boards, set vertically and supported, inside, by cross beams that might eventually be covered with wallboard

when the owner got more money. Since we had so few furnishings, we used the crossbeams as shelves on which to put our radios, flashlights, and alarm clocks.

At night, the place would glow like a Chinese lantern. There was no insulation, and although we had little wind, it would get very cold by 6 A.M. when we had to get up for work. I once woke up with my teeth chattering. The little thermometer read 60 degrees but it felt like 0! The drop from near 100 degrees at the height of the daily heat made it feel that cold. We called the place La Mansión.

Stairs

When we had cleared Operation E in the previous year, a huge amount of cut grass, small trees, and brush had accumulated. To give us maximum working room, we piled the vegetation at the edge of our work area. We put a considerable amount of the stuff in the northwest corner of Operation E, up against the inner side of the barbed wire fence that had defined our boundary, in the area of N25/W15 (fig. 3.2).

As mentioned earlier, part of the work we did in this general area was to place excavation units there, including a north-south trench as well as two rectangular units. This work had indicated that there was a line of stones running roughly west-northwest–east-southeast. At the time that we did this work, we realized that we may have found a feature associated with the infamous line of stones of 1992. We couldn't investigate the matter further, however, because our pile of brush would have required a great deal of effort to move, and we weren't quite sure where to put it without blocking other areas we wanted to excavate.

One of the biggest problems in conducting large-scale excavations is what might seem to be the relatively simple decision of where to put things like brush or, an even more weighty matter, the backdirt pile. Backdirt is the soil that has been excavated, usually screened and so officially empty of artifacts, but which can accumulate at an alarming rate. When soil is "unpacked" from its natural location, it seems to expand in size, especially when aerated by screening. All too often, the hapless field director realizes too late that a mound of backdirt, sometimes several meters high, is in a crucial place for continued excavation, even though its original location seemed out of the way.

In 1994, with the excavations in the central section of Operation E finished, we decided to work where the brush had previously been, now much reduced due to the deterioration brought about by the previous rainy season. Instead of approaching the area from the Operation E side, however, we decided to follow the line of stones, apparently leading to the brush pile from the other direction.

The line of stones had been discovered by accident, on a sojourn away from the work being done at the time in Operation A. Once discovered, I had put a couple of workers to the task of clearing the line as much as possible. This was difficult, however, because the cobbles were buried fairly deeply due to the accumulation of leaf fall from the guava trees and because the low location, at the foot of the Operation A terrace, was a place where sediment buildup had occurred. The line of stones had been followed for 35 meters, after which it seemed to disappear just before the barbed wire fence of Operation E.

In 1994 we took the fence down between Operation E and the line of stones area of the guava grove and moved what was left of the old brush pile farther into the already overgrown area of Operation E, which had been cleared less than a year before. As we worked we found that the line of stones indeed came to an end with only a few meters more beyond the terminal point we had identified previously (fig. 4.1). It ran, however, into a narrow cobble pavement that continued southwestward. It became quite clear that the line of stones was on a course that intersected the other cobble line in the northwestern section of Operation E. This strongly suggests that the line of stones is what we thought it was in the first place. It is a pathway or perhaps the boundary of a pathway that directed foot traffic from the Operation A area to Operation E.

We also had another surprise. As we were clearing the area near the end of the line of stones, we uncovered more cobbles forming a kind of stairway or cobble path leading up the side of the terrace. Although there was some disturbance, it was clear that either a naturally formed path along the terrace face had been modified or a completely artificial cut had been made

and then faced with cobbles to provide easy access from the top to the bottom of the terrace. Although a fair amount of work had gone into this construction, the stairway did not present itself as a highly formalized walkway.

There were a couple of other places along the face of the terrace, one toward the middle of the line of stones, that also were easy to ascend and descend, although it is hard to know if these are the remnants of ancient routes or simply more recent thoroughfares. The stone stairway, however, was ancient, and it seems to have been a route of convenience more than of ceremony. The work put into the arrangement of cobbles, though, suggests that this was a means of communication between two areas of the site that saw heavy traffic and was deemed important enough to receive some extra special attention by the creation of a solid stairway of cobbles. Today it is easy to get up and down the terrace at this locale because of the organization of stones, but it was impossible to determine if these were just natural or the remains of an earlier construction. We excavated in the area, but, other than clearing the cobbles, there were few artifacts there.

We also searched for the end of the line of stones, placing pits at what appeared to be its northern limit, 85 meters north of our datum. Instead, we found what appeared to be some kind of cobble floor, suggesting that much of the area now under grass had a formal pavement at the time of the site occupation. It also indicated that the area of architecture indeed extended well beyond the farthest area mapped in detail, around N70.

The line of stones is interesting because it suggests that there was an important corridor of communication from up-valley into the Operation E area and vice versa. As mentioned in the preceding chapter, a line of very large boulders forms another boundary to Operation E, 18 meters to the east of the line of stones (fig. 4.2). These boulders were on the western edge of the *ballena*. We had noted them in 1993, but in 1994 they were mapped.

We also excavated pits 20 meters north of this area and another group even farther away. The latter, a trench 5 meters long and 1 meter wide at N107–112, was our northenmost pit in the Operation D/E area. Even at these great distances, we encountered cobbles

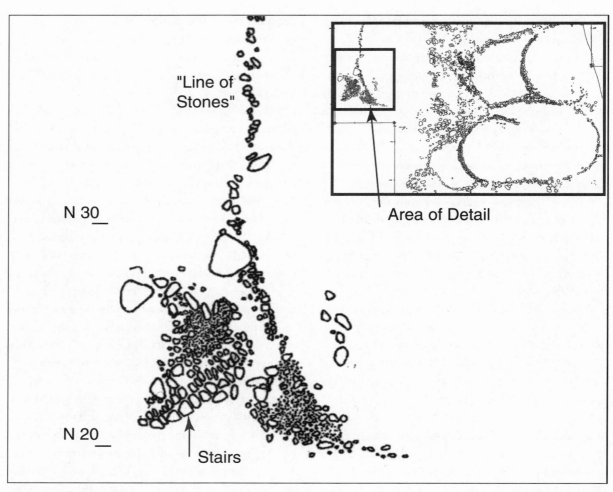

"Line of Stones"

Area of Detail

N 30

N 20

Stairs

4.1. The southern end of the line of stones and the stairs leading to the upper terrace of Operation A. Map by R. J. Frost and J. Quilter.

laid flat, indicating that the site complex continued to this point and likely beyond. The cobbles were buried deeply here, probably because of the deposition of soils eroded from the terrace to the west or washed down from places farther north. We were more than 100 meters north of our datum in the center of Operation E, and we knew that Operation D continued to the south at least as far as the road. Added together, there was more than half a kilometer of cobble formations stretching along the terraces of the Rivas site, with an average width of 50 meters.

All of our probing with *sondas* in the area between the line of stones and the line of large boulders to the east, on the western edge of the *ballena*, revealed no evidence of cobbles. These lines of stones, whether cobble- or boulder-size, resemble the same kinds of arrangements as found in Operation C where we had

located a line of small cobbles set on their edges, which appeared to mark the boundary of the cemetery. Such lines apparently delimit important spaces. Thus it appears that there likely were two paths that led from the upper terrace to Operation E. One is the path found in the southwestern area of Operation E with the large boulder on top of it. We don't know where this path goes, but it runs east-west and appears to have carried foot traffic from Operation E toward the upper terrace. Another, roughly even with the northern edge of the oval, is at the stairway at the end of the line of stones. The line of stones we had discovered the year before in the northwest area of Operation E also probably was part of this system.

But what of the line of stones itself? It may have demarcated the sacred space of Operation E, but it may also have served as a guide for foot traffic coming from

4.2. Boulders uncovered in the guava grove parallel to the northern limits of the line of stones, at N75/W15.

the north. Although some cobbles were on edge, some were flat. It is quite possible that vegetation in this area through the centuries has turned some cobbles on edge and that the original arrangement was of flat-faced cobbles. At the foot of the terrace, it is likely that this area was damp even a thousand years ago. The cobbles of the line of stones themselves may have served as a footpath, though today it does not appear to have the formal characteristics of other, more recognizable ones.

Spiders Big As Kaiser Rolls

Wham! Jeff Frost had gotten up from his bed that doubled as a couch, grabbed a shoe, and in one smooth motion brought it down on something in the middle of the floor of our rickety cabin. "Did you see that?" he yelled. "Did you see that? That spider was as big as a kaiser roll!"

Insect life is abundant in Costa Rica. There were the tiny chiggers that attacked our ankles when we walked through short grass. On the other end of the size range, there were the clumsy flying locusts that local people called *langostinos*, supposedly because they taste like shrimp. They would sometimes lumber into houses on wings that seemed much too small to support them and bounce around, trying to get out. No one killed them because they ate bad insects, so they were usually brushed out with a broom or hat when they flopped to the floor, too tired and apparently too stupid to figure out how to get out of the house they had barged into.

In between the chiggers and the *langostinos* there were all sorts of other creatures. There were tarantulas, known locally as *mata caballos* because their venom can bring down a horse. Then there were the ants. There were the pacific, big black kind and the nasty little red ants that would bite with venom, producing a searing pain. Leaf cutter ants were amazing, traveling in long strings in two directions at the same time over long distances. They carried big pieces of cut green foliage that they use in underground burrows to serve as food, once properly fermented.

There were the swarms of killer bees, also known as Africanized bees. A failed attempt at crossbreeding in South America has produced mean, nasty bees that attack humans and other large animals with little provocation. They had crossbred with other varieties of bees many times and worked their way up to Central America. We heard a story that they had killed a horse, farther up-valley, in Chimirol. One day in 1992, while working in Operation A, I was concentrating on some bit of work when I heard a strange loud buzzing overhead, more like a drone. Too occupied with my task, I assumed it was some kind of aircraft. The next day, at about the same time, I heard the same sound and gazed up to see what looked like a tube of dense black specks undulating through the air only a little more than a meter above my head. It was a swarm of Africanized bees. Luckily, they seemed intent on getting somewhere fast and weren't low enough to consider me or anyone else a threat. It happened several more times. Later, some of our workers were attacked by some nasty bees on the Panteón de La Reina, although they didn't persist in attacking the way some other varieties of killer bees do elsewhere in the tropics.

No Costa Rican houses have screens. There are just too many bugs around to bother trying to keep them out. Despite the occasional misadventure with them, though, insects do not pose the kind of nuisance in Costa Rica that a bad season of mosquitoes or black flies does in northern regions, such as Wisconsin. In the tropics, animal diversity is high but, generally, the number of individuals one encounters at any one time is relatively low, though the Africanized bees swarm, which is partly why they are so dangerous.

Then there were the friendly insects. One day after work, while we were relaxing at the Casa Verde, we were invaded by ants pouring into the house in a line and then heading off in different directions, once inside. Our first instinct was to sweep them away, but Loly Mora, our cook, told us to leave them alone as they would clean out the house of pests. Sure enough, the ants went after every bug, living and dead, that they could find. They killed spiders and other noxious insects and then stripped their carcasses to nothing. After about two hours of their cleaning rampage, the ants all left, leaving us with a bug-free house. This happened at least two other times during our visits to Costa Rica.

There were noisy insects, too. In 1992 we must have been at a peak in the multiyear cycle for cicadas. They made a very loud buzzing sound all around the site and left their molted carapaces on trees, everywhere. They were at least twice as big as the cicadas in the midwestern United States.

One day, one of our workers, Juan Romero Mora, who was also an artisan, asked me if I would drive him downriver to a place known as Pacuar, at the junction of the General and the Pacuar Rivers. Juan Romero wanted to go there to obtain soft stone that he used to produce small carvings he sold to tourists and traded for drinks with bartenders. We drove down to Pacuar, and on the riverbank we found the cobbles that he needed for carving. Nearby, there was a Chiriquí phase site where we found a petroglyph carved on a large boulder. Across the stream, about 50 meters wide, there was a cliff with dense tropical forest in front of it, stretching for about 300 meters. In those trees there must have been hundreds of thousands of cicadas. They didn't just buzz, they roared like some kind of huge electrical system gone haywire. They were so loud that shouted voices could not be heard from a few feet away, as the sound went beyond aural to a physical sensation.

And there were the magical fireflies. Two kinds lit the night. One was a big variety with a blue-toned lamp that made brief tracers in the dark. The other was similar to our northern firefly but a bit larger and with a more intense and slightly longer-lasting glow. The two kinds, together, created magic in the air, especially on dark nights. On clear nights, stars like a million fireflies seemed to glow permanently in the spectacular skies, overhead, far from the strong lights of cities.

Loot Day

We are talking loot. Loot, also known as booty, plunder, treasure, filthy lucre, the shiny stuff. Loot in the form of gold. Gold, also known as *oro*, the purest of metals, the sweat of the sun, the feces of the gods, the riches of the Indies. Rumplestiltskin spun it from straw. Midas got what he deserved. It turned Francis Drake into a hero in Britain and a pirate in Spanish America. It fueled the Spanish Armada and the Renaissance. It drove men to murder, mayhem, madness, and death. It made paupers into kings, kings into paupers, wives into widows, and children into orphans in the towns and cities of Europe. The lust for gold cut a swath of destruction through the Americas.

The Spanish told the Indians they had a thirst that only gold could quench. Once the natives got wind of what the Spanish were up to, they sometimes obliged by pouring melted gold down their throats. The Spanish, in turn, melted down wondrous works of art into blocks of bullion and shipped it off home. Since then, it has been cast into coins and artwork and remelted and reminted again and again. You may be walking around with a fragment of a present from Montezuma wrapped around your finger or a tiny portion of Atahuallpa's ransom packed into a hole in one of your teeth. Your nose ring or tie tack might even be part of the fabulous gold treasure taken from the graves of the Panteón de La Reina.

The desire for gold has driven much of the engine of history. Before the New World was discovered, the same quest drove the exploration of Africa. Gold fever has run high in every century, causing rushes to California, the Klondike, Brazil. The Panteón de La Reina was viewed as a gold mine at the end of the nineteenth century. Gold fever had swept north from Panama, thanks to those Forty-Niners who decided that they could make their fortunes in Central America instead of California. In Chiriquí, ridge-top cemeteries were easily identified by their cobble pavements and stone pillars. All you had to do was dig for a while; it was much easier work than the gold fields of California. You didn't have to travel as far from home if you had sailed from an East Coast city of the United States, and the purity of the gold jewelry found in graves often was very high.

We had been up to the top of the Panteón de La Reina because the Rivas site likely was associated with the ridge-top cemetery. After all, the largest architecture at Rivas was right at the bottom of the Panteón hill. It even was located close to the lowest part of the Panteón ridge. The Panteón summit was mostly covered in thick vegetation. It looked just like what you expected a tropical forest to be. There were tall trees in some areas and thick lianas strong enough for Tarzan to take a swing. But enough light filtered through so that ground vegetation was thick with plants. These included the occasional gorgeous flower, weedy bushes, and, sometimes, nasty plants that seemed to grab on to bare skin and leave stinging welts as painful as bee stings that would last for many hours. Aida told me of a plant that knocked her close to unconscious.

To the uneducated eye this looks like climax vegetation, yet the numerous graves, or at least the remains of them, indicated that a thousand years ago much of the hilltop must have been clear of forest. The Panteón had to have been free of large trees and such in order to put the hundreds of graves up there. The forest floor today resembles an overgrown World War I battlefield. There are looter pits everywhere. Most are old holes with their sides slumped in and overgrown. Sometimes trees have sprung from the bottom of these illegal excavations. In other places, though, the pits have sharp edges and straight sides, indicating recent digging activity. Sometimes there is fresh backdirt, suggesting that looters have been digging quite recently. It was rather depressing as we went up year after year, as the project continued, to start to find looter holes dug neatly, in quadrangular units with straight side walls. It appeared that some of our workers had been learning excavation techniques well.

Any ambitions we had to dig on the Panteón de La Reina were stymied by Costa Rican law and the economic situations of farmers. There were laws of compensation for gold taken from private property, but the farmers didn't trust them. No one had heard of the practice because the economic incentive for campesinos is to dig it up themselves, for sale, or to charge foreign looters for the privilege of looting the national patrimony. They certainly didn't fully appreciate the concept of national patrimony, preferring instead to reasonably consider whatever was on their property as their own. We thus believed that if we found gold we would be getting into a very messy situation, filled with uncertainties for ourselves and for our workers who had become our friends.

We therefore were in a difficult position. We believed that excavations on the Panteón de La Reina were important to understanding the Rivas site. Even if we found no gold, understanding how the cemetery was organized and retrieving information on the numbers of graves in cemetery areas, their arrangements, their associations with stone pillars, and other information would be of great importance. There was also the possibility that there were some graves with gold that had been missed by looters. If we could find even one, it would add a tremendous amount of knowledge about the people who used the Rivas site. But we knew that if we found gold we would have to surrender it to the authorities. At the same time, we would alienate our workers and the landowners who had come to be our friends. We didn't know quite what to do.

In 1992 when we first discovered Operation D, we made another find within the area of large-scale construction about which we had done nothing. Rising sharply on the western edge of the area of large-scale architecture was a distinct terrace, about 3 meters above the level of Complexes II and III to its east. The sharpness of the rise was so distinct that in 1992 we put some workers to the task of clearing a stretch of the face of the terrace. I wanted to see if the natural slope had been altered by human activity and whether there was a cobble facing or other stonework on it. As was the case in so much of our work at Rivas, the work there was inconclusive. There were some cobbles that looked like they were deliberately placed but others that appeared not to be, so we couldn't say with certainty how much human manipulation of the landscape in this locale had occurred.

While Jeff Frost and I were making our preliminary map of the Operation D area, we came to realize that there were some very different cobble features on top of this western terrace. There were two areas, roughly

4.3. One of the pillars in the OpD '94 area. It was on the edge of the cobble pavements (rear), and our workers lifted it to the position seen here.

10 x 10 meters square each, with cobble pavements appearing through places where the grass was thin. These pavements rose slightly, while a swale about 10 meters in width separated them. Most interesting of all was the fact that around the borders of these pavements there were pillars or the remains of them (fig. 4.3).

Stone pillars are one of the most distinctive markers of cemeteries in this part of Costa Rica. In 1992 we found one that had rolled from the top of the Panteón de La Reina almost to the area of Operation A or perhaps had been moved there. In the park of the Central Plaza in San Isidro, a collection of these pillars has been erected to form what appears to be a miniature cousin of something resembling Stonehenge, without the capstones. These likely came from a number of ridge-top cemeteries in the upper General Valley. Pillars that are associated with cemeteries range in size from about 1 meter in height to close to 2 meters. They may have oval or quadrangular cross sections or a com-

bination of both, and they usually come to a rounded point. Some pillars seem to have been modified close to the desired shape, while others had little work done to them. The use of pillars is distinct to the upper General Valley. The use of "standing stones" as markers of important, often consecrated, places is widespread in the New World, from the stelae of Mesoamerica to the *wankas* of Peru.

We began to think that the pillars and pavements were above untouched gold burials. The ridge-top held gold burials, and this terrace was clearly a kind of miniature ridge overlooking the large-scale architecture of Operation D. Perhaps some special graves had been dug right here and not been touched for all the years since their rich contents had been deposited below our feet. We decided that sooner or later we would have to dig in this area. We waited through the 1992 field season and the 1993 excavations. We wanted to get as much information as possible about the main part of the site before we risked the troubles that digging gold burials might bring. In 1994 the time seemed ripe.

I could only be in the field for a short period of time this season. We decided that we would give the excavations on the upper terrace high priority and called this work Operation D, 1994, or OpD '94 for short. It would take some time to get everything in line for our work in this location. We also planned to do some minor work in Operation E that we had not had a chance to do the previous year. An important goal for the field season was a shovel test pit survey of the entire site, to better understand what remains existed between the separate operation areas in which we had worked during the previous two field seasons.

As for the problem of possibly finding gold objects under these pavements and pillars, I decided to take a gamble. I had official permission to dig anywhere at both Rivas and the Panteón de La Reina, officially classified as two separate sites with different site numbers —SJ148RV and SJ109RV, respectively—so that was no problem. If the families agreed to let us work on the terrace, I would take a risk. We would dig only a small portion of the area. We had a long talk with the senior men of the Mora and Mata families. We told them what we wanted to do. We said that we might find gold or we might not. We explained that if we found gold it would have to go to the National Museum, and the issue of compensation was unclear. But, we noted, if we did find gold, the site would be so important that they would reap many benefits. The site might be developed for tourism. Perhaps we could build a site museum. There would be many opportunities to make money that would, well, be worth their weight in gold. They agreed to let us dig in this area.

So it was that we started talking of "Loot Day." We were very responsible, concerned archaeologists. We had our permits, we had our permissions, and we were working in cooperation with everyone with whom we were supposed to coordinate our efforts and to whom we were responsible. But it was a release to sit around the house, late at night, talking of the loot. We had a countdown to the day when we were going to dig the terrace, scratching off each day on the calendar. More seriously, we planned what we were going to do to prevent robbery once we had unearthed the gold. We heard murmurs among the workers about what they would do if we found gold. They knew as well as we did that the cobble pavements signaled burials beneath. We had to develop a strategy to try and cope with the possibilities if we came upon a significant amount of treasure.

Our excavation of the burials could be the first scientific recovery of substantial information on high-status gold interments carried out in Costa Rica. While we planned to work quickly, we would record information on the burials by using photographs and a video camera. The placement of artifacts in graves in relation to the soil stains of decayed bodies and other artifacts would be valuable information. If we could excavate more than a couple of graves, we could evaluate the differences among individuals buried with gold, perhaps making distinctions between higher- and lower-ranking members of those entitled to be buried with this valued material. We also could assess how different symbols expressed in gold—frogs, humanoids, and avians—related to one another in a suite of artifacts shared among contemporary people. And we would be able to state definitively that the gold styles we found dated to the Chiriquí archaeological culture. All of this information would be contributions to the study of prehistoric Costa Rica that had not been made previously.

We finally decided that we would select three or four cobble pavements and excavate them to just above the level of where we expected to encounter the buri-

als themselves. From our work in Operation C, as well as discussions with Aida and other archaeologists, we knew that Chiriquí burials are usually found at about 1.5 to 2 meters below ground level. High-status burials are usually deeper than lower-status ones, so we would expect the remains in OpD '94 to be close to 2 meters in depth, maybe even deeper.

Then, once we were within striking distance of the burial level, we would excavate them simultaneously in a single day—Loot Day. We would notify archaeologists at the National Museum of what we planned to do, and on Loot Day, if we struck gold, we would immediately call them up. We would ask that they provide armed guards and an escort to San José so that the gold could be safeguarded. We talked late into the night of what it might be like, joking that we would be like Indiana Jones in the opening scene of the first movie, with me running with the loot, screaming, "Start the Land Rover," to Jeff and Chris.

On a more sober note, however, we decided we needed our own security prior to any great discoveries since our excavations could be damaged if someone decided to ransack our pits once we had removed the cobble pavements. The work had been going slowly. The cobble pavements had been cleared of soil, and we had slowed down to map and photograph them (fig. 4.4). Only when we had thoroughly documented the pavements would we be ready to remove them and continue excavating to reach the burials below. But while we were exposing the pavements, we feared that we were also exposing the area to looting. We thus decided on round-the-clock protection. Jeff and Chris would camp out next to the cobble pavements and spend the night. In order to give them the opportunity to wash up, do errands in town, and so forth, I volunteered to stay at the site in the late afternoons, after the workday was over, until they could get back for their turn on watch.

So, over a period of about two weeks, after a short run to the house for a little cleaning up, I would come back to the site. It was a beautiful location, with a fine view of Operation D to the east and coffee fields and the Panteón to my back. I took paperwork and books with me, but sometimes I was too tired to work or read.

Sitting out at the site in the late afternoon was an interesting experience. Our workers would pass by as they went out to do their own work in their fields.

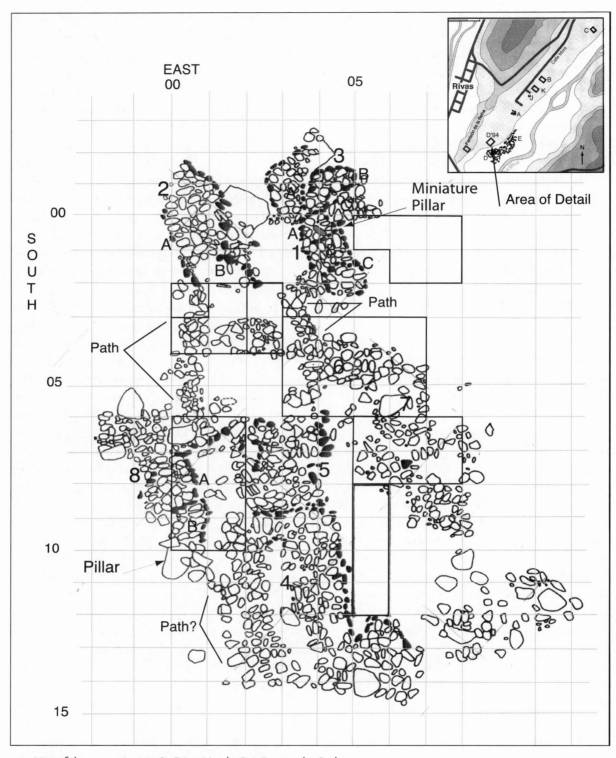

4.4. Map of the excavations in OpD '94. Map by R. J. Frost and J. Quilter.

They would stop and say hello, and I could hear those working nearby from the sound of machetes chopping against coffee plants. I would still be in my spot a couple of hours later as they returned home. It was quiet out there in the country. The distant bark of a dog, the mooing of a cow, the neighing of a horse, and the random cock-a-doodle of a rooster were the only sounds, sometimes punctuated by the straining motor of a vehicle going up the road over the Panteón. A swallow-tailed hawk seemed to favor our area and sometimes could be seen catching the currents off the Panteón. Buzzards circled overhead. The scents of wood-burning stoves, still used by many, and of dinner would sometimes drift by.

When it was still hot, butterflies would flutter about and hummingbirds zip by. Swarms of killer bees would sometimes fly by, luckily high above any human head. They came in formation like a long, angry, buzzing black ribbon, snaking through the sky in their own strange conga dance line.

Gradually, human sounds diminished as the sun took on a more golden hue and started to sink behind the hills, casting long shadows. An hour before sunset there was a flurry of activity as birds flitted about getting ready to take shelter in trees for the night. The flock of white egrets that we had watched fly in formation, low above the river toward the sea in the early morning, flew back on its return trip in the golden sunlight. Smaller birds darted through the open spaces of the pasture, heading for trees.

Close to the equator there are no lingering sunsets. These occur farther north and south where the earth's tilt creates the illusion of the sun sinking at an angle and gradually dipping below the horizon. In the tropics, the sun fairly quickly plunges into the earth, splashing few colors into the sky as it sinks, even though there are subtle changes beforehand. Lévi-Strauss wrote a whole chapter in *Tristes Tropiques* on Amazonian sunsets. Night and day come quickly and with precision throughout the seasons, within a few minutes either side of six o'clock.

Sometimes, when Chris and Jeff were delayed, usually because of Land Rover problems, I was plunged into darkness with the landscape. It was creepy, and I would always worry that something had happened to them. The reassuring sound of the Land Rover would

bring a mixture of relief and annoyance that I had been kept out in this ancient graveyard way too long, hungry and tired. Their nighttime vigils in a tent at the site produced their own worries, and once a wandering cow caused them to leap from their sleeping bags, machetes at the ready to defend the national patrimony of Costa Rica. My guard duty through the afternoons and evenings and their nervous nights in their tent were carried out with a mixture of high anxiety and self-righteous pride that we were doing our duty to protect the precious antiquities just a meter or so below our feet. We were sure our work would make a major contribution to our knowledge of the prehistory of Costa Rica, bring prosperity to the Moras and Matas, and provide significant career advancement opportunities for ourselves.

The actual excavation procedures during the light of day were fairly straightforward, at first. We were working in a small area. We decided to leave the southern pavement and concentrate on the more northern one. We began, as usual, by laying out a grid system. This relied on a local datum, for convenience. We then stripped away as much of the surface grass as we could without disturbing the cobbles, exposing pavements covering an area of about 100 square meters (fig. 4.4).

We then had to begin the laborious task of mapping all of the cobble pavements, especially because our work would likely destroy some of them as we excavated the burials. This slowed work considerably, since everyone had to wait for the mapping team to do its work. The wait was well worth it, however, because in the initial clearing and mapping we revealed a bizarre set of cobble pavements like nothing we had seen before.

We had encountered a series of irregular cobble pavements. Some of these were found immediately upon clearing the surface, while others were a little deeper and not exposed until we excavated them. Like the Operation C cobbles, these pavements were made with stones placed flat-side up and bordered with cobbles set on their edges. But instead of isolated, rectangular pavements, these were densely packed pavements with the cobbles-on-edge apparently used to demarcate subsections within them. This was particularly true in the southern area of our work. In the northern area, there clearly were separate pavements, some of which appeared to be very large. One, Pavement 2, was shaped like the outline of a boat or a projectile point and was 4 meters long and over 2 meters wide. Pavements 1 and 3 were joined together and had many small subunits.

We soon realized that our numbering system of these pavements was mostly arbitrary because it was often difficult to know where one ended and another began. We numbered for our own record keeping, nonetheless, and gave the subunits letter designations. In one of these subunits in Pavement 1, there was a small (53 x 18 centimeters) pillar still in place and almost upright (figs. 4.4, 4.5). We assumed that the subsections represented individual graves. Since no archaeologist had excavated high-status Chiriquí burials before, we didn't know what to expect. These rather baroque variations on the rectangular pavements we had found in Operation C seemed to make sense as elaborate versions for high-status folk of a simpler pavement form for the graves of lower-ranking members of Rivas society.

In addition to these odd-shaped pavements, there were what appeared to be paths between them. While it was clear that many cobbles had shifted from their original places through time and the forces of nature, there was no doubt that paths three to four cobbles wide linked the different pavement areas. The clearest ones were between Pavements 2 and 8, between Pavements 1 and 5, and a Y-shaped one that connected Pavements 5 and 8, ran 5 meters south, and then appeared to stop (see fig. 4.4).

I'd never seen anything like this before, but then again, I hadn't worked long in Costa Rica. It turned out no one else had seen anything like this either. Francisco (Chico) Corrales of the National Museum visited the site. I said, "Well, Chico, are these burials?" He said, "Yes, they're burials, but they're the strangest ones I've ever seen."

The mapping continued, and I was anxious to start digging. I decided to put a trench in an area clear of cobbles between Burial 4 and a disturbed area, which may have been the remnants of a cobble path. We began digging and quickly noticed that there were very few sherds and none at all after 40 centimeters. This continued and we soon abandoned screening the soil altogether. We also dug in 20-centimeter arbitrary levels instead of our usual 10-centimeter levels. The soil was the standard dark material we found in many places

4.5. Pavement 1 in OpD '94. Note the cobbles-on-edge around the perimeter of the pavement. The arrow points to the fallen miniature pillar.

on the terrace, and there were no signs of the orange layers we had found in the big structures of Operation D. Eventually, this trench was dug to 60 centimeters in depth. Near the bottom we encountered a gray, powdery soil similar to our deepest excavations in the main area of Operation D, so we ceased digging in this location.

As the mapping was being finished, we began to open excavation areas. We started cautiously, with a 2 x 2 meter pit east of Burial 1. There were a few cobbles in this location, but it appeared to have been disturbed in the past. Once the stones were removed, we found their negative impressions extending into the soil below to an average depth of about 16 centimeters from where the upper faces of the stones had been. A few centimeters below this, the soil color changed dramatically to the familiar orange hue we had seen elsewhere. This seemed strange since the trench to the south had yielded no such soil. The orange soil continued for about 20 centimeters or so and was followed by large stones that appeared to be naturally in place. By 60 centimeters there were so many of these large stones that we stopped excavation because continuing deeper was too difficult.

We started working elsewhere, with pits both inside and outside of the pavements. In Burials 1 and 2, we encountered the orange PMF soil immediately below the pavement stones. Our most intensive work was in these areas, at first, and we soon encountered odd, circular soil stains as we had found in Operation C. Once again, we carefully excavated one in Burial 2 by profiling it so that we could see a vertical cross section as it went through the soil. It ended abruptly in a sharp point 7 centimeters below the level where it was discovered, at 51 centimeters below the ground surface. In Burial 3, the stains were found beginning at 51 centimeters in the northern subunit (3A) and the southern one (3C) but not in the middle one (3B).

As in Operation C, the fact that these stains are straight and pointed is further support for the interpretation that they are the remains of posts of some sort that either rotted or were removed. In either case, the cavity produced was later filled in with fine-grained soil that compacted through the years. Because they are numerous and apparently randomly placed, it seems unlikely that these soil stains are the remains of the posts of some kind of structure because we would expect a hut, for example, to have a more regular pattern that defined walls and a blank space in the middle. But these post molds were throughout the pit.

It is also curious that the stains began so deep in graves. One possibility is that poles were stuck in the ground at some stage in the preparation of graves and other sacred areas. Perhaps they had banners or flags on them or held the goods or trophies of the deceased. Of necessity, these poles would have been removed before the pit was filled up and a pavement of stones made above it. The preparation of sacred areas is not necessarily done in one construction phase, however, so perhaps the poles were allowed to remain for a while before they were removed and the pavement made. Whether they were in the grave at the same time as human remains is harder to determine but seems unlikely.

Something was troubling me. As we excavated into the burial areas, we didn't seem to be finding any side walls to the graves. When archaeologists find graves, they usually are able to locate the edges of the original grave pit, distinguished from the surrounding soil by the color or the consistency of the soil. When excavating a burial, care is usually taken to excavate soil so that the original contours of the grave are revealed. We hadn't been able to define the original grave pits in Operation C because of the nature of the soil, except for some faint traces of pits seen in profile in our large excavation unit. But here, with the cobbles-on-edge defining the grave edges, I thought we might be able to locate them. Perhaps the cobbles-on-edge were placed just inside the edge of the grave, where the soil was soft. That might explain it—we had left the perimeter ring of cobbles in place to more easily define the different units and subunits of the pavements. Perhaps when we removed the perimeter cobbles, we would find the grave walls, or maybe the soil was such that the side walls would not be easily recognized, as in Operation C.

The other thing that troubled me was that in some places it seemed quite clear that the orange layers extended beyond the perimeters of the graves, under the paths, for example. This might be explained, however, as spillover from filling in the graves, although one would expect spilled soil to be thinner farther from the grave, and this didn't seem to be the case. The orange layers seemed just as thick under paths as they were in the central sections underneath the pavements above the graves. Perhaps a huge pit had been dug for the entire area of the pavements, then the burials were placed in and eventually covered with the orange soil. This might explain why we weren't finding the edges and walls of graves. They must be far out on the edge of the work area. Still, it seemed odd.

We found few artifacts in our early stages of work. In the northeast corner of Burial 1, we found a concentration of carbon from on top of a rock at 55 centimeters depth. In the same pit at the same depth, we found a possible fire-cracked grinding stone. Elsewhere, in Burial 3A we uncovered a metate fragment, also at about 50 centimeters depth. In S4–3/E2, a little path between Burials 2 and 8, we came across a very large rim sherd below the cobbles and then sherds of thick pots below the orange layer, just at the beginning of dark brown soil underneath. Five sherds were unearthed at a depth of 30 centimeters on the eastern exterior of Burial 5. These were all the artifacts we found, and they were very few, indeed, compared to the quantities we found in most site areas. But the excavations of the graves were now getting deep enough that Loot Day was nigh.

We wanted to know as much about the burials before we actually began digging them. We had decided that we had to dig all the burials we had exposed because if we found gold in some and left others unexcavated they would be looted after we left the site. We expected that some graves would contain more gold than others, and if we could determine which ones they were we could devise a plan to give them special attention on Loot Day.

A few years earlier, in anticipation of one day excavating gold burials, I had negotiated with a company in the United States to sell one of their detection devices to the project. Metal detectors are commonly used by all sorts of people to find loose change on the beach or to look for metal artifacts. In the United States, owning them is not illegal, although, unfortunately, many archaeological sites have been plundered through the use of these detection devices. In our case, we had permission to excavate, so we thought that we were turning an instrument that has damaged a lot of archaeological sites to good purposes. The name of this particular device was the Gold Bug. This caused a great degree of mirth, especially for Aida Blanco, who translated the name literally to "Bicho de Oro." In Spanish, "*bicho*" connotes both "bug" and "pest." Jeff Frost, who was partial to technology, studied up on how to use the device, and we took it out to the site on a Sunday, when not many people were around. Jeff inserted batteries and turned on the device, and it seemed to go "nuts." It was beeping and wailing all over OpD '94. At first we got quite excited. But the trouble was, it seemed to be beeping and wailing everywhere else. Jeff was rambling around with this thing, which resembled a dinner plate attached to a bent rake handle with a box on it, and it kept whining and beeping and wailing whether he was down in one of the burial areas or far away from them. We thought that we were either about to hit the mother lode of all gold burials or that the Bicho de Oro was just an incompetent piece of tomfoolery. Then, again, maybe we hadn't quite figured out how to set the thing properly. We soon were to find out.

Excitement was in the air when all of the burials were down to depths of around 50 centimeters. It was Loot Day Eve, and on the morrow we might just make archaeological history á la King Tut: "What do you see Dr. Carter?" "I see wonderful things!"

We had to get ready. We made sure film was loaded in the cameras and that all the excavation equipment was in extra specially good shape. Then we realized we needed a ladder. Burials look best when photographed from above. It was too late to consider using the Floatograph, and we only needed a height of a few meters for good pictures, so a ladder was what we needed to use. After work, Jeff and I left Chris to guard the burial area. We cleaned up and then drove into town to the Museo Regional del Sur in San Isidro. After buying some extra-strong nylon cord and extra bags and boxes to transport complete pots and other precious things we would find, we got a large folding ladder from the museum. We tied it to the top of the Land Rover and started driving back to Rivas. About halfway back to Rivas, as the sun was rapidly sinking, the Land Rover started to act up. We managed to crawl back into town. We had to have the Rover working by the next day, and we found our mechanic who, after taking a quick look at the engine, said he could have it ready by late morning.

We still needed the ladder to take those valuable photos of the burials with all of their gleaming artifacts. No one had a telephone in the Mora and Mata families, so we couldn't call for help. We packed a backpack with the miscellaneous other items we had acquired and then hoisted the ladder on our shoulders, Jeff in front and me in back, and started walking along the road, up over the Panteón de la Reina toward our rented house on the other side.

That walk will stay with me for as long as I live. It was extremely difficult, as we were both tired and the ladder seemed to gain weight with every step, especially as we climbed the road over the Panteón. It was a surreal experience, two gringos carrying an aluminum ladder on a dirt road up a hill in the middle of Costa Rica. Cars passed by, but none of them held people we knew or were of the size that could give us a lift. The moon wasn't up yet, and the stars, as always, were magnificent, like salt thrown on black velvet. We finally got to our house, weary, stowed the ladder, and got to bed, ready for our big day of glory.

Loot Day was officially February 10, 1994. We hadn't been sure exactly when it would arrive, until the last few days before it, but here it was. The sun came up on time, as we expected, and we were already at the site. We hadn't found any sherds or anything else of significance below about 50 centimeters in most pits. The workers knew this was the day; maybe the ladder gave things away. Everyone was nervous and excited. We told all the diggers to "go for it." There were no secrets left to keep, and we were all ready to find whatever lay in store for us. Gold fever had struck, and we dug like demons, planning to slow down, of course, once the first lip of a pot or glint of the shiny stuff appeared.

It was all over by 10:00 A.M. Within a few centimeters of one another, all of the pits revealed huge boulders at about a meter below ground level. We never even dug "Burials" 4 and 5 to the bottom, as it was clear that none of these strange features were tombs after all (fig. 4.6). We couldn't believe it, really. At one point we thought that maybe huge boulders had been rolled into place above the grave contents and the workers

bravely hauled a boulder that must have weighed at least 135 kilograms out of the way. But there were just more big boulders underneath. So much for Loot Day.

In retrospect, all of the signs had been there. There had been no indication of side walls in the graves. The PMF had been spread under all of the cobble pavements, not just in the "graves." When we finally removed the perimeter cobbles, after we had "bottomed out" on the big boulders in the pits, it was clear that there were no edges of pits underneath them. There were no pits at all. But those pavements were just like the burials in Operation C, weren't they? And we had found those strange post molds, just like in Operation C, hadn't we? And what about those pillars, too? There *were* lots of signs that pointed to this being a cemetery. We had concentrated on those signs and ignored the other indications that suggested that these pavements did not cover graves. It was a good example of how the desire to want something to be a certain way can override the evidence to the contrary, even to so-called objective scientists.

Loot Day night found us bewildered and depressed.

4.6. An excavated "burial" in OpD '94. Note the ring of cobbles surrounding the area and the large boulders at bottom.

Instead of driving to San José with the most spectacular and scientifically important grave goods ever excavated in Costa Rica, we were in a bar wondering why those odd pavements were on top of a layer of orange soil, with black soil beneath, and then huge, naturally occurring rocks.

The day after Loot Day, I realized that what we had found was perhaps equally as interesting as any gold burial. I had gone over all of the telltale signs that we had first encountered: pillars, pavements, PMF beneath. I started to think about how to interpret what we *had* found. Since the pavement, the pillars, and the post molds are all associated with graves and cemeteries, the logical interpretation of our finds is that they were related to something involving funerals, even though this wasn't a place where people had been buried. The orange soil that clearly had been brought to the terrace to serve as a foundation for the pavements suggested that it was a special place, likely a place for some kind of ceremonies, like the Operation E oval. We could now be much more certain that the orange soil in Operations D and E was transported and laid down deliberately. We had been somewhat uncertain that the orange soil might have washed into Operation E. Here, on the terrace, the distribution of the orange soil was limited to only the area immediately under the pavements, so the same was true elsewhere at the site.

After the debacle of the morning's excavation we began to call OpD '94 the False Cemetery because it had what appeared to be the signals of a true cemetery, yet there were no graves underneath its pavements. But there is another way to look at this phenomenon. Perhaps both cemeteries and this False Cemetery had drawn upon a common set of architectural features because they were making reference to a more general set of concepts. I began to develop an interpretation of the pavements and pillars as a stage for rituals involving the dead or ancestors. The orange soil underneath them sanctified the area and the activities on the pavements above. We had thought, previously, that the terrace on which these pavements were located was in a perfect position for something special. It was elevated above the plane of Operation D. It was at the base of the Panteón de La Reina with access to a saddle in the ridge, one of its lowest areas. The pavements and pillars likely served for rituals performed in medi-ating between the world of the living, below, and the world of the dead, on the ridge-top, above. Perhaps this was a consecrated place where human remains were included in some kind of public ceremony, in view of a throng below, before they were taken to their final resting place in the cemeteries on the Panteón. Or perhaps the living could perform rituals of remembrance on this upper terrace to worship those buried above them.

It is hard to determine exactly what happened in OpD '94 in ancient times and the meaning of the organization of the pavements, but it seems likely that this was a place for mortuary rituals. We had found something never reported before, and for that all of the trouble to which we had gone had been worthwhile.

Considering further, it is interesting that the pavements were in two sets; we had worked only in one of them. The two pavements indicate some kind of dualism in the social system of the people who used these pavements, although perhaps the space between the two areas may hold pavements buried deeper beneath the grass. The exact arrangement of the pavements is harder to interpret. What we had called "paths" as a simple term of reference likely were indeed paths between the separate cobble areas. The pavements themselves had been disturbed through time, but it was clear that they had been subdivided into smaller units within larger ones. Even allowing for some disturbance, the pavements did not appear to be highly ordered or organized. They weren't disorderly, but they were not highly regimented either. Using this as an interpretive guide suggests that the rituals carried out on these pavements also were rather esoteric and complicated and may somehow be related, ultimately, to the social organization of the people who used these places.

The smallest areas defined by the cobbles placed on their edges—what we had been calling subunits—are too small to lay a corpse on, even considering the likely smaller size of the ancient Chiriquí people. The rituals that occurred in this area, then, likely involved people standing or kneeling on these pavements, or otherwise why demarcate them as they had done? Alternatively, the remains of the dead could have been kept within the boundaries of these small areas if they were secondary burials, such as bundles of bones. Secondary burial is a practice that we know occurred at various times and places in ancient Costa Rica.

The few sherds and stone tool fragments we found below the pavements may indicate an earlier occupation of the area before the ceremonial platform was built, or they may represent activities carried out immediately before construction. The large-mouthed vessels and the grinding stone fragments suggest that a feasting ritual may have occurred. This is a common way construction efforts are carried out in South America today. The area was prepared in a manner very similar to burial grounds, with orange soils laid down, posts of some sort placed in the ground, and then the pavements placed on top. This close parallelism to actual graves, as well as the location in relation to the Panteón de La Reina, is what is most suggestive that this was an area of ritual practices related to burial of the dead.

Our hopes of finding gold burials had been raised high and then dashed, but it was nobody's fault but our own. Anyhow, "half the fun is getting there," and we had had a great time doing our work. We had found something unusual that added to our understanding of mortuary ritual at the Rivas site and the Panteón de La Reina, even if we couldn't say precisely what took place there. And at least we didn't have the headaches that come with finding gold, such as getting people upset and greedy. We could continue our work to understand the site better, and that is exactly what we did.

The Shovel Test Pit Survey

It was time to try and put the site together. How did the areas we had identified and called operations fit together? The only way to address this problem was to conduct a shovel test pit survey. Shovel test pit surveys have become the stock in trade of archaeologists attempting to find sites or determine their extent when remains are not visible on the surface of the ground. It is common for archaeological sites to have the ground surface that was present at the time of occupation covered up by later soil development. At Rivas, with erosion from the Panteón, we expected thick deposits over those ancient living surfaces, and so the shovel test pit would be especially useful to detect buried occupation layers.

In some places, such as the coast of Peru or California, sites may be fairly easily visible by the presence of whitened shells where they don't occur naturally.

Sites can thus easily be identified by visual inspection in a pedestrian survey—walking over the area. Elsewhere, such as in the midwestern United States, plowing farmland turns over the earth, disturbing sites but bringing artifacts to the surface where, again, they can be easily seen. Even in these cases, however, parts of sites may be buried. In many other places, such as in tropical lands with dense vegetation, artifacts and other indications of sites are hidden by accretions of soil, burying them underground. The only way to find sites in such cases is to dig. Lenorha Pohlman, one of our ACM students, had done a shovel test pit survey of Operation A in 1992. Now we would do one for the entire site.

Shovel test pit surveys consist of lining up a number of workers with shovels and, usually, small sifting screens and having them walk through a field, stopping at regular intervals to dig small holes, sift the dirt, and see if artifacts are present. There is a great body of archaeological literature on the best way to do this—on the advantages of uniform lines of holes, staggered lines of holes, and so forth. In our case, we chose the simplest system, with uniform lines of holes spaced 5 meters apart, with each line traversed by a workman also 5 meters apart from the one on his left and another on his right (unless he was at the end of a line, of course). How deep to dig is always a problem. We told our workers to excavate slightly deeper than the length of a shovel blade, 30 centimeters, since most artifacts were found between this depth and the surface at the Rivas site. Pits were to be circular, with a diameter equal to the width of the top side of the shovel blade. Using this system made it easy for our workers to always have the proper measurements for their pits available, since they were based on the dimensions of the shovel blade.

Our workers had never done this kind of work before, although by now they had developed good eyes and hands to recognize and recover artifacts. Keeping a uniform pattern of lines and holes would be easiest to maintain, and rocks and other features interfering with a true pattern would add some variation in any case.

Since we wanted to survey the entire area from Operation D to Operation C, a distance of more than a kilometer, we needed some control over the different areas to be covered. For this, we used the boundaries that were already present: various plots of land defined by fence lines. Each of these bounded units was called a Shovel Test Pit Operation, or a STOp for short. The STOps would be ordered in numerical sequence to distinguish the shovel test pit survey from the excavation operations, which followed an alphabetic sequence.

We began the shovel test pit survey in field 1, just south of Operation A and on the same terrace. As can be seen by the map (fig. 4.7), artifacts were found in the northeastern side of this field but not in the western or southern parts. It was here, of course, where we had first encountered the remains of architecture. It is hard to expect to find a one- or two-row-wide line of circular cobbles; Lenorha Pohlman had only found one in Operation A, though we assumed the area was filled with structures.

In this, our first STOp, we came across an area of compacted cobbles. Following the procedure we had established, we quickly placed two 1 x 5 meter trenches in the area, with their ends catercorner. This exposed more of a cobble feature, and we then were able to set up a grid system to excavate it fully. Our work revealed (fig. 4.8) an irregular cobble pavement very similar to the ones we found east of the structures of Operation A. Artifacts were present but not abundant. We searched for signs of a circular structure to the west of this area but with no luck. The presence of the pavement does suggest, however, that structures similar to those of Operation A are likely in the neighborhood.

I was able to supervise this work, but I had to leave for home soon afterward. Jeff and Chris supervised the remaining surveys. They worked first around the perimeter of the areas where we had done large-scale excavations, then expanded northward and, later, south of Operation D. The terrace of Operation A was followed to Operation D, after which dense coffee plants and a narrowing of the terrace inhibited work. At that point, the fields on the Operation D terrace, south of it, were tested.

This work revealed relatively high densities of artifacts, mostly sherds, from about 80 meters south of Operation B continuing on the lower terrace, south of Operation D, to the Rivas–San Gerardo road, at which point the work halted. This is a distance of 900 meters. If the patches of dense sherds are counted in STOps 13 and 14 (see fig. 4.7), the site as defined by these concentrations stretches over a kilometer. In addition to

the sherd concentrations, we were able to reconfirm the presence of a cemetery originally identified by Bob Drolet (Operation K; see chapter 5). Although not tested, the survey brought the workers to another likely cemetery, marked by a petroglyph on the other side of the Rivas–San Gerardo road.

Very few sherds were found north of the Operation B petroglyph. There was another concentration, however, in the vicinity of a petroglyph in STOp 23, about 500 meters north of the one in Operation B. Another high concentration patch of artifacts was found in STOps 30 and 31. These were intriguing because we were particularly interested in trying to identify habitation areas in the vicinity of the Operation C cemetery. We couldn't work in many lots in the area because they were occupied by the houses of the Mora family.

The shovel test pit survey was of great use, even if some areas remained in question regarding previous habitation or use. We encountered sherds almost everywhere in the 1.5 kilometers surveyed, and even a few sherds suggest fairly heavy traffic since one broken pot probably indicates that many other activities occurred in the area at times when no pots were broken or other objects lost or discarded. It thus seems reasonable to propose that areas of very high sherd concentration represent or are very close to areas of considerable activity, most likely occupation areas or similar kinds of activity areas. On the other hand, STOps 15–22 were extremely light in artifacts, suggesting a real separation between the dense concentrations to the south and the patches of concentrations farther north.

One point will be raised here, and it can only be mentioned at all due to another serendipitous event. The money we had been paying our workers for several weeks each year had apparently flowed into the local economy. A considerable amount of this had been literally pumped in liquid form through great consumption of beer and *guaro*, the local clear hard liquor; Mondays were often light days for work, as many of our crew nursed hangovers. Some had saved their money, however, and rather than be consumers they became providers of liquid refreshments.

One manifestation of this entrepreneurial spirit was the establishment of a small cantina known as La Troja de Mi Abuelo (roughly, the storehouse of my grandfather), or La Troja for short. This was a small struc-

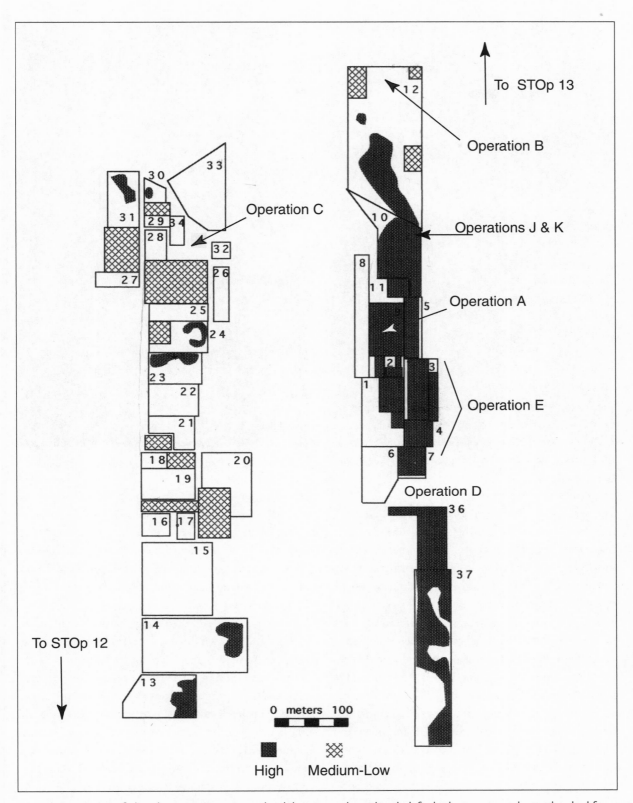

To STOp 13

Operation B

Operations J & K

Operation C

Operation A

Operation E

Operation D

To STOp 12

0   meters   100

High   Medium-Low

4.7. Schematic map of Shovel Test Pit Operations. Sherd densities indicated as dark for high amounts and cross-hatched for medium-to-low amounts.

4.8. Cobble pavement found in Shovel Test Pit Operation 1. View to the west.

4.9. Bands of dark soil below lighter ones in the pit behind La Troja de Mi Abuelo.

ture made of wood, cane, and straw on the Mora Road, near the southern end of the cluster of Mora family houses and conveniently across the thoroughfare from one of the co-owners. Inside La Troja, one could sit at a small table or at the counter and quaff a cold beer, surrounded by a combination of old ox yokes, gourd water containers, and other antiques of farm life vying for attention with beer company posters depicting scantily clad buxom young women.

A year later, in 1995, Jeff and Chris were relaxing in La Troja one afternoon after work. The owner, serving as bartender, mentioned that he had recently had a trash pit excavated in the field immediately in back of the bar. In the Costa Rican countryside, this is a common way of disposing of trash—dig a pit and throw the trash in, sometimes burning it to reduce the volume. The restroom also was out back, and heading toward it, Jeff glanced at the newly dug pit. There he saw a dark band of soil, several centimeters below the orange topsoil. Below the upper dark layer, another band

of PMF was followed by another black band running the entire length of the pit, as was the case with the upper one. After a "leapin' lizards" moment, Jeff rushed back into the bar and asked if the archaeologists could study this phenomenon before the trash pit was put into service (fig. 4.9).

Permission was granted, and eventually four other pits, 2 x 3 meters wide, were placed behind La Troja, at intervals 50 meters apart. The pits were placed to determine how far the soil levels extended along the terrace and if the soil horizons decreased in thickness moving farther away from the Panteón. Two layers of black soil were found: one varied between 75 and 95 centimeters below ground surface, and the other was 130 to 145 centimeters deep. The black levels remained relatively uniform, but the orange soil thinned in the pits farther east, away from the Panteón. This suggests that the orange soil was laid down by a natural event such as heavy erosion or a landslide.

Three of the pits yielded cultural materials, though

none were diagnostic, revealing their type of manufacture or decoration. The orange soils contained small flecks of carbon perhaps from natural fires but possibly from deliberate slash and burn farming techniques. Since the orange soil is derived from the Panteón de La Reina, the burning likely occurred there or in a space on the terrace between the base of the ridge and the place of deposition. The fact that there is little mixing of the orange soil with the black soils beneath suggests that the orange material was laid down quickly. The lower parts of the black soils, however, blend into the orange soil, suggesting that they were laid down over time and that activities—probably human—mixed the accumulating dark soil with the orange soil beneath it.

The discovery of these deeper layers of earth and the occupations that they represent, made in 1995, occurred three years after our first work in 1992, two years after our biggest field season in 1993, and a year after our shovel test pit survey in 1994. I have jumped ahead of myself in telling the story of La Troja pit because this is the appropriate place at which to mention this discovery. We had put a lot of time, money, and energy into our work at Rivas. We thought of ourselves as quite clever at having noted the two major phases of occupation in the large-scale architecture. We also thought that we had been very thorough in our shovel test pit survey. But the fact is that without the deep pit in back of La Troja, dug by the owner of the bar, we would have finished the project without ever having known of the earlier occupations. Granted, we had some indications of earlier use of the site area because a few early sherds were found in the STOps. But without a fairly wide and, especially, deep pit, we wouldn't have found the lower dark layers. Our shovel test pits were too shallow to have detected them.

The black earth is indicative of burning and the deposit of organic materials. At least two periods of the intrusion of nutrient-poor orange soils occurred, each burying one of these layers. How old these deposits are is hard to tell. One or both of them may even represent the same occupation period as the operations in which we worked. Perhaps this area was just lower and more susceptible to inundation by PMF than other areas of the site. The cause for the inundation is likely deforestation, and it seems reasonable to suggest that the cutting of trees to prepare the Panteón de La Reina as a cemetery may be the specific agent for one or more orange layers.

There is a fascinating project to be done exploring the history of relations of humans to the landscape in the Rivas area. We were not able to follow the lead we had discovered very far, but our research does suggest that the Rivas area may have looked very different during Chiriquí times than it appears today. There may have been many fewer trees and many more open spaces. The "natural" landscape we see today is not natural at all but rather the product of many years of alterations, probably both intentional and unintentional, by the people who lived in Costa Rica for thousands of years before the Spanish arrived (see Hoopes 1996a).

Summary of the 1994 Work

Although we had been disappointed in not finding high-status burials in OpD '94, the field season was a success in greatly expanding our understanding of the Rivas site. The failure of Loot Day was compensated for by clear indications that the pavements on the upper terrace were a ritual platform for mortuary rites. This, in turn, linked the activities in the large-scale architecture with the burials on the Panteón de La Reina. Although we didn't realize it at the time, or for years afterward, this was the first major step toward our present understanding and interpretation of what the Rivas site was all about. It was the great turning point in my thinking about the site because it made me reconsider what the large architecture below the pavements was all about. The experience of OpD '94 also reconfirmed my conviction that finding gold was less important than understanding the roles Rivas and the Panteón de La Reina played in the lives of the people who built and used these sites.

The first work we did in the 1994 field season at the edge of the guava grove and Operation E where we found the stairs going up the face of the terrace perhaps was not a major contribution to the project overall. But the work did help satisfy a nagging question about the role of the line of stones in the architecture of the site. Working at a site for long periods over many years, archaeologists often develop little questions for which they hope to find answers, even if for nothing more than satisfying their curiosity. The line of stones first found in 1992 was one such problem. I derived as much satisfaction in finally figuring out what that mysterious line of cobbles was all about as I did in solving some of the issues about much grander questions at Rivas. The fact that the line of stones was a path and that it connected to a stairs going up to the next terrace, where Operation A was located, was important though. The connection demonstrated beyond a doubt that people who used the big buildings moved back and forth from there to the upper terrace where smaller structures were located and vice versa.

The 1994 work thus helped to stitch together different parts of the site into an integrated suite of architectural forms and inferred activities between them. We realized that the fine details of what was occurring in these different areas of the site and when they occurred in the past might only be revealed through laboratory work, but these field studies had provided information that laboratory research could not address. Nevertheless, we needed to start to review more carefully what the numerous bags of sherds and other artifacts we had collected in three field seasons might tell us.

In addition to the people we hired every season to wash and process artifacts as we were excavating them, we had hired two local university students, Edwin Montenegro and Olman Vargas. They worked throughout the year, even while we were away, to draw and catalog artifacts, especially sherds. By 1994 we had several hundred thousand sherds to go through, and, given the quantity, Edwin and Olman were still working on materials from 1992, two years earlier.

We reviewed their progress to date, and it was clear that the general pattern we expected was revealed in their drawings and measurements: the ceramics consisted of bowls and jars of Buenos Aires Polychrome, Turucaca White-on-Red, Sangria Fine Red, Papayal Engraved, and Ceiba Red-Brown. We would have to wait a little longer to start to tease out fine-grained differences in the quantities of different types of ceramics and vessel forms in different areas of the site and in different stratigraphic levels.

The obvious differences were apparent, notably, the lack of metates in the large-scale architecture. In addition, we had no explanation as to why Operation C appeared to be isolated from the rest of the site and lacked a nearby residence area. Other than these issues, however, we were happy to have a better understanding of the site, to be fairly confident that we were beginning to put the pieces of the Rivas puzzle together.

During the 1993–1994 North American academic year, Aida Blanco and I began writing an article based on our work at the Rivas site through 1993. In this article, published in the *Journal of Field Archaeology* in 1995 (Quilter and Blanco 1995), we announced the presence of the large-scale architecture at Rivas, the presence of two phases of construction, and the distinct architectural zones at the site. We interpreted the spatial segregation and architectural differences of Operations A and D/E as perhaps reflecting status differences, with lower-ranking members of the Rivas community living in the small-scale architecture of Operation E and higher-status people living in Operations D/E.

The two programs of field research we undertook in 1994 both yielded negative evidence. We did not find burials underneath the pavements on the terrace overlooking Operation D, and we did not find signs of habitation around Operation C or in the northern area of the site in general. Not finding things might be considered as a failure, and, in fact, immediately after our work we still had some lingering frustrations at not having our expectations met for the field season. But this work was a turning point for the project. It made us reconsider all of the assumptions we had built up about the site since we had begun. Although we did not immediately develop a new interpretation of Rivas, we did have to start the process of reevaluating the significance of our findings, both in terms of the positive evidence of the architecture and artifacts and the negative evidence of their absence. In this state of uncertainty and the beginning of reformulating our ideas, we decided to return to Operation D in the next field season in the hope of finding more satisfactory interpretations of Rivas.

CHAPTER FIVE

REFINING OUR KNOWLEDGE OF RIVAS, 1995–1997

Assessing the Situation

After three field seasons at Rivas we had learned many things. The Rivas site was quite different from other Chiriquí communities, as far as we could tell, since few had been studied. It had circular houses, similar to Murciélago, but it also had a complex of large-scale architecture. Two major construction phases had occurred. Although the nature of the first phase was unclear because it was deep and hard to expose, the second construction phase resulted in large buildings and spaces apparently for the gathering of many people. Some of the activities of those gatherings appear to have involved mortuary practices for the burial of people on the Panteón de La Reina. At the same time, however, there were cemeteries associated with Rivas itself, so some people were not buried on the ridge-top.

Our shovel test pit survey work indicated that the site area had been occupied earlier than the Chiriquí phase, but previous occupations had been small. The survey had not entirely clarified the relationship of the different occupations, even of the relationship of different site sectors apparently occupied contemporane-

ously, but it did indicate that the later occupations were even more extensive and intensive than could be observed without the survey.

We had gradually answered the most important questions about the site that could be investigated through fieldwork. We knew when Rivas was occupied and the nature of the spatial patterning of architecture and artifacts. We now had to start to focus on how to finish the project. There were several pressure points that encouraged us to consider this. First, there was the issue of our funding. We had spent our money very carefully, so that we still had considerable financial resources available to us. We asked for and received an extension of the deadline for the completion of the grant from the National Endowment for the Humanities. That, at least, gave us more time in which to finish the work.

Among the problems we faced were the changes in the personal lives and fortunes of the core members of our research team. This happens in any research project but was a particularly significant challenge for Rivas. Research projects carried out through universities with the aid of graduate students working on their doctorates can rely upon those students to continue to return to the site because they have a vested interest in finishing the work. Ripon College is not a research university, however, and I had no graduate students. Even with grad students, projects face the problem of key personnel dropping out of doctoral programs, getting married or getting jobs, and the other vagaries of life that result in the loss of continuity in personnel and research. I was lucky. Bill Doonan had received his Ph.D. from Tulane but was still committed to devoting as much time as he could to Rivas. The other key member, Jeff Frost, had graduated from Ripon College in 1990. He had spent extensive amounts of time through the years at Rivas, but he was planning to go to grad school and once in, his time would be taken up with classes and other commitments. For the moment, however, he was free to continue to work on the project.

I was also subject to these changes. In the autumn of 1994 I applied for the position of director of Pre-Columbian Studies at Dumbarton Oaks, a combined library, museum, and research institute in Washington, D.C. I had been lucky enough to be offered the position, and I took it. My new job offered me all sorts of opportunities, but it was not an academic position that gave me my summers off. I would be working on a twelve-month contract, although I did receive three weeks of research leave per year. Still, this meant that I would not be able to spend as much time at the site as before. Furthermore, the summer of 1995 would be devoted to moving my family and setting up a new household, so I could only spend a couple of weeks at Rivas before returning to Wisconsin to pack up and move.

The personal situations of Bill, Jeff, and myself meant that the 1995 field season might be the last opportunity that any of us had substantial amounts of time to spend in the field. We would have to concentrate on work that would provide key answers to understanding the Rivas site.

Picking Priorities

If this was to be our last opportunity to answer key questions about Rivas, we would have to concentrate on the large-scale architecture. There were two areas of the complex for which we had little information. The first was the coffee field separating Operations D and E. The second was Complex IV, the "plaza," the area south of Operation D, in pasture, which had a sunken area between a high *ballena* on its eastern side and a terrace remnant to the west. We also needed better mapping of Operation D. Since 1992, we had been busy working in Operation E, digging the False Cemetery of OpD '94 and conducting the shovel test pit survey. That survey had been linked to our master grid system, set up in Operation E in 1993. But we hadn't had the time to return to the main area of Operation D to produce the high-quality map we had done in Operation E; we were still working with the crude map we had made in our original work in 1992.

I was very preoccupied with packing up my office and family in Wisconsin for the move to Washington. Both Bill Doonan and Jeff Frost had worked long and hard enough at the site in the previous years that I designated them as co–field directors. Because everyone had prior commitments, our field season was to run from the beginning of May to the end of June. Jeff was to go to Costa Rica first, to set up the coordinates to remap Operation D. That map would serve as the master document for our planned excavations. He would be followed by Bill and then me. I brought two recent graduates from Ripon, Matt Reynolds and Jim Schumacher, to help with the mapping since Jeff would have less time to map as his supervisory role had increased. Chris Raymond, who had been with us for every field season in the past, was eager to participate, too, and his skills and energy were most welcomed. Paul Dolata, a man about my age who had returned to Ripon College for classes, and Gabriela Castro, a Costa Rican student who had been at Ripon, also joined the project and were essential in getting the work done. We had a relatively great number of gringos in this field season. This was partly because we had fewer local farmhands available due to their own needs to be in their fields in a critical time in the coffee-growing season.

Jeff began the 1995 Rivas field season on May 4, and I arrived on May 22. With his typical thoroughness, Jeff had extended the 0/0 north-south running line from Operation E all the way from Operation E through the intervening coffee field to Operation D and beyond. Although the coffee field was only 70 meters in width, Jeff had extended a master line, with bright pink fluorescent painted stakes at 5-meter intervals, each one labeled with its coordinates, for a total distance of 300 meters. It was not only a masterpiece of precision but presented itself as a work of landscape art, as the pink stakes appeared to march through the coffee fields and pastures with surreal precision.

The main target of our desires to finish the work was the coffee field separating Operations D and E. From our observations in walking through this field, it was clear that there were some very impressive large structures there. We wanted to be able to clear coffee plants in crucial areas in order to map and to make some selective excavations. Coffee fields are valuable, however, bringing cash to local farmers. Many of the local men in our crew observed that the coffee plants in this field were getting old, not producing as much anymore, and that we should be able to strike an arrangement with the owner to remove plants at a reasonable price.

One of Jeff's first tasks was to count coffee plants. He and his assistants counted the number of plants in five 5 x 5 meter areas in the field, calculating an average of 16.4 plants per 5 x 5 meter unit. We hoped we could excavate at least two or three such units. When approached, however, the owner asked a very high price for the removal of each coffee plant, far beyond what we were able to pay. We encountered this same problem in the coffee field that covered most of the area of Complex III. This was the famous "square" structure on the southwestern side of Operation D.

We were disappointed. Fieldwork in the coffee field was crucial to help determine the relationships between the circular structures in Operation D and the more varying shaped structures in Operation E. Still, there was not much we could do if the owners wouldn't allow us to work in their fields. The owners did compromise so that we could continue to map in their fields, however, and we were able to at least record the general outlines of structures. Jeff, Chris, and a couple of the local fellows mapped the architecture in the coffee field later in the season. It was tough work. The old coffee field still was pretty thick in places, while in other areas it was overgrown with weeds. They spent two months crawling on their hands and knees with tape measures, drawing boards, pencils, and such, mapping each structure and connecting it to our large grid system.

With the coffee field between Operations D and E not accessible for excavation, we had to find other opportunities for work. We decided to excavate in Complex II of Operation D. This circle of cobbles was the first structure we saw when we discovered the large-scale architecture in 1992 (fig. 2.17). It was on what appeared to be a river terrace remnant and thus higher than Complex I, already excavated, and at a lower elevation than the False Cemetery of OpD '94. Most of the large stones and cobbles appeared to be visible on the surface of the ground in the short grass of this area. We wanted to be able to map the structure and conduct excavations to see if there was evidence of two building phases, as we had found elsewhere. The owner did not want us destroying his grass, important for his dairy cows. We therefore agreed to open only a minimal number of excavation units to help answer our questions and to reseed the excavated areas so that grass would be available to his cattle for the rest of the rainy season.

The other area in which we would concentrate would be the plaza, or Complex IV. Again, the owner prized his pasture, so we made the same arrangement to reseed excavated areas. We also hoped to excavate another cemetery on the Rivas terraces for comparison with Operation C.

Excavations in Complex II

With limits as to the number of pits we could excavate in Complex II, we had to choose our excavation locations carefully (fig. 5.1). We put a trenchlike 1 x 3 meter pit across the western side of the inner ring of the structure. The trench revealed the usual pattern of more artifacts outside of the ring than inside of it. The section of the trench inside the structure was dug to a depth of 30 centimeters. There was no evidence of any kind of artificial fill. We decide to stop work in this trench and open up a larger unit adjacent to it, on the inside of the ring. This 2 x 2 meter pit would give us more room to see if there was an earlier construction phase. We had not dug very deeply and were only in the second excavation level (10–20 centimeters) when we encountered the dense gravel known as *rípio*, similar to Complex I, and so we halted excavation.

The work suggested that, as in the case of Complex I, Complex II had been built on top of the gravel deposits of an ancient river terrace. At least in the area in

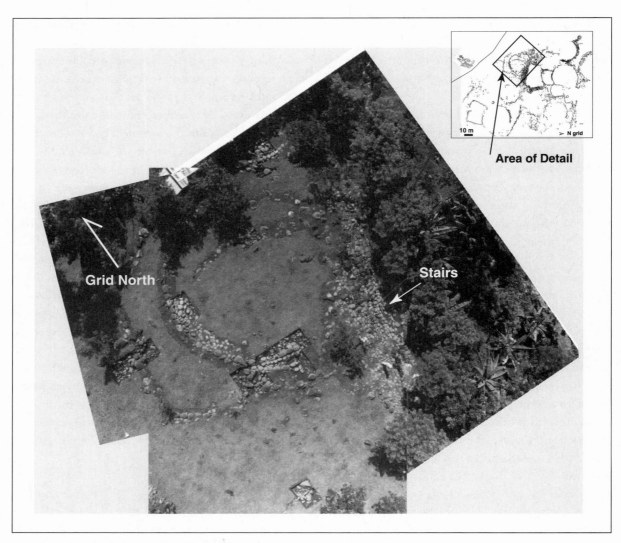

5.1. Composite aerial photograph of Complex II, Operation D.

which we worked, there was no possibility of an earlier construction phase. We set up another trench running across the outer, western ring of the complex to see if perhaps there were signs of an earlier construction phase there. Sherd densities were higher than outside the inner ring, to the east. In the third level (20–30 centimeters), we encountered *rípio* again. We stopped work in this pit at 40 centimeters in the inside of the wall.

We then turned our attention to the southern side of the complex. We opened up a large 5 x 5 meter pit, subdivided internally into separate excavation units. This area did not reveal a continuation of the stone rings visible on the surface. The excavations did not attain great depths because within 20 centimeters from the surface we encountered boulders that completed the upper circles.

All of the evidence we found indicated that Complex II had been built on top of *rípio*, and if there was an earlier structure we didn't encounter it. It is likely that there was no earlier structure, however, as the terrace with its *rípio* would have been as difficult to excavate in the past as it was in the present. Work in Complex II was thus complete.

We next turned our attention to an area to the east of Complex II and which might even be considered part of it. We had noticed this area before. There appeared to be some kind of wall running roughly grid northwest to southeast. This appeared to be a retaining wall built on the eastern edge of the terrace on which Complex II was located. A barbed wire fence running parallel to the ancient construction was only a few meters eastward. The other side of this fence was the old cane field where we had uncovered large-scale architecture in 1992. It was now planted with a few banana and maize plants. The eastern end of the causeway excavated in that earlier field season ran onto the terrace a few meters from the southern end of the apparent wall to which we were now about to turn our attention.

We began to place large excavation units spread from the bottom of the wall, across it, to the terrace above. Eventually, these were joined into one large 5 x 5 meter unit (S105–101/W45–41). At the northeast corner of this large unit, we also placed a 3 x 1 meter trench (S100–98/W40), mostly to work on clearing the face of the wall and to excavate at its base.

It is remarkable how the contemporary landscape can influence an archaeologist. Since the beginning of the project we had worked with the full knowledge that when the site was occupied there had been no barbed wire fences or coffee groves. Much of the land probably was cleared for human habitation with only a few trees for shade or fruit and probably plots of maize, beans, and squash in areas away from the ceremonial center. Likewise, the Panteón de La Reina must have been mostly clear of trees in order to serve as a cemetery, as the discovery of the layers behind La Troja de Mi Abuelo, later in 1995, were to show. Any project member, when asked, could have easily discussed the general differences between the ancient landscape of the Rivas site and the present-day one. Nonetheless, modern fences act as subconscious barriers. We are trained from infancy to think of them as separating distinctly different spaces.

Thus it was that for three years we had considered the "causeway" we had cleared and mapped in 1992 as a distinct feature connecting Complex II with the terrace of Complex II. A barbed wire fence ran parallel to the terrace just a few meters away from what we thought was the end of the causeway, perhaps emphasizing the linearity of the architectural feature. It was only as we began to study the maps we were making in detail and began to excavate on what we thought was a retaining wall that it became clear to us that our understandings had been biased. The raised, cobbled pathway that we had called a causeway was actually the

southern arm of a large patio extension of Complex II. This was a patio-on-a-patio, and its northern side was rather weakly defined by a single row of boulders, some of which were disturbed at the time of our work. Even in antiquity, however, the southern and western ends were more elaborately and better made than the northern and eastern sides (fig. 5.2).

The western end of this formation was the area in which we were now working. It did not take very long for us to realize that we were not, in fact, excavating a wall but probably a stairway. The steps consisted of two risers with a pavement at the bottom made up of three lines of cobbles. In some places, large boulders were left in place during construction, incorporated into the design of the stairs. Neither photographs (fig. 5.3) nor drawings show the stairs very well because the cobbles of the stairway have been disturbed through time, but in the field the steps were clearly visible. In general, the ceramics found on the stairs and at their base were plentiful and of fine quality. There were a couple of complete vessels and the foot of a ceramic figurine on the stairs.

Summary of Work in Complex II

Our research in Complex II revealed no evidence of more than one construction phase. Resting on hard, compact gravel, it is unlikely that the main circular structure would have undergone more than one building effort. We had no way to know, however, without artifact analysis or radiocarbon dates, if Complex II was earlier or later than either of the two building phases in Complex I to the east. Complex II was much more carefully made than Complex I. The higher circle had cobbles of more uniform size, and they were laid to form the circle and patios very carefully. Complex I is much larger than Complex II, however. The large quadrangular patio of Complex I, with its stairway on its wide, western side, likely played a pivotal role in activities taking place in Operation D in ancient times. As noted above, the patio is so large that it becomes the dominant structural feature in the area, set apart from the round structures nearby. The form of this grand patio appears to have been based on the simple, smaller house patio such as that of Structure 1 in Operation A. We determined that the "causeway" was not made primarily for foot traffic. Nevertheless, the wide south-

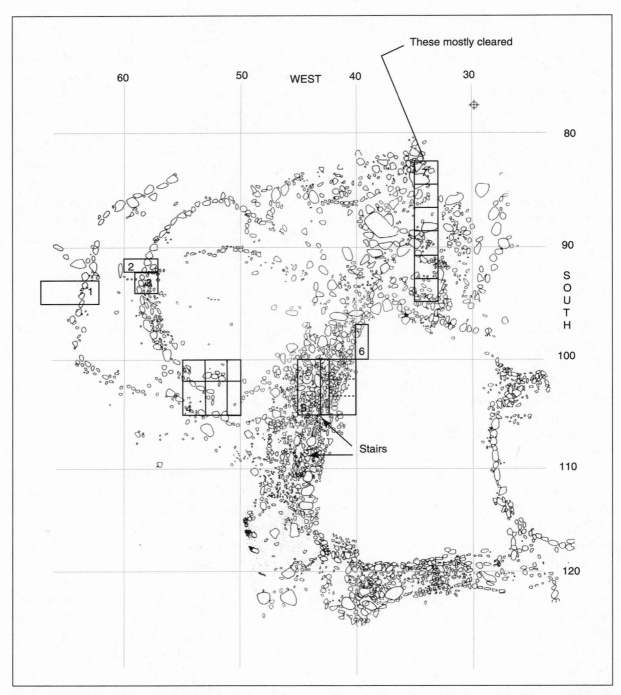

5.2. Excavations in Operation D. Coordinate system of 1993 and later. Note that Grid N is to the right. Map by R. J. Frost and J. Quilter.

ern arm of the structure could have served as a walkway connecting the southern edge of the semicircle attached to Complex I to the higher terrace on which Complex II is located. At about 3 meters in average width, it could have been used for processions. The stairs at the western end would have served as another route up to the Complex II terrace or down from it. The area of this quadrangular space is quite large. At about 117 square meters, the space within it is as big as many circles in Operation D. It seems quite likely that this space was used for public gatherings.

A combination of mapping and excavation just south

5.3. The stairs east of Complex II. View toward Grid W.

of Complex II revealed the presence of a large circle almost tangent to the southwest corner of the quadrangular structure. It was different than most of the other structures at the site because it was made of a single line of cobbles. This circle is intermediate between Complex II and the huge stone circle of Complex III (see fig. 3.1). A pit was placed on its northern edge to confirm the cobble perimeter stones there. This pit can be seen near the bottom of figure 5.1.

The large boulders forming the northern corner of the patio of Complex III were first thought to be a quadrangular structure, and it was only through crawling through dense coffee plants that we discovered a very large circle attached to it, to the east. This Complex III unit is one of the most impressive structures at the site. It is made of very large, uniformly sized boulders, and its plan was carefully laid out. It stands apart from the interconnected architecture to its north and east. Of all the architecture in Operation D, Complex III is the closest to the False Cemetery of the OpD '94 terrace abutting the base of the Panteón de La Reina ridge. It is likely that Complex III was one of the most significant structures at the site, considering its size, the quality of its construction, and its proximity to the False Cemetery. Unfortunately, we could not conduct extensive excavations in it because most of the structure was in a healthy coffee field that was thick with plants. We had placed a few pits at the northern juncture of its patio and circle in 1992. At that time, we had not realized the significance of the structure, other than that it may have been quadrangular in form.

The artifacts we did recover during that excavation were similar to others we encountered in Operation D in general.

Complexes II and III are separated from the more integrated architecture of Complex I and Complex IV by a large stone wall to the east (see fig. 3.1). This wall once ran in a continuous line northward, to connect with the complex of stones forming the upper part of the stairway just discussed. The line was broken when an east-west running dirt farm road was made and the local farmers moved the large boulders out of the way of their carts and other vehicles. Once again, modern land use had obscured the presence and possible significance of this feature for us until we had made a detailed map of Operation D and carefully studied it.

All of the major architectural features defined in Operation D—Complexes I, II, and III—have westward-facing patios. These features were in privileged positions in comparison to the other structures at the site. They conform to the general format of domestic architecture but are much larger. The circle between them does not conform to domestic architecture at all, being a simple but elegant circle. Although coffee fields filled most of the space to the south of Complex III, we did walk in them and observed no other architecture on the west side of the wall. In other words, Complexes II and III and the intervening circle appear to be the only structures between the wall and the False Cemetery ridge.

Walls, even if they are not very high, are built to demarcate spatial relations: to make people conscious of being on one side or the other or to actually separate people. The north-south running wall that placed Complexes I, II, and the large circle of single cobbles on one side, and the rest of the Operation D architecture on the other, thus might indicate something important about what occurred at the site. Given the fact that the False Cemetery is divided into two components and that dualism is a common feature of Native American social organization, perhaps the two circular structures closest to it and the Panteón are part of a system of dual division that was expressed in mortuary rites.

Excavations in Complex IV, the Plaza

We turned our attention to work in Complex IV, an area that we commonly called the "plaza." In 1992, when we first encountered the large-scale architecture, this was one of its most notable features. We only named four complexes at the time, and this was the last one. We referred to it as a plaza because that is what it appeared to be.

Complexes I and II form a suite of architectural features running east-west. Barbed wire fences form a boundary to this general area on its southern side. A few meters south of the fence there is a rough farm road, mentioned above, that also runs east-west. A healthy coffee field covers most of Complex III, to the south of the road, with only the quadrangular patio extending out into a pasture. On the western side of the Complex III circle runs the wall discussed above. Between that wall and the edge of the terrace on which all of the Operation D architecture sits is Complex IV.

There is a distance of about 70 meters between the causeway and the northern edge of the plaza (fig. 3.1). This roughly large area is in short grass underneath a few guava trees. Its central section is slightly higher than either side. We found traces of a circle in this area. The eastern terrace of the area drops off sharply, and a 10-meter-long line of large boulders marks this edge. Heading south, the terrace edge swings eastward, however, opening up into the large space of Complex IV.

The Complex IV (fig. 5.4) field covers an area of about 4,200 square meters. About a third of the way from the eastern terrace edge a large *ballena* rises, running north-south. The other side of the *ballena* is what

looked like a plaza to us. The *ballena* served as the western side of a large flat area. About 50 meters farther west, there appeared to be a remnant *ballena*. It was not as high as the eastern one, but a rise in the ground surface created another edge to the plaza. Viewed from the northern fence line, the ground grades downward to the central field of the complex. The feel of a sunken flat area with heights to the north and east was what gave us the impression that this place may have been a plaza area. With no trees and shin-high grass at most, kept short by grazing cattle, the open feeling of the area may have contributed to our impression that this was a gathering place.

In 1992 we had done some preliminary work in the plaza. In the area just south of the northern boundary fence, we put in a large 2 x 15 meter trench running north-south. Our aim in doing this was to see if there was any formal entryway, such as a stairway, descending from the higher level at the north down into the plazalike area. Work in this huge trench produced a great number of ceramic sherds but no evidence of architecture. We now wanted to do more work to see what exactly was in the flat, low spot between the *ballena* and the high ground to the east.

Because I had to return to the United States to move from Wisconsin to Washington, D.C., Bill Doonan and Jeff Frost took charge of the plaza fieldwork. The final phase of excavations in Complex II and all of the work in Complex IV were carried out under their leadership after we had planned our tactics together.

There was no clear evidence of circles or any other structures in the work area. The grass was fairly high, and the soil seemed to be thicker here. Here and there were lines of cobbles, but they didn't run for very far and were easily hidden under grass or in soil. We laid out a series of eight very large (5 x 5 meters) excavation units in a row, like a trench. It ran over the *ballena* on the eastern side of Complex IV. Although we laid out a work area that stretched 40 meters, our workers only completely scraped three units in the western pasture area where the grass was thickest. Eventually, Bill and Jeff added a cross section of similar-size units running along the *ballena* itself. Since the *ballena* had only a little grass on it due to its rocky nature, we were free to scrape off as much of the grass and topsoil as possible, though this was difficult to do.

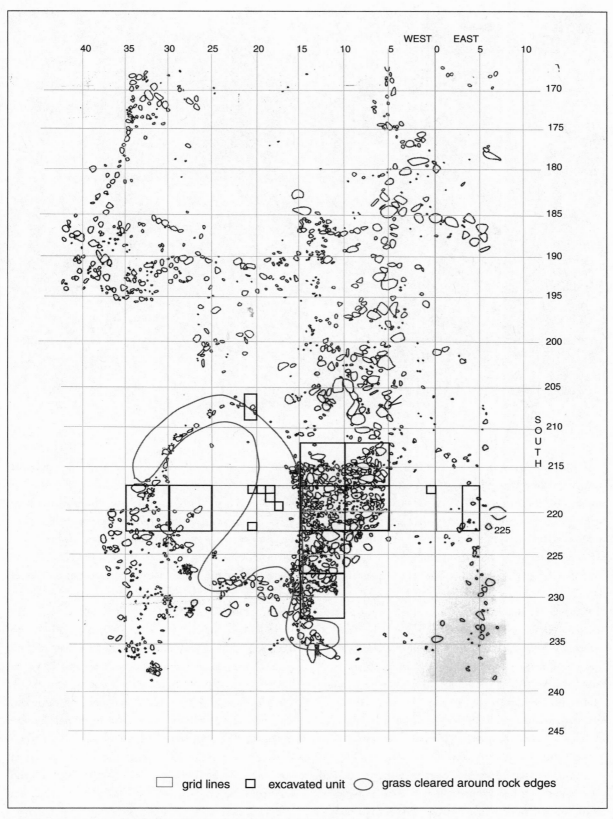

WEST EAST

40   35   30   25   20   15   10   5   0   5   10

170

175

180

185

190

195

200

205

S
O
U
T
H   210

215

220

225

225

230

235

240

245

▭ grid lines   ▢ excavated unit   ⬭ grass cleared around rock edges

5.4. Map of excavations in Complex IV. Map by R. J. Frost and W. Doonan.

5.5. Aerial view of the work on the *ballena* in Complex IV. Arrows point to the bench.

In the flat, grassy areas, Bill and Jeff could trace lines of stones. Once the grass and root layer of soil were scraped clear, they could see that most of the architectural features were close to the surface, 10 to 20 centimeters deep. All scraped earth was sifted through ¼-inch mesh screens, as was our standard procedure in almost all of our excavations. Sherds were very abundant, in greater quantities than in Complex II.

West of the *ballena* ridge and north of the line of 5 x 5 meter units, Bill and Jeff found a half circle of stones. They placed a 1 x 3 meter unit in this area to retrieve a sample of sherds. The work in the large units revealed little evidence of architecture. There were many stones, but they were all jumbled. In one area, there were seven stones in a line, and a pit was placed to see if they continued farther but with no success.

Work then turned to trying to examine what appeared to be steps or a bench on the western side of the *ballena*. A pavement made of flat stones was found on the surface of the "riser" of the first step or bench. Work at the edge of the step also retrieved a fair number of mano and metate fragments, artifacts that were

generally rare in other parts of the site, and many polychrome sherds also were recovered.

When Bill and Jeff finished supervising work on the step or bench area, the bottom step was visible for a distance of more than 9 meters (fig. 5.5). An upper row of boulders that served as a second bench tier was 4 meters in length. The reason why these lines of boulders appear to be benches rather than stairs is because of their dimensions. The bottom bench was 42 centimeters high, and its "tread" was 1.5 meters in width. This is much too wide and high to make a stairs, but it would have been convenient as a place to sit. The construction was clearly made with some care. A few of the boulders even appeared to have been modified to fit snugly in a row. The stones were about half a meter in length. The top row of boulders was harder to define or understand. They appeared to be somewhat larger, unmodified boulders in a row, set back 1.5 meters from the edge of the first row, with the pavement between them.

In the case of this bench, the aerial photographs we took with our balloon system came in particularly handy (fig. 5.5). From the ground, only about 9 meters of the lower bench can be seen clearly, as noted above. But using an aerial photograph, a line of relatively uniform cobbles can be traced running much farther, almost the entire 20 meters of cleared area. The same is true for the upper row, although the total distance that appears to show a line of stones is shorter, only about 10 meters.

The work on the benches and in all of Complex IV was a reprise of our research in many other areas of the large-scale architecture at Rivas. Despite a large crew, plenty of resources and time, and the opening of very large areas to study, there were still many unresolved issues by the end of our investigations. This was due to a combination of problems already discussed: the scale of construction at the site is huge, and the mixture of natural boulders and manipulated ones in combination with changes through time make interpretations difficult. Even taking into account that, over time, human and natural activities, the latter including earthquakes, may have severely altered the arrangement of cobbles in this area, it is hard to envision how this area looked at the time it was in its prime. The careful arrangement of cobbles to form steplike risers and the cobble pavements on the surfaces surely would have not produced a view of well-ordered space because of the very large boulders in their midst. As elsewhere at the Rivas site, the users of the site seem to have been comfortable with space that included artificially organized areas mixed with large, rather unorganized areas of natural boulders and smaller rocks. They maximized use of the natural landscape of terraces, *ballenas*, and the Panteón into a dramatic monumental landscape. This efficient use of landscape forms still required great efforts of labor to move huge boulders into place in many areas of the site.

The size of the risers and treads of the feature excavated on the *ballena* makes them too large to be considered steps. They appear to be more like a bench or a terrace upon which to sit or stand. Why the best-made bench only ran 9 meters and then stopped, apparently in a clutter of natural boulders, is hard to guess. Even taking into account the deterioration of features at the site, perhaps through rebuilding efforts and certainly through time, this imposition of rather formal architecture onto an unmodified landform immediately next to it is hard to understand. This is especially so because these bench features do not appear to have been connected to other features above or below them.

The same uncertainty exists for the flat area to the west of the *ballena*. The high densities of artifacts we uncovered suggest that there were considerable numbers of people in this place. The arc of stones indicates some kind of structure. We also found evidence of other circles or parts of them outside of our main area of work. But there was no clear pattern of domestic architecture in this outside area. One thing, however, was clear: this space was not a plaza. If it had been a plaza, we should have encountered empty spaces and perhaps extensive cobble pavements. Instead, the space appears to have contained circular structures. We couldn't tell if those structures were built on residential models or if they were more like ceremonial spaces such as the Operation E oval or the single-cobble circle between Complexes II and III. The bench on the *ballena* is curious, though, suggesting that some kind of ceremony took place. Perhaps the area had been residential and then later remodeled as ceremonial, or vice versa.

During excavation, the plaza area had seemed particularly rich in artifacts. Later laboratory studies showed that the quantities and kinds of artifacts we had found were not different than those from elsewhere in Operation D. Without more information, we can only state that Complex IV generally conforms to the rest of the architecture of Operation D. It may have indeed been a plaza during one phase of its use, with the benches serving to seat people watching events below. But at some point it appears to have been an occupation area, or at least to have been a place where circular structures had been built. Without stripping much more of the valuable grass and spending more time working in the area, we could not say more than this.

Searching for Residences Near Operation C

There was one final phase for research in 1995. As noted in the preceding chapter, we wanted to try to locate a domestic area associated with Operation C. We had been informed of the location of other cemeteries at the Rivas site. Most seemed to be relatively close to domestic architecture, such as Operation A. Operation C had been an opportunistic excavation, however, quite far from the rest of our work in 1992 and in subsequent years, too.

We had detected a few concentrations of artifacts near Operation C in our shovel test pit survey in 1994. The sherds were found close to the modern houses of members of the Mora family. It is an archaeological truism that places of preferred residence today commonly were desirable places to live in the past, especially if present conditions of the site area are similar to the environment in the past. While the present-day cluster of dwellings at the northern end of the site likely is due to the desire to be close to the main road of the region, these houses also are near small rivulets of water running off of the Panteón ridge. They also occupy flat ground relatively clear of boulders and rocks. And the original placement of the houses was done in the 1940s, when the Moras were among the first Euro–Costa Rican families to settle in the area. At that time, there was no running water or electricity, and therefore the Moras probably picked the locations of their houses following many of the same considerations that ancient people made. Thus the general area seemed to be a likely place for the prehistoric habitation, having both flat ground and access to water.

The first locale that the crew selected for examination was the front lawn of the Casa Verde, which we had rented as a residence for most of the gringos for our 1993 field season. The excavators set up a trench consisting of six 1 x 1 meter units running north-south. In all of these investigations, units were not tied to our master grid system but had their own coordinates based on cardinal directions. Decisions on where to place pits were made on the basis of the 1994 shovel test pit survey. The crew chiefs chose locations that appeared to suggest relatively high artifact concentrations and which were close to the Mora houses. The crew dug six 1 x 1 meter pits, placed in a row, to 40 centimeters but only found two sherds in the entire trench and no evidence of architecture.

The crew then moved to the other side of the dirt road, to the area of STOp 31. Again, six 1 x 1 meter pits were lined up as in a trench. The crew found a few sherds in this work, so they extended the excavation units to form two perpendicular trenches, 15 and 20 meters in length each. Sherd densities were low, about 10–15 per 10-centimeter level, and the excavators encountered no architecture.

The crew placed a third and final trench on the property of Martin Mora. His house was about 100 meters south of Casa Verde and Operation 31. This was a 15-meter-long set of 1 x 1 meter pits. The crew found two sherds and no architecture in the trench.

At the time this work was completed, the crew was disappointed. The field season was not ending on an upbeat. We had hoped to find low-status architecture near the Operation C cemetery but had not encountered any. There are several possible explanations for this failure. First, there is simply the problem of trying to locate structures in a large area. Fifteen-meter-long trenches are impressive and take a lot of work to excavate, but in an area of several hectares they only reveal a fraction of what is below ground. The same is true for the shovel test pits dug in these areas in 1994. The circular cobble rings that define architecture at the site usually are less than half a meter in width and thus can easily be missed. Added to the problem of the elusiveness of ancient architecture was the presence of numerous modern-day buildings and the vegetation surrounding them, which limited where we could dig.

Another issue is the question of the location of cemeteries in relation to domestic areas. We assumed habitation sites would be relatively close to the cemetery, but this is not necessarily the case. Larry Conyers had noted that the Operation C cemetery likely was placed in its location because of the availability of deep soils relatively free of rocks, unlike areas of the site where *rípio* began below the grass roots. It thus may be that families or other social groups associated with the cemetery did not live in immediate proximity to the grave sites. It also may be that the criteria for burial in one cemetery or another were not based on residence but on kin affiliation or some other social distinction that may not have been expressed in location of residence during life. If this were the case, then again it is not necessary to expect a habitation site near the graveyard.

A final consideration is the issue of what constituted nonelite residences. The history of the way in which we investigated the Rivas site instilled preconceptions in our views later in the project. We had started in Operation A and then discovered Operation D with its much larger structures. Given the disparity in size and the spatial separation of the Operation A structures from the complex in Operations D and E, we came to consider the small structures on the higher terrace as "low status" compared to the huge structures farther south.

It was only later, when we started to do the laboratory analyses, that we realized that the inhabitants of Operation A were living quite well. This was made quite clear later in the project when Francisco Corrales did a detailed study of the Operation A artifacts. He found lots of what appeared to be high-status artifacts. There were fancy objects such as whistles, ocarinas, ceramic figurines, and so forth. It made us reconsider what we thought when we viewed these smaller structures since, in terms of the inventory of artifacts and quality of construction, they were equal to the larger ones. It appeared that the occupants of Operation A were not necessarily of lower status than those people who dwelled in the larger structures, but rather they may have had different social arrangements—different roles in society not necessarily related to "wealth" or "status" as we might consider them. Indeed, if there had been low-status occupants of Rivas, it seemed likely that they would have lived in houses made of perishable materials, in which case finding evidence of them would be difficult. Alternatively, the observed differences may be the result of different periods of occupation of the two areas, but making such fine-grained temporal divisions is difficult.

In the end, we cannot say conclusively whether the people who were buried in Operation C had lived nearby. If they were low status, perhaps their houses had been located where we excavated trenches in the front lawns of the Mora family houses, but their living structures had been made of materials long since vanished. The low quantities of sherds we found in our work suggests some human activity had taken place there, but not much. Perhaps residences or other signs of regularly occurring activities had been a few meters away. Although not finding structures was disappointing, we can at least say that there is no evidence of intense human activity close to the cemetery.

Overview, 1995

We had accomplished much in our 1995 field season. The work was piecemeal, in a way, touching on three different issues.

First, our work in Complex II and the nearby stairs gave us a better understanding of how this area of the large-scale architecture connected to other structures and places in which we had worked in 1992. We also discovered that Complex II did not have two major construction phases. Through this work we developed a theory regarding the relative ages of structures on *ballenas* and other hard, gravel surfaces compared to those buried in softer, deeper soils.

Our work in Complex IV produced mixed results. We were able to conclude that this was part of the site and that it was as intensely occupied as elsewhere, if not more so. The artifacts we recovered showed some differences from other areas of the site, though at the end of the field season we were not able to say what those were or what they meant since we had not been able to analyze the artifacts in detail. We found equivocal evidence that this place was a plaza. The bench-like constructions on the western side of the *ballena* hint that this may have been an area to sit and watch activities below or, alternatively, to perform activities for a crowd looking up, but the evidence was not clear as to any of these possibilities. In the plaza area itself, we did find evidence of stone circles, suggesting that at least at one point in the history of the site this was an area in which people had made structures similar to other large-scale architectural features.

Our work at the northern end of the site did not yield many artifacts, but it did open discussion about this apparently isolated cemetery, far from habitations, and how to interpret it. In some ways, this was better, in the long run, than if we had found the remains of structures, as it made us think of alternate possibilities to the assumptions we had built up through the years. We weren't through with cemeteries, anyway.

Throughout this period of our research, our continuing efforts in mapping the site in more detail and our resulting interpretations of that work, in conjunction with excavations and simply spending more time in this part of the Rivas site, yielded some new ideas. In particular, we came to understand the north-south running wall separating Complexes II and III from the rest of the site as significant. Focusing attention on it made us think about how the large-scale architecture was organized in relation to the False Cemetery. This, in turn, made us consider how the architectural layout might reflect the organization of the behavior of the people who used the site and the conceptual categories of their social organization. In terms of examining issues about how Rivas was used and how the people who used the site were organized, this relatively light-weight work may have yielded the most important results. Sometimes, just spending long periods of time at a site or in an area of it yields the most important results.

High Jinks, Continued

Lest you think, gentle reader, that the high jinks discussed in earlier pages of this book had ceased in the sober regularity of the fieldwork of later field seasons, be not so deceived. There were plenty of adventures. Some of these occurred when I could not be in the field, such as some strange and peculiar events involving the short-term presence of a few disgruntled North Americans who had volunteered to work on the project but found it not to their liking. Tales of temper tantrums that had to be quelled, including the unthinking throwing of a chaining pin (a large, thin metal stake used in surveying) that landed, daggerlike, in a project member's leg, could be told. I refrain, however, from delving into such unfortunate events that worked themselves out, in one way or another.

At the beginning of the 1995 field season, we decided to take some of the new North Americans, a couple of Ticos, and the old hands on an educational trip to Palmar Sur. We crammed an amazing number of these people into our trusty Land Rover and headed south to experience the tropical clime of lower elevations and to see the famous stone balls in the vicinity of the town. We spent most of the day touring sites worthy of a visit, though perhaps not under the circumstances in which this one occurred. Tempers ranged from extremely irritated to downright hostile throughout most of the day due to some rather complex previous relationships—relationships involving love and lust, won and lost and, during our trip, under negotiation. Grumpiness was cranked several notches higher than it might have been by heat and humidity, especially in the sardine can–like environment of the Rover. The stone balls are perhaps the best-known remains of pre-Columbian Costa Rica and they were interesting, but it was very hot and humid and the banana plantation was a rather nasty place to be. We knew that the whole place was regularly sprayed with chemicals, and there were drainage ditches, everywhere, with foul water in them.

At the end of the day, we repaired to a hostelry in Palmar Norte, that is to say, a sodden cantina serving beer over ice cubes (a Central American tradition from pre-refrigeration days) and small snacks known as *bocas*. It had started to rain, and the whole place had the unique rankness that a former plantation town now mostly serving as a low-rent commercial and transportation center in a delta in an out-of-the-way corner of Central America in the rain can have. Beers were drunk and only potato chips eaten, despite gnawing hunger, due to the unattractive offerings of the cantina: the meat passing by the tables as the supposed *bocas* of choice seemed to be the end-cuts from fatty hams. I decided that for the sake of all, the newcomers should take a bus back to San Isidro. It would be good for them to experience the standard means of public transportation in Costa Rica. Everyone would thus be more comfortable on the way home, and those of us in the Rover could pick up the bus contingent in San Isidro for the shorter drive back to Rivas. The Rover left before the bus with Jeff Frost, Bill Doonan, Chris Raymond, Costa Rican archaeologist Ifigénia Quintanilla and her baby boy, and me.

The rain stopped as we steadily rose out of the delta on the Panamerican Highway. We stopped briefly to refuel at a gas station near Buenos Aires. I was driving and suddenly, about twenty minutes into the journey, heading around a curve in the road, the engine sputtered a couple of times and died. It died so suddenly that I couldn't coast the Rover over to the side of the road, especially since we were going up an incline at the time. We jumped out of the car and quickly pushed it to the side of the road, out of the way of any traffic behind us. There then followed a long examination and discussion of what might be wrong with the vehicle. At one point, a couple of project members got their dander up at the thought that the gas station had given us watered-down gas. It was decided, in any event, to go back for more gas, and Jeff and Chris hitched a ride back to the Buenos Aires turnoff. The rest of us waited. I could tell it would be dark in half an hour, and I was not optimistic that this problem would be solved any time soon. At about this time, the bus to

San Isidro passed us, and we saw the other project members stare at us with a mixture of puzzlement and glee as they rode by in comfort.

The guys came back with the new gasoline and poured it in the tank. It didn't make a difference. With the tropical nightfall about to descend, we had to plan for a long stay in this spot, in the middle of nowhere. We had to perform the difficult and dangerous maneuver of pushing the Rover so it faced downhill and then coasting it for about 100 meters. We could then turn off into a wider area of brush, on the other side of the road, where we might have to spend the night. Although we almost got hit by a semitrailer in doing this, we were finally able to get the vehicle over to this makeshift lay-by. It was now pitch black.

Jeff had his Land Rover cap on, and he tried to make a serious appraisal of the engine in the hope of fixing it. We didn't have any flashlights, so we had to light matches to see. This didn't work very well, and Jeff couldn't find any obvious problems. We started to talk about what to do. Worried that if we left the car by the side of the road it would be stripped of anything useful by morning, we began discussing who was going to stay in the car all night, ready to fend off anyone anxious for a spare tire or a headlight.

Costa Ricans are famous for being friendly and helpful. The threat of having the car stripped was simply the reality of living in a country in which there are people desperate or ambitious enough to take advantage of an abandoned vehicle. Still, cars kept pulling over, their drivers asking us if we needed help. We mostly politely thanked people for their concern and sent them on their way. Finally, we accepted an offer, and we sent one of our group with the passers-by back to the gas station to try and bring a mechanic out to see if he could help us. Soon after this, another Good Samaritan car pulled up with three Costa Rican men in their midthirties. They were evangelical Christians and hell-bent on doing a good deed. The next thing we knew, two of them had whipped out flashlights and the third was standing on the front bumper of the Rover with his nose somewhere in the engine. His arms started flailing with his hands in a blur, pulling out wires and small engine parts with what appeared to be great confidence. He kept on saying things like, "We'll have this fixed in a jiffy," in Spanish, of course.

Somewhere in the midst of this our team member arrived with the mechanic. The evangelicals dominated the proceedings, however, and the guy from the gas station couldn't find a space or muster the authority to elbow his way into the fray. He left, in a huff, I was later told, though with all of the wire pulling and confusion, I hadn't noticed that he had gone. After about twenty minutes of the masterful performance by the evangelical maestro of machines, he shouted to someone, "Turn on the engine!" Nothing happened. "Well, it looks like you've got bigger problems than we can handle," he said, and the next thing we knew, he and his companions were gone.

All we could hear were the sounds of insects in the jungle around us. Traffic had dropped to a trickle on the road. Finally, Bill Doonan said he remembered that there was a *finca* about a mile back down the road, toward Buenos Aires. Since we were uphill from it, there was a good chance we could coast the Rover all of the way there, and maybe the *finquero* would let us keep the vehicle safe behind his locked gate for the night. It was the only reasonable option that we had left. We put the only woman on the trip and her baby in the car. The remaining guys heaved and pushed the vehicle up from the lay-by to the road and then downhill.

The vehicle started to roll, gradually gaining speed. Jeff was in the front, ready to jump in the driver's seat to steer the car. (I guess because he had the Land Rover cap on he thought he was the best person to do this.) Chris was on the other side, and Bill and I were at the back. At one point there was the magical feeling of when the vehicle began to coast on its own, leaving our hands that had been pushing so far, only a few moments before. People started jumping into the car, while others jumped onto the running boards. I was at the back, and the only space to jump onto was the small metal hitching plate. Bill had jumped on it, already, however, and I could find no place to attach myself on the Rover. All of this happened very quickly, and suddenly the vehicle was rapidly accelerating. I ran faster, but there was no place to jump, and it was getting harder to keep up with the vehicle. In a moment, the Rover was 10, 20, then 30, then 100 meters away, and speeding up. The last I saw of it was the silhouettes of project members sitting on or in the boxy outline of the Rover, whipping around a bend.

So, there I was, the project director of a major research program, walking along the Panamerican Highway in the dark, abandoned by my project personnel and vehicle. Was this some kind of land-based inversion of a captain going down with his ship: a director not coasting on his Land Rover? I walked within the insect sounds and cooling air, feeling the heat rising from the highway in the dark. Rather than be upset, this was such a unique experience that I actually relished it. After all of the hubbub of the whole day, it was just nice to be by myself. When I rounded the bend, I saw the *finca*, and soon it was clear that the Rover and crew had made it to the driveway of the farm. The owner was gracious in allowing us to park the car behind his gate.

Perhaps I was so relieved that we had the vehicle safe for the night that I blanked out subsequent events, but the next thing I knew we were all crammed into a large, late 1970s vintage Chevy with bad springs trundling toward San Isidro. We were going at a speed no faster than about 35 miles per hour. The owner and driver who had given us the lift was another Tico evangelist, though of no acquaintance with our erstwhile mechanics of an hour before. He tried to proselytize us all the way back to San Isidro.

Upon arriving in San Isidro, we thanked our driver, offering him money for the ride, which he graciously declined. Suddenly, all of the muscle and mental strains of the day began to make themselves known, and we achingly made our way to the Tenedor Restaurant where we ordered two very large pizzas and many beers. There was no sign of the bus contingent that was supposed to meet us here. But the hour was very late. We eventually got taxis back to Rivas where we were reunited with the bus group who had arrived on time, ate their pizzas, and took taxis back to their bunks in Rivas.

The next day, we sent our mechanic and one of our crew back to the Rover at the *finca*. The problem had been a minor glitch in the alternator. It was nothing we could have easily fixed ourselves. The damage done by the evangelists had not been great, and the vehicle was fixed on the spot and driven back the same day.

All of these events are not directly related to what we found out about prehistoric Rivas. These kinds of escapades, however, can affect relations between project members—sometimes building camaraderie, sometimes resentment, sometimes both. They are the kinds

of stories that get told by project members many years after the field and lab work are completed and the publications done. There weren't too many bad feelings over this incident; it was another adventure for the crew. It didn't give us much confidence in our aging Land Rover, though.

Operations K and J, 1996: A Low-Status Cemetery and a Large Circle

Our next field season was in January 1996. We wanted to excavate another low-status cemetery in order to have a comparative sample for Operation C. What kinds of social and other differences might be in evidence by comparing the artifacts and mortuary practices of two low-status cemeteries?

We knew of another low-status cemetery located close to the northernmost boundary of what we had designated Operation A, on the uppermost terrace (see fig. 1.8). It was here where Bob Drolet had come across looting and had confiscated some ceramic vessels now at the Museo Regional del Sur, in San Isidro. He also had taken notes and did some cleanup work of the area. The "looters" had been local people. As in the case of their digging in Operation C, they had not thought that they had been doing anything wrong. It was their property and their artifacts; these were resources for their use and profit, like anything else on their farms.

To review Operation A, we had found Structures 1–3 in a grove of guava trees at the southern end of a rectangular area that was mostly in pasture (see fig. 2.1). This rectangle was about 100 meters wide and 250 meters in length, north-south, bounded up-valley by the southern end of the Mora Road, which turned eastward near its terminus. The flat, boulder-free pasture on the terrace consisting of the southern part of Operation A continued beyond the road, where it ended in a coffee field.

Our studies of the area closest to the structures of Operation A, including our two shovel test pit surveys, yielded evidence that the area was filled with circular houses similar to those we had excavated. North of the Mora Road, the presence and nature of prehistoric remains were less certain. The shovel test pit operations had found no definite evidence of circular stone rings, although cobble pavements and some stone alignments were in evidence. At the northernmost end of the northern field, however, just before entering the coffee field, the shovel test pit crew working under the supervision of Jeff and Chris found a very nicely made stone circle. In fact, it was one of the best made stone rings we found at the site, and it measured 17 meters in diameter. We planned to work in this area and called it Operation J.

My time again was limited, so after some initial investigations of Operation J, for the remainder of my time at Rivas we concentrated our work in Operation K, a low-status cemetery. After I left, Jeff finished supervising work in Operation J. I will discuss Operation K before I describe our work in Operation J because they were finished in that order.

OPERATION K

We were once again working among coffee plants, and once again we were faced with the problem of damaging crops valuable to their owners. We found a space among the coffee plants, however, that was clear and appeared to be higher than the surrounding ground and decided to concentrate our work in this location. We also wanted to maximize the area in which we were to do our research. Our workers told us that they had dug up about 30 burials in this area when they were children. The area we were now in was also said to be where some of the Moras had found a stone statue that we had been allowed to examine in 1992.

The rows of coffee plants edging the cleared area formed a rectangular shape (fig. 5.6). After we set up the rectangle, however, we realized that the geometry of the area was askew from our grid system. In addition, we were very far north, more than 300 meters from our master datum for the site. This would make labeling bags quite tedious, having to use three-digit numbers. Given these two facts, we decided to link our work area in the coffee field to a known datum point that was part of the master grid system and treat it as a secondary datum. This point was N335/W115 on our master grid but became 0/0 for our local work. We established a second point 25 meters west of this point (N0/W25) and then measured 3.5 meters to the south to establish the northwest corner of a rectangular area for our excavations on the mound. The southwestern corner of our rectangle, established from this point, was S7/W25. The pit was 5 meters long, east-west, and 4.5 meters wide. It was later expanded to greater dimensions, however. Finally, we decided to refer to this rectangle as Operation K2, whereas any other pits we opened that were on the master grid system would be in K1. In addition to the rectangular area, we set up a long trench running close to our "B" datum. We worked between two rows of coffee plants, so the width of the trench, at 1.8 meters, was determined and limited by the coffee plants on either side of it. Coffee has a relatively small root ball, so it was feasible to work between rows of plants without hurting them.

Work in the rectangular area started off with some uncertainty. During the first day of work, a cavity was encountered almost in the middle of the pit (fig. 5.7). We weren't quite sure what this was until we realized it was the remnant of a looter hole that had somehow been covered up with soil, above it, but retained an empty space that had been dug into during the looting. As work continued, we found the majority of the burial remains in the southern area of the rectangle. The central area had been looted and also, possibly, the northeastern corner of the pit. On the other hand, the northwestern area of the excavation unit yielded undisturbed remains, while the central western and southwestern areas were undisturbed but revealed no mortuary materials. Perhaps this area was a boundary between two sectors of the cemetery, or perhaps it was simply a section of the cemetery that never had been used. More likely, it represented a space between two or more sets of burials each grouped together because the dead were members of the same family or some other social unit.

When we had excavated Operation C, we had encountered problems in keeping track of burials. Because single pots or groups of them had no associated human remains, we couldn't be sure where the original burial had been located in many cases. This time, we tried to keep better track of things. Every time we found a single pot we gave it a precise grid designation, based on our coordinate system, and determined its depth below the ground surface, which also became part of the reference information for the ceramic vessel. When we found two vessels close to each other, they became a "group," and their coordinates and depths were also noted in our record books. As we exposed more of the area around such groups, only if a soil stain was present did we finally designate it as a *tumba* (tomb— technically, these are graves, but I have retained the

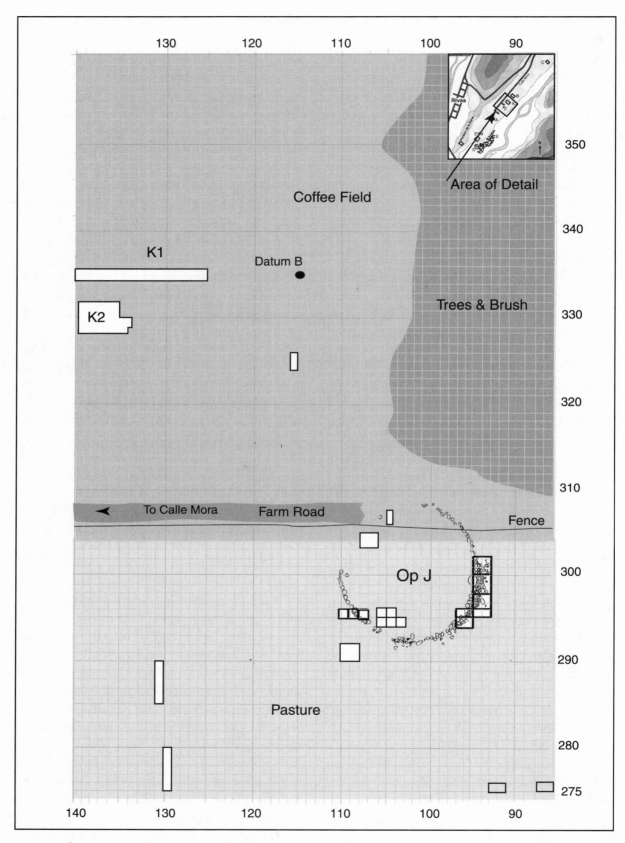

5.6. Map of excavations in Operations K and J. Map by R. J. Frost and J. Quilter.

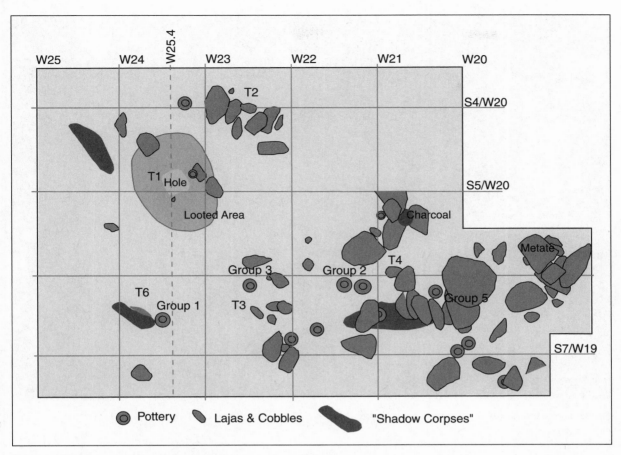

W25.4

W25　　W24　　W23　　W22　　W21　　W20

S4/W20

T2

T1 Hole

Looted Area

S5/W20

Charcoal

Metate

Group 3

Group 2

T4

T6

Group 5

Group 1

T3

S7/W19

◎ Pottery　　◗ Lajas & Cobbles　　▬ "Shadow Corpses"

5.7. Excavations in Operation K2. Map by R. J. Frost and J. Quilter.

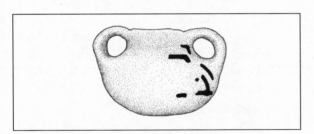

5.8. Small Buenos Aires Polychrome jar found in Tomb 2, Operation K 2. Height: 5.1 cm. Illustration by Jennifer Ringberg.

English term "tomb" throughout this book following our use of the word in our work) and then associate a group with it. We sometimes found groups of pots long before we found the soil stains. Group 1 eventually was associated with Tomb 6.

We found three distinct soil stains similar to those we sometimes found in Operation C. Two were in the northwestern area of the excavation unit. One was in the northwest corner of our excavations at a depth of

108 centimeters and measured 70 x 25 centimeters, with its long axis running northwest-southeast. No grave offerings were with it (fig. 5.7). The other, to the south, was designated as Tomb 2. It was beneath a jumble of *lajas* (stone slabs). The stain merged into the soil and was impossible to measure with accuracy, although it was clear it ran east-west and was at a depth of 190 centimeters. At the approximate center of the stain, we found a small, two-handled Buenos Aires Polychrome jar (fig 5.8). These two soil stains were about 10 centimeters in maximum thickness.

Two vessels designated as Group 2 later were associated with Tomb 4. After initially identifying the ceramic group, we found a soil stain in the extreme southeast portion of the excavation area where a grave pit could be traced in the excavation profile. We extended the excavation unit half a meter eastward in order to trace this feature, although the end of the grave was almost exactly at the edge of the original wall. Overall, this was one of the most complete and distinct graves

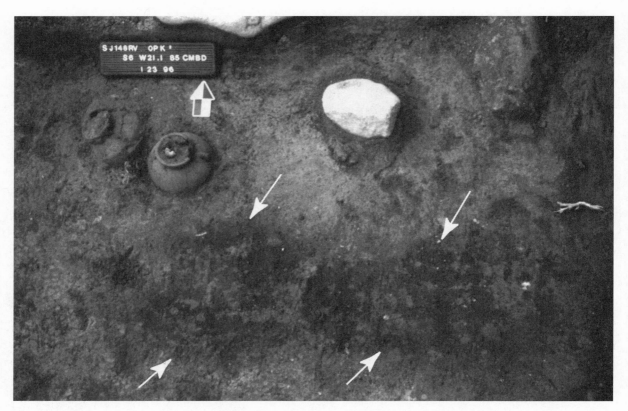

5.9. "Shadow corpse" with vessels. The vessels (Tomb 4, Group 2) are at S6/W21.2, 85 cm depth. The arrows point to the edges of the "corpse."

with offerings we encountered (figs. 5.7, 5.9). The stain was rectangular in shape, 30 centimeters wide and 1.4 meters long. It was found at a depth of 94 centimeters and was 3 centimeters thick, roughly lenticular in cross section. We found two simple jars at about the same level as the stain and to the north of what had been either the head or feet of the burial.

We found other pottery vessels near the Tomb 4 soil stain but deeper than it, including one directly below the stain at 160 centimeters depth. So, too, we encountered four *lajas*, stacked in a row, at a depth of 106 centimeters. Further excavation failed to reveal another burial below the one found at 94 centimeters. It seems unlikely that these deeper artifacts were part of the burial offerings of Tomb 4. Rather, they probably were part of the grave assemblage of an earlier burial that had left no trace of the remains of the deceased.

We found single ceramic vessels in various parts of the K2 excavation. One of these was a rather spectacular, complete, large, tall-necked jar in the southern sidewall of the pit at S7/W21.5 and 41 centimeters in depth (fig. 5.10). It had been buried upright, close to

the surface, and we had never seen vessels of this type before. We had found a large rim sherd of similar shape, however, directly under a cobble pavement in OpD '94. Perhaps these large jars were used to hold *chicha*, a beerlike drink of maize or fruits, for burial ceremonies and were interred or broken at the graveyard once the contents had been consumed.

We found other groups of pots. In some cases they were stacked together, often with wide-mouthed bowls with tripod legs inverted over jars (see fig. 5.11). These appear to be food-serving bowls judging by their wide, open form. Furthermore, they often show swipe marks, as if they had been cleaned or as if someone had reached in them to gather food by using their fingers. The fact that they were inverted over jars is a further indication that these were dining vessels. The jars may have been filled with food, but the vessels from which the dead would eat such food were laid in the grave empty, waiting for their ghostly service.

One vessel was originally a globular jar with tripod legs, but the legs had clearly been broken off during use. We could infer this because there was no trace of

5.10. A large jar found in the south side wall of the Operation K2 excavations. Large sherds of this vessel have been removed as excavation advanced, but the profile of the jar can be easily seen.

any of the legs nearby, and this area of the site was undisturbed. In addition, once we cleaned the vessel we could see that the area of the body vessel where the legs had been attached had been worn during use—the breaks were not fresh as we might expect if the vessel had been damaged in excavation. The only conclusion we could reach, then, is that one or more legs had broken during the "life" of the vessel, but it had continued in use. Probably, one or two legs had broken, and the owner decided to break off the remaining legs so that the vessel could more easily be used and not be lopsided. This little bit of evidence is important because it is another indication that the person who had owned this pot had been relatively poor. Given the amount of broken pottery at the site, it is easy to imagine that a more affluent person could have easily afforded to get a new tripod vessel for his or her use.

In addition to our area excavations in our large pit, K2, we also excavated a long trench, which we referred to as K1 (see fig. 5.6), where we uncovered more ceramics. In only one case, however, did we find evidence

of formal burial practices. Close to the northern edge of the trench in the vicinity of the W17 mark, we came across three *lajas* in a row, under which were two ceramic vessels. It is likely that this was the edge of a burial, although further work yielded no more artifacts.

The maximum excavated depth, in general, in both the trench and the rectangular unit was deeper than 2 meters. In the eastern half of K2, workers dug to 256 centimeters below our datum, at which point they encountered big rocks that serve as the equivalent of bedrock as far as cultural remains are concerned, just as in the False Cemetery of OpD '94. In the trench, a maximum depth of 266 centimeters was reached. The soils remained black, but there were lots of big rocks and no cultural materials. No artifacts were found at great depths. One artifact was found at 190 centimeters and another at 192, in the rectangular unit, but most were found at about 160, 130, or 95 centimeters in depth or higher.

Comparing the Operation K burials with those of Operation C reveals similarities and differences. In

5.11. Post molds around pottery vessels in Operation K2.

general, mortuary practices are quite similar. The depths of graves are about the same in each cemetery, as is the absence of human remains except for an occasional "shadow corpse." Because the area had been looted and then used for a coffee field, causing further disturbance, we didn't find clear indications of surface pavements in Operation K as in Operation C. If there had been cobble pavements, they had been removed relatively recently during planting. We never got a clear answer from the workers if this had been the case.

We found the same small, circular post-mold stains in different colors again in Operation K. Once again, we carefully excavated examples of and cross-sectioned some, for vertical cutaway views of them (fig. 5.11). And once again, the cross-sectioning revealed that the post molds had tapered ends. In some cases, the patterns seemed to be around groups of pots, perhaps marking off one group from other deposits. In other cases, however, the stains revealed no apparent patterns. As before, we must consider that numerous marking events could have created an apparently random pattern as one set of markers was placed near others.

The post molds seemed to appear in the soil surrounding the level at which artifacts and the occasional shadow corpse are found or somewhat slightly above and below them. As in other cases, the post molds never extended to the present-day ground surface or even to upper levels of soils filling cemeteries. As interpreted in OpD '94, this suggests that the posts were placed in open graves or in graves with only enough soil to cover the human remains and grave offerings. Again, the purpose of these posts remains unknown. While cobble grave pavements helped to mark graves, if posts were left in and around burial areas, perhaps they also served to warn later grave-diggers of burials nearby.

The post molds suggest that the rituals of death in the Rivas cemeteries may have consisted of more than one phase. A burial pit was excavated, and human remains and offerings were placed in it. The grave may have been kept open or partly filled with soil and posts stuck around the contents. At some later date the grave was filled completely. The shadow corpses might be the remnants of processed bodies, perhaps bundle burials, as they are rectangular in shape, suggesting a package of bones. Unfortunately, the soil stains are so few and hard to study that this cannot be said with certainty, and the possibility of interment of a body with little postmortem treatment is just as likely.

The artifacts found in the Operation K burials are generally similar to those we encountered in Operation C. In both cases, it appeared that the offerings were materials likely used in the everyday lives of the deceased. Evidence for use wear on vessels and the specific example of the tripod jar with its legs snapped off as well as other examples of broken vessels and sometimes even sherds as grave offerings suggest that these were remains of objects that had seen service before they were given as offerings.

Another observation that we first made in Operation C, but which was confirmed through our work in Operation K, regarded miniature vessels. Small versions of larger pots were commonly found in different excavations at various levels of work. There was a tendency, however, for small pots to be found in the upper levels of cemeteries, sometimes quite close to the surface. There are two possible explanations for this.

One is that the miniatures were associated with the burial of infants and young children, who were not buried very deeply. The second is that the miniatures were deposited near the surface of cemeteries because they were used in some sort of postburial rituals, after a grave had been filled with soil. In Operation C, miniatures were sometimes found with no cobble pavement nearby; they were simply buried in an upright position below the surface of the ground. Miniatures are not necessarily associated with children, and they are not necessarily toys, so a full explanation of miniatures and their locations in cemeteries must await excavations in contexts where human remains and the details of mortuary rituals are better preserved than at Rivas. The small Buenos Aires Polychrome vessel we found in Tomb 2 was not a miniature, however. It was simply a small pot, perhaps used to contain a condiment, spice, or pigment. Its shape has no analogue in larger vessels, whereas the miniatures are indeed small versions of larger ceramic vessels.

There are differences between the cemeteries. The use of *lajas* within a grave was found in only one instance in Operation C. In Operation K, however, despite disturbances, *lajas* were much more common. Could it be that *lajas* came to substitute for the cobble pavements? Some graves in Operation K appear not to have had these stone slabs on the body. For example, the shadow corpse of Tomb 4 was in an undisturbed area and had no *lajas* over it, although some were found beneath it, likely on an earlier burial.

Lack of cobble pavements above graves in Operation K made it very difficult for us to estimate the number of graves present in the cemetery. Even in cases in which we had shadow corpses, we could not be sure which vessels went with which graves because the grave pits were so hard to identify. Group 2, for example, appeared to be associated with the shadow corpse of Tomb 4, but it might have been part of the burial goods of Tomb 5. There also appear to be distinctions between the two cemetery assemblages in general.

In Operation C, Sangria Fine Red and Turucaca White-on-Red were the predominant pottery types, and we only found a few examples of Buenos Aires Polychrome. The Operation K assemblage generally had fewer decorated vessels and no definite examples of either Turucaca White-on-Red or Sangria Fine Red. Granted, the slips seem to have deteriorated more completely in Operation K than in Operation C, which may be due to minor but significant variations in soil acidity, drainage, or other factors. We worked in the dry season in Operation C and in the rainy season in Operation K. The ceramics in the first cemetery were quite dry when removed from the ground, while some in Operation K often had the consistency of wet clay, resulting in more fragmentary pieces. This difference in the apparent quality of ceramics in the two cemeteries also could be the result of better-fired ceramics in the Turucaca and Sangria wares than in the pottery from Operation K, however.

We excavated about the same number of graves in both cemeteries. The Operation K graves had no burials with many offerings, such as Tomb 5 in Operation C. There were fewer offerings per tomb in Operation K, in general, and fewer of the small jars so common in the other cemetery. The standard burial offering in Operation K appears to be one or more medium-size jars or bowls. Of the 22 complete or near-complete Operation K vessels, 3 were examples of Buenos Aires Polychrome, 2 were Papayal Engraved, and 1 was Ceiba Red-Brown. Of the remaining vessels, two tripod bowls had no traces of slip remaining and were of forms that could be decorated in either Buenos Aires Polychrome or Turucaca/Sangria styles.

While the total number of ceramics from each cemetery is small, the striking difference in the dominance of the Red Wares in Operation C and their virtual absence in Operation K seems noteworthy. Keeping in mind that the small sample sizes may be biasing the distribution of these wares in the collections, there are other possibilities that might explain this patterning. One possibility is that the differences reflect different contemporary social groups that favored or identified with different pottery styles as marks of social distinction. Another possibility is that the different assemblages reflect temporal change as Red Wares decreased or increased in popularity through time. This would make one cemetery later or earlier than the other. If this were the case, we might expect to observe differences in the styles of the Buenos Aires Polychrome vessels in comparing each assemblage. There are so few examples of Buenos Aires Polychrome in both collections, however, that such a comparison is difficult to make. The issue is complicated by the fact that two of the Buenos Aires Polychromes in Operation C

are the tapir figurine and the human-head whistle, which are distinctively decorated even within the Buenos Aires style. But this might be telling us something, also. Depending on whether the Operation C cemetery is earlier or later than the Operation K cemetery, this use of Buenos Aires Polychrome might indicate that the decorative style began or ended by only being used for decorating figurines. This, however, is a hypothesis to be tested in some future archaeological project.

For more than two years after Operation K was excavated, we were unable to investigate the possibility of temporal differences between the two cemetery assemblages. As noted earlier, we had only one radiocarbon date from Operation C (see appendix), and it was not highly reliable as an indication of the age of the cemetery. The date was slightly later than the rest of the radiocarbon dates we obtained for other areas of the site. It was only when we began our laboratory phase of research that we had the time to find other carbon samples and have them processed to try and clarify this dating issue.

There also were two tantalizing indicators of something quite different in Operation K compared to Operation C. One was the presence of a possible pillar. As it was found in the hole left by looters, we could not be sure of the original archaeological context of this stone. But this piece certainly resembled a pillar and may have marked an area of the cemetery, perhaps a family plot. We found no pillars in Operation C, but, then again, we found no others in Operation K. It is quite possible that pillars were in both cemeteries but were taken away, relatively recently, to adorn house lawns in the region. The other intriguing evidence was the presence of metates and fragments in Operation K. We found no metates in Operation C, and, again, this may be due to the circumstances of where we happened to excavate. Metates are rare throughout the site. The presence of metates in Operation K, then, suggests that the era in which the burials were made in this location may have had a different character to it than when the rest of the site was constructed.

The most important result of the Operation K excavations is the additional evidence we obtained for cemeteries next to the Rivas site in contrast to the Panteón de La Reina burials. Why were some people buried down on the terrace near the structures while other people were buried on the ridge-top? Once again, as in

Operation C, no gold was found in the Operation K burials, and our workers reported that they had found no gold when they had dug in the area when they were boys. It was thus obvious that there was some very distinctive patterning in the site complex as a whole. There were at least two cemeteries on the terrace of the Rivas site in which the dead were not buried with gold, while there was evidence that the people on the Panteón de La Reina had been buried with the precious metal. We knew of a third cemetery on the Rivas terrace. We did not excavate it, although all reports were that there was no gold in those graves, either.

Precise dating was critical to working out the puzzle of the presence of gold in the Panteón cemetery and its absence in the Rivas cemeteries. There is always the possibility that the different cemeteries could represent changes in burial customs and the use of gold jewelry that had occurred too quickly for our ability to detect them. But there is also the likelihood that the cemeteries were used at approximately the same time, by the same culture, and that some people had privileges and others did not. One way to examine that question was to see how similar the ceramics of the Panteón graves were to those of the Rivas cemeteries. But we would have to wait a while before we could work on the Panteón. I wanted to save that work until we had resolved some remaining issues about the Rivas site. I wasn't sure whether, once we started to work on the Panteón, we would find ourselves in a situation that would make it hard to work anywhere else.

OPERATION J

We discovered Operation J (fig. 5.6) during our shovel test pit survey in 1994. It was located at the far end of two large pastures, the southern one of which was Operation A. It consisted chiefly of a large stone circle.

Our discovery of the circle of Operation J was a testament to the value of the shovel test pit survey. The ring of stones was completely invisible from the surface, and we only found it thanks to the small pits we excavated in the 1994 operations. These helped us to locate evidence of cobble pavements, alerting us to the possibility of more extensive features. Trenches then helped reveal the general contours of the structure. Without the shovel test pit survey, we could have walked quite close to this area and never have spotted the structure.

5.12. Operation J excavations. The east side expansion of the cobble ring. View toward Grid N.

By 1994 we had seen many stone circles and other cobble pavements at Rivas. After a while, one comes to develop a discerning eye for these things, and thanks to such training we immediately appreciated the quality of artisanship in the Operation J structure. It was a beautiful formation, with cobbles carefully picked to be of uniform shape and size and carefully laid end-to-end (fig. 5.12). Not only were the stones carefully selected and laid, but also the geometry of the circle was highly accurate. In addition, the circle was large, at 17 meters in diameter. Although there were larger circles at Rivas, few were both this large and finely made, especially north of Operation E.

Jeff Frost was in charge of most of the excavations in Operation J. Work began by clearing the topsoil while following the circle of stones. After that, workers laid out a line of 1 x 1 meter pits to cut across the wall of the circle on its southwestern side. Then a series of large pits in trenchlike formation were laid out running over and just outside of the eastern side of the circle. The archaeologists placed additional pits in the northwest quadrant of the circle to see if it was complete or if it lacked cobbles there as so many of the "circles" at Rivas seemed to do. Finally, a 2 x 2 meter pit was established 3 meters to the southwest of the circle to see what lay outside of it but relatively nearby.

There were a number of interesting features of this large circle. The trenchlike pits quickly revealed alternating layers of black and reddish soil, just like in Operations D and E. In one unit, in a cluster of five pits immediately inside the circle on its southwest side, we found what appeared to be a hearth (fig. 5.13). This consisted of three plate-size cobbles in a semicircle, open to the south, with small, fist-size cobbles arranged as if in a miniature pavement or cobble ring between them. There was a dense deposit of charcoal, curiously, mostly outside of the center of this semicircle. Most of this feature was at a depth of between 40 and 50 centimeters. Hearths are almost nonexistent at Rivas, and the fact that there was no charcoal inside this feature is unusual. Perhaps it was scraped clean and filled with clean soil before it was buried, or perhaps it is not so much a hearth as some kind of dedicatory offering that included perishable materials now vanished from the center of the semicircle.

Two significant architectural aspects of the Operation J ring of stones were in patterns that were the exact opposite of what we had previously encountered at the site. First, as was noted earlier, most "circles" are not complete; there usually is a gap in the ring of stones. In most places, that gap is on the southern side of structures. In Operation J, however, the gap is on the northwestern side of the circle. Two pits placed there showed no evidence of a continuation of the stone cobbles, although a smashed pot was found in one pit.

Another contrary pattern in this structure was the elaboration of the eastern side of the ring of stones (fig. 5.12). In this section, the single line of stones forming the perimeter expanded into a carefully made five-tiered arc. Again, such expansions are not unknown, but they almost never are located on the eastern sides of structures, being more common on the south or west.

Another distinctive feature of Operation J is that the circle lacked a quadrangular patio. The lack of a patio on the Operation J circle suggests that whatever activities were carried out in the circle, there were no "external" activities as associated with patios in other structures.

Other unusual patterns in Operation J consisted of dense accumulations of artifacts inside the ring of the structure with fewer remains outside. Again, this is the reverse of what we found in all other operations. So, too, there was a relatively great amount of lithic debris in the materials we recovered compared to elsewhere at Rivas. Just to make things more confusing, however, the 2 x 2 meter pit outside and to the southwest of the ring of stones was extremely rich in artifacts, including a large Buenos Aires Polychrome figurine head.

Jeff conducted some additional work in Operation J. He placed a 1 x 5 meter trench, running north-south, 20 meters to the southwest of the stone circle and another trench of the same dimensions south of the first one. He selected these locations because high concentrations of artifacts were found in this area during the 1994 survey; perhaps there was a structure or a cobble pavement nearby. Jeff found no architecture in the trenches, but he did discover soil horizons and fairly dense deposits of artifacts. He also placed two small 1 x 2 meter pits on either side of a definable line of stones to the southeast of the circle, about 15 meters south of it (see fig. 5.12). This line of stones appears to have been a boundary marker close to the edge of the terrace. In this case, more artifacts were found "outside," to the east of the line of stones rather than to the west.

One explanation for the apparent contrary organization of the Operation J circle is that it was somehow linked with the cemetery to its northwest, the same direction as the opening in the circle facing the cemetery. Operation J is not only a magnificent structure, but it also is the last structure of a complex of architecture stretching southward to Operation A and beyond. Just as the OpD '94 pavements served as some kind of ceremonial space before the dead were taken up to the Panteón de La Reina, perhaps the Operation J structure served as a center for mortuary activities before the dead were buried in Operation K. Jeff commented that the "smashed pot" features in Operations D and E also seemed to be in vacant spaces, on the southern sides of those architectural complexes. Per-

5.13. Hearth in Operation J.

haps the smashed pot feature in Operation J, in the northern vacant space, was tied to rituals of burying the dead beyond, to the northwest.

It might be argued that the great amount of stone tools and fragments found in Operation J suggests some function for the structure other than mortuary activities. But we do not know the details of burial rites. Whatever the case, the distinctions of the Operation J structure in contrast to the Operations D and E architecture seem appropriate. The more southern, larger structures were oriented and focused on burial rituals on the Panteón. Perhaps earlier or poorer folk living at the northern end of Operation A made a relatively small and simple but very finely constructed mortuary facility for the burial of their kith and kin. They oriented their mortuary rituals and the very structure of their ceremonial space itself in different directions than those of the rich folks down the street.

Last-Day Discovery

One of the great archaeological truisms is that the most important discovery is always made on the last day of a project's field season. Many a tale is told of finishing up work on the final day—just before backfilling and other tidying up work—when suddenly the most spectacular burial or most important, interesting, or beautiful feature or artifact is discovered. Often, the project must be extended a day or more to take care of this discovery. More often, work is intensified to try and get the object or feature properly excavated while at the same time keeping to schedules for closing down the project.

Why does this happen? Perhaps it takes so much excavation or other investigation to reach a point at which important discoveries are ready to be made. There is a kind of geometrical progression of knowledge that happens in digging, so that by the final days the archaeologist in charge knows much more than when the project began. Often a "hunch" is really the accumulated, partly subconscious, knowledge about how a site is organized that builds from time in the field. Sometimes discoveries are made near the end of work because the archaeologists might finally have time to look around a little more than when they are concentrating on a narrow set of tasks during the main field season. Perhaps the saints or gods of archaeologists like their little jokes.

In 1996 it was a case of finally having a little time. I was about to leave, and Jeff and I decided to go and look at the top of the Panteón de La Reina. Jeff had been up in the area previously and had found a number of features he wanted to show me. We climbed up to the ridge-top via a road commonly used by local farm folks, about halfway between the tip of the Panteón and the road that crosses the ridge between the town of Rivas and our farm and site area in Guadalupe de Rivas. We walked around and saw a number of interesting features, including stone pillars, looted areas, and areas where no looting appeared to have been done.

In the northern end of the area over which we trod, there was a moundlike rise at the top of which was a looter hole. To the east, however, there were what appeared to be a series of steps or retaining walls made of river cobbles, running roughly north-south in the same general direction as the ridge itself. After having looked around, we realized that we could descend from the ridge, down to the area of Operation D, by a trail leading directly from this cobble feature.

As we descended the trail, we realized that there were steps or terraces running down the slope of the Panteón among the coffee plants. The section we saw ran down the hill for about 20 meters. Within this space there was a set of at least six risers and treads formed by the river cobbles. In the middle of this stairway there also appeared to be a small raised platform, about 2 meters in width and running 1.5 meters deep, into a tread. As we proceeded down the side of the Panteón, we lost sight of the stairs, but it was clear that erosional deposits were thicker lower down, probably covering up any stairs there.

We were excited by our finding of the stairs, as we thought we had made a great discovery. Later, back home, we found that a stairway had been mentioned for the Panteón de La Reina by María Eugenia Bozzoli de Wille (1966), although no details had been offered as to its location. Still, it was exciting because the stairs provided a clear link between the Panteón de La Reina and the Rivas site. In fact, it appeared that if they continued in the direction that we estimated, they would link directly to the False Cemetery of OpD '94. Thus Rivas and the Panteón were demonstrably each part of

a complex. The stairs and the Panteón beckoned us to study them.

Stairway to Heaven: Work in 1996 and 1997

In less than 12 months we were back at Rivas in a field season that lasted from mid-December 1996 to mid-January 1997. Due to a variety of circumstances, none of the key Rivas project personnel could spend more than a month in the field. The 1996–1997 field season was therefore devoted to tying up some loose ends, such as taking care of some miscellaneous mapping and testing the area between the observable stairs on the Panteón slope and the OpD '94 terrace as identified in the previous January. Jeff Frost was in charge of all field operations during this period (fig. 5.13).

When work began, four separate sections of architecture were known on the Panteón. Section 1 was the steps we had found on the ridge slope the previous January. Section 2 was the area slightly higher up-slope where we had found the cobble platform in the middle of the stairway. Still farther up hill, the contemporary footpath crossed the ancient stairway. This was Section 3. Finally, at the summit of the ridge was Section 4, the architectural feature of steps or walls around the looted mound. None of these sections were clearly connected, however. As work proceeded, additional "sections" were added in areas worked at the top of the stairway.

Jeff shot a coordinate line from OpD '94 westward toward the stairs and other features, and then he established local datum points within the various work areas. He concentrated work in the area between the stairs and OpD '94 to see if the stairs continued toward the False Cemetery or if there were pavements or other features between them and at the top of the stairs near the looted mound.

Jeff placed 16 excavations units, mostly 1 x 1 meter pits, in the space between the stairs and the False Cemetery. He found no stairs or architecture in any of them, even though most were excavated to depths greater than a meter, presuming that there was a lot of erosional deposition in the area.

The work in the mound area was of interest. What had appeared to be terraces, once cleared, revealed themselves to be a continuation of the steps, rising to the very summit of the ridge. There were flat areas of pavements near the summit, however. These had features resembling the pavements over burials. Whether they were like the False Cemetery below, at the base of the ridge, or were actual burials could not be determined as they were only mapped, not excavated.

This brief field season yielded much useful information. In addition to filling in some blanks on our maps, we identified an additional circular structure in Operation D, to the east of Complex I. We had studied the stairs and found they did not continue all the way to OpD '94. Perhaps they were built only in the steep part of the Panteón slope. Because this area was entirely in coffee, we were restricted in opening large excavation units that might better determine how the stairs were architecturally linked, or not, to the structures in Operation D.

Summary of 1995–1997 Work

The three field seasons conducted from 1995 to 1997 had increased our knowledge of the site. Combined with our previous work, we now had a highly accurate map of the large-scale architecture. We also had defined an area of smaller architecture and an apparent ceremonial structure, the circle of Operation J, and an associated cemetery at its northern end. We had retrieved substantial amounts of data from various sectors of the site that remained to be analyzed. We also had a clearly defined link between Rivas and the Panteón de La Reina.

Through the years, our work at Rivas had continually pointed us, literally and figuratively, to the Panteón de La Reina. All of the evidence we accumulated suggested that the large-scale architecture was tied to the ridge-top cemetery. So it seemed unavoidable that we should conduct research on the Panteón. But time and funds were beginning to run short. We had been given extensions for the research and we had conserved our money, but our last extension was to end on July 1, 2000. We had to be completely finished by then. We would need at least a year within the remaining grant extension, and possibly another year beyond that, to take care of the laboratory analysis of our materials and writing up the results of our studies. That meant that we could only afford one more field season before we restricted ourselves from doing any more fieldwork in order to concentrate on laboratory work and writing. Thus, if we were going to do any work on the Panteón at all, it should be in our next field season, in January 1998.

CHAPTER SIX

THE PANTEÓN DE LA REINA AND BEYOND

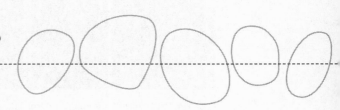

The Power of the Panteón de La Reina

The Panteón de La Reina was always there (fig. 6.1). It was the first thing to catch your eye rounding the bend on the road from San Isidro (see fig. 1.2). It defined the right-hand horizon driving up the main street of Rivas. It was where the blacktop ended and the dirt road began. It was the hill we had to climb over and back again, in the car or on foot if the Land Rover was in for repairs. It loomed over us when we sweated in the pits at the site. For five years we had mapped and shovel test–pitted and dug the Rivas site, but we hadn't touched the Panteón. More than a thousand years had passed since the last ceremony had been held at Rivas, the last of the dead had been carried up the stairs from the great cobble circles, and the last gold had been covered by soft earth. And still the ridge-top maintained its power over the land. Perhaps this is why a modern cemetery had been made up there in a spot where no ancient graves were known.

A visitor to this part of the valley is always aware of the Panteón ridge, thrusting out into the valley from the mountains behind. Clearly, the reason why the ridge

was so important and why it became the focal point of extensive constructions and elaborate ceremonies is due to its unique physiographic nature. It juts out from the mountains and is imbued with even greater spiritual power by its dominance of the river intersection, a *tinkuy*, over which it holds sway.

Across the ridge and up-valley, about a half an hour's walk from the site, and up a nearby hill there are hot springs. The landowner has extensively modified any earlier pool that may have been present before Europeans arrived, and there is not a trace of artifacts in this very popular spot for locals who want to soak in the luxury of unending hot water. We thus have no evidence of use of this place in ancient times. But if this warm spring was bubbling a millennium ago, it likely also was a place of importance for local people and could have easily been associated with nearby Rivas and the Panteón.

Although the Rivas site first was discovered in the 1980s by Robert Drolet, the Panteón de La Reina has been known since the late nineteenth century as a rich source of gold. By 1891 it already had been severely looted, as testified by the early explorer Henri Pittier

6.1. The Panteón de La Reina. View from the north. The great mass of trees in the middle distance is on the Panteón ridge. The Rivas site is on the valley floor to the left.

(1892: 72): "At an angle formed by the joining of the Chirripó and Buena Vista Rivers there is a vast cemetery the tombs almost all of which have been opened. From these were taken many gold figures (*muñecos*) and pieces of pottery" (translation by Quilter).

No archaeologist before us had dug there, but a pockmarked, cratered landscape had been formed by industrious *huaqueros*. There had been the widespread epidemic of gold fever that raged in the Americas in the mid-nineteenth century, and a wild frontier culture remained well into the 1950s in many of the more remote parts of southern Central America, such as the upper General Valley. Costa Rica is known as a prosperous country by Latin American standards, but there are still plenty of campesinos who could use extra cash. Like their nineteenth-century forebears, many country folk look upon the gold in cemeteries on local ridgetops as mines that have valuable resources worthy of exploitation. At the same time that these heights are viewed as a source of ready cash, they also are seen as dangerous, liminal places where strange things take place.

Some of our workers told of their days of *huaquerismo*. One vividly recounted how he had dug for hours and finally saw the glint of gold at the bottom of his hole. Dropping onto his hands and knees he began to scrabble for his prize. The little gold figure drove itself deeper into the soil, saving itself from being taken.

There is also a classic tale told throughout the lands of gold. A naive campesino takes a gringo or other foreigner up to the Panteón, or sometimes the local man is by himself. They dig and find a fabulous hoard of treasure. For one reason or another, the treasure cannot be taken at the moment, and they must return the next day. Of course, upon returning, the treasure has not only vanished, but the earth is sealed up and the site cannot be found.

There is supposedly a true tale of triumph about the Panteón, though. Sixty years ago, when looting was semilegal, a young Rivas man got up before dawn, gathered his work tools, and walked all the way to General Viejo, where he had heard farm labor was needed. When he arrived, however, he was rudely told to go home, he wasn't needed. By now it was hot, and as he trudged back down the road, almost home, he passed by the Panteón de La Reina. A group of men had been digging hard with no luck, and, after exchanging casual conversation, he asked them if he could come up and have a try. They said certainly he could. He climbed the Panteón slope and in his first hole came upon a treasure that, in an instant, made him the richest man in the valley. He bought a large *finca* and lived happily ever after, establishing one of the most prominent families in the community. It is a tale such as this that stokes the fires of gold fever.

These tales each reflect conflicting attitudes about gold and express the frustration of the poor subsistence-based farmer confronting a cash economy. Wealth, in the form of gold, is elusive in the first tale; what appears to be an easy road to fortune is not. There is also an element in this story of the sacred realm in which gold exists, with powers not held by ordinary objects. The "lost mine" tale can be spun to reflect the same elusiveness, or, when a gringo is added to the plot, the implication often is that he has robbed the local man of his rightful claim. The final story, while hopeful, still emphasizes the arbitrariness of luck, which might bless the unfortunate soul miraculously made into a millionaire through little effort while others who had dug all morning remain poor.

Because ridge-top cemeteries are so visible and hold such esteem as sources of wealth, any excavation occurring on them is soon known in the neighborhood and attracts attention. While surreptitious excavation at night can be carried out by looters, it is not the way archaeology is done. Thus we faced a problem: if we wished to dig on the Panteón de La Reina, we would have to do it openly and thereby attract a lot of attention. The problem was compounded by the fact that once a project began there, a high state of vigilance would have to be maintained to protect excavation pits. If any gold, especially in quantity, were to be found, we would not only have to contend with potential conflict with workers and landowners over issues of compensation, but we also would have to worry about a massive invasion of the site by fortune hunters once we left. Such an invasion could not only damage any remaining archaeological remains but also cause property damage or more to the landowners and their families who were our friends. The term "gold fever" is appropriate, for, like a disease that damages a person's

health, the thought of easy riches can turn friends into enemies and produce dangerous situations.

We wanted to avoid such troubles. True, we had had our "Loot Day." That was a calculated risk, however. We had thought that our activities had so exposed the "cemetery" in the OpD '94 area to local scrutiny that, unless we excavated soon, it would be looted by someone else. As noted earlier, the fact that there were no gold-bearing burials in that area was greeted by me with mixed emotions. It was disappointment mostly, generated by the increasing emotional state into which I and the others had worked ourselves—a touch of gold fever, perhaps—but I also had felt relief that we wouldn't have the headaches that come with finding gold.

By the last field season, in January 1998, however, we thought that we should try to learn a few things about the Panteón in order to help us better understand the Rivas site. We were not particularly interested in finding gold at this point. It still would have been welcomed, in a way, due to the information it might provide. We were much more interested and felt compelled to better understand how the Panteón cemetery had been organized and how it linked to the Rivas site, since so much of the site seemed tied to the ridge-top cemetery. We therefore embarked upon a research program that concentrated on mapping, ground surface inspection, examination of patterns of looting, and some limited use of shovels and screens to retrieve information of interest to archaeologists but of no value to those who seek financial wealth. We could have our cake and eat it, too, by trying to do everything we could to retrieve information except actually dig for gold burials.

If we had decided to seek gold burials and had been successful, the information recovered would have allowed comparison of high-status burials in our region with the few archaeologically excavated in southern Central America. One of these was at Sitio Conte, excavated by the Harvard–University of Pennsylvania expeditions of the 1930s and 1940s (Lothrop 1937, 1942; Mason 1942). Samuel Lothrop (1963) reported on gold looted in the Diquís Delta in the early 1960s, although he never actually dug a cemetery.

Finding rich gold burials would help define local styles of gold jewelry and identify imported pieces, thus aiding in addressing questions of long-distance contact (Helms 1979). Happily, this has recently come to pass in the excavations of Richard Cooke (Cooke et al. 2000) and his colleagues in Panama at the site of Cerro Juan Díaz. At the time we were doing our research, however, Cooke and his team had just begun their work, and the site in Panama is earlier than Rivas and far away from it. There is no doubt that the discovery and careful excavation of one of more high-status gold burials on the Panteón de La Reina could contribute much to our understanding of many important issues regarding Chiriquí and Central American archaeology and the nature of complex nonstate societies. The excavation of more than a single intact burial would be even more valuable because it would help us understand social differences within the Panteón cemetery, thus contributing to understanding how this chiefdom society was organized and offering opportunities to compare it with others.

In addition to the gold, there was much more information to be found in excavating an undisturbed burial. Often, the fanciest ceramics and stone tools are found in graves. Again, as in the case of gold, issues of long-distance contacts, status ranking, and so forth could be addressed by finding one or more complete burial lots of grave goods. Archaeologists are frequently frustrated because the finest and most complete ceramics shown in museums often come from illegally excavated burials, while the archaeologist must be content to excavate fragments or complete vessels of lesser quality.

When all was said and done, I just couldn't bring myself to deliberately go after burials on the Panteón de La Reina. My reasons were varied, including a mix of altruism and practicality. The farm family members saw the gold as theirs. They looked upon gold as a resource, similar to any other on their farms—fertile soil, water, plants, and pasturage—that was theirs by right of ownership. Costa Rican law was contradictory and vague about compensation. Although looters generally conduct their illegal excavations clandestinely, they often make agreements with landowners to pay them if they find gold. The landowner is at the bottom of the profit chain and the looter often not much higher, because the big profits are made when pieces are sold to wealthy collectors in Europe, the United States, or Asia (see Kirkpatrick 1992). Even if I could find a source to fund paying for gold, I had no idea, before I

began work, how much money I might need to reimburse the farmers. Furthermore, I would create a very bad precedent. Word would soon get around that a gringo archaeologist was paying for gold, and any future archaeologist then would be required to pay for gold found in excavations in Costa Rica. National archaeologists could not duplicate such an arrangement, due to lack of funds. In short, paying for gold by archaeologists, given current laws and arrangements, is considered unethical.

Through the years we demonstrated to the local families that we were interested in information that could be revealed by studying bits of broken pottery, stone tools, and the like and that we were not *huaqueros* seeking fortunes. I also had explained to them that excavating at the Rivas site and the Panteón could bring them wealth in the long term, especially in the form of tourist dollars if the ruins were developed as an attraction. They understood this and supported our work. Still, once gold was found it is hard to know how people might react.

Another issue that contributed to my decision not to excavate on the Panteón was my growing awareness that a project on the ridge-top would be a considerable undertaking. Of course, we could plan to simply dig in a relatively small area and hope for the best. If we found a burial with a fair amount of gold, that would be a significant achievement, and the work could end there. But once the archaeologists left, the ridge and surrounding farmlands might be invaded by hundreds of looters struck with gold fever who would have no consideration for anyone's rights.

We also knew that there were hundreds of looter holes up and down the Panteón ridge. Did all of the burials looted on the Panteón date to the same time period? Were there internal divisions within the cemeteries, representing social units within the general population of those who had the privilege of being buried on the ridge? Were there other patterns of significance? To answer these questions would require an extensive long-term project. To guarantee the least amount of trouble during and after excavations, we would need support for armed guards and continued protection of the Panteón. All of this required more research funds than I had left in our account and commitments of time that I was not at liberty to make. With the hope that I might develop a future project on the Panteón and find significant time in which to do it, I decided that a more limited project would be appropriate—one that would at least give us a general idea of the patterning of burials on the ridge and an indication of the kind of information that could be obtained there.

The Panteón was one of the first places I had visited when I came to the region. It had all of the elements of an Indiana Jones movie. There were huge trees with lianas as thick as a ship's cable wound around them. There were exotic wildflowers and lots of nasty plants, too. During our time on the Panteón in 1998, Jeff Frost and Andrew Gordon, who had joined our team, encountered a huge snake at least 2 meters long and as thick as a man's thigh. It surely was the guardian of the tombs.

We all had visited the Panteón many times over the years. It was only in 1996, however, that Jeff Frost and Chris Raymond carried out a semisystematic review of the ridge-top. They had found numerous pillars lying on the surface of the ground, areas bearing the scars of intensive looting, and other places where there were no looter holes at all. Our initial impression of the ridge had been that it looked like an overgrown World War I battlefield. You could not walk on flat ground because there were so many looter holes, some more than a meter in depth. Most of these were covered in vegetation, although some were freshly dug. But only certain sections of the surface of the ridge were pockmarked by looting. We quickly identified two distinct disturbed zones separated by an unlooted area (fig. 6.2). Looters must have left the intervening area alone because there were no prehistoric burials there. This unlooted area also has no stone pillars marking ancient cemeteries. Furthermore, the recent Christian cemetery in the western part of the vacant zone is another indication that no ancient burials are in this area. We asked local people if they had ever come across pottery sherds or other evidence of ancient activity in the modern cemetery, and they replied in the negative.

We conducted an unsystematic survey of the Panteón ridge. In other words, we walked over as much of the ridge-top as we could to see where the looter holes were located. We probably could have set a formal grid system to walk straight lines (transects), but that work would have been extremely difficult and laborious. We established a local datum point for mapping the top of the stairway that we had found in 1996 and linked it to

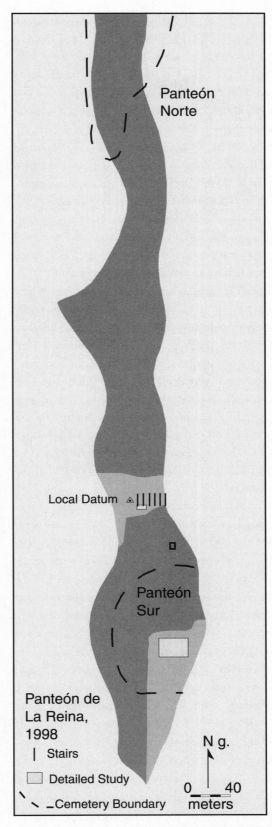

6.2. Work on the Panteón de La Reina. Dark and light shading represent heavy and light vegetation, respectively.

our grid system at the Rivas site below. We then shot another survey line along the Panteón ridge to areas where we planned to work. The great distances covered, the angle of the slope of the ridge, and the dense vegetation on its top made accuracy questionable, but at least we could generally coordinate our mapping on the top of the hill with the Rivas site.

We named the cemetery area south of the vacant area the Panteón Sur and the area to the north the Panteón Norte. In the Panteón Sur, we observed looter holes, with a few near the top of the ancient cobble stairs and many more farther south. The greatest concentration began about 60 meters south of our local datum and covered an area of approximately 6,800 square meters on the eastern side of the Panteón de La Reina. The first looter pits in the Panteón Norte began to appear at 350 meters from our datum. The distance from the northernmost looter pits in the Panteón Sur to the southernmost looter pits in the Panteón Norte was about 500 meters. Lack of time prevented us from determining how far the Panteón Norte cemetery extends up the ridge. Later, Jeff determined that this area of looting stretches for a distance of 200 meters and is between 30 and 50 meters in width, with an estimated total area of 7,100 square meters. Thus the estimated areas of each cemetery were about the same, especially considering that looter pits only provide an approximate measure.

We focused our work on an area of the southern Panteón Sur and a smaller section of the Panteón Norte. This included recording the location and dimensions of several pillars (fig. 6.3). We found eight pillars in the densest area of burials in the Panteón Sur, one was found near the top of the stairway, and another was found on the Panteón Norte. We could see no clear patterning in the distribution of the pillars in the various cemetery sectors. We did note, however, that two were near the outer edge of the Panteón Sur burial area.

In walking around the Panteón and mapping the various areas, we noticed that there were pot sherds and other materials in the mounds of looters' backdirt. When we came across a stone adze lying on the surface of the ground, we realized that the looters had likely not been interested in anything other than gold. Perhaps they also had taken complete ceramic vessels, but, for the most part, it appeared that they were only after precious metal. This was likely to have been especially true in the early days of looting, when local *huaqueros* probably had little opportunity to sell ceramics and could more easily turn gold jewelry into cash.

The mound of dirt on which the adze lay was next to an old, abandoned hole. Although time and the elements had compacted the looters' backdirt, it was easy to estimate where the ground surface had been at the time the illegal excavation had been done. We shoveled this old backdirt pile, which we called Looters' Hole (LH) A, into a screen and found pot sherds. We then decided to investigate additional holes and backdirt piles in a more systematic manner.

We staked out a 20 x 30 meter area in a place of relatively light vegetation, in old coffee plants in the Panteón Sur (fig. 6.3). We identified a total of about 60 holes inside the unit, or 10 holes per square meter. Using ¼-inch mesh screens, we sifted the looters' backdirt around 7 holes in or near the 20 x 30 meter unit. We worked in another 7 holes away from the 20 x 30 meter unit following this system. On the Panteón Norte, we sifted backdirt from 8 holes, for a total of 22 looter holes investigated.

We also conducted some geophysical work under the direction of Larry Conyers. He used a variety of techniques to attempt to detect burials below the ground surface. We also made a "false" grave in an area a local man told us contained no graves. We dug a rectangular pit 1 meter wide, 2 meters long, and 2 meters deep. We filled it with stones such as the cobbles or *lajas* sometimes found in graves. We then ran Larry's equipment —ground-penetrating radar and electromagnetic conductivity meters—over it to produce a "signature" of what an undisturbed grave might look like on the printouts produced from these machines. Of course, a grave filled with gold or many ceramics would probably give a slightly different signal, but we had a baseline from which to judge such things. Unfortunately, because we never dug deep for a real grave, we never were able to confirm whether Larry's techniques would work.

Although the geophysical analyses could not be advanced further, the sifting of looters' backdirt produced a great number of sherds as well as some stone tool fragments (table A3). As in the cemeteries at the Rivas site, some areas around holes produced very few and plain sherds, while others produced great quantities. Because these are disturbed deposits, it is hard to know for certain if these differences represent distinc-

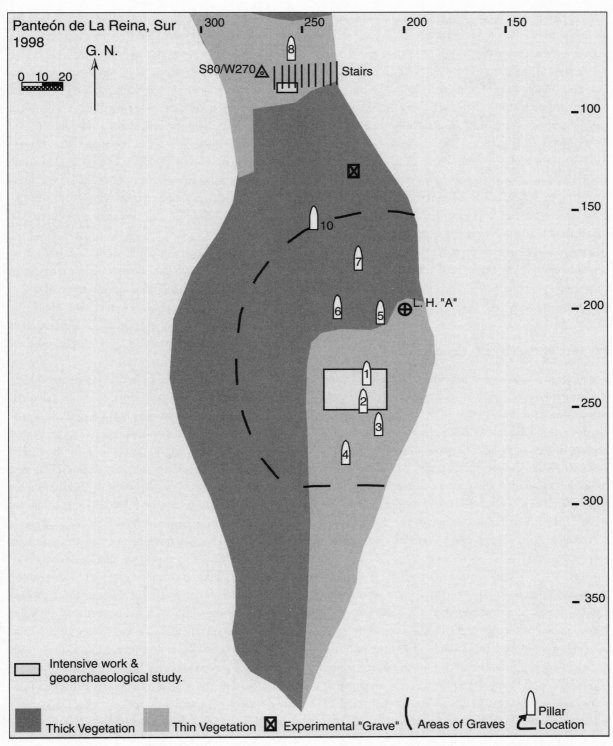

Panteón de La Reina, Sur
1998

G. N.

0 10 20

300   250   200   150

S80/W270   Stairs

8

⊠

10

7

6   5   ⊕ L. H. "A"

1

2

3

4

— 100

— 150

— 200

— 250

— 300

— 350

Intensive work &
geoarchaeological study.

Thick Vegetation   Thin Vegetation   ⊠ Experimental "Grave"   Areas of Graves   Pillar Location

6.3. The Panteón Sur. Cemetery boundaries and pillar locations noted. The rectangle at center is an enlarged view of the 20 x 30 m area of looter pits that was cleaned, examined, and mapped. Modern cemetery in vicinity of 300 mark at top of page.

tions in the quantities of grave goods in different burials. It seems likely that this is so, however. The looters probably indiscriminately dug out burials and tossed the ceramics and lithics in the backdirt next to their holes. Although we cannot make a one-to-one correlation of materials with any particular grave, the artifacts collected around any one hole probably approximate the nonperishable grave goods of one or two burials, excluding gold jewelry and perhaps one or two fine, relatively intact pottery vessels. Fine examples of stonework might also have been taken. But the artifact groups we recovered and identified generally do seem to confirm that there were distinctions in the artifact quantities and richness of grave lots. Retired *huaqueros* stated to Aida Blanco (personal communication) that some graves on the Panteón had only gold, some only ceramics, and some had both.

Interpreting the Panteón de La Reina

Because the Panteón de La Reina produced so much gold more than a century ago, we have a relatively early description of it. The explorer Henri Pittier first made a report after a visit in the late years of the nineteenth century, as previously mentioned. In 1907 Pedro Pérez Zeledón also discussed the Panteón de La Reina, describing it as "one of the richest cemeteries of the region" (Pérez Zeledón 1907–08: 16; translation by Quilter). In his recounting of his visit to the cemetery, he describes its form as a complex series of platforms or sections:

> It is of a unique construction: at the front it has three sections, one elevated in the center to 18.50 meters and two lateral sections at a lower level, each one at 7.50 meters (in height). The three sections have a base of more than 100 meters going to the north. The quadrangular construction is well squared and was defined on all sides by use of flat stones of the same oval shape laid on top of one another. In the main section there are three "orders" or lines of graves and in the two lateral sections two "orders" in each. The ridge top was cut and excavated to produce a single horizontal plane and then refilled to produce the three defined horizontal levels. The remains (*cadáveres*) were deposited facing to the east. (Pérez Zeledón 1907–08: 28; translation by Quilter)

Pérez Zeledón seems to imply that there was some sort of terracelike system, with the highest terrace in the middle and two lower ones on either side. He also states that there were stone walls separating these different cemetery areas. Presumably the use of the term "*cadávares*" refers to the state of the burials when they were placed in the grave and is not a reference to any sort of preservation of human remains. Still, the reference to the position of the burials suggests that some human remains were unearthed. Given the great numbers of burials excavated, perhaps enough had been uncovered to establish a general orientation of corpses in graves.

We searched for land modifications as described by Pérez Zeledón, but we did not find them in the entire 2-kilometer length of the Panteón from its tip to where the road from Rivas crosses the ridge. The terraces he describes are so distinct that they would not disappear in a hundred years, nor would they be obscured by vegetation.

Some Chiriquí cemeteries in the region are known to have walls, such as a ridge-top cemetery called El Chiricano, near the town of El Cajón farther downriver and which Pérez Zeledón (1907–08: 28) stated was the second most important cemetery in the region (see fig. 1.1). He described it as consisting of an area 80 meters long by 40 meters wide, with a perimeter wall .75 to 1.5 meters in height. He also noted that the wall at El Chiricano resembled the one at La Reina.

On a visit to the Chiricano site we saw the remnants of a wall that probably was the same one described by Pérez Zeledón. It was made of river cobbles of about the same lunch-plate sizes as our features at Rivas. The cobbles had been arranged to form a low retaining wall that matched Pérez Zeledón's description in its height, and it was elliptical in shape. Interestingly, one of our local guides was another "reformed" *huaquero* (looter), and he stated that there had been burials outside of the wall as well as inside. He said that outside the wall only small gold objects had been found in graves, while inside the wall gold objects were larger in size and more plentiful in graves.

If walls once defined cemetery areas on the Panteón de La Reina, we did not find them, particularly in the Panteón Sur, where we spent most of our time. There may be other ways to interpret Pérez Zeledón's statement, however. It may be that he came across the top of the Panteón stairs and was referring to the cobble arrangements there, though this seems unlikely. But it is also true that we found the upper part of the stairs before we found the section on the slope, and we, too, were under the impression, at first, that this was some kind of structure. Indeed, it is not altogether clear whether the stairs are or are not modified to create a kind of series of flat, terracelike areas at the very top of the Panteón. This possibility seems unlikely, however, because Pérez Zeledón gives exact measurements of the feature he found, and these do not conform to the top of the Panteón stairs.

Another possibility is that Pérez Zeledón was somehow referring to the large divisions we noticed of the Panteón Sur, the vacant area, and the Panteón Norte. Perhaps there had been stone walls defining these boundaries, which were easily dismantled for local building efforts between the time of his visit and our work. Again, his description is too specific and detailed to refer to the general features we observed.

A third possibility is that Pérez Zeledón is referring to some other part of the Panteón that we did not visit. The evidence suggests that graves extend very far up the ridge. We do know that much higher up there is an earlier site, possibly Aguas Buenas in date. Perhaps he saw some structure in this or another locale, or he may have misinterpreted secondary natural terraces that occur on the ridge-top area itself. In some areas the ridge is quite flat, while in others steep clifflike areas lead to other, lower, secondary terraces.

A fourth possibility is that looting has been so intensive on the Panteón de La Reina that all traces of the structures have been churned up by *huaqueros*. This seems unlikely because if there had been terraces and retaining walls, at least one local person should have remembered seeing them or have been told of them by a grandparent. A couple of our workers did mention, vaguely, that they had seen walls. Still, while the looting was intensive and extensive, the very distinct forms described by Pérez Zeledón should have survived long enough for someone to have recalled them fairly well. No one had done so.

Finally, perhaps Pérez Zeledón refers to some ridge-top cemetery other than the Panteón de La Reina, even though he gives the correct site location. There are many ways in which this confusion could have occurred, such as his mixing his field notes when he returned home and such. Personally, I tend to favor this explanation or the fourth one, that any traces have been obliterated.

In addition to the distribution of looter holes, the location of the pillars on the Panteón may help in understanding the organization of cemeteries there. We found a total of nine pillars. Pillars, like the famous stone balls farther south in the Diquís Delta, have commonly been thought to be cemetery markers. Buenos Aires appears to be the point south and east of which stone balls were popular and north and (perhaps) west of which pillars were employed in sacred places (Drolet 1992: 232). Just as research in the Diquís Delta suggests that stone balls may have had a wider role as markers of important places or spaces (Fernández and Quintanilla 2003), the same seems true for pillars, as we found them in OpD '94, where no graves were located. It seems safe to suggest, however, since we found no pillars anywhere else at the Rivas site, that they marked important places closely related to mortuary ritual in general—perhaps highly sacred places, the most common of which were cemeteries.

The sources of the stone for pillars are places where volcanic magma was extruded into distinct shapes of columnar basalt. The specific locales are yet to be identified, but they were not nearby, indicating that much labor was invested in going to the quarry, selecting the right pillars, and carrying them back to a cemetery or ceremonial site. This fact also suggests that bigger pillars likely indicate higher-status individuals or groups, on the assumption that the greater labor invested in procuring them was proportional to the status of the deceased. Occasionally, pillarlike-shaped boulders can be found in streambeds, and there are plenty of rocks in them, so that the rivers may have been another source for pillars. But there are so many pillars in the general region of the upper General Valley that it is likely that there was a specific source of columnar basalt.

Our examination of pillars at the site, particularly studies done by Jeff Frost, indicated that most are in their natural forms with only slight modification to their surfaces. A few have been modified substantially. We have not been able to weigh many pillars, but a small one, of about a meter in length, weighed well over 45 kilograms. It must have taken a very great effort, probably by several people, to find a pillar and then transport it many kilometers to a ridge-top cemetery, and those pillars more than a meter in length would have been a considerable challenge to carry long distances.

Many stone balls have been removed from their archaeological contexts to grace the lawns of private homes and public places in modern Costa Rica. The pillars are less impressive than the balls, perhaps, in that they are not as highly transformed from the appearance of having been made by nature to having been culturally manipulated. Although a few pillars have made their way to public spots, such as the main plaza in San Isidro, many probably lie close to where they were originally erected. It may be that the pillars on the Panteón de La Reina have moved several meters as *huaqueros* pushed them out of their way in order to sack ancient graves. It is doubtful, however, that pillars were moved very far because investing energy in such activities would have detracted the looters from finding gold.

We can thus infer that the locations of the pillars in the Panteón cemetery areas approximate their original locations. Though perhaps moved slightly, their present locations are interesting because it appears that they were placed among groups of graves. An alternative explanation might be that pillars had been erected around the perimeters of cemetery areas. Of course, it is possible that pillars marked the edges of family plots or some other social division of the graves. The important point, though, is that they are close enough together and in proximity to former graves to indicate that the social units that erected them or which they marked by their presence were at a level below the cemetery population as a whole. These were not erected as a recognition of the community of the dead, much as a modern cemetery fence does, but rather for some smaller social unit. This is in the manner in which some families in Christian cemeteries place a large stone monument with the family name in the center of a cemetery plot, around which individual graves are placed with smaller headstones.

Although we could infer that burials were grouped in clusters judging from the pillars, it was much more difficult to investigate individual graves. The Panteón looters almost certainly excavated quite haphazardly, including tunneling from the bottom of one grave to another. They did not respect the outlines and shapes of graves or the cobble architecture above or in them. This method of excavation means that there was little preserved to study individual graves. It also means that there is no one-to-one correlation between the number of looter holes and the number of graves. But working with artifacts from backdirt piles as if they represented one or two burials can give us a rough idea of the kinds and approximate quantities of burial goods interred with the people buried on the ridge.

We screened the dirt next to 14 holes for the Panteón Sur and 8 for the Panteón Norte. As a whole, the Panteón artifact assemblage (table A3) is striking in its quantity and variety of materials compared to the materials in the Operation C and K cemeteries. For example, we encountered two separate instances of ground stone metate fragments on the Panteón, in LHs F and V, while there were no examples at Rivas. Stone tool fragments were more numerous, in general, on the ridge than in the Rivas cemeteries. Even though we cannot make accurate estimates of the numbers of pottery vessels per burial, the fact that hundreds of sherds were found in some Panteón backdirt piles suggests great numbers of ceramic offerings or very large vessels buried in graves. LH V is the richest of those studied, and if its burial assemblage is associated with a single or even three or four burials, it manifests a great wealth of grave goods, especially since it only is a partial representation of the total goods buried.

Even those areas with fewer artifact totals still show high diversity in the kinds of materials represented. We cannot necessarily assume, however, that those backdirt piles that contain few artifacts clearly indicate that the corresponding grave was similarly poor in grave goods. The materials may have been tossed to a different side of the looter hole, or perhaps it was one of the graves high in gold but low in ceramics. Overall, however, the fact that some piles were low in artifacts and others were high affirms the notion that there were differences in grave wealth between different graves and likely between family groups.

The Panteón assemblage includes fancy ware ceramics but also utilitarian vessels. This indicates that a suite of vessels was included in each grave. It also implies that, like the Rivas burials, each set of grave goods on the ridge likely represents the inventory of pottery used in the lifetime of the dead individual with whom it was associated, including everyday wares that held food. Whether some goods were added as offerings to the grave assemblage by family members or other individuals in any particular cemetery is hard to assess. But it appears that the ceramics are those that were used in the lives of the honored dead. So, too, none of the Panteón ceramics would be out of place if found at the Rivas site. But while any individual pot or sherd is interchangeable with Rivas materials, the consistent high number of fine-quality ceramics in the Panteón de La Reina graves is notable.

Overall, the Panteón graves appear to be richer in fine-quality wares than the Operation C burials and markedly richer than Operation K graves, which were notable in the paucity of fancy goods. These differences may be due to factors of sample size, but the overall impression is that the Panteón dead had more fancy goods placed in their graves than the people buried in the sites below. Some Rivas burials were fancier than some Panteón burials, though. Our inability to distinguish between the sexes and ages of the individuals represented in such cases makes it hard to more finely examine the possible meanings of such differences. For example, if males generally had higher status in Rivas society and if age conferred greater status, then we might expect an old man in Operation C or K to have more goods and fancier ones than a young woman buried on the Panteón might have.

If we could make such observations regarding age and sex of burials, we could know a lot more about the social system of ancient Rivas. For example, if young women or children who were buried on the Panteón did receive more and fancier goods than old men buried at the Rivas site, it might indicate that social ranking based upon inherited status in a clan or class was in operation. If that were the case, then we could infer that there were social strata representing a form or forms of social inequality and limited social mobility in operation in the ancient society.

The Panteón de La Reina was not an isolated phenomenon in many respects. First, it was associated, in some way, with the large-scale architecture at the site below. Second, perhaps there was some relationship between the two sectors of the Panteón and the cemeteries at Rivas, with a sector associated with one or more of the Rivas graveyards. Third, the Panteón was fabled as one of the richest ridge-top cemeteries in the region, but there are others similar to it, such as El Chiricano. Finally, ridge-top cemeteries are phenomena that came into existence at a particular time and place, and, eventually, the practice of burying people following these patterns ceased. The only comparable data available for considering some of these issues are the results of research by Bob Drolet and his team in and about the Muricélago site, with less extensive data available from other sources. We will examine this information and then return to the Panteón de La Reina and Rivas to compare them and discuss them in greater detail.

The Murciélago Cemeteries and Others

Bob Drolet (n.d.) conducted a site survey using the Murciélago site (P-107-MC) as a central point and radiating outward from it for a distance of 2 kilometers (fig. 6.4, top). By doing this he located a total of 23 new sites. These included an additional residential zone of Murciélago, several cemeteries located around the entire site, and a new site, Limón (P-249-Ln), with its associated cemeteries, 1.5 kilometers south of Murciélago. He identified clusters of cemeteries in what he defined as funeral zones. He encountered a total of eight such zones, two of which consisted of only a single cemetery and the rest with four to seven cemeteries each and covering between 1 and 6 hectares in area. Only two funerary zones were directly associated with the Murciélago site, however. The rest appear to have been associated with the Limón site and other sites farther away, some of which remain to be identified.

The cemeteries ranged between 250 to 700 meters from the Térraba River and between 560 and 1,100 meters from the Murciélago site. Most of them were about 500 to 700 meters from Murciélago. Sites also were commonly located on high points and plains close to the river or smaller *quebradas*, while others were close to residential areas. There was a high degree of variability for these cemeteries. Many had artificial mounds covered by river cobbles; others had no mounds but had elaborate pavements; still others had no distinguishing features other than graves with simple pavements above them. Most cemeteries were internally subdivided into burial clusters. A student working on Drolet's project, Ursula Iwaniec (1986), carried out a detailed investigation of such a Murciélago-related cluster in La Pista Cemetery (P-220-LP) (fig. 6.4, bot-

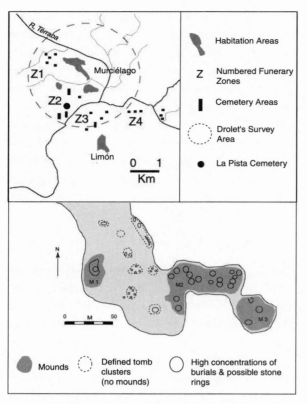

6.4. Top: The Drolet survey of cemeteries around the Murciélago site. Illustration courtesy of R. Drolet. Bottom: La Pista Cemetery. After Iwaniec 1986.

tom). This cemetery appeared to be midway in the range of funerary elaboration of these sites and was located about a kilometer from the Murciélago residential area. It had three mounds and 28 pavement clusters. Iwaniec excavated Cluster 15, selected because it had the least signs of looter disturbance.

Cluster 15 contained 16 burials. As noted earlier, there was no correlation between the surface cobble pavements and the graves themselves (Iwaniec 1986: 3), a pattern we also observed at Rivas. The bottom of the graves ranged between 60 and 200 centimeters in depth, again similar to Rivas. There was no clear orientation of the graves. It seems as if it was more important to cluster graves close together than to point the heads of the dead in one direction or another as is the case in some cultures.

Of the 16 burials, 4 had no grave goods, 5 contained a single grave offering, 4 interments yielded two grave goods, and a single tomb had three offerings. The most common grave good was a tripod jar, either of Panteón White Line (six examples) or Ceiba Red-Brown

(five examples) wares. Two globular jars were found, both of which were Ceiba Red-Brown. The only examples of Buenos Aires Polychrome were two figurines, each found in a grave with another artifact accompanying it. A metate was found as a single offering in one grave, and a polished cylindrical stone likewise was a lone offering in another grave.

Unlike Rivas, there were bone fragments in a few of these graves, thus allowing some inferences to be made regarding the age of the interments and their modes of burial. Four burials (6, 8, 12, and 15) appeared to have been in extended positions. Teeth in these graves suggest that two of the burials, at least, were adults. One burial, T3, appeared to be a child or youngster. Burials 14 and 16 may have been secondary remains, perhaps bundles of bones made after the flesh had decayed or been removed from cadavers. In addition to the bones and teeth, the sizes of graves might also indicate the age of death, though some smaller ones could have been for secondary burials. Six of the 16 graves were less than a meter in length. These had the greatest numbers of offerings. It may be, then, that young people or secondary burials were accorded more offerings than adults. Whether there was a positive correlation between the number of burial goods and age at death or other social statuses is hard to judge, especially if many valuable grave goods were made of perishable materials.

There may have been a great deal of variation in styles of cemeteries and forms of burial in the land of the Chiriquí. In the Caracol area on the Térraba River, there were seven cemeteries similar to those described for Murciélago and, like them, on lower-level terraces. They ranged in size from small sites, half a hectare or less, with relatively tightly packed burials, to others with burials in rows covering 4 to 7 hectares (Drolet 1984b: 260). One cemetery had two associated petroglyphs, while another had a large stone ball.

Drolet also describes a second class of cemetery for the region, restricted in size but more elaborate than the first type. They tend to be on second-level terraces, above both the other cemeteries and the habitation zones. Found at the sites of Curré, Caracol, Cola de Pato, Macho Monte, and San Andres, they have mound constructions and stone cist tombs (Drolet 1984b: 261). At Caracol (Drolet 1984b: 261 citing Haberland 1961b: 32–33), there were a series of rectangular mounds faced with straight-sided retaining walls with river cobbles and containing hundreds of tombs. Pillars were used at this site as was also the case at Finca Remolino, near the Ceibo River. Petroglyphs have been found at some such sites, and a stone ball was found on the south side of Finca Remolino. In addition to these, Haberland (1959b) and the Minellis (Laurenchich de Minelli and Minelli 1966) excavated mound cemeteries. The Minellis found more elaborate grave goods, including fancy ceramic types, gold, and small stone sculptures ("*sukia*" figures), than were encountered at La Pista. The excavators do not report stone pillars, large stone pavements, or other indications of great investments of labor other than that represented by grave goods.

The Minellis excavated at a funerary complex in the vicinity of San Vito de Java in southern Costa Rica at an altitude of 1,200 meters. This upland locale is similar to the location of Rivas and the Panteón, although San Vito is farther south, closer to Panama. The cemeteries were on a small hill overlooking a lagoon near a hamlet known as El Zoncho. The excavators identified four cemeteries, which they named El Zoncho A, B, C, and D. As usual, the graves had been looted extensively, but the investigators estimated that Cemetery A had 300 graves, C had about 150, and D only 20. Cemetery B also was large, but an estimation of the number of graves could not be made.

River cobbles were found inside graves, perhaps used in a manner similar to the *lajas* found immediately above the area of bodies at Rivas. Cobbles do not appear to have served as pavements, nor do the Minellis mention the presence of stone pillars. Apparently, burial was not done by placing the dead in clustered groups but rather in rows oriented east-west.

Despite the looting, the Minellis recovered a great number of artifacts. These included simple and elaborately carved metates, crude stone sculptures, adzes or celts, and a great quantity of pottery. They also reported that they found four examples of metal objects but provide no details on the specific contexts of them or of their characteristics. The metal objects were found in burials located in the center of Cemetery A. Some of the characteristics of recovered pottery suggest that this cemetery may date to a transition period between Aguas Buenas and Chiriquí.

What does the information from these other cemeteries contribute to our understanding of the Rivas and Panteón de La Reina cemeteries? The information about El Zoncho is of interest in its apparent early date and apparently quite different cemetery organization compared to La Reina and the Murciélago cemeteries. Although more early cemeteries need to be excavated to provide a good comparative sample, the change from a cemetery structure in which burials were aligned in rows to one in which they were clustered in groups may be of considerable significance.

Organization in nested sets is common at La Reina and the Murciélago sites: larger units contain smaller ones, each distinct from the higher order level of organization. For El Zoncho, sets are in evidence in the separate cemeteries on the hilltop. The significance of the rows of graves is hard to determine. The nested hierarchy at Murciélago, from highest to lowest, is: village complex, funerary zone, cemetery, cluster, grave. In trying to interpret the social equivalents of these archaeological remains, we can confidently equate the grave with an individual and, probably, the village complex with the community. The intermediary groups are more difficult to interpret because social categories can vary widely. Given the information we have for a burial cluster, it seems reasonable to suggest that each represents a family, probably an extended family of grandparents, parents, and children. Less certainly, a cemetery may represent an extended family over a period of many years.

Throughout the Americas, native people commonly organized themselves by dual divisions. The largest of these are sometimes referred to as moieties, in which all of society is divided into two groups. Often, these groups would also be divided in two, and sometimes there would be another division of the smaller groups. Drolet determined that only two funeral zones were directly related with Murciélago and, more clearly, that the site itself was divided into two different zones. It is tempting, therefore, to suggest that the funerary zones correspond to the habitation zones at the site.

The Murciélago residential complex consisted of two sectors with a total of 50 circular houses clustered into six groups. The southern sector is quite small, however, and was not investigated in detail. It may be a ceremonial precinct rather than a residence. Also, there is a problem of microchronology, as we can't be sure that all six groups were occupied simultaneously.

Perhaps one or more of the groups were established late in the life of the community as the population grew. Even with six residential units or more, they all could be accommodated by a dual social system with corresponding dual funeral areas. It may even be that where one was buried was not directly linked with where one resided in life.

After a moiety division, defined by the two major funeral zones, individual cemeteries may each represent a "house," as first proposed by Drolet (n.d.: 10). The concept of "house" here is not just in the literal sense of a structure but also in terms of a social unit (see Carsten and Hugh-Jones 1995). With diameters of 10 to 30 meters, it is likely that the round houses at Murciélago were occupied by a great number of nuclear families, all of whom were related by reference to common grandparents, uncles, aunts, and the like. These house kin groups may have been similar to the social groups in the large circular structures known as *malocas* in the Amazon. There, however, a single community occupies one large structure. At Murciélago, a number of *malocas* appear to have been clustered in different arrangements to support higher populations in a single locale. Together, the social groups in these houses probably saw themselves as descendants of a common ancestor: unity was stronger within the house than to more distant relatives in other houses. But the house social units, combined, could reference themselves to one another by claims of links between the ancestors, who each house kin group considered as its founder in a system known as segmentery lineages. Below the level of the house, a more closely related family group, probably nuclear families with occasional sisters, brothers, and other kin, may have been defined and was expressed in the clusters of burials. Finally, the individual was marked by his or her own grave.

Interpreting the social organization from the Murciélago cemetery data as I have done offers explanations as to why some cemeteries had many graves and others fewer. Through time, some house kin groups were more successful than others in community politics. In nonindustrial societies, one of the main routes to prosperity is to produce more offspring who can take care of the elderly, grow more food, engage in more trade and crafts, and otherwise increase the reputation and importance of the group. For a variety of reasons, some houses did poorly and left only a few of

their dead before the line died out or merged into another group, while other houses did well, producing many descendants who eventually found their way to the cemeteries of their house group ancestors.

Another problem in interpreting the arrangements of residential areas and cemeteries in the Murciélago region is the way in which funerary zones seem to cover all of the available landscape. If Murciélago and Limón were two separate communities, we might expect a kind of "no-man's-land" between their spheres of influence, but this is not the case. Perhaps there were boundaries that did not leave archaeological traces, or perhaps they are present but we contemporary archaeologists cannot see them. Another possibility is that either the Limón or Murciélago community was an offshoot of the other. Examples from many places in the world abound in which once a community reaches a certain size, a group of people decide to move to form a new community. Relations between the "parent" and "child" communities may vary from friendly to hostile, and, of course, over time, such relations may vary.

It is likely that such patterns occurred in Costa Rica. If part of a community did separate, the use of a system of dualism to maintain relations would be quite useful. In fact, such a dynamic might explain why the dualism in such systems is always slightly unequal or organized in what is called asymmetrical dualism. The moiety half with slightly greater status—often described as "higher" or "older"—probably was given to the original community, while the "child" community took on the role of "lower" or "younger." In the case of Murciélago and Limón, we may be seeing the archaeological traces of such a pattern. Murciélago appears to be the larger community, judging by its more extensive archaeological remains, and so it may have been the "parent." The apparent overlapping of funerary zones of the two sites may be due to the fact that both residential sites saw themselves as part of a larger system of organization. No distinct boundaries were maintained because of a sense of common community shared between the residents of Limón and Murciélago. A future study in which the two sites are carefully dated might help clarify the matter.

One striking feature of the Murciélago cemeteries is the fact that while there are so many of them and even more clusters and graves within them, nowhere on the landscape near the habitation site was there a ridge cemetery like the Panteón de La Reina. This suggests that there were significant differences between the way in which the people of Murciélago organized themselves and the organization of the people of Rivas. At Rivas, there appear to be only two residential zones and two distinct funerary zones. The residential zones are the architectural complexes of Operations D/E and A, and the funerary zones are the Panteón de La Reina and the Rivas terrace cemeteries. Since we never conducted an intensive survey around the Rivas site, as was done for Murciélago, we cannot be sure of the total number of non-Panteón cemeteries. We know of at least three, two of which we excavated. Compared to Murciélago, these cemeteries are rather simple, with no mounds or other elaborations; they have simple pavements over graves. On the ridge, there are two major divisions to the Panteón funerary zone, and there are clusters of graves within them, probably marked by pillars. If the *huaquero* was right, and there is no apparent reason why he would have told us an untruth, the ridge-top cemetery at El Chiricano also was divided in two, inside and outside the wall, with status differences marked by the size and, presumably, quantities of gold jewelry in graves. Located close to the river, perhaps the Murciélago inhabitants simply did not have a prominent ridge-top nearby on which to bury the elite of their community. Perhaps they marked social differences in ways that have not yet drawn the attention of archaeologists. But Drolet's study was quite thorough, and to date there do not appear to be any indications that suggest that one funerary zone or the other was as distinctive as the ridge-top cemeteries of El Chiricano and the Panteón de La Reina.

For the present, we must assume that the presence or absence of ridge-top cemeteries is a significant indicator of social differences between sites that have them and sites that do not and that the way in which people organized themselves was different in each, to some degree. Why, then, was the Rivas-Panteón complex organized on different principles than Murciélago? What do the differences imply for understanding the nature of chiefdom societies in the western Chiriquí culture region in late prehistory? We may not be able to answer these questions or even address them well. We did not do an intensive survey around Rivas, but we did get to know a lot about local sites and landscape features. Reviewing some of our observations

may be useful in more fully developing our understanding of the site, the Panteón de La Reina, and the times in which they were built and used.

Shaping Nature

What can we say about how the Rivas area appeared between about A.D. 900 and 1300? We can be fairly certain that the most imposing landforms we see today were present then. The Panteón de La Reina was there, used as a cemetery and jutting into the basinlike valley. The steep hills and mountains rose all around. The rivers ran down the valley, and the Río Chirripó del Pacífico may have been much closer to the site.

The Panteón was probably clear of trees. It would have been impossible to excavate graves if it had been as forested as it is today. The tropical forest on the ridge today appears to be climax vegetation but must have been reestablished in the thousand years, perhaps less, since the Panteón was in use as a graveyard. There may have been plantings on the ridge, however. It is very likely that there are relict trees and other plants on the Panteón summit continuing from its use as a cemetery, but we have not conducted a systematic search for them.

At the Rivas site itself, there was no coffee or bananas, of course. Again, much of the site area probably was devoid of significant vegetation but probably supported shade trees and perhaps small plots of fruit trees and other useful plants. Perhaps the guayabo grove of Operation A is a relict of some ancient grove used by the inhabitants for shade and fruit. Study of the pollen and phytoliths from the site by John Jones suggests that there were many grasses there, implying that the climate was wetter and that there were trees nearby, at least, to shade the ferns that also are in evidence.

Pedregales, Petroglyphs, and Piedras de Indio

One of the most curious aspects of interpreting the appearance of the Rivas site when it was occupied is the presence of concentrations of boulders in certain areas of the site. It is likely that the main areas of occupation were cleared of most boulders, and many were used in construction, but in many places boulders went unmoved. In Operation A, the Piedras Southeast apparently served as some kind of stela or monument, given the stone pavement placed around it, and the Operation B petroglyph may also have served a similar purpose.

Elsewhere at the site there were huge boulders left in place on the *ballena* that runs to intersect the northwestern side of the Operation E oval and the circular addition to it, on its western side. Farther north, large boulders of relatively uniform size were clearly placed on the western edge of the *ballena*, and there may be others covered by soil. Another area of the site with a large *ballena* and boulders scattered about is the "plaza," Complex IV. Tectonic activity alone cannot explain the presence of these boulder scatters, since they may have been moved several meters but are unlikely to have moved tens of meters. Apparently, the site occupants were perfectly comfortable to maintain quite organized and structured architectural features adjacent to piles of boulders in a way that seems hard to appreciate today.

In addition to the *ballenas*, there are rocky areas known in Spanish as *pedregales*. None are immediately next to occupation areas, but it is interesting to reflect on how such areas were incorporated into the inhabitants' perspective of their site. In many other parts of southern Costa Rica, such areas are filled with petroglyphs, commonly of the spiral and circle varieties such as we discovered in Operations A and B. In Quebradas, the valley adjacent to the upper General Valley, there are many petroglyphs. Down-valley, at Finca Longo Mai, about halfway from San Isidro to Buenos Aires, hectares of land are filled with isolated boulders and clusters of them with elaborate carvings.

It is unclear why some *pedregales* are laden with rock carvings while others are not. Aida Blanco, who is conducting a long-term study of petroglyphs in the Southern Zone, suggests that the recent and rapid deforestation of the region has played a role in this patterning. In areas that have been cleared of trees and tall grasses that protect the carvings, the petroglyphs are exposed to rapid deterioration through cycles of rain and sun, as we saw in the case of the Operation B petroglyph.

It thus may be that many of the boulders that we walked by every day had borne petroglyphs in the past. In Complex II of Operation D, I once thought I could trace a remnant of a spiral carving, but the traces were so faint that I could not be certain. It is extremely difficult to know how petroglyphs were patterned in the

landscape or how sites such as Rivas were marked by them. Aida Blanco's project to record as many petroglyphs as possible before they vanish from the region due to deforestation is thus extremely important. Were the petroglyphs incorporated into a ceremonial site, or were petroglyphs only placed in areas away from settlements? Perhaps petroglyphs were carved by people on vision quests that required leaving the familiarity of a community and awaiting a vision in some unfamiliar place. The carving might have been a mark on the landscape that an individual had received such a vision.

The fact that petroglyphs are carved on rocks is so basic and obvious that it is easy to overlook the potential significance of the act of making an inscription on a stone. We live in a world of material things that do not easily go away. Even in poor countries in tropical climes, garbage heaps grow bigger every day. But a thousand years ago, most of the constructs and residues of human life were evanescent in tropical America. Objects of cloth, wood, calabashes, shell, and bone all disintegrated with the passing of a few rainy seasons unless great pains were taken to preserve them. Only the stone foundations of structures and the broken bits of pottery from last night's fiesta had staying power. Even these were only partial remnants of formerly complete things, for a house needed a roof and thatch to be a house, and ceramic sherds were mostly useless except to rework as spindle whorls or pottery tools. But a petroglyph, carved deep into a rock, held a mystical aura of longevity. While today exposure in open fields quickly fragments the surface of a rock, erasing a thousand-year-old carving in a year, a petroglyph carved into a rock under the forest canopy might be visited and revisited for many lifetimes.

The concepts connected to petroglyphs are hard to imagine, whether they are records of spirit roads or trance visions. What we can say, however, is that these markings endured, and their ability to remain relatively constant while everything around them changed may have been a key aspect of their significance to those who made or later saw them. The spiral forms of petroglyphs of southern Costa Rica are common, worldwide, and associated with visions seen in trances. It is possible that they were carved for centuries before late prehistory. Their association with late period sites, however, suggests that the religious complex associated with their making was a relatively late prehistoric

6.5. The Piedra del Indio. View toward magnetic northeast, up-valley.

phenomenon, and there appear to be no precedents for them in the region. While it is also a supposition, the great number of them in the General Valley implies that many people may have participated in whatever cult practices included inscribing spirals in stone. This, in turn, suggests that at least one component of religious activities in late prehistoric Costa Rica involved relatively individualistic actions in which a person expressed a religious sentiment by making a permanent mark on the landscape. This interaction with rocks as significant landscape features found other expressions in the form of Piedras del Indio and in the use of stone pillars at sacred sites.

There are many large boulders in Costa Rica known as Piedras del Indio. We encountered our first one as we drove to the Rivas site in the upper General Valley. The Piedra del Indio is a sculpture, though it appears "natural" in form at first glance (fig. 6.5). It sits on the edge of the ridge by the modern highway between San Isidro and Rivas. Its name was given to it by local people, not by us. The stone measures 6.3 x 5.2 meters, stands about 2 meters high, and is oriented roughly on the same axis as the ridge and valley. The monument is

shaped something like an aircraft carrier: there is a large flat area on the side facing the valley and then a high ridge along the other side.

Local people commonly point out that the silhouette of the ridge on the Piedra del Indio conforms to the line of the ridge of the hills in the distance. This is true. In fact, the form of the distant mountains is maintained in two completely different views. If one stands perpendicular to the long axis of the stone, to its east, and looks west, the silhouette and distant ridge on the far side of the Quebradas conform quite closely. Similarly, looking from down-valley to up-valley, northward, along the long axis of the Piedra, produces a similar result. If the Piedra del Indio has weathered more rapidly than the surrounding hills, the conformity may have been even closer in ancient times.

The Piedra del Indio shows numerous signs of human modification. The most obvious are circular holes located in places on its upper surface that make no clear sense to modern understandings. Perhaps they denote sacred springs on a three-dimensional map of the region. The highest part of the Piedra has scalloped sides replicating the effect of erosion of moun-

6.6. The Piedrón del Indio. The indentation in the lower center of the rock, as seen in this view, overhangs a natural spring. The spiral petroglyph is on the other side of the boulder.

tain peaks. Presumably, these concavities are also due to the work of ancient carvers. To what extent the stone has been modified from its original form is hard to determine. It is unlikely that this huge rock was moved into place, and it probably has been in this location since early in the geologic history of the valley.

We had visited the Piedra del Indio several times. Although we agreed that the holes were made by humans, we were uncertain how much of the rest of the stone had been modified. It was only after three or four visits, however, that we realized that the rock was undercut at its base, making it look as if it were resting lightly on the ground. This undercutting is unlikely to have occurred through the agency of natural forces because it is uniform around the base of the stone, whereas we might expect differential undercutting if it had been produced through erosion. The final proof that this was indeed a stone of importance to ancient people was found when we discovered a cobble stone ring around the base of the stone. This was a sure sign

of human activity that perhaps served to increase the sanctity of the stone. If the cult of Piedras del Indio is somehow related to petroglyphs, then the presence of this cobble ring might lend support to the traces of what appeared to be some kind of cobble pavement at the base of the large petroglyph stone in Operation B and the apparent significance of the pillarlike Piedras SE in Operation A.

A few years into the project, we visited the Piedra del Indio to show it to some visitors to our project. A young man came from out of the coffee field, across the road, and said, "This isn't the Piedra del Indio. The Piedra del Indio is over there." We followed him through the coffee plants into a *finca* that was being developed as a kind of working farm for tourists. Down the slope off of the ridge, about 30 meters, we came across a large flat area with an immense boulder the size of a house (fig. 6.6). I remarked that this was not the Piedra del Indio but the Piedron, the "-on" ending used in Spanish to mean "big."

This boulder was positioned as if it were diving into the ground or rising from it. From the southeastern side, the top edge of the boulder appeared to be scalloped. On the other side, this huge stone resembled the Piedra del Indio in possessing a large flat area. Jeff Frost, who was a member of our group, was the first to notice that in the middle of this space there was a neatly carved spiral. Walking around to the southwestern end of the boulder, we came across a beautiful sight. The boulder here rose up from its base, jutting out at a steep angle. Beneath the overhanging rock there was a small spring of water that formed a pool. The potential for interpreting this rock as a sacred site was not hard to understand.

We found another Piedra del Indio while working on the Panteón de La Reina in 1998. The top of the Panteón is not as narrow as it appears from the ground. In certain places, at least, there are old terraces formed by the river when this land was the surface of the earth. In the area we called the Panteón Norte, there is one such terrace on the western side. It is here that we found another large stone similar in shape and size, though not identical, to the first Piedra del Indio we studied. It was in fairly dense vegetation and our attention was elsewhere, so we could only measure its general dimensions, which were similar to those of our first Piedra del Indio. There certainly must be many more such large stones throughout the region.

From a geological perspective, these Piedras del Indio are simply isolated large examples of andesite boulders found throughout the region. Was every one of them considered something special? Until a thorough study of them is undertaken, we cannot answer this question. I would speculate that all such large stones appearing to stand alone may have been viewed as having special significance and power, but some may have been seen as more powerful or important than others.

Unlike European megaliths, these great stones probably were not dragged into place but were discovered in their locations. This, admittedly, is a supposition. If the ancient Costa Ricans had wanted to move huge stones they could have done so, but my impression is that these stones were found in place. The people who built Stonehenge and Carnac took natural rocks and made them do unnatural things, rising out of the ground where they do not belong. The ancient Costa Ricans did something different. They took a huge stone, in situ, and modified it to make it appear peculiarly natural. If the shaping of large rocks to mimic the landscape holds true for other cases, it opens a window into the minds of these ancient people in pointing to their interest in creating a resonance between microcosms and macrocosms and being acutely aware and appreciative of scalar values. The builders of Stonehenge, in one sense, created a cosmic center. The people who made Piedras del Indio appear to have found a place of spiritual power that they then enhanced or, through carving, brought out its true nature.

If this interpretation has merit for Piedras del Indio the size of the one on the San Isidro–Rivas road, how it relates to larger examples or, perhaps, to petroglyphs is uncertain. The very large boulder nearby may be related to different concepts associated with water and fertility. The fact that a spiral petroglyph was carved on it may indicate that these designs were associated with similar symbolism, and it is interesting that there are no traces of such spirals on the other Piedras del Indio we have seen. Of course, perhaps spirals on the other boulders have eroded over time. There may have been different ideas about the nature and importance of different large boulders, with some having different pedigrees and importance than others.

It is certain that throughout the native cultures of the New World, large rocks that attract attention usually have some special stories connected with them. It is interesting to consider that the elaboration of the Piedras del Indio bears a marked resemblance to the ways boulders are treated in the Andes. The Inca and their ancestors were master stonemasons, moving and carving great stones with skills that still astound contemporary visitors. Nevertheless, some of the most sacred stones in the Central Andes were those that had unusual forms or were found in impressive locations. These were sometimes left untouched by the hand of stonemasons but viewed as sacred; they were commonly thought of as heroic ancestors. Elsewhere, such as the site of Qenqo outside of Cuzco, Peru, they were elaborated by carving on their surfaces and even modifying of parts of their interiors while their basic forms were left unchanged. This sensibility seems to have been shared in the Rivas area and is another testament to the South American ties of the culture of its ancient inhabitants.

Although the Piedra del Indio by the road presumably was in its location due to chance, we attempted to determine if it could have been seen from the Rivas site. This was hard to do because vegetation today obscures the view. Our best estimates indicate that it could indeed have been seen from the site, especially from the Operation D area. We wondered how the stone might have related to the site. If vegetation had been cleared in the past, the stone might very well have served as some kind of marker. Perhaps it denoted the limits of the region of influence, or it may have served as some kind of ceremonial way station —perhaps something like a roadside shrine—to people traveling up-valley. It certainly would have been a signal that the Piedrón was nearby, and since this larger stone is completely invisible from the site and from the valley, it could have served as a guidepost to visit that more impressive stone. It also bears consideration that, as in their shared approach to standing stones, this part of Central America and the Andes appear to have shared notions of dualism. The chance propinquity of two Piedras del Indio, one on either side of the valley ridge where the highway now runs, may have increased the sacrality of this part of the valley. The fact that one boulder is huge and the other even bigger fits nicely with concepts of asymmetrical dualism.

Whereas petroglyphs require an individual to step outside of the envelope of culture to make a mark on the natural world, pillars represent the opposite action, bringing a piece of nature inside the bounds of culture. We do not know how a particular stone or *pedregal* was selected to be the site of a petroglyph. We can know, however, that finding a stone suitable for a pillar would have taken a great deal of time. I have already mentioned that the sources of stone pillars probably were far away at places where geological conditions produced columnar rock formations, while another source may have been river boulders. When found, it must have required the efforts of many people to lift and carry the pillar to its final resting place. It would have been a long haul to the top of the Panteón de La Reina, no matter where the sources of the pillars were located.

Of the pillars we have examined, most have very little evidence of modification. There may have been some slight trimming and grinding to make them thinner, although there was no attempt to make them perfectly smooth and uniform in shape or cross section. Perhaps when no stones wholly shaped by nature were found, one that was close to form could be selected and slightly modified, but the "natural" shape of the stone was maintained. These were special stones, rare among other stones, and created by nonhuman forces.

Pillars marked special places, such as the ceremonial platform of the False Cemetery in Operation D, but all appear to have been associated with places of the dead ancestors. The evidence also suggests that a pillar marked a place, perhaps a central place, of a group of burials, likely a group of graves containing the remains of family or other kin-group members.

Standing stones are found over a wide area of the ancient world and in the Americas took forms as stelae among the Maya and as *wankas* among the Inca of Peru. Their use in southern Costa Rica appears to be in the upper General Valley, ending somewhere in the vicinity of Buenos Aires, after which stone balls seem to have been favored instead of pillars. Among the Maya, stelae were carved with depictions of living rulers and remained in place as memorials to them after the living had passed into the underworld. In the Andes, some standing stones were thought to be the ancestors themselves, transformed into the enduring substance of stone.

We do not know the specific ideological complex that was associated with pillars among the ancient inhabitants of the upper General Valley. It is likely that some sense of permanence and remembrance, as was the case with so many stones in so many distant places, was part of the belief system that caused them to be found and erected in parts of Pacific Costa Rica. If petroglyphs were singular acts made by those on vision quests, venturing beyond the bounds of security into a liminal state and literally making their mark on the world, pillars were the opposite. They were retrieved by the group for the group, incorporating a (super)natural object into the cultural realm and repositioning it in the culturally created liminal setting of the cemetery or sacred precinct. Pillars may have been particularly appropriate for cemeteries because, in the highly charged sacred grounds of the graveyard, the interplay of nature and culture is most powerfully in action. Once-living members of the community were integrated back into the natural medium of the earth but at the same time took on the supracultural role of revered ancestors.

Roads and Entries

Although the Piedra del Indio might have served as a guidepost on the landscape, the route next to which it lies probably was not used in ancient times to enter Rivas. The stone certainly could have served to guide travelers across the grain of the landscape, though, if one wished to travel from the Chirripó valley to the Quebredas valley, beyond.

A good route once found is rarely abandoned. Judging from the account of Alexander Skutch (1991) and other early visitors to the region, the old path out of the mountains passed by Rivas and then cut diagonally across to the southeastern side of the valley to General Viejo. From there, the road entered the large General Valley, swinging farther east. This would have been the most economical route to take the foot traveler to the next big Chiriquí sites known for the region, El Chiricano, Las Brisas, and Pacuar, the latter, like Rivas, located at the junction of two rivers. It seems likely that this is an ancient route, and it was probably used at the time Rivas was occupied.

The Chirripó del Pacífico River is unnavigable here due to large rocks, and the river probably was of little use for all but the shallowest draft canoes or rafts, and only at certain times of the year, in most of the valley above Pacuar. Today, the river crossing to El General, while spanned by a modern bridge, is next to a large island. Either a rope bridge spanning the space of the modern bridge or some other construction that took advantage of the solid ground provided by the island may have served to cross the river in ancient times. In 1992 we made a brief reconnaissance of the island and found some evidence of Chiriquí phase presence there, including a possible stone platform. Rivers can vary from slow, low streams in the dry season to raging torrents in the wet season, and they can change from one to the other quite suddenly. It is thus likely that some kinds of bridges were in use in ancient times in Costa Rica.

Along the modern Rivas–General Viejo gravel road there are houses that are mostly occupied by members of the Mata family. Behind them, to the north, is a mixture of overgrown coffee fields and dense second-ary growth. This area is about 250 meters long from Operation D, through this area, to the river, and we had little time to explore it in detail. There are no signs of large-scale architecture southwest (Grid South) of Structure III in Operation D, however, although there is a low-status cemetery on the property of a member of the Mata family directly across the Rivas–General Viejo road. No detailed studies have been made beyond this cemetery, but there are no obvious signs of large-scale architecture proceeding on a straight line farther south. There do appear to be large-scale structures behind the houses on the north side of the road, following in the same direction toward the river. The Rivas site may thus extend well beyond the area in which we worked, and it is likely that this southeastern area, toward the river, was the entry point for people visiting the site from lower in the General Valley.

On the northern side of the large-scale architecture, a possible entry is also in evidence. The line of stones running below the Operation A terrace and on the west side of Operation E (see fig. 2.2) seems best interpreted as a symbolic boundary defining one side of the large-scale ceremonial architecture. One of the *ballenas* at the site runs parallel to this line, and, as noted before, a large line of boulders is on the western side of this mound. On the other side of the *ballena* there is large-scale architecture, but although they are of grand dimensions, the structures are made of small cobbles. Proceeding southward, the architecture is composed of cobbles of greater size. This long bounded space, with no architecture in it, might be interpreted as a ceremonial entryway for those entering the site from the north. Perhaps those visitors who came from across the mountains, from the Central Valley and Atlantic Watershed regions, entered the site along this route.

How would people who came to the site have interacted with the built spaces there? One striking aspect of the large-scale architecture is the lack of a clear sense of organization. Even if there are other big structures we have not identified, we have found more than 15 circular structures, the exact number depending on how one distinguishes between patios and circles, and organizational patterning of them might be expected to be in evidence. While the plan of the site may elude us, in many other cultures axial lines and symmetry are clearly in evidence for such architectural complexes. The only pattern clear in the Rivas ceremonial area is the orientation of patios toward the Panteón stairs or, more likely, toward the cemetery on the ridge-top.

The other clear pattern is that most of the structures are built on the model of a house. There is no clear explanation as to why some structures are completely circular with no patios, losing the similarity to houses, though. We must take into account remodeling of structures, but some clearly were made with no patios. In addition, there are some structures with dark black soils in their interiors, others with orange soil, still others with *rípio*. Is there any functional difference we may infer due to these differences? We found no post molds in the structures, suggesting that walls and roofs were made by supporting slanting poles—like a tipi—wedged next to or into the circles of stones. Some structures are huge, and it is hard to interpret how they could have been roofed at all. We are thus faced with a number of questions about the structures, ranging from basic issues of construction to interpretations of use, none of which is easily answered.

Our work in Operation A identified a small circular structure with a patio and two small circular structures much less well made, nearby. This may be a residence consisting of a main house and adjacent outbuildings, either for children and their spouses and families or some other form of extended family arrangement. Alternatively, the structures could be for different functions of one household group, such as cooking and storage in the secondary structures. Although no metates were clearly in evidence, a distinctive pottery inventory somewhat strenghtens the argument that the structures were basically domestic in nature. While I might continue these speculations indefinitely, the strongest argument to make from the available evidence is that the circular structures with patios were of more importance than nearby circular structures that appear to have served ancillary roles to what occurred in the circles with patios.

Why were patios built on some circular structures? Perhaps the circle and the patio had different symbolic values, different functions, or both. It appears that the ideal patio was made in a quadrangular shape. Structure 1 in Operation A and Complex III in Operation D both appear to have been made as planned structures, neither reutilizing older architecture nor adding much to them during their use lives. In both cases, the patios are sharply quadrangular, whereas in Operation E, for example, old circles appear to have been reworked into patios. The large patio between Complexes I and II is quadrangular also, although a somewhat rounded smaller patio is between it and Complex I.

The circle and its adjacent quadrangle likely had different symbolic values. Since spaces are used we can infer that different activities also with different symbolic ties took place in the quadrangle and circle. In many places in the New World, the circle and square play different roles in rituals. In early Peru (see Quilter 1991), the circle is the more ancient form. In temple complexes, sunken circular rooms, resembling the kivas of the American Southwest, have been interpreted as sites of gatherings that emphasized relative equality among the participants, calling upon primeval sentiments of solidarity in the circle around a central hearth. In contrast, quadrangular structures evoke feelings of hierarchy and opposition. In a circle, all can be equidistant from the center, whereas in a quadrangle, groups must literally "take sides."

Patios, by their very nature, are projections out from the equality of the circle toward a larger world. Drawing upon the fundamental properties of these shapes as well as the Peruvian example, it may be reasonable to argue that the quadrangles were where the social group presented itself to outsiders, just like the front porch of a modern American home. Thus these spaces may be where public presentations of the group of the circle were made, in a space still linked to the particular social unit but presented to a larger public. Hopes that these distinctions might be in evidence in differing kinds of artifacts or percentages of them have not been realized in our analyses.

Houses at Murciélago did not exhibit patios. Either patios are a distinctive feature of houses in the upper General River Valley or they are specialized features for houselike structures used for mortuary rituals. The extent of research in the region is so little that this question cannot be answered at present. The fact that there were a great number of fancy objects in Operation A and an absence of metates suggests that although the main structure is small, it, too, may have been a site for funerary rites. Let us move from the issue of patios, then, by stating that it may be reasonable to suggest that the patios served as places to hold mortuary rites. Furthermore, these rites likely were the first public ceremony probably succeeded by some ritual on the upper terrace platform (the False Cemetery) and eventual burial on the Panteón de La Reina.

The upper General Valley of today and that of a thousand years ago are very different places. The Spanish came to Costa Rica halfway between those two points in time. Many years after the fall of Tenochtítlan, far to the north, they penetrated into southern Costa Rica for a brief while and then left. It seems that whatever tremors ran through the local populations, whether the decimation of numbers by disease, the shaking of faith by foreign gods, or the secondary disruptions that either or both of these might have caused, life settled back into something resembling earlier ways.

We do not yet have a clear idea of how forested the valley was at the time that Rivas was a place of renown. The circles, plazas, and ridge-top must have been cleared of tall vegetation, though a few shade trees may have been left in place. At the time of the Spanish arrival, *pejibaye* (peach palm) trees, with their trunks filled with spikes, rimmed the perimeters of some settlements for defense. There is a single *pejibaye* tree at the site, and Rivas is not a location where it grows naturally, hinting that it may be a relict from previous cultivation. Except for this tantalizing single example—and it or its ancestors could have been planted at any time in the thousand years since the site was abandoned— there is no evidence of remnant vegetation that might suggest Rivas was protected from intrusion. In fact, all of the evidence indicates that Rivas was open and inviting for people to visit from far away. Although weapons may have been made from perishable materials, there are few signs of warfare at Rivas except for the single example of a human head ocarina from the Operation C cemetery (see fig. 2.16). Rivas either was a place of sanctuary from interethnic disputes or it was occupied at a time of relative peace.

The most striking aspect of the site is the way it appears, to our eyes, at least, to mix natural landforms with geometric human constructions in a pattern that is not wholly "natural" or completely "artificial" in the way in which we think of these terms. The site was re-worked and rebuilt a number of times, so the palimpsest of building phases may obscure ordered construction from our eyes. Nevertheless, the overall impression is one of architectural planning in relation to the landscape that neither fully integrates human construction into the natural world nor fully imposes the architectural plan on top of what nature offers in the place where roofs were raised and dance floors demarcated. What was most important, apparently, for the ceremonial center was the orientation of the structures to the Panteón de La Reina cemeteries—that and a belief that activities of those below its ridge were in harmony with the realities conceived to be expressed in the rites and obsequies carried out in regard to the living and the deceased ancestors.

If we now consider the proposition that the site lacks an overall plan and that the circles and patios served as sites for mortuary practice, this leads us to another inference. Mortuary ritual at Rivas was not based on a grand program that utilized the entire complex but rather on a number of specialized points of activity. Instead of a papal mass at St. Peter's Cathedral, Rivas may have served to support a number of separate rituals in separate chapels. At this point, the archaeological data fail us in going further. It is quite possible that extended families, "houses," or some other social units were pulled into a common experience after some ritual phase occurred in individual structures. Such rites of solidarity could have taken place in the large oval dance ground in Operation E and on the False Cemetery below the stairs. What the social dynamics and rituals were that emphasized the autonomy of separate social units or, alternatively, the fusing of these units into a larger whole cannot be interpreted from the evidence we have at present.

Let us now turn from a macroview to a microview, in the next chapter, looking at the artifacts and other remains we found. Then, in the concluding chapter, I will try and integrate these various strands of information into a whole, including drawing upon ethnographic accounts of the peoples of the greater region.

CHAPTER SEVEN

THE ARTIFACTS

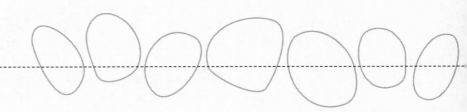

Our Changing Perspectives on the Site:
Rivas and Murciélago

When we walked down the slope of the Panteón de La Reina at the end of January 1998, we concluded our last major field season. One phase of our work had ended and another had begun. Our excavations were finished, and now we had to devote time and attention to interpreting the results of our digging and other investigations. Things are rarely black and white, though; we had been doing some lab work all along as well as making interpretations as the work proceeded. We also have since been back to the site numerous times to check details of our maps and to reacquaint ourselves with various aspects of our work. But it was only after excavations halted that we could devote the time to study the artifacts and other information in detail and to attempt to interpret these material fragments of the past to reveal something about the people who made and used these objects when they were whole and complete. While we continued to visit the site and our friends there, we were in a different phase of research in which we had to turn our raw data—pot sherds,

lithic debris, maps, photographs, and other materials —into information that we then had to examine to interpret past human behavior.

Our intention was to understand Rivas within the context of what was known about Chiriquí phase archaeology in southern Costa Rica and western Panama. We also wanted to see how the Rivas site and the society and culture it was a part of could be understood in light of theories of ranked societies or chiefdoms. Before we could attempt to address either of these issues, we had to have an understanding of what occurred at the Rivas site itself. Even in 1998, at the end of six years of study, we could not approach answering that question through our knowledge of artifacts, since they had not been studied in detail. We could start to attempt to formulate some ideas, however, by considering what we knew of the organization of the site. The size and locations of structures in relation to one another were avenues of investigation. This information, combined with our general knowledge of artifacts and their distributions, could give us some leads for more detailed investigations in the laboratory.

We had begun with the assumption that Rivas was

somewhat similar to Murciélago, the site that Bob Drolet had excavated. Bob had reported the possibility of quadrangular structures, but otherwise his estimation of the organization of Rivas was that it was generally similar to Murciélago. Through our research, we had been able to reinterpret Bob's view of quadrangular structures as the corners of large patios, particularly the northwestern corner of the patio on Complex III in Operation D. But we still were unclear about many things. For example, we thought that we had found a causeway projecting off of Complex I. Only later did we realize that this was a widened arm of a large patio. It could have served functions similar to a causeway, but it was not a structurally separate elevated walkway. In looking at what Bob had reported about Murciélago and what we had found at Rivas, however, it became clear that there were significant similarities but also many differences. Some of these already have been discussed in the previous chapter in regards to cemetery organization.

Drolet (1984b: 258) described Murciélago as covering 4 square kilometers on the valley bottom of the Térraba (lower General) River with six residential sectors within it, each ranging from 5 to 6 hectares in area. In two mapped residential sectors, he found circular cobble house foundations measuring 30–35 meters in diameter and in clusters of two to three units. Dense clusters of refuse pits and built-up piles of debris were around the cobble circles. Hundreds of manos and metates far outnumbered all other artifacts found around the houses, and there also was a variety of other tools, including those used to manufacture, maintain, and repair the grinding stones.

In his research, Bob found up to 30,000 sherds on the surface of the refuse deposits surrounding houses in a single residential sector at Murciélago. These included fragments of bowls, plates, and jar forms. Jars often had incised and punctated circular handles, and modeled frog heads formed handles on some. There was a homogenous range of ceramics dominated by Ceiba Red-Brown (fig. 7.1: 3, 4), with tiny amounts of Buenos Aires Polychrome (fig. 7.1: 1). For example, in Cluster A, Sector 1, there were 10,442 Ceiba sherds and 67 examples of Buenos Aires Polychrome. The greatest number of Buenos Aires Polychrome sherds was in House C, Sector 6, where there were 208, but they were still overwhelmingly outnumbered by Ceiba, which

had a total of 18,460 (Drolet 1992: 228, table 3). Bob suggested that the scarcity of Buenos Aires Polychrome sherds at the site might indicate that they were manufactured primarily for interment in cemeteries because they were common in such settings in the Murciélago complex.

At the southern end of the major habitation area, Bob identified Complex 4, containing the remains of structures of different sizes and shapes than the round residential ones. A causeway linked these structures to circular house structures in the same complex. The archaeologists also found a platform mound in another complex at the site (Complex 5) (Drolet 1984b: 258). Other nondomestic site components consisted of cemeteries, as already discussed.

How does Rivas compare with Murciélago in its general features as outlined above? If the Panteón de La Reina is included as part of the site complex and if the site area extends to Operation C, then Rivas is half the size of Murciélago, at about 2 square kilometers. If the Operation B area is considered the northern site limit, then Rivas is even smaller than Murciélago. But while Rivas is smaller in overall size, its ceremonial area is much larger and its residential area much smaller than at Murciélago. At the latter site, the ceremonial sector identified by Bob measured about 5,000 square meters in area. At Rivas, Operations D and E cover 60,000 square meters. So while Murciélago is mostly residential with a small ceremonial area, Rivas is mostly ceremonial with a small residential area. Also, Rivas has the Panteón de La Reina, with no comparable cemetery at Murciélago. The Murciélago cemeteries, however, are similar to Operations C and K at Rivas.

Size differences between the two sites are also manifest at lower levels of analysis. Six residential clusters at Murciélago contrast with two at Rivas: one is the assumed residence area incorporated in the architecture of Operations D and E and the other is the Operation A area. While our work at Rivas suggested house clusters consisted of two or three structures, like Murciélago, the houses in Operation A were small, about 10 or 11 meters in diameter at most. Even in the large-scale architectural zone, the largest circles are 20 to 25 meters in diameter. At Murciélago, diameters of 30 to 35 meters were frequent.

There are other differences. Bob noted the abundance of pits around the perimeters of houses, but we found few such pits at Rivas. There was a considerable amount of debris on the cobble perimeter walls and in the cobble pavements east of the Operation A circles, but there were no pits. At Murciélago, there were huge numbers of grinding stones and associated tools, but at Rivas we found very few. At Murciélago, there were very small amounts of Buenos Aires Polychrome, but at Rivas sherds of this type were abundant.

All of the differences suggest that very different activities occurred at Rivas and Murciélago. Some of the contributing factors may include the fact that Rivas is located high up in the valley, lacking adjacent high-quality agricultural land, whereas Murciélago was next to very fertile floodplains, where its inhabitants may have grown maize in surplus (Drolet 1992). Another factor may be that Murciélago appears to have been inhabited at a slightly later time than Rivas, though both are within the Chiriquí phase.

Understanding what happened at Rivas, why the site developed as it did and then was abandoned, requires a wider view than simply comparing it with Murciélago. We need to understand the site first in and of itself, then in the context of events in greater Chiriquí and from the perspective of southern Central America in general. In the following sections, I will review the state of knowledge we have on the internal chronology of the site and then examine other lines of evidence.

The Origins and Growth of the Rivas Site

A relatively small settlement was established on the upper terrace of the Rivas site sometime during the Aguas Buenas phase. We know this from the few examples of early sherds we found during the shovel test pit survey. Some of the black soil layers found behind the La Troja (see chapter 4) may have been formed by human agency during this early occupation, although we do not know this with certainty. The presence of ceramics in some of the layers at La Troja suggests a sedentary occupation, although we have not found traces of houses.

Based on the radiocarbon dates we have for the site (see appendix), sometime between A.D. 900 and 1000 the first Chiriquí settlement at Rivas occurred. As in the case of the earliest settlement, we do not know much about this occupation. Later construction trans-

formed the remains of the earlier settlement to such an extent that our excavations, though quite large in size, could not detect specific features of the first Chiriquí phase. We have indications that the earlier settlement was at least partly comprised of circular structures that likely were houses. Perhaps the plan of the site at that time was not too different than that of Murciélago, consisting of circular houses and cobble pavements where daily activities occurred. We have found evidence of circular structures both in the excavations in Operation D and in the interpretation of the large oval in Operation E. In Operation E, especially, we identified what appeared to be remnants of circles from an early site phase that were reworked into the later oval shape.

Sometime during the two- or three-hundred-year occupation of the site, it underwent a radical transformation. Some structures were modified, while others were deliberately buried with new constructions placed on top of them. Whether remodeling and burial were two separate events or part of a single reconstruction phase at the site is difficult to know with certainty. Although the general format of the architecture remained the same—a circular house form with a quadrangular patio—the area now called Operation D/E became a center of ritual activity, much of which was focused on funerary ceremonies. Old metates were reused in cobble construction. The residents of the site may have been supplied with food from outside, perhaps by people who came to participate in the rituals. The absence of metates and of storage pits stands in sharp contrast to the huge amounts of broken crockery scattered about the site. We do not know if the resident population was small or great, but the number of burials on the Panteón de La Reina suggests that the use of Rivas as a ceremonial center lasted for several generations.

Eventually, sometime between about A.D. 1250 and 1400, the political/religious system that had sustained Rivas and the Panteón de La Reina as a ceremonial complex was transformed into something else, resulting in the site falling into disuse. If a remnant population remained at the site, its presence cannot be separated and distinguished from the mass of material left during the heyday of the complex.

This narrative is a basic, unadorned interpretation of the history of the rise and fall of the Rivas–Panteón

TABLE 7.1. Distribution of Decorated Rim Sherds at the Rivas Site
1,023 sherds: 128 (13%) identified by type

	BAP	Papayal	Red Wares[a]	Ceiba	Other	Total
Count	77	11	37	1	—[b]	126
%	61%	9%	29%	<1%	—	

[a]Sangria = 25; Turucaca = 12.
[b]2 sherds of Rivas Incised identified.

TABLE 7.2. Distribution of Decorated Body Sherds at the Rivas Site

	BAP	Papayal	Red Wares	Ceiba	Other	Totals
Op A[a]	17	6	8	8	32	71
Op D[b]	391	37	14	5	28	475
Op E[c]	491	94	10	13	90	698
Totals	899	137	32	26	150	1,244

[a]9.1 kg total; 2.3 kg sample (25%).
[b]4.2 kg total; 2.1 kg sample (50%). Complexes I and III combined.
[c]29 kg total; 7.2 kg sample (25%).

de La Reina complex. Even this simple outline requires considerable interpretation of the archaeological remains and other inferences that may be made from the data retrieved by our work. Still, I think that this is the best interpretation of what happened based on my experience of working at the site and with the artifacts that we found. A closer examination of the results of our artifact analyses may allow us to offer a more detailed and perhaps more refined interpretation of these events, however, and to put the Rivas site in a broader interpretive context. Let us therefore review the results of artifact analyses to attempt to better understand what occurred at Rivas.

Ceramics

Broken pottery is the most abundant remnant of ancient life at Rivas. We estimate that we recovered approximately 600,000 sherds at the site. Most of these were body sherds with a plain-colored slip or, more often, only trace remnants of one. Given our limited time and resources, we decided primarily to concentrate our analyses on rim sherds because they hold more information regarding the original shape and size of vessels. For quantitative analyses, we further reduced the sample size to include only those rim sherds large enough to estimate the original rim diameter. For the most complete analyses, it is best to know both the original form of the vessel and the style in which it was decorated. Of the great number of sherds we gathered, however, we could assign both form and style to only 126 sherds (table 7.1). When we counted decorated body sherds, we reached a total of 1,244 (table 7.2), but for most of these, we did not know the form of the original vessel.

The most striking aspect of the Rivas ceramics when compared with those found at Murciélago is the different amounts of decorated pottery at each site. As noted above, Buenos Aires Polychrome comprised a tiny portion of the sherds found at Murciélago, but at Rivas this type was very common. The dominant ceramic type at Murciélago was Ceiba Red-Brown, but it appears that it was less popular at Rivas. Ceiba was the least numerous type in both the decorated body sherd and the rim sherd samples (tables 7.1, 7.2). We may have misidentified some Ceiba sherds. Ceiba is identified primarily by the red-brown paint combination on a single vessel, but a sherd may be either red or brown.

7.1. Ceramic types found at Rivas. 1: Buenos Aires Polychrome (17.3 cm rim dia.); 2: Papayal Engraved (11 cm rim dia.); 3: Ceiba Red-Brown (14.6 cm high); 4: Ceiba Red-Brown/Carbonera (11.5 cm high) with detail of leg to left; 5: Sangria Red Fine (Negative); 6: Turucaca White-on-Red (28 cm rim dia.). Illustrations by Jennifer Ringberg.

Without any other decorative features plus the fact that slips didn't always preserve well, it is likely that many Ceiba sherds were identified as something else or as "unknown." Nevertheless, the fact that Buenos Aires Polychrome comprises 60 percent of the rim sherd sample and 72 percent of the decorated body sherds indicates that it was plentiful at the Rivas site and more frequent than any other type (fig. 7.1: 1).

Sangria Red Fine and Turucaca White-on-Red (fig. 7.1: 5, 6) are two variations of what we class as Red

Wares. These two types have only recently been designated by French archaeologists (Baudez et. al. 1993), based on perceived differences in vessel shape and application of a band of white paint on the exteriors of Turucaca bowls, below the rim. I prefer to keep the older term of Red Wares (Lothrop 1926, 1963: 69), however, for a number of reasons. Chiefly, when working with sherd collections, it is often impossible to distinguish between the two types. Body sherds are virtually identical in appearance, and even when rims are found, paint often is eroded so much that the former presence of white or red slip in the appropriate area cannot be determined with confidence.

The distribution of Red Wares at the Rivas site shows interesting patterns when the rim sherd and body sherd samples are compared (table 7.1). They are the second most common type among the rim sherds, at 29 percent, with Sangria dominating the assemblage. The preponderance of the monochrome ware may be real or may be due to the erosion of some white bands on Turucaca vessels. Among the body sherds, however, Papayal is much more common, at 11 percent, while the Red Wares are only 3 percent. This must be due to the nature of the ceramics themselves. Perhaps slips were thicker near rims and thus preserved better. The upper parts of vessels would receive less wear than the bodies, set on the ground or exposed to fire. We believe that the figure for rims more accurately represents the presence of Red Wares at the site than do the body sherds.

It is also worth noting that Turucaca and Sangria pottery dominate the Operation C cemetery assemblage. Perhaps Red Wares were popular during the time when the section of the Operation C cemetery where we worked was in use for burial. Since we excavated only a small portion of a large cemetery, it could be that a larger excavation that uncovered more than seven burials would find more of the other pottery types. Alternatively, Red Wares may have been more popular or associated with the social group represented by the graves we excavated.

Papayal Engraved (fig. 7.1: 2) is generally thought to be the "everyday ware" of Chiriquí (Corrales 2000). Its relative frequency in the two separate Rivas samples is about the same: 9 percent among the rims and 11 percent among the decorated body sherds (table 7.1). If Papayal was a "common" Chiriquí pottery

type, then its low percentage at Rivas supports the notion that uncommon things were taking place there. Still, many Papayal vessels were made with great skill and care, while some Buenos Aires Polychrome ceramics were carelessly made. A well-made Papayal bowl may have been quite valued and would have been striking in appearance, especially if the incised lines were highlighted after firing with light-colored pigment rubbed into them. Traces of white pigment are found in some Papayal bowls in museum collections. How these two wares related to each other in the value systems, chronology, and regional distribution in Chiriquí remains to be more fully explored. If it was the case, however, that a Buenos Aires Polychrome vessel, no matter how carelessly made, was considered more valuable or more appropriate as "fiesta ware" than Papayal, then Rivas was a party town indeed.

All other ceramic types at Rivas occur in very low quantities, and some are not present at all. The rare types include Panteón White Line (Haberland 1961a) and Silena Winged (Corrales 2000: 355–356). The French team led by Claude Baudez (Baudez et. al. 1993) at Palmar Sur cites Silena Winged as another style common in their collections, and the type is also discussed by Francisco Corrales (2000: 355–356). The style is named "winged" because of the tab handles that rise like wings from a large, shallow, tripod bowl. We only found a few fragments at Rivas that may be Silena Winged, including some large tripod legs that generally conform to the style. Once again, the scarcity of the type suggests it may be earlier than the Rivas occupation or more common farther east.

For those interested in Pre-Columbian ceramics, Tarragó Biscuit is one of the best-known wares for Chiriquí culture. It is beautiful and striking in the emphasis placed by its manufacturers on simple forms, often highly burnished, with little *adornos* used as the sole decoration. Tarragó is present at Rivas (fig. 7.2) but is about as common at Rivas as Buenos Aires Polychrome was at Murciélago or less so. It was difficult to identify because it is most easily recognized when small *adornos* can be found, since the bodies are plain. One way to identify Tarragó is by the thinness of its vessel walls. In Panama, studies have shown that Tarragó ranges in thickness between 4 and 7 millimeters (Linares de Sapir 1968: 38). But this could not be used as the single criterion at Rivas because many other ceramic types

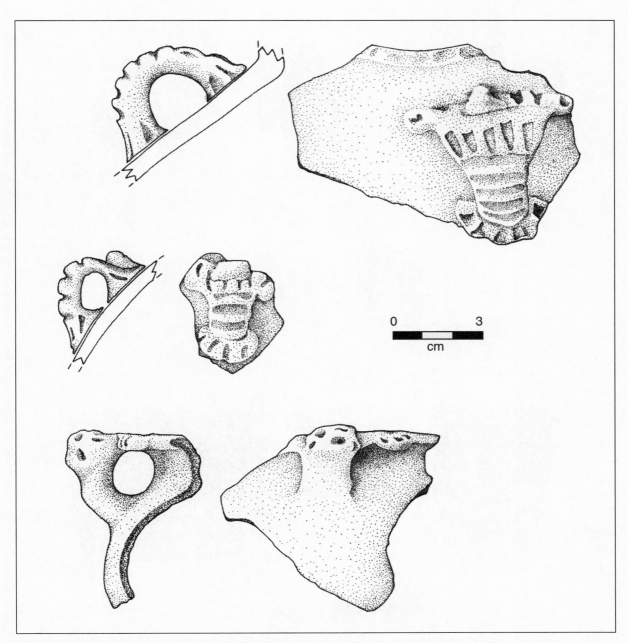

7.2. Tarragó Biscuit *adornos* and strap handles from Operation E. All from the area of S2–1/E20–21. Illustrations by Jennifer Ringberg.

also are finely made with thin walls, and many sherds with lost slip can't be assigned as Tarragó or something else. It is clear, however, that Tarragó was present but rare at Rivas.

We identified a new pottery type, Rivas Red Incised (fig. 7.3). This type consists of thick-walled pottery. The examples we have come from large, deep, open bowls with almost straight sides. The body is covered in an orange-red slip with unslipped decorative bands,

often incised. Two sherds show traces of white paint that may be the remains of the application of postfire pigments. We only found a total of nine sherds of this type, and two of these were joined into one piece. Based on where these sherds were found and the features of their decoration, they probably represent the remains of only seven vessels, at most.

The characteristics of Rivas Red Incised—thick vessel walls, straight sides, and incised zoned decoration

7.3. Rivas Red Incised sherds. All from Operation E. Sherds 7–9 appear to be from the same vessel.

—are typical of ceramics of an earlier age. We found fragments of other vessels that also resembled earlier styles. Some loop-shaped tripod legs and human head *adornos* are similar to those found on El Bosque Red on Buff pottery, which was common in the Atlantic Watershed region ca. 100 B.C.–A.D. 50 (Snarskis 1982; see Katz 1985: 212, plate 120). A sherd with features similar though not identical to Zoila Red Engraved was recovered. Zolia Red Engraved is from the Atlantic zone and is dated slightly earlier than Rivas, ca. A.D. 500–1000 (Brook and Minardi 1976: 215).

Knowledge of Costa Rican ceramics is still underdeveloped in many ways, so it is uncertain if some of the styles we identified as foreign were really from distant areas or if Chiriquí ceramics were more diverse than previously thought. While there is evidence to suggest that many ceramics were imported into the area, some of the exotic wares may represent pottery from relatively nearby areas done in styles thought now to be more foreign because they are only known from distant regions. For example, we found most of an elaborate pedestal bowl in which the supports are in the form of atlantean humanoid figures (fig. 7.4: 3). This resembles pot stands found on the Atlantic Watershed. But the Rivas example has an upper section decorated with incision similar to Papayal Engraved. Is this from the Chiriquí zone? Is it a Chiriquí copy of a foreign vessel? Could it be from some regional style not yet identified? More research is needed to resolve these questions. The same questions exist for those ceramics that appear to be in earlier styles. Many ceramics likely were imported, however, such as an open-work vessel stand (fig. 7.4: 2). This and other examples often are made of different clays than the majority of ceramics at the site. Studies of pastes and tempering agents will be one of the best ways to determine manufacturing origins in future analyses.

We found a sherd (fig. 7.5: 1) from central Panama. Its style is so different from Chiriquí that there is no question as to its origin, probably more than 200 kilometers distant. We also found a single sherd from Guanacaste or Nicoya, also about 200 kilometers away (fig. 7.5: 2). Examples of pottery from great distances are realtively few. This suggests that contacts with people very far away were rare. We do not know if the exotic ceramics were brought directly from their places of origin or exchanged hands through intermediaries along the way. Most of the nonlocal sherds we found at the site resemble styles from the Central Valley or the Atlantic Watershed region, and so it seems that the greatest amount of contact with outside peoples was across the mountains rather than down or up the Pacific shore. As already noted, we are not sure whether some styles may be local, such as from the poorly known region of Pacific Costa Rica between the upper General Valley and Guanacaste. It may thus be that there are many more exotic sherds in the collection, but we just cannot recognize them at present.

Some examples of this internationalism serve to illustrate this point. In the area of the Operation C double wall, we found most of a vessel, previously noted, consisting of a shallow open bowl supported by masked atlantean figures on a ring base (fig. 7.4: 3). The bowl is incised on its exterior in designs similar to Papayal Engraved. The base, though, is similar to atlantean figures found in the Atlantic Watershed region. The origins of the Rivas example are uncertain, but the piece shows that there were widespread shared design motifs in Costa Rica at the time the site was occupied.

There are many charming and elaborately made figures that likely were *adornos*, the feet of elaborate tripod vessels, or atlantean figures. One fragment (fig. 7.4: 1), is of a bent-over coati. Others like it were found, and this one is apparently part of the leg of a tripod bowl.

Although most of the ceramics that appear to be nonlocal have been cited as possibly coming from the Atlantic Watershed or the Central Valley, some could have come from elsewhere. Two sherds that we found are noteworthy for their punctate designs (fig. 7.5: 3, 4). This type of fine "stipple" punctate decoration does not appear to be typically Chiriquí and seems more like early pottery from the Atlantic region, but, again, we need more information on the kinds of ceramics used in many different parts of Costa Rica. We think it likely that there are sherds at Rivas from the northwest but that we have not been able to recognize them. Future work may help clarify this uncertainty. The west coast of Costa Rica is poorly known, and ceramics from the few sites that have been investigated in this region have not been widely published (cf. Corrales Ulloa and Quitanella Jiménez 1996). Chiriquí sites are known for Dominical, the nearest beach resort to Rivas and San Isidro, but there appears to be some shift farther north. Ceramics from this area have not been published, and so contacts with the closer northwest cannot be determined at present, though surely they existed.

Ceramic Figurines

Some of the best-known Chiriquí artifacts are figurines of humans (fig. 7.6). Photographic plates of them are standard illustrations in art books that have sections on southern Costa Rica. These figurines are made of solid clay and are usually fairly small, about 5–7 centimeters in height or less. They are always decorated in the distinctive red and black paint on white slip of Buenos Aires Polychrome. The heads also are made in

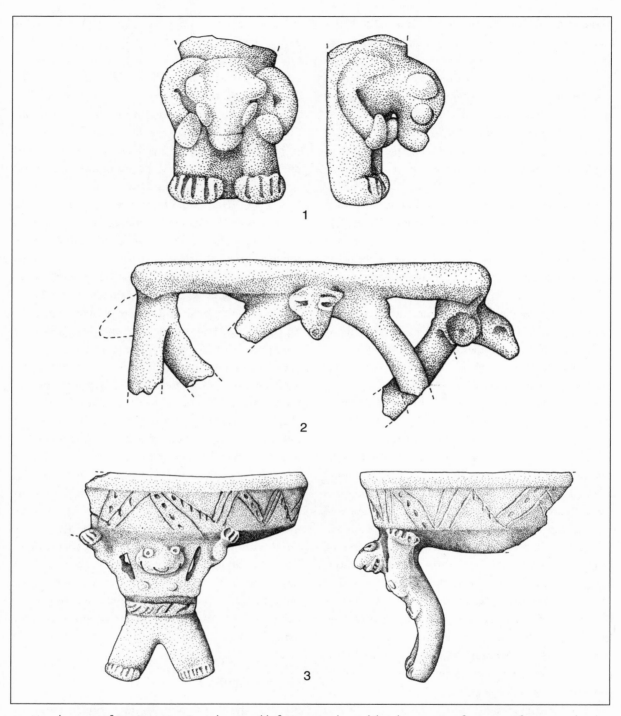

7.4. Vessel supports from Operation E. 1: a leg, possibly from a tripod vessel (height: 5.7 cm); 2: fragments of a pot stand (length: 11.9 cm); 3: a leg with part of the vessel attached (height: 11.7 cm). Illustrations by Jennifer Ringberg.

a distinct form, with hair shown as parallel black lines running vertically from the top of the head to the neck and two planes to define the sides of the face, undercut to form the nose. Each figure has an incised mouth enhanced by red paint. Oval eyes are painted in black, with a central dot to represent the pupil. Arms are shown as curved loops extending out from the shoulders and connected high on the thigh or above the pelvis with hands minimally represented or not depicted at all. Legs are splayed and end in points, with no effort

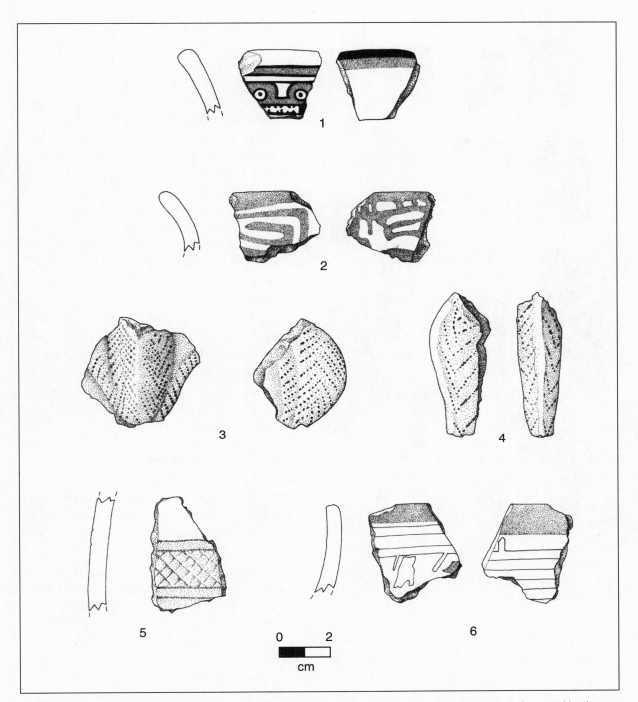

7.5. Unusual sherds from Rivas. 1: Panamanian import; 2: Guanacaste import? (red on white); 3: punctate decorated knob similar to early Atlantic Watershed ceramic; 4: punctate fillet or leg resembling Atlantic Watershed ceramic; 5: Zoned incised-white slip on buff background; 6: linear incised sherd similar to 5. Illustrations by Jennifer Ringberg.

to render feet or toes. Holes often are located toward the back of the head on a line with the mouth or higher, at the level of the eyes.

These figures are almost always represented as women through the application of clay buttons to form breasts or by a distinct triangle for the pubis. Sometimes a small incision to indicate the vagina is present. Some figures are not clearly gendered. The splayed leg with arms akimbo is the most common form, but museum collections show some variations, including a figure seated

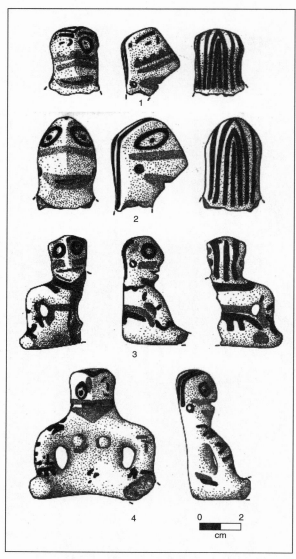

7.6. Buenos Aires Polychrome figurines. Illustrations by Jennifer Ringberg.

examples had a single line, while a fourth example had two parallel lines across the nose (fig. 7.6: 1). This same head also had painted eyebrows, which were generally absent on the other figurine heads.

Our sample of figurines is too small to know if minor differences in decoration are significant cultural markers for different subregions of the Chiriquí style or simply represent variation due to the whims of individual artists. Doris Stone (1962: 20) reported that in the nineteenth century, the bishop of Costa Rica stated that he saw some women and children in the Chirripó del Pacífico with face paint consisting of two bands of black paint below their eyes and on their cheeks. The paint on the figurines may indicate that a similar facial decoration was practiced in antiquity, perhaps with different color preferences.

The figurines are quite tough and are made in a compact shape that resists breakage. Nevertheless, figurine head fragments are common, and there appear to be breakage patterns that suggest they may have been deliberately snapped off of the bodies. The explicit pose of the figurines, drawing attention to the pubic area of predominantly female representations, suggests that these clay objects were associated with concepts of fertility. Perhaps a figure was deliberately broken once a prayer had been answered or some ritual activity related to fertility or childbirth was carried out. This might explain why the figurine fragments were found in the ceremonial area of the site and less commonly in cemeteries or areas more domestic in nature. Two were found in graves in the La Pista Cemetery, however. It may also simply be a matter that the neck was the weakest part of these little statuettes, and so that is where they broke after discard.

Most of a Buenos Aires Polychrome figurine of a small figure carrying a large jar by means of a tumpline was found on the Panteón de La Reina (fig. 7.7). Although more rare than the seated figurines, this figurine type appears also to be part of a repertoire of images used in Chiriquí ceramics. A similar, complete example is in the collections of the Museo del Sur. It seems significant that this is the only representation of human labor depicted in Chiriquí art. The large jar suggests that the figure is carrying *chicha*, perhaps for consumption at a ceremony. A raised area on the preserved section of the chest of the Panteón example more

on a feline-shaped stool, resembling some of the stone metates known for the region. In fact, the figure may be represented as seated on such a metate. Other figures are shown holding a single infant or small child.

We found about a dozen fragments of this kind of figurine at Rivas, although some fragments were so small that it was hard to know if they truly were parts of figurines. Six fragments of figurines were complete or complete enough that the original appearance could be judged with confidence. Some of the slight variations noted include the presence or absence of a horizontal red line painted across the nose. Three of our

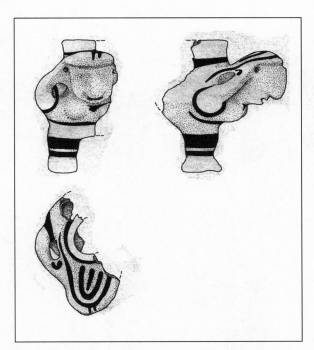

7.7. Figurine of a woman (?) carrying a large vessel through use of a tumpline. Height: 6.4 cm. Illustration by Jennifer Ringberg.

strongly implies that the figurine represents a woman. The burden figurine in the Museo del Sur stands upright with hands over the breasts, holding the strap that carries the jar on the figure's back. This position obscures the secondary sex characteristics. What kinds of tensions or politics between males and females might be played out in the production of these figures? Why were they made, in any event, and who made them? Were they made as toys to instruct young girls in their future roles to provide *chicha*? Were they made to express a more ambivalent or outright subversive message, that it was women who toiled for the benefit of others? As with so many other issues, more research is needed to explore these questions further.

We also found other types of figurines at Rivas. The head of an Aguas Buenas style figurine with a conical hat or helmet was found by one of the Mora family boys and presented to us. He claimed that he found it on the Panteón de La Reina, though he could not tell us the precise location. We know that there is an Aguas Buenas era occupation in the area and also probably burials of the period farther up the ridge than where we worked. Conical hats were symbols of social power in ancient Costa Rica and Panama, and so the figurine

from which this fragment came may have represented a high-status individual, possibly a male.

We also found figurine fragments of styles different than the Buenos Aires Polychrome seated females (fig. 7.8). These were all found in Operation E, and most of them were from the double wall area of the oval. Some of these may therefore be imports from other regions, but we can say that they probably were contemporary with the Buenos Aires Polychrome figurines. It may be just a question of chance, but these different figurine types are represented only by legs and lower body parts, with few exceptions. No heads were found, although a torso was recovered. Because ancient Costa Ricans were so fond of tripod vessels, it is possible that some of these legs are not from figurines but from bowls. We will treat them here, however, as figurine legs.

One form of leg was made as a solid cylinder with red slip (fig. 7.8: 5–8). The foot was represented by an expansion of the cylinder or an added round lump of clay at the end of the leg, and toes were made by incising the spaces between them. Two examples (fig. 7.8: 5, 6) have incised lines to indicate knees or perhaps ligatures below them. Other figurine parts include one with a foot with incised lines to represent toes, while the other foot was club-shaped with three conical projections (fig. 7.8: 3). This figure is reminiscent of God K of the Classic Maya (see Schele and Miller 1986: 49), who has a snake for a foot. His image formed the scepter of rulership, and he was associated with sacrifice and with self-inflicted blood-letting in particular. Other distinct figurine foot fragments include a tabular one with curvilinear designs and punctates above incised toes (fig. 7.8: 9), and another form of foot was rendered red slipped, ovoid in cross section, and pointed at the end (fig. 7.8: 13, 14).

Animal figurines were relatively few in number compared to human representations. A Buenos Aires Polychrome tapir was found in an Operation C burial (see fig. 2.15). It was hollow with pellets inside so that it would rattle when shaken. The head of a similar hollow figurine was found elsewhere. It has traces of white slip. Whereas the Operation C figurine had a pointed, downturned nose, the second example has a flat nose projecting from the face. The other porcine creature made into figurines is the peccary (see fig. 2.5). A com-

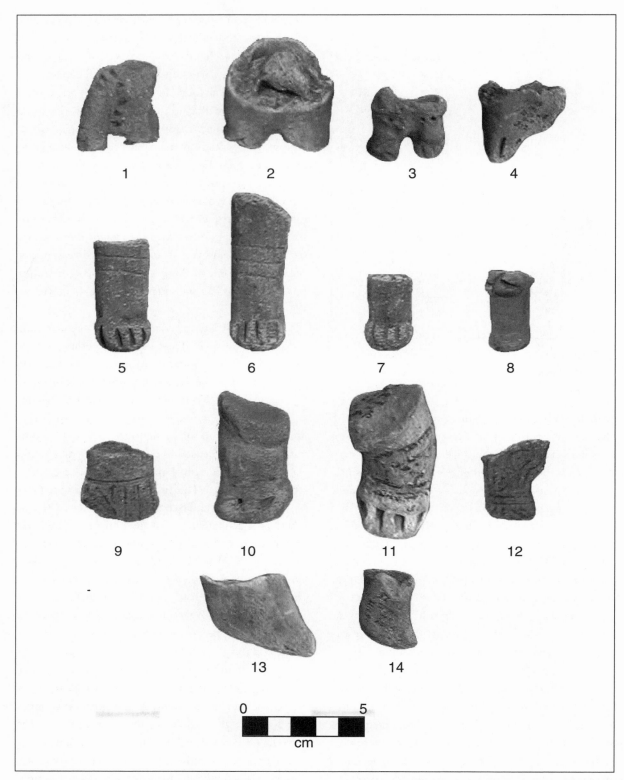

7.8. Figurine body parts. All Operation E. 1: right arm and torso fragment; 2: torso and upper legs; 3: lower torso and leg; 4: stylized right leg?; 5: leg and foot; 6: leg and foot; 7: leg and foot; 8: leg and foot; 9: foot; 10: left leg and foot; 11: right leg and foot (match to 10?); 12: incised, flat, right leg and foot; 13: thin, stylized foot (?) side view; 14: solid foot, similar to 13, side view.

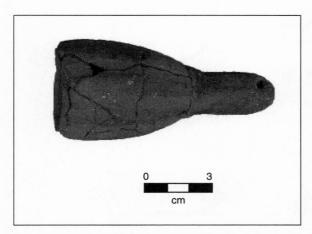

7.9. A rattle in the shape of a gourd or squash. Length: 9 cm.

plete example of one was found during the shovel test pit survey in Operation A. It is solid, not hollow, probably because of its small size. A transverse hole below the ears suggests it may have been suspended from a string.

The final class of elaborate clay objects with significant numbers in the Rivas collections is that of musical instruments. These include rattles, whistles, and ocarinas. Only one rattle was found: a complete but broken example in Operation C (fig. 7.9). The fact that it was broken allowed us to note that clay pellets were used to make the sound. This rattle style is another example of a form found throughout the Chiriquí region. It appears to be in the shape of a squash blossom, folded for the night.

Whistles have, at most, two stop holes, while ocarinas have more. We rarely found complete examples of large specimens. The best example we found was the human head, slipped white with black-painted decorations, in Operation C (fig. 2.16). When suspended by the hole at its rear it would have resembled a small trophy head, and it is the only overt symbol of violence we found. We also found a small whistle in the shape of a bird with its wings folded. It appears to have been made in Buenos Aires Polychrome style, although the color was dark, possibly due to overfiring.

The rest of the ceramic artifacts at the site include spindle whorls, ceramic disks, and miscellaneous objects. Both spindle whorls and ceramic disks were commonly made from pottery sherds, and we found examples of all ceramic styles. The most recognizable spindle whorl type was a relatively flat body sherd that had

been reworked into a circular form and punctured with a hole in its middle. Presumably, they were used to spin cotton thread and fibers of other plants. They were found throughout the site wherever other debris was encountered, and if women were the spinners, then women were present in all areas. We found spindle whorls in a range of sizes from more than 3 centimeters in diameter to small ones about 1 centimeter in diameter, suggesting that everything from coarse to fine thread was spun.

What ceramic disks were used for is uncertain. In addition to disks, there also are sherds reworked into semicircular and triangular shapes. Many of the edges of these objects appear to be worn. Perhaps they were used to scrape food from bowls or as tools for smoothing hand-built pottery. Ceramic disks may also have served as stoppers for gourd containers. Some old-timers still use gourds as water bottles, although they do not use ceramic disks to stop them.

Miscellaneous artifacts mostly consist of objects of uncertain use. We found clay beads in a small container in an Operation C burial. Larger objects may be beads, spindle whorls, or labrets. Some artifacts likely are fragments of decorative parts of elaborate ceramic vessels. We found tubular fragments that might be the remains of pipes. Most tripod legs are either solid or hollow but with a slit in them in which a ball would be placed as a rattle. Two tubular fragments we found had relatively straight shafts. If they were the remains of tripod legs, they would have been very long.

Quantitative Studies of Jars and Bowls

Ceramic styles convey one kind of information, while vessel form may be used to make different inferences. Bottles are used to preserve and serve valued liquids, for example. Ideally, it would be best if we could ask questions of the data, such as What is the relative frequency of Buenos Aires large, open bowls in Operation D compared to the frequency of small ones, or of large, open Papayal Engraved bowls? Unfortunately, despite the great numbers of sherds we recovered, the sample is very small to answer such detailed questions with confidence. Nevertheless, using the Rivas master database of rim sherds, we were able to ask some questions that compared different vessel forms (fig. 7.10).

As we studied the kinds of forms in the Rivas ce-

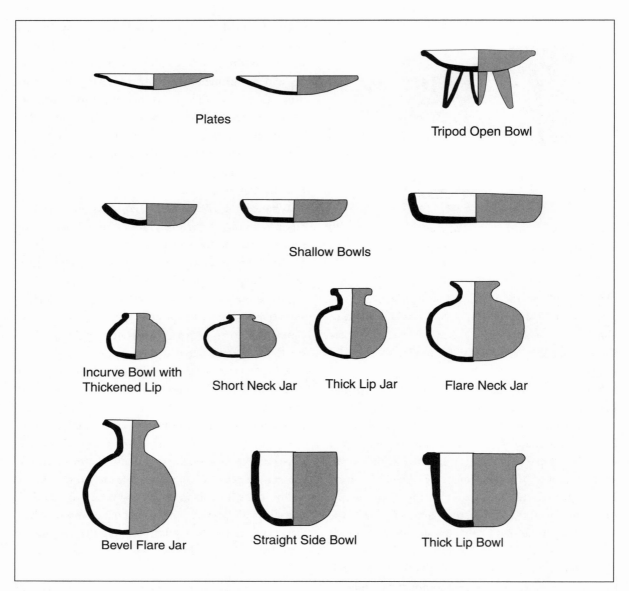

Plates

Tripod Open Bowl

Shallow Bowls

Incurve Bowl with
Thickened Lip

Short Neck Jar

Thick Lip Jar

Flare Neck Jar

Bevel Flare Jar

Straight Side Bowl

Thick Lip Bowl

7.10. Vessel forms found at Rivas.

ramic assemblage, we defined two major categories: bowls and jars. In general, bowls are vessels with wide mouths, and jars are vessels with narrow mouths in relation to the maximum diameter of the body of the vessel. Within each formal category, we identified subcategories. Making such decisions was difficult. Even the categories of bowls and jars can merge in vessels that have mouths not quite wide enough to call bowls but not quite narrow enough to label as jars. For subcategories, distinctions were even more difficult to make. For example, at what point is a bowl no longer "shallow" but rather "open"? In the case of a category such as a "thick lip bowl," there clearly were vessels in

which the top of the rim had deliberately been thickened with extra clay, presumably to make the vessel stronger. There were other vessels, however, with a slight thickening perhaps just due to the random variation as the result of different pottery maker's styles of work. We did not establish rigid categories to separate such cases but rather used our intuitive sense of things.

The kinds of wide-mouthed bowls found at Rivas appear to be ones used to serve food. Most of these likely had tripod legs such as the bowls found in the Operations C and K burials, where the form is expressed in Red Wares and Buenos Aires Polychrome styles. We found no signs of burning on the bottoms

TABLE 7.3A. Distribution of Bowl Rim Sherds at the Rivas Site
445 bowls: 335 (72%) identified by form

Form	Count	% of Total	% Identifiable Rims
Bowl	130	28	
Shallow	92	20	27
Open	83	18	25
Incurve	81	17	24
Thick Lip	73	16	22
Incurve Thick Lip	3	>1	1
Straight Side	3	>1	1

TABLE 7.3B. Distribution of Jar Rim Sherds at the Rivas Site
537 jars: 260 (48%) identified by form

Form	Count	% of Total	% Identifiable Rims
Jar	277	52	
Thick Lip	95	18	37
Flare Neck	87	16	33
Incurve	21	4	8
Short Neck	18	3	7
Open Neck	17	3	7
Bevel Flare	16	3	6
Straight Neck	6	1	2

TABLE 7.3C. Chi-Square of Bowls vs. Jars in Rivas Operations

	Op A	Op D	Op E
Small Jar	28	65	175
Large Jar	46	77	135
Small Bowl	29	144	45
Large Bowl	49	146	37

df = 6; chi-square = 194.9 P < .001 at 22.457, so distribution is highly unlikely to be by chance.

Small jar </= 12 cm rim diameter; large jar >/= 12 cm rim diameter.

Small bowl </= 16 cm rim diameter; large bowl >/= 16 cm rim diameter.

TABLE 7.3D. Chi-Square of Jars and Bowls in the Operation E Oval and the Rest of Operation E

	Oval	Other Operation E
Jars	128	182
Bowls	42	40

df = 1; chi-square = 2.56; P = 20–10%.
No strong suggestion of nonrandomness.

TABLE 7.3E. Chi-Square of Flared Jars vs. Nonflared Jars in Major Rivas Operations

	OpA	OpD	OpE	Op J
Flares	12	58	30	41
Nonflares	62	84	280	95

df = 3; chi-square < .001.

Operation D has more flared jars and Operation E has more nonflared jars than would be expected in a random distribution. Operation J is somewhat like Operation D, although the distribution is not as striking. Operation A does not show unexpected patterning.

of complete bowls that might suggest they were placed over fires. Instead, it appears that legs served to raise a bowl above the surface on which it was placed, probably the ground, and thus facilitate taking food from the bowl. The surfaces of some bowls were so flat that they could be classed as plates. We classed bowls that probably were on tripod legs as Open Bowls in our sample (table 7.3A), although with only a sherd as evidence, we couldn't tell if tripods had been part of the vessel. The generic category of Bowl was used when the original shape was uncertain, but it is likely that the majority of these also were Open Bowls.

The second most common form after the combined Open Bowl/Bowl category was the Shallow Bowl. Sherds were assigned to this category when the original height could be determined, often because there was clear evidence of the wall turning at an angle to form the bottom of the vessel. This style of bowl, also commonly with tripod legs, was more popular for use in Papayal Engraved pottery than Buenos Aires Polychrome. It is likely that large varieties of this vessel form were used for the same purposes as Open Bowls. Some Shallow Bowls have small diameters, however, and perhaps were used for foods supplementary to the main course served in the large Open Bowls.

Thick Lip Bowls and Incurve Bowls are almost equally common in our sample. Some Thick Lip Bowls had very wide mouths and straight or nearly straight sides. The thick lips of some of these vessels would have offered an easy way to carry them. These vessels likely held great quantities of liquids that could be easily accessed by their wide mouths. Incurve Bowls are sometimes called *ollas* or *compoteras* in some parts of Latin America. In these bowls, the maximum diameter is often much larger than that of the orifice. This shape makes Incurve Bowls similar to jars in their potential functions. The accidental spilling of contents is less likely to happen than in other forms because of the restricted diameter of the mouth. Unlike jars, however, it is awkward to pour liquid from Incurve Bowls. It is likely that this shape was used to store granular materials or, when used for cooking, to create an environment in which evaporation of liquid was minimized by the closed shape.

As in the case of bowls, we recognized a number of jar shapes. Some of these categories, particularly Incurve Jars and Straight Neck Jars, represent vessels that seemed to occupy the intermediate zone between more distinguishable bowls and jars. The Thick Lip Jar and Flare Neck Jar are the most frequently occurring types. We found several complete examples of these in our cemetery excavations. They often were slipped in a simple brown color with no decoration. Many of the whole jars had soot on their lower areas. Their relatively small size of about 12 to 15 centimeters in height, in combination with these other observations, suggests that they may have been used to heat small quantities of liquids for consumption. They seem to be a rather utilitarian vessel form and could have served a wide variety of purposes.

I developed a suspicion that small jars, such as the Ceiba Red-Brown/Carbonera jar illustrated in figure 7.1: 4, served as drinking vessels. My hypothesis seemed to be confirmed in an experiment conducted in the Museo del Sur archaeological laboratory. Two complete Carbonera tripod jars that are part of the collection were filled with water, and I drank from them. Both served quite well for drinking, although one with a slightly more flared rim did slop a bit between cup and lip. Carbonera tripods and a related form known as Fish Ware (see fig. 1.7: 4) tend to be decorated in Ceiba Red-Brown style. They are often elaborately decorated either by rendering the tripod legs in the form of fish, from whence one variety gets its name, to adding incised fillets of clay around vessel necks or ornamenting vessels with little *adornos*. Such an elaborate example of this style is represented by the example in figure 7.1: 4.

It is very likely that the sherds we designated as Bevel Flare Jars and probably many of the Flare Neck Jars are from drinking vessels. We know that in the mid-nineteenth century *chicha* was drunk in quantity at ceremonies among the Bribri peoples of the Atlantic Watershed (Gabb 1875). These people likely were continuing many practices from early times and may be the descendants of the people who lived at Rivas or related to them. The presence of maize at Rivas indicates that the essential component of *chicha* was available to the Rivas people. Chocolate also was consumed as a liquid in historic times and was highly valued. We know less of the recipes of the chocolate drink among the Bribri. If their practices were similar to those of the Maya, they may have drunk it both hot and cold, and, on occasion, they may have laced it with substances to produce psychotropic effects.

Now, if bowls were mostly used for consuming food and jars were used for drinking, the distribution of these two vessel classes might tell us something about what happened in different parts of the Rivas site. Of course, both jars and bowls may have been used for storage or the preparation of food or *chicha*. Jars, though, might be considered as the best way to store and transport liquids, while bowls are more likely used for consumption. Even if the straight-sided or thick-lipped big bowls mentioned above were for beverages, they likely served more as "punch bowls" for consumption on the spot than for storage.

To test this hypothesis, we performed a chi-square analysis of the distribution of bowls and jars in various operations. Chi-square is a statistical analysis that describes the likelihood that an observed distribution of things among a set of other things—in this case, the distribution of jars and bowls among different areas of the site—is the result of random forces. This is usually expressed as a range of percentages. The lower the percentage, the more likely the observed distribution would not occur randomly (table 7.3).

The results of the study were clear in showing distinctions (table 7.3). The raw data themselves are telling, with 311 jar rim sherds and only 82 bowl rim sherds in Operation E. Operation D also has a significant number of jars in comparison to bowls, while Operation A has more bowls than jars. If the assumption that jars are for drinking and bowls are for eating is correct, then more drinking occurred in the large-scale architecture than in the small-scale area of Operation A.

Because we found a high concentration of exotic ceramics in the southern area of the oval structure in Operation E, we wanted to see if there were particular activities that occurred there. Consequently, we ran a second study comparing jars to bowls in the area of the southern part of the oval (S3–N3/W5–35) with distributions in the northern part of the oval (table 7.3B). The result was a probability between 10 percent and 20 percent that the observed distribution of more jars outside than inside the oval would occur at random. A 10 to 20 percent chance that something occurred at random might be considered fairly low, but in archaeological analyses it is usually not considered highly significant. We might interpret this pattern as suggesting that drinking was widespread throughout this area of Operation E, and not necessarily concentrated in our outside-the-oval architecture. But it also suggests that there may have been slightly more drinking—or, more accurately, more disposal of drinking vessels—away from the oval than in it.

We also wished to examine whether jars with flared rims occurred in greater numbers in different parts of the site compared to nonflared jars (table 7.3C). The analysis suggested that there was a distribution very unlikely to have occurred at random. Operations A and E had distinctly fewer flared jars while Operations D and J had significantly more flared jars than might be expected in a random distribution. This is of interest because, on the basis of architectural features, both Operations D and J are interpreted as areas where mortuary ritual took place. If flared jars were indeed beer mugs, then drinking rituals took place in mortuary rituals at Rivas in patterns similar to those known for the Bribri of the nineteenth century.

Ceramics in Overview

The Rivas ceramics are abundant and varied. The great amounts of Buenos Aires Polychrome suggest that "fancy" vessels were used in activities there. It is hard to know for certain if the dominance of ceramics by this pottery type is because of special activities at the site or because this pottery style was more popular in this part of the range of Chiriquí culture. The fact that the amount of Buenos Aires Polychrome is high and that of Tarragó Biscuit is low at Rivas, but that the reverse is true in western Panama, suggests the relative percentages have more to do with time and space than with the special status of Buenos Aires Polychrome as "fiesta ware." Or it may mean that the "fiesta ware" of northern Chiriquí peoples was Buenos Aires Polychrome and that Tarragó Biscuit was the party favorite in southern Chiriquí communities. This is certainly a hypothesis that will need testing in the future, however.

Better temporal controls of changes in ceramics would help answer many questions about the relations of different site components to one another and of relations between different sites in the region. There is, for example, the position of the Red Wares in the overall chronology that still needs to be more finely documented. Another case in point is the ceramic assemblage recovered from El Zoncho cemeteries by Laurenchich de Minelli and Minelli (1966). Some of the ceramics from El Zoncho are of Aguas Buenas style, which is definitely earlier than Chiriquí. Others, such as "Chocolate Incised" (Papayal Engraved), White Line, and Tarragó, are part of what is recognized as Chiriquí. The presence of gold ornaments in a few burials suggests that El Zoncho dates to late in the Aguas Buenas phase or early in the Chiriquí. There are no representatives of Buenos Aires Polychrome in the assemblage, however. It may thus be inferred that the Buenos Aires Polychrome pottery style is relatively late, that it was not popular in the El Zoncho area, or possibly both. There are some jars, however, that are decorated with stylized animal motifs in red paint outlined on black placed on an unslipped surface (Laurenchich de Minelli and Minelli 1966: fig. 17). This decorative motif is continued on white-slipped pottery in Chiriquí times. It may be that this decorative style, as found in El Zoncho burials, is an early style that was a precursor to Buenos Aires Polychrome. Once again, this is another topic on which further study certainly is needed.

One other important point to reemphasize is that the style categories used to type Chiriquí pottery are very cumbersome. Although some of the earlier categories' mixing of vessel forms, distinct decorative techniques, and more general paint schemes have been straightened out, a confounding of attributes in ceramic classification remains, making use of the categories awkward at best. Furthermore, these styles invariably were first defined on the basis of whole, well-preserved vessels and are not easily applicable to sherd collections, which make up the bulk of most archaeological assemblages. Again, future work should be invested in trying to improve this situation.

As the artifact class with the greatest number of representatives at the site, the Rivas ceramic assemblage offers much information. There are lots of fancy pots, even if Buenos Aires Polychrome was not as rare as previously thought and even if many of the "exotic" pots may have been produced closer to Rivas. The distribution of jars and bowls also seems to be significant in offering evidence for activities at the site, while the figurines suggest that activities associated with them also occurred. In order to make the most of this information, though, it is best if we integrate the ceramic analyses with the study of the other artifacts.

Stone Artifacts

Based on method of manufacture, archaeologists commonly discuss two major classes of stone tools: chipped stone tools and ground stone tools. The latter may include tools that also were pecked or polished even though grinding is a specific technique. Chipped stone tools (fig. 7.11: 1–3; table 7.4) were made by knocking large flakes off of a core of material and then either used for the sharp edge produced or further shaped to a desired form. Ground stone tools mostly consisted of hand-held manos and passive metates (fig. 7.12: 1–2). As noted earlier, metates were rare at the site. Stone adzes and similar tools such as celts and chisels (fig. 7.11: 4–5) were first pecked and then later ground and polished. The same is true with statuary and fancy metates.

Jeff Frost has been the project stone tool analyst, and the following discussion is drawn from his studies. All of the material for chipped stone tools is either andesite or basalt. Most of the celts also were basalt. The andesite is available locally, in the form of river cobbles and larger boulders, while the basalt source is unknown. We found only two flakes of exotic, good-quality chipping material, both in Operation E. Both

were very small fragments of a bright red chert. We found another red material throughout the site. It was in small chunks, unworked, and unidentified as to stone type. We also found several quartz flakes and crystals that were not worked. Quartz is locally available. In many societies in South America, quartz crystals were associated with shamanism (see Saunders 1998, in press).

The acidic soils and wet and dry spells of the area create a thick patina on chipped stone tools. Edges that once were sharp become dull, and the outlines of flake scars are muted. It is only with careful examination that tools and debris from their manufacture may be recognized. We identified a total of 8,632 stone artifacts in our collections. Of these, only about 35 were not chipped stone tools, fragments of them, or the debris from making them.

The main categories of chipped stone tools are flakes, in the majority, cores, blades, scrapers, perforators, and rare items (fig. 7.11: 1–3). Flakes are almost all made from fine-grained basalt. They tend to be large and thick, and Jeff did not divide them into subcategories. Cores are mostly multidirectional—with flakes knocked off from many different angles—with one example of bidirectional flaking and no examples of unidirectional ones. Some of these may be scrapers (fig. 7.11: 1) because some large examples of these tools have prepared striking platforms and microflaking along their working edges. Blades—flakes twice as long as they are wide—are rare at the site (fig. 7.11: 2). They usually are single crested, suggesting that they are flake blades or flakes that by chance have the correct proportions to categorize them as blades. All of these artifacts are fairly evenly distributed across the site.

Scrapers are the most common tool type in all operations. Operation A has 16, Operation D has 34, and Operation E has 45. They range in size from less than 3 centimeters to almost 10 centimeters in length. They have a steeply angled scraping surface and exhibit unifacial flaking. Preliminary studies suggest that there are two types of scrapers: flat and thick.

Perforators (fig. 7.11: 3) are also common, though less frequent than scrapers. Operation A yielded 3, and 16 were found in Operation D. Many have been retouched, though most are too weathered to identify such work. Several other types of chipped stone tools were found in small quantities. We also recovered two

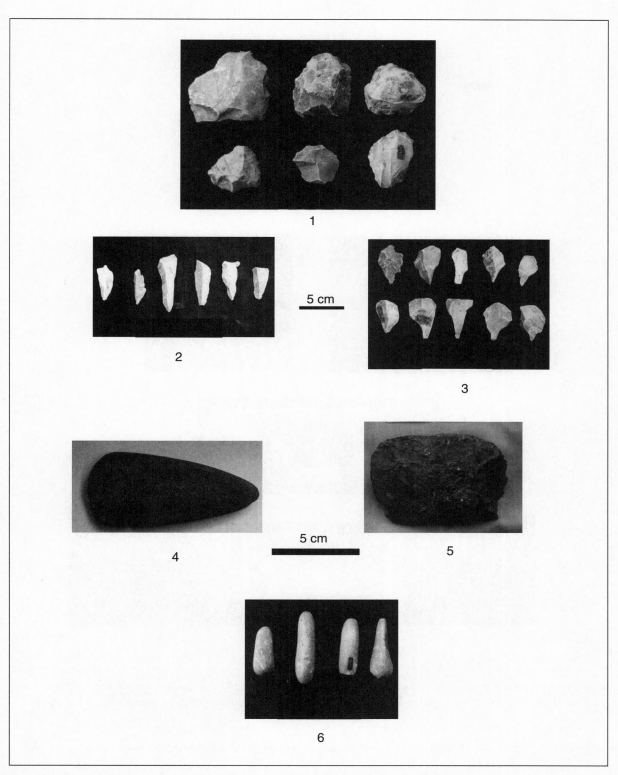

7.11. Chipped stone tools. 1: scraper-cores; 2: blade flakes; 3: perforators; 4: celt; 5: celt perform; 6: chisels.

7.12. Ground stone tools. 1: manos; 2: slab metate fragment; 3: slab metate fragment; 4: jaguar metate at Museo Regional del Sur; 5: feline head fragment (front); 6: feline head fragment (side); 7: fragments of lower legs of anthropomorphic sculpture.

possible spokeshaves as well as one biface and a couple of unifacially worked tools.

Celts, adzes, and chisels are tools commonly thought to have been used for agriculture or woodworking (fig. 7.11: 4, 5). Celts are convex-convex in cross section, while adzes are plano-convex in cross section. Only one adze was found, in Operation E. We found eight complete or nearly complete celts as well as 14 proximal end fragments. We found no celts or fragments of them in Operations A and B. We found two complete celts in the Operation C cemetery, one in the Operation K cemetery, and one on the Panteón de La Reina. We found a celt fragment in Operation J and another one in Operation H. Operation D yielded 10 celt frag-

TABLE 7.4. Stone Tools and Remains at Rivas

Artifacts	Operations							
	A	B	C	D	E	J	K	Totals
Bifaces	0	0	0	1	1	0	0	2
Blades	18	19	0	12	11	2	1	63
Celt Flakes	9	2	0	9	38	1	0	59
Cores	6	3	0	39	29	1	0	78
Debitage	1,442	249	16	2,907	3,381	31	13	8,039
Drills	0	0	0	0	1	0	0	1
Perforators	3	0	0	16	0	0	0	19
Scrapers	14	9	2	45	55	0	2	127
Spokeshaves	0	0	0	1	3	0	0	4
Adzes	0	0	0	0	1	0	0	1
Carved Stones	3	0	0	2	11	0	0	16
Celts	0	0	2	6	7	1	1	17
Manos	9	4	0	11	31	0	2	57
Metates	19	0	0	0	0	0	2	21
Nutting Stones	0	0	0	1	0	0	0	1
Pestles	3	0	0	16	0	0	0	19
Polish Stones	7	10	0	5	6	0	0	28
Others	5	0	0	2	6	0	0	13
Totals	1,538	296	20	3,073	3,581	36	21	8,565

ments, and 6 fragments were found in Operation E. The lack of distal (working) ends of celts in our collection of fragments may be due to the fact that they could have remained in use as small cutting tools after the celt broke. In Operation E, we recovered 25 fragments of the basalt used for celt manufacture in an 11 x 22 meter area immediately to the south of the patio on the western side of the oval (between S10–N1 and E3–25). Just to the north of this area we found a celt preform that had snapped in half, probably due to a flaw in the material (fig. 7.11: 5). Jeff Frost's study of these materials suggests that they minimally conform to stages of production for celt manufacture as defined by Sheets, Rosenthal, and Ranere (1980: 410).

Chisels (fig. 7.11: 6) are also convex-convex in cross section but have an equal width from cutting edge to poll, unlike the teardrop shape of celts and adzes. We found six complete or fragments of chisels. Two were surface collected on the Panteón, one was found in Operation A, and three were recovered from Operation E.

One of the hallmarks of the Rivas site is its lack of metates (fig 7.12: 1–3). A small metate was found on the north side of the Operation E oval. I tripped over a broken one many times in the large circle extending south of Complex II in Operation D before I turned it over and realized what it was. Two relatively large metates were found in the Operation K cemetery. Those metates were complete or nearly so, so were evidently made of large slabs of stone unshaped except for the basin made by grinding on the flat surface.

Manos occur, although not in the quantities reported by Drolet (1984a: 126) for Murciélago. We only have a few examples instead of scores of them. Several examples of single-handed grinding stones were found in various locations (fig. 7.12: 1). Manos large enough for two-handed grinding are unknown at the site. All of the manos we found were discoidal in shape, suggesting they were held in one hand. Two-handed manos are best employed if extensive time is to be spent grinding material, such as maize. The fact that no two-handed metates were found is another indication that little preparation of maize or other bulky starches was done at the site.

Fancy metates were made from a volcanic tufa that must have been imported from far distances, as Rivas is outside the range of volcanoes active in the recent geologic past. The "standard" form for fancy metates in the area is a sculptural representation of a feline (fig. 7.12: 4). The flat, usually oval surface of the metate forms the body. A carved head protrudes from one end, while on the other a tail curves around to attach to one of the rear legs. We found a feline head that probably came from one of these metates in Operation A. In Operation D, we found a tail fragment and a small fragment of a piece of a jaguar metate leg. Operation E yielded the greatest number of ground stone fragments likely from metates. There, we found two feet similar to those found on feline metates, though they could be from freestanding stone sculpture. They are of different shapes, suggesting that they may be from different metates, although front and rear feet may differ on a single grinding stone. In addition, four cylindrical fragments also were found in Operation E and may also come from jaguar metates or similar grinding stones. In our sifting of looters' backdirt on the Panteón de La Reina, we found part of the grinding surface of a finely made metate with chevron designs worked into its side.

Evidence for standing stone sculpture is very rare at the site. In an excavation unit in Operation E, in the area of the cobble path on the southwestern side of our work, we found a fragment of a human right arm and hand carved from andesite. In the next level excavated, we found a human foot carved out of the same material and of proportional size to suggest it came from the same statue. The only other clear evidence of the sculpted human form was a small head from Operation A, carved out of the soft, decaying andesite known locally as *piedra muerta*. It likely is an example of "folk art" as it does not partake of the great carving tradition as the other pieces we found.

One of the Mora family members showed us a roughly carved figure that he claimed he found at the site, though he did not provide a specific location. There also is a very large quadruped carving in the Museo del Sur gift shop. It weighs several hundred kilos, and no one knows its place of origin. The simple form looks unfinished, but its general proportions and blocky shape conform to known Chiriquí stylistic conventions. It may have come from Rivas, though given its size and weight, perhaps its origins are closer to the museum.

It is difficult to determine the significance of the nature of the stone tools we found at Rivas or of their distribution around the site because so few studies of stone tools at Chiriquí sites have been published. Often in the tropics, hard woods are used to produce cutting edges, so there is a further complication in that we cannot have great confidence that the stone tools and remains we found approximate the full range of cutting, scraping, and similar implements used by the site occupants. Perhaps it need not be noted that the ubiquity of scrapers suggests that some activity that required scraping was done with some frequency and that other activities were also carried out but to a lesser extent. If the large-scale architecture at Rivas hosted feasting, then we might infer that the scrapers were used in some kind of food preparation or the making of structures, such as racks for roasting or similar gear.

One striking aspect of the stone tool assemblage is the relatively high number of stone tools in Operation A compared to Operations D and E. The area we excavated in Operation A is tiny in comparison to the other two operations, yet Operation A has about half the number of stone artifacts found in each of the other two study areas. This might mean that the people in Operation A were doing a lot more work that required stone tools in comparison to those who were in the other operations. We have no "normal" standard of activity to use as a comparison for this observation.

We also do not know whether the number of fancy metates in various areas or in the site as a whole is significantly higher or lower than we might expect from a common residential area. It does appear that more such objects were in Operation E, although this may be due to the fact that we excavated more extensively there than anywhere else. On a visit to the site and in subsequent conversation, Michael Snarskis (personal communication) noted that he had expected us to find many more examples of freestanding stone sculpture than we did. In ceremonial centers in the Atlantic Watershed, they are fairly common. Given that Rivas is in a fairly vulnerable area for looting, it may be that much of the stone sculpture was carted off during the same period as when the Panteón was extensively looted. Stone sculpture was almost as valuable as gold, especially for antiquarians. Another possibility, however, is that the nature of the Rivas site ceremonial zone was such that the purposes to which it was put did not re-

7.13. The Rivas textile evidence. Top: Three conjoined sherds with the impression of a textile. Bottom: William J Conklin's reconstruction of the possible structure of the original textile that made the impression in the sherds. Photographs by William J Conklin.

quire stone sculpture. Perhaps the sociological and ideological dynamics of what occurred at Rivas called on different displays of prestige goods and activities than took place at ceremonial sites in other areas. The stone pillars, discussed earlier, are the largest and most prominent stone monuments for the upper General Valley, and while they may have been modified to some degree, they clearly involved less craftsmanship than the stone balls in the southern part of the valley or statuary across the mountains.

A Trace of Textile

One artifact deserves special mention even though it is the only example of its kind at the site. In the materials we recovered from LH Q on the Panteón de La Reina, there were three small sherds that fit together (fig. 7.13: 1). Joined, the three comprised a single piece measuring 12 centimeters in maximum length, 6 cen-

timeters in width, and 1.5 centimeters in thickness. This was not a pretty piece of pottery. The paste was of medium quality and the color varied, suggesting uneven firing. What made these fragments special was the impression of a fabric on the interior, concave side. This was the only evidence of textiles found at the site.

William J Conklin, a noted expert on textiles, kindly agreed to examine the structure of the now-vanished textile based on its impression. All of the following observations are his unless otherwise noted. The first issue he addressed in his analysis is why there is a textile impression on the inside of a vessel. Fabric impressions are sometimes found on the bases of vessels because the vessels were placed on a cloth or mat after manufacture when the clay was still tacky and receptive to marking. Conklin notes, however, that if a larger vessel had been used as a kind of mold in which to make a smaller, perhaps thinner, pot, a damp cloth may have been laid between the two surfaces so that the newer, smaller vessel could be removed from the larger one. If the pot that had served as the mold itself had not been fired, it could easily have been impressed as the clay for the second vessel was pressed against it. Since it appears that some vessels were made in this manner, Conklin's observation seems quite reasonable.

The textile itself has the characteristics of having been loom woven. Most of the fabric impression seems to represent a simple, plain, balanced weave with neither warps nor wefts predominating and each consisting of elements about 1 millimeter in diameter. A portion of the impression is different, however, with one set, possibly the warp, having created alternating large and small impressions. Linear troughlike impressions have been created in every other row, suggesting that there had been a continous ridge in the textile itself. Conklin suggests a number of possible explanations for this distinct pattern. The three most likely explanations are (1) that there was some smearing of clay onto parts of the textile, slightly altering its visible patterning; (2) that there were separate elements, locally carried as "floats" in the textile, producing local ridges within a plain weave; or (3) that the textile was constructed using columns (or rows) or elements in "over-and-under" construction alternating with rows (or columns) of twined elements (fig. 7.13: 2).

A piece of cloth used for pottery making probably

was little more than a rag. Nevertheless, this evidence is extremely valuable because so little is known of the textiles of the ancient people of southern Central America. The fact that rags existed means that cloth was present in some abundance. Thus the people at Rivas were clothed, not nearly naked as Gabb encountered them. The Kogi of Colombia (Reichel-Dolmatoff 1976, 1985) wear long shirts today, and perhaps similar fashions were popular at the time of Rivas. Elaborate textiles may have been made, now vanished save for a few imprints on sherds. It would be well worthwhile looking for other examples, although this was the single find among thousands of sherds examined.

Summary of Artifact Analyses

Artifact analysis is often similar to a child's Christmas: the reality does not always match dreamed-of expectations. Questions posed often aren't answered, and always, new ones are raised. The big questions with which we started the project were: What happened at Rivas? and How may knowledge of the Rivas site and the people who built it and used it add to our knowledge of the Chiriquí archaeological culture? and How do our understandings of what happened at Rivas and of Chiriquí culture contribute to theoretical issues in anthropology regarding the nature and origins of those socially ranked societies known as chiefdoms? These three questions move from specific to more general subjects and issues.

Our studies of artifacts can help address these questions. Here, I will mostly concentrate on the first two, saving the last one for the end of this chapter. We can say that the artifacts show that eating and drinking were certainly important activities at the site. If Buenos Aires Polychrome pottery was the "party ware" of Chiriquí folk, then there were lots of fiestas at Rivas. I think that this statement is not quite correct, though. The high amount of Buenos Aires Polychrome and the low amount of Tarragó Biscuit at this site, at the upper end of the valley, is in reverse proportion to the ceramic assemblages at sites in western Panama. The great amounts of Buenos Aires Polychrome thus seem to be partly due to a regional popularity for the ware compared to other regions. We might also consider whether the high amount of Buenos Aires Polychrome at Rivas compared to Murciélago is due to the fact that the lat-

ter site is later and perhaps the style lost some popularity. In this case, however, I think that the distribution is reflecting the use of Buenos Aires Polychrome as specialty ware for fiestas.

Not only do the dominant ceramic types at Rivas suggest fiestas but so does the range of vessel forms, which is very narrow. Diverse activities, such as those carried out by a household, would require diverse vessels of different sizes and shapes. Instead, the Rivas assemblage consists mostly of open bowls; small to medium-size jars, some of which may have been drinking mugs; and large jars and bowls that appear to have been useful to carry and serve liquids such as *chicha*.

The narrow range of vessels is a supposition. No other Chiriquí site has been studied or reported in the way we have conducted the research at Rivas, so we have no comparison at present. But further support of the argument that limited activities were carried out at Rivas is found in the similar narrow range of stone tools at the site. This is especially true for ground stone tools, particularly metates. Almost none were found in the upper layers of the site, and those found were broken and reused as cobbles in the stone circles and other structures.

Another aspect of the site that appears to be unusual is the great amount of exotic ceramics in Operation E. At least they appear to be exotic. Many could be regional styles with which we are not familiar. Since Rivas appears to be at the western edge of the Chiriquí region, some could be from not too far away. Nevertheless, given current information, many of these ceramics do appear to be from distant regions. This does not necessarily mean that people from distant lands brought these ceramics to the Rivas site, however. Such could be the case, but it also is possible that these were prized goods obtained from foreigners by Chiriquí people through some sort of exchange system who then brought these valued exotic ceramics to Rivas. What is interesting is that the concentration of these exotics is exceptionally high in Operation E, especially but not exclusively at the southern end of the oval. Thus we may infer that whatever events occurred in Operation E were different from those in any other area of the site. Such activities entailed the breaking, perhaps deliberately, of rare pottery vessels. Since most of the vessels in question are relatively small, we may assume that it was the ceramics themselves and not their contents that were brought to the site. Special drinking and eating vessels were taken to Rivas, were used to consume foods and liquids, and were broken and discarded.

Another point to consider is the role of the figurines of women and animals. Why were women, tapirs, and peccaries the only creatures to be portrayed as complex, three-dimensional figurines? There are many animals depicted in Chiriquí pottery such as birds and felines as legs on tripod vessels and so forth. The triangles painted on Buenos Aires Polychrome pots were interpreted to represent alligators by William Henry Holmes (1888: 82), who conducted the first detailed study of Chiriquí area ceramics. He subsequently named what we now call Buenos Aires Polychrome as Alligator Ware. The stylized armadillos on the handles of Tarragó Biscuit pottery similarly led George MacCurdy (1911) to name the ceramic type as the Armadillo Group. There are one or two Buenos Aires Polychrome vessels in museum collections in the form of alligators. The armadillos are clearly present in Tarragó Biscuit ceramics, although they are done casually in their execution. There also are a few representations of the stylized tortoise or armadillo quadruped bowl style such as we found in the Operation C cemetery.

Armadillos play a prominent role in the folklore and mythology of South American Indians (Wilbert and Simoneau 1992: 755). They are portrayed as culture heroes, the oldest of animals, the scout sent out after the deluge, and magical helpers. These armored creatures are frequently rendered in a casual style as handles on Tarragó pottery, but mostly tapirs, peccaries, and humans are elaborated much more as fully rounded figurines at Rivas.

There is an extensive literature on the symbolic role of the tapir in the mythology of Middle and South American Indians. The tapir is seen as a powerful sexual symbol, a seducer of women, and a tricksterlike figure (Benson 1997: 44; Roe 1982: 192). The creature is often portrayed as the master of animals or of crops, a spirit helper who sometimes transforms itself into a human (Wilbert and Simoneau 1992: 1239). Tapirs are hunted and valued for their meat and hides, but it is their symbolic power that must have given them the status to be rendered as figurines.

Peter Roe (1982: 192) cites Lévi-Strauss (1969: 276) on the sexual ambiguity of these animals, which is nonetheless powerful. They are famed for their large penis.

At the same time, Phillipe Descola (1993: 79) states that the Achuar, formerly known as the Shipibo, consider the tapir as the "corpulent symbol of ideal maternity." Tapir pregnancy lasts for more than a year, and mothers suckle their young for many months.

Perhaps the idea that tapirs can transform themselves into humans is due to their preferred habitats. A forestry study (Fragoso 1991) determined that tapirs prefer to feed in the earliest successional stage habitat of floodplains and disturbed areas, such as recently logged forest. These areas support the greatest density of all food plants, especially herbs, which tapirs favor. Logged areas and floodplains are where humans plant gardens. Thus tapirs and humans would have competed for the same territories. Although no studies are available on the topic, it is likely that tapirs would actively prey on garden crops. Just as deer populations increase with the introduction of maize fields, tapir populations may also have risen. Tapirs and humans therefore share characteristics of sexuality and gestation and may be linked in their preference to spend time in gardens. Tapirs prey upon the fruits of gardens and, in turn, are preyed upon by humans, yet both are similar in their behaviors, especially in regard to sex and procreation. Tapir figurines may thus be bundles of these symbolic relationships.

Peccaries, like humans and tapirs, have few young at birth (Emmons 1999: 178–180). Infant peccaries quickly learn to walk and stay close to their mothers. The most significant behavioral difference between tapirs and peccaries is that the latter are distinctly social, traveling in herds in the forest, away from humans, where they are the favorite prey of jaguars and pumas (Benson 1997: 44). If tapirs are competitors to humans, intruding into the cultural space of the garden, then peccaries comprise a separate, parallel community. They are a society of the forest—living in groups, like humans; raising their young, like humans; and fearing big cats, like all but the bravest hunters. Perhaps the "cute," solid clay peccary figurine with a suspension hole, found in Operation A (see fig. 2.5), was for a child: be like the peccary young and stay close to your parents or the big jaguar will eat you.

What do figurines that may be associated with fertility and reproduction have to do with drinking and eating in quantity? Both are affirmations of the continuity of life and commonly are tied to funerals. Both tapirs and peccaries are animals like humans but different from them. The tapir is both competitor and prey. It may eat the garden crops, but it can be killed and eaten itself. The peccary is also a food source, and it is part of an analogous social community, apart from humans. In a world with no domestic beasts, in which animal protein was rare and prized, the fertility of these two porcine creatures was most desired. Although it is speculation, the continued abundance of both tapirs and peccaries may have been seen as vital to the continuity and prosperity of human society. Figurines of tapirs and peccaries thus took their places alongside figurines of humans so that all might increase in numbers.

Many mortuary rituals incorporate activities that reaffirm the social system that is endangered by the loss of one of its members through death. Ritual or verbal statements that life continues or is even nurtured by death are part of the same sentiments, differing only by the degree to which they do or do not emphasize the individual instead of the social group. The Irish wake or even a simple meal served after a burial ceremony both are common expressions of such sentiments in contemporary Western culture. What better place, then, to reaffirm the life force that will guarantee babies, whether human or porcine, than at a mortuary ritual center?

In sum, the artifacts at the Rivas site suggest common, everyday activities of eating and drinking, but there are some important absences in what we would expect if the site were simply a village. For example, there is the absence of metates. There are exotic ceramics, in great numbers and great amounts of fancy pottery as well. It is now appropriate and necessary to try and combine the evidence from artifacts and architecture with other lines of evidence to interpret the site in full. In the next chapter, I will attempt to put some anthropological meat on the bones of the archaeological skeleton I have managed to assemble.

CHAPTER EIGHT

THE PHYSICAL AND SOCIAL WORLDS OF ANCIENT RIVAS

Archaeology and Ethnography

Everything I have written up to this point has been designed to lead you, the reader, to the same conclusions I made, some time ago, that Rivas was a special ceremonial center for mortuary practices to bury elite on the Panteón de La Reina. I came to this conclusion after the fateful Loot Day. Although I had an "aha!" moment, I can't remember exactly when it was. It certainly wasn't in the days immediately following the frenzied morning of excavations through the pavements on the upper terrace of Operation D. My research thus did not follow the strict scientific method of hypothesis testing that I had been taught in graduate school to rigorously uphold. In that approach, the archaeologist sets up three or four possible explanations such as: "If the Rivas site was primarily a residence, then we would expect the archaeological data to be patterned this way. But if the Rivas site was primarily a ceremonial center, we would expect the archaeological data to be patterned that way." Then, trusty trowel in hand, the archaeologist goes out to excavate, discarding all of the hypotheses he or she has

created that clearly don't fit the data. The hypothesis that remains after this work is the one used as the explanation for the observed phenomena of archaeological data.

I should note that I did not deliberately attempt to avoid the scientific method. It is just a simple fact that the most important lines of evidence I followed were ones that I hadn't expected at all and therefore could never have built into a series of "if/then" statements about the site. It is true, though, that as I found out new things, I used a series of "if/then" statements, but they weren't always constructed with multiple hypotheses to be tested.

I started out with some general notions about what I expected to find, based on Bob Drolet's work at Murciélago. When I found things that didn't fit into my expectations, I had to develop explanations for them, and those led me to new interpretations of Rivas as something different from Murciélago. In a general way, I did follow a method of hypothesis testing, but it was not with the precision that many scientific archaeologists hope will happen. For sites or situations in which there is a considerable amount of previous discussion, it is easier to build detailed hypotheses. But for areas in which very little is known, it is more difficult to make a set of alternatives. In these latter cases, the hypotheses that can be developed are very general, because knowledge is general and vague. What is more appropriate to say, perhaps, is that my "if/then" hypotheses are so generalized that I might not even formulate them as such. Some future archaeologist may take our research at Rivas and develop a more precise set of hypotheses based on the increased amount of knowledge on Chiriquí culture.

Now that I have concluded that Rivas was a ceremonial center, though, I feel obliged to hammer away at that idea and see if I can come up with alternate explanations. Frankly, I don't think so. There is too much evidence that points to Rivas as a place for conducting rituals for the burial of the dead. The orientations of the structures to the terrace and to the stairs are the strongest lines of evidence, but they are well supported by the analyses of the artifacts. I think that the more interesting and perhaps more important question is not *if* Rivas was a mortuary ceremonial precinct but, rather, to what degree was it a specialized center? This raises the question of how the site and its occupants fit into the larger social world of Chiriquí culture in late prehistory. It brings us to questions of social anthropology.

Sixteenth-Century Panama

For the New World, and in other places, too, early colonial period accounts are available that describe native cultures at the time of contact. For use as a baseline by which to compare archaeological data, they must be treated with caution due to the decimation of populations brought about by European diseases. Lacking resistance to Old World viruses, native populations were traumatized in the sixteenth century. The diseases usually traveled much faster than Europeans, so that by the time the first Spaniard, Frenchman, or Englishman entered a region, the native social system had already been shaken or collapsed. The degree to which societies were affected varied, though. The coast of Peru suffered huge losses of people, for example, but depopulation was apparently less severe in the highlands.

For southern Costa Rica, we lack detailed information on such events. We know that Europeans entered

the region briefly in the sixteenth century and that most did not stay very long or write very much, but there is one exception. Gonzalo Fernández de Oviedo y Valdés (a.k.a. Oviedo) deserves to be much better known than he is. As a youth, he served as a page in the court of Ferdinand and Isabella and was present at the siege of Granada. He was 22 the year that Columbus discovered America and was soon in the New World. In 1513 he was appointed the Royal Warden of Gold Mines on the isthmus, and in 1526 he became governor of Antigua. He started writing about his experiences in the New World in 1515, one of the earliest chroniclers writing about terra firma. A version of his report was published in 1526 and his magnum opus began to be printed in 1550, but his death seven years later cut short publication of the full 50 volumes of his writings. It was not until the nineteenth century that the full work finally was printed and distributed, and further editions were rarely printed (Oviedo y Valdés 1959). Part of the delay was due to the fact that later historians tended to disparage Oviedo because he, in turn, made it clear that he did not like Columbus. But if Oviedo's personal agendas are taken into consideration, his work is quite valuable in providing a firsthand account of life in the New World less than a decade after initial contact by Europeans.

Early chroniclers frequently don't quite say everything that a modern scholar would like to know. Often, they state something such as "and there were many interesting other customs that I will recount later," and never do, which leaves the scholar frustrated. Other than these general problems common to all early reports, there are two aspects of Oviedo's account that make use of it for insights into Rivas tenuous. The first is that even though he was a very early chronicler, he was writing two centuries or more after the Rivas site was abandoned. Thus there is not only the problem that cultures likely changed as a consequence of dramatic population decreases from introduced diseases a few years prior to Oviedo's experiences. There is also the problem that cultures likely changed in the 200 years between the times of Rivas and Oviedo's era. The second problem is that Oviedo's experiences were mostly in central Panama, far from the Rivas area. We might expect that the ways in which societies were organized in central Panama were different than in southern Costa Rica. We know, for example, that the forms of burial seem to have been different. The grand graves at the famous Conté site in central Panama (Lothrop 1937, 1942; Mason 1942; Hearne and Sharer 1992) were not on a ridge-top, like at Rivas, but in the ground. Many features of them, as well as their later date and distant location, make them interesting for comparison but not for much enlightenment. Nevertheless, it is worth reviewing what Oviedo said about the chiefdom societies he encountered. They offer issues worth considering in interpreting Rivas. This is even more so because a very influential scholar on southern Central American chiefdoms, Mary Helms (1979, 1994), uses Oviedo's information in her own interpretations.

In sixteenth-century central Panama, society was composed of two distinct strata: common folk and those of high rank. There were three ranks within the elite: *quevis*, who occupied the highest offices; *sacos*, who had vassals but were inferior to *quevis*; and *cabras*. The *cabras* were a category that offered upward social mobility for commoner men who had distinguished themselves in battle. Following Oviedo, Helms interprets the *quevis* as high chiefs who held sway over a given territory, with *sacos* and *cabras* administering districts within the *quevi*'s domain.

Populations were dispersed, with no cities or large towns. The *quevi* lived in a large compound, however, called a *bohio*, consisting of a number of structures. One of these buildings was reserved as a kind of temple, and it held the dried remains of the *quevis*'s ancestors, richly adorned and arranged in the order of the rank that they had held in life. A later seventeenth-century account of the Darien region, in southern Panama, reported that a "patriarch" controlled a large extended family, focused on daughters and granddaughters with their husbands and families (Wafer 1956 [1699]; see Helms 1979: 8–9). The titles of these people were not mentioned, but it is likely that higher-ranking men had increasingly larger households. Helms believes that political alliances were sealed through marriage, a common practice throughout the world. She also suspects that the varying marriage and family alliances were founded on lineages that were ranked, relative to one another (Helms 1994: 55).

Different forms of dress, different rituals, and endogamy distinguished the two major classes of elites and commoners from each other. The status symbols of elites included gold ornaments, distinctive clothing,

elaborately decorated houses, litters for the highest ranks, and elaborate mortuary rituals and graves (Helms 1994: 58). Complex political alliances among elites were likely related to making truces or joining forces in warfare, to gain access to fishing and hunting grounds, and perhaps to attain prestige goods and access to trade routes (Helms 1979: 33). Food was plentiful and probably locally controlled, although chiefs may have had access to lands to produce abundant surpluses beyond their basic needs.

Even the less than fully attentive reader may have noted descriptions of sixteenth-century Panamanian chiefdoms that might easily apply to Rivas. The description of two distinct classes might find an analogy in the two burial populations on the Panteón and at Rivas, for example. But, as already noted, sixteenth-century Panama is several hundred miles away and at least two centuries later than the last occupation of Rivas. Before I examine how we might use the Panamanian data, I will first discuss information later in time but closer to the upper General Valley. Finally, I will compare all of this information with the Rivas and Chiriquí evidence, taking into account theories on the nature of chiefs and chiefdoms.

Cabécar and Bribri

There are two principal sources with relatively detailed information on the native peoples of Costa Rica that pertain to Rivas. The first is by William Gabb (1875), an American who collected objects for the Smithsonian Institution. The second is by Doris Stone (1962), daughter of a U.S. executive for the United Fruit Company. While Gabb has the advantage of providing an early account, Stone was a pioneering archaeologist and ethnographer who had extensive knowledge of Costa Rica and its past and present peoples.

Both authors discuss the peoples of the Talamancan Mountains. By the nineteenth century, and still today, the greatest number of native people in Costa Rica resided in the mountains, hills, and plains of the Atlantic Watershed southeast of San José. These Talamancan tribes, as Stone refers to them, also populated the flanks of the mountains on the Pacific side and today consist primarily of two groups known as the Cabécar and Bribri. Attempting to define distinct social groups, especially in relation to prehistoric populations, is complicated by layers of postcontact historical events. For example, a group apparently unrelated to either the Cabécar or Bribri, known as the Brunca, today live in the town of Rey Curré and the nearby hilltop settlement of Boruca. Excavations at Rey Curré (Corrales 1983) revealed continual occupation from prehistory to the present, with Buenos Aires Polychrome sherds and other artifacts directly under the feet of modern Brunca people. As inhabitants of one of the oldest continuously occupied communities in the New World, the Brunca, then, are clear candidates for claims of descent from Chiriquí ancestors. But the Brunca consider themselves as distinct and apart from the Cabécar and Bribri.

If we could know for certain that the people of the upper General Valley were the ancestors of the Brunca or the Cabécar and Bribri, it would be most useful information in attempting to interpret Rivas. Unfortunately, we do not have that information. Nonetheless, I am going to use the information on the Cabécar and Bribri for two reasons. First, the systems of social organization described for these groups covered a great area, including the Pacific slopes of the Talamanca Mountains. Second, the Rivas site is much closer to the Cabécar and Bribri than it is to the Brunca heartland; indeed, it is in the foothills of the Talamanca Mountains. Most of the following discussion of these groups is based on the work of Doris Stone, who knew Gabb's publication and added to the information in it.

The ways in which people define themselves as ethnic or social groups are malleable, depending on historical circumstances. Peoples formerly distinct unite in some circumstances only to redefine themselves as separate when conditions change. The rearrangement of social identities is all too obvious in the past and recent history of the Balkans, for example. We may never know how many different languages or how many different social identities defined one village, group of villages, or subregion a thousand years ago. When people from the upper General River all the way into western Panama used similar dishware and lived in similar houses, and so forth, how did they perceive the boundaries between "us" and "them"? Just as in the modern world, those identities likely shifted and changed depending on many different factors. Without becoming entangled in issues that might never be resolved, it is best to move on. The evidence for simi-

larities between Talamancan tribal practices and Rivas will become evident, or at least argued, presently.

It does seem clear that there were many different social units occupying or controlling particular territories in times past. By the mid-nineteenth century, though, when Gabb encountered them, the Cabécar and Bribri numbered greatest. These two groups are distinctive mostly due to the fact that each has a language unintelligible to the other. They occupied the same region but lived in separate villages so that some areas were more Cabécar while others more Bribri, but with considerable intermingling of populations over the Talamancan range. Both groups agreed that the Bribri had conquered the Cabécar and dated the event to 1827 (Gabb 1875: 489; Stone 1962: 7). In Gabb's time, one family claimed to have the hereditary right of chieftainship. The chief had full powers of government, and upon his death the power passed to the most able person in the royal family, not necessarily his son.

Both Gabb and Stone state that the Cabécar were learned and intelligent and the Bribri aggressive. The Cabécar learned to speak Bribri, but the reverse was not true. The Cabécar were recognized by both groups as possessors of esoteric knowledge for curing and the control of spiritual forces. According to Gabb, the Cabécar high priest, the UsegLa, was the spiritual leader of both the Bribri and his own group, while the Bribri "king" ruled over both peoples in temporal affairs. This is an important point and deserves emphasizing: the "dominant" group, the Cabécar, claimed special spiritual powers, but the affairs of daily life were under the rulership of a high chief of the "subordinate" group, the Bribri. Thus the people living in the same region recognized a "high" group and a "low" group; "power" was conceived of as spiritual and temporal (to use a Western term not completely inappropriate), and power was split into two roles.

Stone (1962: 35) states that both the Cabécar and Bribri were divided into matrilineal clans that "developed from moieties." What she means in referring to moieties is unclear. So, too, how a "clan" is defined has varied considerably in the anthropological literature. In the present case, Stone states that clans were based on rules of marriage and, on the Caribbean side, with land ownership in particular locales. On the Pacific side, she states that land was owned jointly by two or three groups, presumably referring to clans. In the

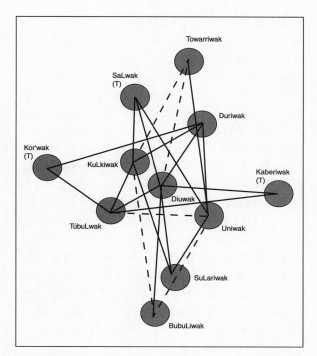

8.1. Bribri marriage patterns. Dotted lines leaving the center of a circle signify a clan whose males can marry women in the clan where the dotted line stops. These marriages are not reciprocal. Solid lines represent marriage between clan members of both sexes. (T) indicates the clan resided only on the Atlantic Watershed. Redrawn from Stone 1962: 16.

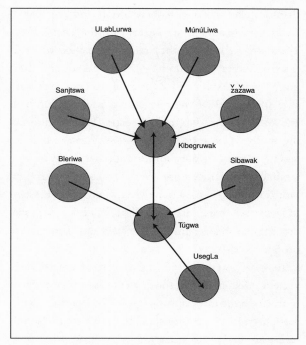

8.2. "Husband Givers" among the Cabécar in the 1950s. The direction of the arrows indicates where men may find brides. The Bleriwa, for example, find brides among the Túgwa. The UsegLa, Túgwa, and Kibegruwak were on both sides of the Talamanca Mountains, while the other clans were only on the Atlantic side. Redrawn from Stone 1962: 36.

1940s there were 9 Cabécar and 11 Bribri clans (figs. 8.1, 8.2). Some of these clans were ranked higher than others, and there were specific marriage rules about in which clans a man or woman could find a husband or wife.

Interestingly, for our purposes, Stone (1962: 35) notes that Gabb interpreted Talamancan social structure as a system of classes rather than clans. The UsegLa came from a single clan of the same name. The most respected medicine men were Cabécar who came from a single community, San José de Cabécar, in the upper Coen River, the same area that Gabb had said was a center of special shamans. It is likely that Gabb simply lacked the terminology to describe what he understood; he was not an anthropologist, and the discipline was only just beginning to take shape in the 1870s. Nevertheless, the fact that he interpreted social structure as stratified is significant. It becomes even more significant when we examine marriage patterns as outlined by Stone. In the 1950s, when Stone wrote her book on the Talamancan tribes, both clan systems had

very specific marriage rules. The Bribri system was quite complex and exhibited no clear patterning (fig. 8.1). The Cabécar pattern, however, was quite clear (fig. 8.2).

Three Cabécar clans intermarried. UsegLa men or women could marry men or women in the Túgwa clan, a "noble" clan that produced chiefs. The Túgwa men and women could marry into the UsegLa clan and the Kibegruwak clan. Kibegruwak men and women could marry Túgwas. In addition to these rules, Túgwa women could marry men from either the Sibawak or Bleriwa clans. Kibegruwak women could marry men from any of the other four Cabécar clans. If we look at the marriage rules from the perspective of men seeking wives, the men of four clans could find wives only among the Kibegruwak, and the men of two clans could find wives only among the Túgwa. The Kibegruwak and Túgwa men could find wives in each other's clan, while the UsegLa could find wives among the Túgwa. Túgwa men had a distinct advantage in having two clans in which to find spouses. Perhaps the extra opportunity for Túgwa men to find spouses in more than one clan was one of their "noble" prerogatives.

Descent was matrilineal except for the Túgwa clan. Túgwas were bilineal; they could trace their descent through either their mother or their father and thus claim "noble" status. Everybody else traced their kinship through their mothers, their mother's mother, and so forth, through their ancestry. This meant that the mother's brother or a person equivalent to him was the man of greatest importance in a family group. Unilineal descent systems—tracing ancestry through only one "line"—tend to be used when it is necessary to keep resources, such as land, tightly held. A single descent line means half as many heirs and claimants to property compared to bilineal descent. Although the status of women is often slightly better in matrilineal societies than in others, the descent system is designed more to avoid breaking up groups of women who work together, such as sisters, than due to any sentiments about equality between the sexes. Another situation encouraging matrilineal descent is when men are away from home for long periods of time, on trading expeditions or fighting wars, or, more recently, working as laborers. The Iroquois are a case of classic matrilineality. Groups of sisters worked the maize and squash fields while Iroquois warriors went on raids as far away as North Carolina or Wisconsin.

Matrilocal postmarital residence sometimes is practiced in matrilineal societies. In such cases, the groom moves to the household or community of the wife, thus keeping the wife with her female workmates. The groom then becomes an additional member of the local community, adding his labor and other abilities to the family of his bride. This seems to have been the case in sixteenth-century Panama, judging from Oviedo's report, as discussed earlier in this chapter. Among the Talamancan tribes, however, the wife moves to her husband's community. Nevertheless, the suitor contributes a substantial amount of labor to the family of his fiancée. On both sides of the mountain range, in the late 1950s, once a marriage was arranged, the suitor would live with his prospective bride's family for a length of time, during which he would work for his soon-to-be in-laws. On the Atlantic Watershed, this sometimes was many years because marriages were arranged when brides were still girls, and the suitor would have to wait until she reached puberty to marry her (Stone 1962: 28–29). Four wives were permitted

a man, and he usually would marry sisters. Such an arrangement could result in substantial energies devoted to one's in-laws.

In such a society as described, political advantage occurs when a man has many sisters who have many daughters. A plethora of female kin of the same age or younger offers opportunities to make alliances with other men who will take your female kinfolk. Returning to the charts of clans, the three clans who interchange women and men among one another are at a distinct advantage. This is especially true for the Kibegruwak and Túgwa because their women are more "in demand," and whereas other clans have to get their women from them, they have a reciprocal relationship between each other. The Túgwa "nobility" perhaps have the best arrangement. They can exchange men and women with the Kibegruwak and the UsegLa religious specialists *and* have two other clans solely dependent on them to provide women.

We do not know to what degree the clan relations described by Stone for the 1950s reflect earlier patterns, especially in remote times. Does the less elegant and more complicated system of Bribri represent a closer approximation of an earlier system or an arrangement resulting from their conquest of the Cabécar and subsequent realignments of older political relations from some previous homeland, which may have had its own dynamics? Is the story of the conquest true, for that matter? Stone notes that clans were known to have been created, to have merged, and to have disappeared. Some Cabécar clans have been "taken over" by the Bribri. We cannot address these questions fully. More to the point, however, there likely never was one set "pattern" of clan relations. They probably were constantly undergoing change through time due to many different factors. Nevertheless, it is clear that the Cabécar clans in the 1950s were ranked and that the ranking was heightened by three clans with status differences in sharp contrast to the other six.

Religious Specialists and Funerals

The final ethnographic information we should examine concerns religious specialists and funerals. The UsegLa were the highest rank of Cabécar priests, but their numbers had diminished by the time of Gabb and Stone, or perhaps their numbers and activities were kept secret from the two outsiders. There was a second group of specialists who apparently were more involved in medicine, as we would call it, than in esoteric practices. These were called *jarwá*. There were both Bribri and Cabécar *jarwá*, although the former were supposedly not much respected and were accused of black magic. It took between two and six years to learn to become a *jarwá*. This long apprenticeship is reminiscent of the complex training for similar knowledge among the Kogi of Colombia (Reichel-Dolmatoff 1976, 1985) who, in many ways, seem to offer analogies to the peoples of ancient southern Costa Rica.

One of the most important rituals for the Talamancan tribes was the burial of the dead. The body of the deceased was taboo, and so specialists had to take care of the remains. The specialists included buriers, known by different names in Bribri and Cabécar, who handled the body and lit the funeral fire. Singers chanted in a sacred language during the funeral ceremonies. There also was a position of Organizer of Feasts who planned and oversaw the rituals and celebrations, serving as a kind of master of ceremonies at the events. Although Gabb said that the role of Singers was hereditary, both he and Stone note that extensive training was necessary to achieve this rank, which was considered second in importance only to the UsegLa. Buriers had to pay fees to a teacher for their training.

Both Gabb and Stone state that there were two phases of burial. The first involved preparing the body and wrapping it in bark cloth tied with cotton string. In the backwoods, the deceased's clothes, ornaments, and other items were buried with the corpse. Miniature tools were often placed with the dead. After a ceremony, the bundle was taken into the woods. In a funeral witnessed by Stone (1962: 11), the corpse was taken about 455 meters from the house. Purification rituals for kin and other activities were carried out for ten days after the disposal of the corpse, ending with a feast.

It was the old practice to retrieve the bones of the dead about a year after the ceremony just described. In Stone's day, however, it was prohibited by Costa Rican law and only practiced in remote areas. The bones were rewrapped, and an extensive ceremony took place. Gabb (1875: 500–501) witnessed the burial of the "last King of Talamanca" and described the ceremony:

I had the rare good fortune . . . to be present at the death feast of the chief Santiago. That is to say, I saw all that happened on the first and last days; the intervening thirteen or fourteen being all alike; a succession of eating, drinking, dancing; a disgusting scene of carousal and debauch that did not possess even the merit of variety.

The feast was held in a large house, adjoining the residence of the chief Birche. . . . A little rack, made of wild cane was tied up to the sloping side of the house, about eight feet from the floor, and on this was laid the bundle containing the disjointed skeleton of the murdered chief.

After the lighting of the fire, singing and dancing began in earnest interrupted occasionally by eating and drinking.

The dances are kept up nearly all [day], and sometimes all night at the funeral feast; the participants retiring from time to time and sleeping an hour or two, when exhausted, and returning with renewed vigor to chicha drinking, eating, and dancing. It is particularly on these occasions, when the older people are too drunk, or too busy to keep strict watch, that the younger folks manage to evade their vigilance and ———. These eminently practical courtships almost invariably preceded the asking of the father's consent by the would-be bridegroom.

After more than two weeks of this license and debauchery, during which three cows, about a dozen pigs, hundreds of bunches of plantains, several quintals of rice, and hundreds of gallons of chicha had been devoured, the *bi-ka-kra* or steward announced that the commissary had given out and the riot must come to an end.

After this event, the bone bundle was carried to a special clan cemetery, a considerable distance away, where the remains were interred.

Chiefly Feasting

The ethnographic record discussed above provides extensive information on tribal and clan organization and funeral rites, among other subjects. How can this information be used to interpret Rivas? We have three sets of information from written sources: the Oviedo account, the report by Gabb, and the writings of Stone.

Each report offers different information, some of which is complementary to the others and some of which is not, for the purposes of interpreting Rivas. Gabb's description of the funeral feast is the most detailed discussion of the behavior of people in a relatively circumscribed space and has the most bearing on interpreting the similarly small space of the Rivas site. Other descriptions, supplied by Gabb and the other writers, are more germane to larger questions about the nature of Chiriquí chiefdoms. I will thus begin on the relatively small scale of the funeral feast described by Gabb and how it pertains to the archaeological data from Rivas.

Gabb witnessed rituals for an important political leader. Presumably, the resources available to the celebrants were considerably less than when populations were greater and had more access to and control over resources. Funeral rites at Rivas might have been even more elaborate than what Gabb witnessed, but his general emphasis on feasting, drinking, and sexual license could be envisioned on a grand scale in the plazas and large houses we uncovered.

Several points that Gabb makes are worth considering. First, the ceremony lasted for about two weeks and consisted of eating, drinking, and dancing. Presumably, much of the victuals had been prepared in advance, but a fortnight of celebrations likely required some cooking and other domestic-like duties while the celebrations were occurring. Thus we might expect the site of such a carousal to leave some residues that resembled regular domestic life, such as fires, broken pots, and tools to keep fires burning, cut up meat or plant foods, and other things involved with the ceremonies and festival. But, on the other hand, everyday work probably was not done. We found evidence for domestic activities at Rivas, but perhaps these were only "domestic" in the sense of keeping the funeral feast going.

Gabb mentions that a little rack was made and tied to the sloping side of the house on which was placed the remains of the chief. Perhaps the post molds we found in various sectors of the site also served to support racks or hold other objects related to burial rites. He also notes that the chief's skeleton was disjointed. Earlier, he states that the body of the chief had been taken out into the bush and left for many months so that all that remained were bones, and Stone reports the same practice. Our evidence is too slim to know if

secondary burial was practiced at Rivas. Some of the "shadow corpses" we found in Operations C and K appeared to be rectangular in shape and might indicate that bundle burial was practiced, but the soil stains are not precisely defined enough to be certain. Pittier's (1892) report on what he witnessed on the Panteón de La Reina suggests that he saw complete burials, but perhaps he did not observe the arrangement of bones carefully.

The large-scale architecture at the site likely was a grand complex for elaborate funeral rites that began in the grand patios of the grand circles. Perhaps such rites entered a final phase of solemnity in the OpD '94 terraces and culminated by carrying the bodies or bundles up the stairs for burial on the Panteón de La Reina. Most of the large-scale architecture likely had few permanent residents. This might explain the smaller structures in Operation A. Perhaps this area was the true residential area for the Rivas inhabitants who lived well by running elaborate funeral services in the plazas below. This still does not explain why some people were buried in Operation K or C, however, but it helps resolve another nagging issue about the site.

Ever since 1992, we were struck by the relative scarcity of metates at the site. Some kind of passive grinding stones are an essential part of any community dependent on maize agriculture. We found charred maize kernels, and a sample of residue from an Operation K pot also yielded evidence of maize. There is no reason to doubt that maize was an important food source for Chiriquí people. Bob Drolet had found so many metates and manos at Murciélago that he thought the community might have specialized in producing maize flour in abundance, perhaps for trade with other communities. But at Rivas we found relatively few manos and almost no metates, as the artifact analyses have shown. Lack of metates makes sense, however, if the large-scale architecture was mostly a place for fiestas, similar to the place Gabb visited. A large-scale party would leave debris very similar to everyday living, but few metates suggests that not much everyday work was carried out. The maize had been ground elsewhere, perhaps, and only food and *chicha* made from *masa* (maize flour) that had been brought to the site was consumed. The corn kernels we found in Operation A again might signal that this was a neighborhood of latter-day funeral parlor directors and party organizers who did go back to their houses and live more typical lives. Even there, though, metates were rare. Perhaps they took home leftovers from the funeral parties or were given food as part of the payment for their services.

Nearly all the metates we found were broken and incorporated into architecture. In 1999 we began to realize that these broken metates likely came from the earlier construction phases in Operations D and E. Older structures were likely robbed of stones for the later, higher constructions, and old metates found on the ground were incorporated into the new building efforts. In other words, it appears that Rivas may have begun as a village not much different than others but that at some time in its history it was remodeled and converted into a specialized mortuary ceremonial center. We suspect that if large-scale excavations could open up areas of the lower construction phase in Operations D and E, we would find many more metates there than in the upper phases. But resources, time, and reluctance to damage the upper architecture prohibited us from opening up such large areas at lower levels.

The final piece of evidence that supports the proposition that Rivas was a mortuary complex are the orientations of the patios of the circular structures. The patios in the central part of Operation D—Complexes I and II—point almost directly west. The patio of the huge Complex III, however, points somewhat northwest. The patio of Structure I in Operation A points southwest. If lines are drawn through the centers of the circles of the houses and the patios, they all intersect at the pavements on the upper terrace (the False Cemetery), in front of the Panteón stairs. Thus the terrace pavement was literally the focal point of the site, and so were the activities that took place there, the last rites of the honored dead.

A volume on the role of feasts in ancient and modern societies has recently been published (Dietler and Hayden 2001). Throughout the case studies presented, spatial differentiation of the feasting area is a clear pattern in the archaeological and ethnographic record. The same is true at Rivas, with the clearly distinctive architecture in the large-scale area of the site and, particularly, the dense accumulations of drinking and eating vessels in the Operation E oval. The Rivas pattern also conforms to other examples in the abundant evidence of large serving vessels and "fancy" pottery for consumption. Where Rivas differs from most such feasting sites, however, is in the absence of clearly identifiable festival food and drink preparation areas and tools. In fact, as noted many times now, Rivas lacks or has very few of the tools necessary to prepare food and drink, that is, metates and large manos to make cornmeal.

While Rivas may contribute to the archaeology of feasting, it is perhaps more important to note that the archaeology of feasting informs us much about Rivas. Clearly the protracted and elaborate ceremonies and feasting of the burial of the dead at Rivas were tied to the complex politics of chiefdom societies. Mortuary feasts and ceremonies at Rivas and similar sites served as contexts in which families and their leaders could attempt to assert their claims to greater recognition and access to power positions by linking the claims of the living to the revered ancestors. Whether this included potlatch-style competition to construct more impressive funeral facilities than another lineage or clan is hard to determine. Due to factors of preservation at the site, with a lack of food remains, the role of feasting per se in competitive funeral ceremonies is hard to interpret in detail. But the lack of an overall organization of the site might be due to a lack of a central authority dictating order to the site plan. Quite possibly, most of the circles or similar complexes each represent a separate social unit that had its own mortuary house at the site.

Archaeological Kin and Clan

The information just presented on the clan organization of the Talamancan peoples is much more detailed than the sixteenth-century report by Oviedo. Nevertheless, there are interesting points that resonate in the discussions of both native peoples. First, in both early colonial Panama and later Talamanca, society was stratified into two distinct classes of elite and commoners. The most distinct difference appears to be the emphasis on power in the hands of the quevís in Panama and the Talamancan arrangement in which the highest temporal leader was a member of the Bribri while the elite Cabécar were prominent religious specialists. Rivas does not appear to have the characteristics of the residence of a quevi; it seems much more like a special religious center such as San José de Cabécar. The *quevi* who Oviedo encountered kept the mummified remains of his ancestors in a structure in his chiefly compound. Of course, such a practice could have been done in earlier times since the numbers of the ultraelite would have been few. The dead on the Panteón de La Reina could have represented the majority of the high-ranking people of the region, just not the very few of highest status. But this seems like something of a stretch of interpretation.

In general, the Rivas data seem to be much more amenable to interpretation using the reports for the nineteenth- and twentieth-century Talamancan tribes than for early colonial period Panama. Before we turn to that issue, however, let us look a little more closely at the Rivas data in light of the Talamancan social systems.

The earlier detailed discussion of Bribri and Cabécar clan organization cannot be easily applied to ancient Chiriquí society. Too many events occurred in the millennium between then and now. First, there is the period before the arrival of Europeans, at least a century, if not more. Michael Snarskis (1992) noted, some time ago, that large sites in the Atlantic Watershed zone appear to have been abandoned by about A.D. 1300. The same is true for Rivas. Those sites, such as Guayabo (Aguilar Piedra 1972; Fonseca Zamora 1979), appear to have served formerly as centers that brought people together, perhaps on pilgrimages or something similar, in relatively peaceful times. Afterward, however, the region seems to have fallen into a balkanized state of petty chiefdoms at war with one another. This is the system encountered by the Spanish.

If chiefly systems in the sixteenth-century upper General Valley were like those of Panama, these societies were organized quite differently than those of the tenth through thirteenth centuries, the time of Rivas. But if the more recent ethnographic evidence for Talamanca fits Rivas so well, it suggests one of a number of possibilities. One is that upper General Valley societies never resembled the chiefdoms of central Panama. While changes occurred in many specifics, the basic clan system of the Bribri and Cabécar is a continuation of social systems of great duration.

A second possibility is that the kinds of chiefdoms described for Panama could have been in operation within a clan system very similar to that described for Talamanca. Perhaps the system of *quevis*, *sacos*, and *cabras* lies in the remnants of the special ranks of the three highest Cabécar clans, with the *cabras* transformed from an achieved category to an ascribed social rank. I cannot interpret the Rivas data to make this claim, however. Perhaps if we had more detailed information on the distinctions in mortuary features on the Panteón de La Reina such a case could be made.

A third possibility is that the social system of Rivas resembled Talamancan tribal organization in its basic structure, though perhaps differing in some aspects. Then, when Rivas was abandoned, there may have been a period in which chiefdoms similar to those described for Panama emerged. Perhaps depopulation and other effects of the Spanish intrusion caused the chiefdom system to collapse, resulting in further changes that led to the situation described for Talamanca of a half a century and more ago but which also resembled the earlier Rivas-like system.

These possibilities are hypothetical constructs. They need to be investigated by conducting archaeological research at many more sites in the valley system. They also raise issues of how we might view the peoples of Rivas and its time from the perspective of different theories on chiefdoms.

Starting sometime between A.D. 800 and 900 and lasting until A.D. 1300 or 1400, though, Rivas was a thriving center of ceremonial activity. All of the research we have conducted suggests that these ceremonies involved the burial of the dead. They likely were carried out over many days, if not weeks. The architecture and activities in the ceremonial precinct generally resembled those of everyday houses and eating and drinking, respectively.

We do not know when or how often such events took place. Rivas was certainly a busy place for at least a brief period during the year. Although it is possible that the site was used intermittently, whenever a distant group made the trip to bury their dead on the Panteón de La Reina, it seems more likely that there was a specific time of year when there was a large gathering at the site. While the site is not highly structured or apparently organized, the fact that circular structures are crammed together and are oriented toward the upper terrace and stairs suggests that the whole place was designed to support large gatherings and spectacle. The honored dead could have been preserved through a number of ways, including drying by heat or by allowing the flesh to disintegrate, preserving the bones. The opportunity to meet other people and to participate in common rites focused on the dead of one's own group, while maintaining distinctions, would have been attractive. A congregation gathered for such feasting of the dead also could have taken advantage of the meeting to plan marriages and make other alliances.

If a single gathering did occur, it was likely at the end of the dry season. There may not have been a distinct dry season, but there likely was a time of year when there was less rain in contrast to wetter times. If it was a fairly distinct period, as today, some of the foliage would be brown, and the air would be dusty. While southern Central America has plenty of rain, the end of the dry season today is an unpleasant time. While the ending of the rains and the beginning of warm, sunny weather are welcomed in December, by March the heat and dust begin to wear on the soul, and people long for the soft early rains, turning the brown fields green and the dry air soft again with humidity. The end of the dry season may easily be associated with death, as plant life shrivels and dies and rivers shrink in size. It would have been easy to link these phenomena with the burial rites of loved ones, much in the same way that Halloween and All Souls Day were associated with the end of harvest and the dying off of summer growth in Europe.

Celestial phenomena may have been linked to the timing of mortuary rites at Rivas. With its heavy cloud cover, Costa Rica is not the best place to rely on seeing the stars every night, but they appear often and are brilliant. Throughout New World cultures, the rising and the setting of the Pleiades were used to mark time. They served to mark the Aztec New Year (Clendinnen 1991), and possible evidence for their importance is found at the ancient site of Chavín de Huantar in Peru (Burger 1992). The borderland tropical forest between Ecuador and Peru also lacks few distinct seasonal markings, as in Costa Rica. There, the Achuar mark the disappearance of the Pleiades from the western horizon in April as a raft journey to the underworld (Descola 1993: 239), and they emerge from their subterranean trip in June in a kind of rebirth. Today, the end of the dry season in southern Costa Rica also is in April. Thus the death of the Pleiades may have been tied into the timing of rituals at Rivas as well.

The Rivas structures face toward the Panteón, which runs in a northeast-southwest direction. The west is the land of the dead in Mesoamerica and Peru, perhaps because the sun sinks into the western sea. The dead of the Panteón de La Reina were thus placed in proper position in relation to their living descendants on the terraces below. But due to its orientation and because the ridge rises so prominently in the valley, late in the day the lower terraces are in shade while the Panteón ridge is briefly lit in a golden glow before the sun rapidly sinks behind the farther western hills of the valley. For a moment then, the living stand in the shade while the ancient ones receive a benediction from the solar orb before they, too, are cast into the dark.

There must have been a resident population to maintain the ceremonial center when it was not in use. The occupants of Operation A could have served this purpose. They certainly had fancy goods. It is also possible, however, that the large-scale architecture was inhabited by a priestly elite and that their everyday life is mixed among the fiesta debris we encountered. Although we (Quilter and Blanco 1995) once thought that there were two distinct classes at Rivas of high and low status, we no longer think that the situation was that straightforward or simple.

The clan organization and social roles for the Cabécar as described by Doris Stone likely represent vestiges of a somewhat more complex system. How more complex it was cannot be said with certainty. There probably were more clans, and perhaps there were more status rankings of priestly specialists and other "professionals." We cannot even be sure if matrilineality was practiced a thousand years ago. Kinship systems can change quickly if there are compelling reasons to ally oneself with others differently. What is striking about the Cabécar clan system is the clear differentiation between the three clans (Kibegruwak, Túgwa, and UsegLa) and the others. These three clans freely intermarry, in pairs. Two of them had special hereditary rights to chieftainship and the highest religious office, and the third, the Kibegruwak, demanded that four other clans marry their sisters and daughters.

Given the Native American penchant for quadripartite division, the Cabécar clan system is hard to fathom. Perhaps the Túgwa and UsegLa were a pair of noble clans, and the Kibegruwak and the other clans were seen as part of a dual division of commoners, with the Kibegruwak as the higher-ranking member of the pair. Perhaps the three highest-ranking Cabécar clans are the transformed ranks of *quevis*, *sacos*, and *cabras*, with the latter transformed from an achieved to an ascribed social rank, though this is but conjecture. What is more important, however, is the basic division of "elite" and "commoners." On the most basic level, this dual division may explain the difference between ridge-top cemeteries and village cemeteries we have seen at Rivas. If the number of clans was greater and perhaps if there were divisions within the "nobility," such organization might explain the divisions between the Panteón Norte and the Panteón Sur or the separate cemetery areas at the El Chiricano cemetery.

It bears repeating here that a critical point in this interpretation of the Rivas burials is the contemporaneity of the Panteón de La Reina burials and those at the Rivas site itself. In general, all of our evidence suggests that the two different sectors of the Panteón were in use simultaneously, as were the separate cemteries on the Rivas terraces. But we should remember that archaeology rarely is able to measure temporal change with a fine scale. Archaeologists must settle for decades, at best, and often, as is the case at Rivas, for centuries. It is quite possible that the different cemeteries were used within decades of each other, and such differences could be the results of rapidly changing social arrangements that we cannot see. Despite this caveat, however, the available evidence does suggest that all the cemeteries on the ridge and below were in use at more or less the same time and therefore that these different mortuary groupings reflect important social differences. High and low in life were reflected as high and low in death, while, at the same time, separate social units—families, clans, or "houses"—were distinguished by separate cemetery areas on both the ridge-top and the terrace.

The fact that there is more than one ridge-top cemetery in the General Valley also must be addressed. The Panteón de La Reina is one of the richest such cemeteries in the region, but it is not the only one, as El Chiricano and others demonstrate. We do not know if these two and the other ridge-top cemeteries were

used contemporaneously, but it is reasonable to think that they were. If we consider the clan diagram (fig. 8.2) for the Cabécar as a stylized model of the organization of a set of clans, it is easy to imagine that there were many other sets as well. Population density in the region was probably high, and through time the landscape had been filled with groups that had fissioned off of earlier, smaller groups but that had replicated the social system of their parent community. In other words, there wasn't just one group of Cabécar or people like them but several subdivisions of them. These different groups may have shared common ways of life and beliefs. Since the site location of Rivas suggests that defense was not a concern and there is no abundant evidence of warfare in the artifacts we found, relations between these different, larger clan groups may have been played out in feasting and other activities associated with funerary rituals, perhaps in a way similar to that suggested for the Hopewell of the eastern United States (Knight 2001).

From a larger perspective, there may have been "maximal units" of organization within the general Chiriquí social and cultural system. The largest unit was Chiriquí in general, stretching from western Panama to southeastern Costa Rica. Within that, there may have been divisions based upon distinct social units expressed in ideology as different practices—for example, the region in which pillars were used as grave markers, north of Buenos Aires, in contrast to the stone balls south of Buenos Aires. It may be significant that there is a "gap" of no large settlements in the major sites mapped by Drolet. The two clusters, one in the upper General Valley and the other along the lower part of the river, likely refer to two large, distinct social groups (fig. 8.3). Stone (1962: 5) cites Juan Vásques de Coronado as stating that there were only two provinces in the region between the Talamancan Mountains and the Coastal mountain ranges, one known as Coto and the other as Turucaca. Together, they were comprised of 13 villages. Although Rivas was abandoned by the time of Coronado's visit in 1563, it is tempting to see the major sites in the valley and the separation between them as analogous to this description. If so, the southern province would have been Coto, and the northern was Turucaca.

Many archaeologists are loathe to assign specific regional or cultural names reported in early colonial

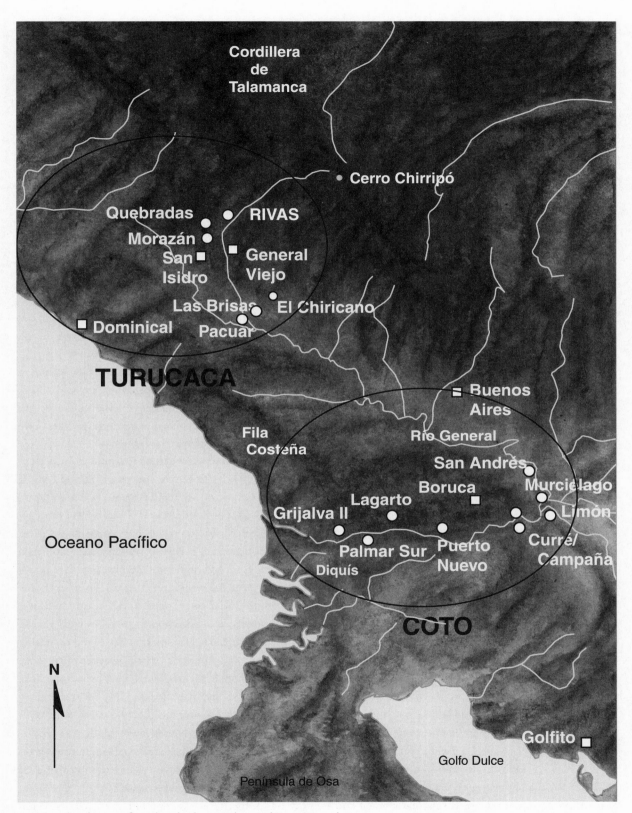

8.3. Suggested names for cultural spheres in late prehistory. Boundaries are approximate.

times to archaeological phenomena for fear that we are projecting a late pattern back into an unknown time. I think it is worth using these terms for the greater Diquís region, however, for a number of reasons. First, the archaeological data, at present, closely conform to a pattern similar to what we would expect from the Spanish descriptions. Second, while western Chiriquí society likely was very different by the time the Spanish arrived than 200 years earlier, when Rivas was a thriving center, it equally could be true that larger cultural patterns had not changed. Third, in proposing this nomenclature, I am providing a clear archaeological problem to test in future work. There also is a tendency in the archaeology of southern Central America to use the term "Greater" for various regions, such as "Greater Chiriquí." Furthermore, everything below these grand areas is called a Subregion, such as the Diquís Subregion. It is time that we start to define distinct cultural units, and with careful work, especially for late prehistory, we might be able to make reasonable linkages between the distribution of archaeological remains and reported social units.

One key to supporting this interpretation is understanding how marriage arrangements, postmarital residence, and mortuary customs were interlinked. Unfortunately, this kind of information is some of the hardest to retrieve through archaeology. If some kind of clan or similar corporate group membership was in operation that crosscut the separate groups living in the valley and if there was a rule that the dead had to be buried not where they lived but where their clan center was located, it might explain why certain places had ridge-top cemeteries but others did not. Alternatively, each ridge-top cemetery may have simply been a central place for a regional group that buried their dead on one particular hilltop.

A critical question that must be answered in order to test the hypotheses just proposed is the issue of how the population was spread across the countryside. Stone noted that Cabécar and Bribri settlements were scattered throughout the landscape. Such dispersed settlement is the kind of situation that would make a place like Rivas an important focal point for a population spread around a region. Rivas clearly had a considerable number of people living there in Operation A, but were there even greater numbers of other people living in hamlets or farmsteads in "rural" areas?

We do not know, and future research would be well directed if it could address this question. For the present, we must be content that our research at the site has advanced knowledge regarding many issues about Chiriquí culture and ridge-top gold cemeteries. By raising new issues, we have helped advance knowledge on the particulars of Costa Rican prehistory and larger matters as well. While previously we could only discuss social organization in Costa Rica in general terms (e.g., Creamer and Hass 1985), we can now offer some very specific proposals as to how society was organized at one time and place in Pacific Costa Rica.

Interregional Dynamics in Late Prehistory

Rivas flourished between about A.D. 900 and 1300. It was not alone. There were many large sites throughout Costa Rica that were built and which thrived during this time. But things fell apart. Why?

The period between A.D. 900 and the 1300s was one of great social unrest to both the north and south. Classic Maya civilization ended at about A.D. 900, and there was trouble in central Mexico, too. To the south, the Chimu empire of the north coast of Peru was only just beginning to organize itself, while the political center of gravity in the central Andes was located much farther south, at Huari and Tiahuanaco, which themselves fell apart sometime in this period. Our understanding of these events is not very good, and dates for the rise and fall of major political and economic powers in both Mesoamerica and the Andes are under seemingly constant revision. It is also hard to know how events so far away may have affected communities in Costa Rica and neighboring regions. We do know, however, that long-distance contacts were operating throughout many periods of antiquity and that these contacts, whether for trade, religious proselytization, or imperial expansion, ebbed and flowed. It therefore seems reasonable to argue that the turmoil in both Mesoamerica and the Andes in the tenth through the early thirteenth centuries may have been in some ways related to the rise, prosperity, and then collapse of events in southern Central America.

The southern Classic Period Maya sites in the Petén region of Guatemala and vicinity appear to have gone into severe decline in A.D. 800 due to increased population, environmental degradation, warfare, and other factors (Sabloff 1990). In the northern Yucatan, however, the Maya thrived, including centers in the Puuc Hills and at the great city of Chichén Itzá, which had its heyday between about A.D. 850 and 1200. Chichén's power was based to a considerable degree, as best can be determined, by its control of long-distance trade systems, many of which were sea routes trading along the Caribbean coast. The Terminal Classic Period, when Chichén rises to power, is also the time when the first gold ornaments make their appearance in significant numbers at Maya sites. In fact, the Sacred Cenote at Chichén Itzá yielded numerous gold disks and other ornaments that appear to have come from Costa Rica (Coggins and Shane 1984).

The evidence suggests that Chichén's fall from power was rapid. When it occurred, the city of Mayapán rose to prominence. Mayapán probably took over some of the trade routes, but it may not have had the great reach of trade routes that its predecessor had controlled. In the Postclassic Period, Mayapán appears to have maintained local power but lost out in the larger political games that increasingly placed the center of political gravity in Mesoamerica in the valley of Mexico, where the Aztecs eventually became masters of an empire. It seems reasonable to suggest that events in Costa Rica are tied to these larger dynamics.

The appearance of the first gold jewelry in Costa Rica is usually interpreted as having spread from the south, from Colombia and Panama. This interpretation suggests a "pushing" of metallurgy up from equatorial regions. But the gold did not travel by itself. It was people who decided to start working gold, and they made their decisions based on complex calculations of what they wanted to do and why they wanted to do it. If we want to talk of a "push" from South America, though, we could also think in terms of a "pull" from Mesoamerica. But, again, these events have to do with people making calculations about their strategies for success in the world in which they find themselves. Costa Rica and southern Central America, in general, are often seen as irrelevant to events happening in Mesoamerica or South America. The fact that the rise of large ceremonial centers in Costa Rica occurred at the same time that a particular kind of long-distance trading system was in operation and that it collapsed when that system ended strongly suggests that Costa Rican native peoples and others in between

Mesoamerica and the Andes were not just passive recipients of culture but were active participants in culture change.

At the same time that we should see events in late prehistoric Costa Rica as involved with those occurring in other, distant locales, we should not lose sight of the unique ways in which people in southern Central America found their own solutions in their own ways to the problems that life put before them. Burying the dead and holding ceremonies and a feast as part of the funeral rites are widespread patterns of human behavior. In the upper General Valley, though, these old traditions were reworked in the context of changing social circumstances apparently related to binding together regional groups. These patterns were part of other changes that had to do with the incorporation of goldworking and gold jewelry as technological and social tools for promoting one's family and self into higher social ranks than others in what was probably a very competitive and confusing time.

Feasting the dead was a ceremonial format that drew upon ideas of family, ancestors, and community. Concepts of equality and common purpose are expressed in such feasting at the same time that they can be manipulated to promote one's own group and interests above those of others. Such tensions and contradictions were being played out at Rivas and many other sites. These dynamics were set in a larger world context, stretching to Mesoamerica and, most likely, South America. When that world system changed, the collapse of the larger context was such that it could not support the increased social ranking or even stratification that was emerging in Costa Rica. The collapse of the system deflated former sharply differentiated social groups into somewhat more equal ones, though the vestiges of the earlier system remained among the Cabécar. Perhaps Murciélago had a gold ridge-top cemetery, or perhaps it simply was a community that had gone through that social trauma. The report by Columbus that everyone wore gold may be further evidence that social distinctions had ended and that former prestige goods were now available to anyone who could get them. The endemic warfare that the Spanish later saw also seems to be a consequence of a system out of balance from an earlier period in which trade and honoring the dead with the proper ceremonies briefly kept the world in order.

Chiefdoms

Now that we are in the final pages of this book, it is time to turn to the issue of chiefdoms. As I stated many pages previously, southern Central America is a place considered to be a kind of "type region" for chiefdoms. I do not plan to offer an extensive review of the historiography of chiefdoms, as the reader may find many other books and writings that discuss the topic in depth (e.g., Earle 1977, 1991, 1997; Pauketat 1994; Redmond 1998). I also do not want to spend a great amount of time discussing whether the term "chiefdom" or some similar concept is appropriate, useful, correct, or accurate in regards to issues of larger anthropological theory. The fact is that many scholars and laypeople do use the term and will undoubtedly want to know how the Rivas and Chiriquí data fit with current understandings of chiefdoms or will attempt to do so even if I choose to ignore the issue. I will thus briefly discuss some of the main contemporary issues concerning the theory of chiefdoms and then discuss the information gained from research at Rivas in light of them.

Robert Carneiro is undoubtedly one of the great paramount chiefs of chiefdom studies today, having written a number of notable articles on the subject (especially Carneiro 1981). In a more recent article (Carneiro 1998), he notes that Klarevo Oberg (1955) was the first to define the chiefdom. He also points out that Oberg's definition stressed the spatial arrangement of this social type: "a chiefdom is an aggregate of villages under the centralized rule of a permanent political leader" (Oberg 1955: 484, cited in Carneiro 1998: 19). Carneiro states that the two leading scholars who are considered the "founding fathers" of the study of chiefdom societies in Americanist anthropology ignored this multivillage aspect. Elman Service (1962) emphasized the social ranking of different groups in a society, and Morton Fried (1967) did the same, even preferring the term "ranked society" over "chiefdom." Carneiro believes that the multiplicity of villages is the essential feature of the chiefdom and defines it as "an autonomous political unit comprising a number of villages under the permanent control of a paramount chief" (Carneiro 1981: 45).

In a review of changing conceptualizations of the chiefdom, Timothy Pauketat (1994: 2) characterizes it as generally consisting of a "form of nonstate polity based on sacral authority, a nonbureaucratized administrative hierarchy, and a tributary mode of production." He traces how different scholars have emphasized different aspects of what they see as chiefdoms, however. Elman Service, who perhaps more than anyone else was a proponent of the idea of "chiefdoms" in the 1960s and 1970s, saw the chief as a manager and integrator of society. Service, Fried, and many of those who followed their theories saw the primary role of the chief as collecting surplus food and other goods and redistributing them, thus serving to even out imbalances in resources. The research of Timothy Earle (1977, 1981), particularly in Hawaii—another "type region"—challenged the notion that chiefs were redistributors of resources. In later research, Earle developed a perspective (see Brumfiel and Earle 1987) that used the concept of political economy. From this perspective, the growth of chiefly roles involved increasing control over things that only are separable analytically but not in the everyday world of real human beings—such things as religion, prestige goods, and the ability to make the many conform to the wishes of a few.

It should be noted at this point that most of the previous discussion of social types involves what are called "complex chiefdoms" (see Wright 1984). In such societies, classes may emerge, a phenomenon often seen as the hallmark of the state. These ranked groups crosscut kin ties and other social relations, and members of the upper class uniformly appropriate the labor and surpluses of lower classes at the same time that they compete among themselves. Class loyalties outweigh any other social ties. Unlike states, there is no qualitative separation between classes in complex chiefdoms: there are still kinship links between them. But Pauketat (1994: 10) states that there is a quantitative separation, as fewer commoners are tied by bonds of kinship to members of the higher classes.

Pauketat (1994: 13–14) proposes a different theory for understanding chiefdoms, one that is based in a "Theory of Practice," sometimes also referred to as Agency Theory. In this view, the focus is on the way in which the actors in a given, but evolving, social setting conceive of their realities: the cultural meanings and symbols through which people act in the world. How these actions take place within the constraints of the cultural system and the objective conditions of their realities is what drives culture change. The theory also assumes that people act within these frames with the intent, generally, to preserve the status quo as they understand it. But their actions produce unforeseen and unintended outcomes that change that status quo. Medieval warlords, for example, adopted guns to pursue their ambitions for power. They lived in a world in which elite privilege was literally and figuratively based on their roles as horsemen (*chevalliers*, *caballeros*). But the introduction of gunpowder allowed a common foot soldier to bring down a mighty knight and tumble down the walls of the castles of barons and earls. Thus actions within a status quo had tremendous, unforseen consequences.

Having reviewed these various theories of chiefdoms, we may now ask how well the Rivas data may be interpreted in light of them. If we follow the "classic" definition of a chiefdom as consisting of a multivillage community with a paramount chief in his capital town, then the Rivas data are wanting at first glance. There is no evidence that permits us to interpret Rivas as the residence of a paramount chief. Furthermore, our burial data do not exhibit anything that might suggest that one family group was exalted above all others, as we might expect in the case of the highest-ranking leader.

The burial data are hard to use because the Panteón de La Reina has been so badly damaged by looting. A careful study of this cemetery and others like it might yield more fine-grained information that might address the issue, however. In terms of the Rivas site itself, again there is no evidence that a single or even a few families were exalted to a higher level than others. It is possible that some of the large structures in the large-scale architecture were occupied and that they were the dwellings of such an elite. But the structures can just as easily be interpreted as specialized ritual facilities for visiting kin groups that used the facilities for a short time to bury their dead on the Panteón, and this is the interpretation I favor. Absence of a wide range of artifacts that suggest long-term domestic activities is the critical factor in my judgment. The Operation A area may be the residence of the caretakers of the complex, and the great amounts of fancy pottery and other valued artifacts seem to indicate that they had high status. But the fact that there were many houses on the terrace of Operation A suggests that this was a large group of people who held some kind of special status, not a small coterie of a chiefly family. As far as this issue is concerned, though, future comparative studies of other sites may help to clarify the issue of how elite and special the occupants of Operation A may have been.

There is another way to approach the issue of the Chiriquí region as a realm of chiefdoms. While we do not have good information on villages, we have at least some information on ridge-top cemeteries. We know that the Panteón de La Reina was one of the richest ridge-top cemeteries in all of southern Costa Rica. There was another elaborate one near Buenos Aires, however, and there are smaller ridge-top graveyards throughout the region, as I discussed in the preceding chapter. Did every ridge-top cemetery have a ceremonial center and residential complex associated with it? We do not know, but the little evidence available suggests that such may be the case. Much more work needs to be done, but apparently the cemeteries were roughly contemporaneous. If they were, then it is reasonable to assume that each represents a social unit of some sort within the larger world of Chiriquí times. A critical question to address is whether cemetery/residential sites that differed in size reflect some regional hierarchy or whether they were independent units, differing in size due to a variety of reasons. We might expect that the situation was somewhat analogous to the Classic Period Maya, with each cemetery/residential complex representing an independent unit but one that made alliances and shifted its role as something equivalent to ally, vassal, or lord depending on changing political circumstances through time. Who was negotiating such political arrangements, however, currently cannot be known. How the process of making treaties, marriage arrangements, warfare, trading partners, and the like was carried out is uncertain. Presumably, some members of the elite such as were buried on the ridge-tops did so, but how power was gained and wielded cannot be determined with any certainty.

The fact that ridge-top burials appear to be organized in units that increase in size from individual grave to family plots to some kind of lineage or clan suggests that it was the highest-ranking families within these largest units who likely wielded the greatest power. Whether one such maximal unit rose to prominence at any time and place to assume the highest rank of the chieftainship, however, cannot be determined at present.

Continuing with reference to various interpretations of chiefdoms, it does appear that something similar to classes had emerged in Chiriquí times. The distinctions between the people buried on ridge-tops and the people buried on the river terraces is sharp enough to suggest that Chiriquí society was composed of two very distinct strata. There even appears to be a qualitative difference between the two groups as marked by the use of gold jewelry by one group and its absence in the graves of the other group. Archaeological data are coarse, though, and perhaps there was more permeability of the system than can be seen through artifacts and poorly preserved burials. It is hard to imagine, however, that burial in two such different areas would have taken place without the concept that these two groups of people were real classes: they had no association in life and none in death. As I have noted many times before, this interpretation is dependent on the contemporaneity of the terrace graveyards and the Panteón de La Reina burials. Evidence for such coexistence of two modes of burial and two classes is fairly strong, judging by artifacts, but it is not as strong as it might be with better radiocarbon dates and other supporting evidence, such as genetic studies of the bones of the dead. Perhaps excavation at a Chiriquí site with better preservation of organic materials may one day help to answer these questions.

As for issues of agency, I have already suggested that the elaborate mortuary center of Rivas grew out of earlier traditions and humbler means of disposing of the mortal remains of the honored dead. Ancestry and kinship clearly were the means by which people made claims about who they were and what they could do. At some point in time, probably tied to a number of other changes including population growth and the arrival of gold-working technology, among others, the simpler patterns of early times were elaborated. They were elaborated in such a way that some people claimed special privileges—in death, to be buried on the ridge-top, and in life, very likely to demand that others work for them or fulfill their desires in a number of ways. For some time, perhaps as long as three centuries, this ideological and ritual complex was able to support a system of institutionalized inequality. The priesthood and other ritual specialists were able to convince others that this was the way the world was supposed to be and that any attempt at change would bring disaster. Perhaps the inequalities did offer a relatively stable world in which warfare was diminished and competitiveness occurred among the elite, with their retainers, in staging more elaborate ceremonies for their dead than others.

A recent review of issues and theory in North American archaeology by Michelle Hegmon (2003) notes that there has been a shift away from the study of "the" social organization to investigating organizational strategies. Nevertheless, the chiefdom concept still holds interest for many scholars. In the southwestern United States, however, at least one recently published volume (Mills 2000) shifts away from the concept because leadership seems to have taken on a variety of forms. I think that with further study, the same may be true for southern Central America. The term "chiefdom" might still hold some relevance, but as more work is carried out and different organizational strategies are revealed, such work will provide a richer database for those interested in chiefdom variability but also offer more to consider for those interested in the details, rather than in generalizing categories.

We still have much to learn regarding the density of population in southern Costa Rica and the kinds of demographic and other pressures that may have contributed to the complexity we can see in the case of Chiriquí. Although there appears to have been great inequality between two major sectors of the societies of the people who used Rivas, other forces, probably a combination of social and environmental, appear to have prevented the consolidation of power in a ruling class that would have led to a true state. The Rivas center was a powerful magnet for people to come to and to engage in displays and feasting to emphasize their lineage and their other claims to power, but it could not hold them for long. How power was distributed once they returned home is a subject that remains to be studied in the future.

EPILOGUE

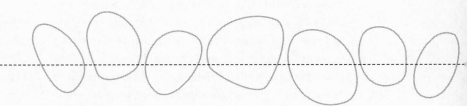

Archaeologists try to objectively study how cultures change but they cannot escape change themselves. Whether members of large civilizations or small tribes, individuals, including students of the past, are caught in the flow of transitions and transformations. I write this short epilogue in the summer of 2003, only a few weeks before this book goes to press and ten years after our major excavations in Operation E. After our 1998 field season we went back to Costa Rica regularly for the next two years to do laboratory work and analysis. Then three years slipped by before I was able to return to Costa Rica, and this year I found many changes.

The Musoc bus line is no longer in that section of San José known as the Coca Cola. It has moved across town to its own new concrete-and-glass building, complete with a stained glass window and a fountain replicating a tropical waterfall. The buses are bigger and more comfortable, though they still wind through the mountain mists and often pause for long periods while landslides are bulldozed off the road ahead. A huge billboard located on the edge of San Isidro offers an answer to the question regarding the general who gave the valley his title: "En Esta Valle el General Es

Jesu Cristo" (In This Valley the General Is Jesus Christ). The ice cream shops full of exotic flavors, which we once frequented in San Isidro, have closed down, as has our former favorite place for lunch, the Soda el Jardín. Now, a two-story McDonald's shines in bright colors of red and yellow along the highway, a favorite place for young couples on dates. Along the road to Rivas a few new houses and restaurants have opened, with one enterprising establishment featuring the Piedrón del Indio as a main attraction.

Although the main street looks about the same, the town of Rivas has grown. It has spread up side valleys where the bright orange of new roads can be seen cutting through the green hills. Happily, the people of the Rivas site—the Mora and Mata families—are all doing pretty well. There have been a few deaths of the older folk, but the "Dons" remain fit and active. Many of the younger men have left the valley for work in New Jersey, almost all returning with money to remodel their houses, to build new ones for their married kids, or to invest in small businesses. Most of the families still rely on coffee for their cash even though coffee prices have sunk to historic lows. One local large landowner is even rumored to be planning a switch to pineapples.

The Rivas site has slowly become overgrown, for the most part, as the tall grasses, trees, and vines of the *monte* have reclaimed the spaces that we so carefully denuded for our studies. We have analyzed our sherds and stone tools and packed them in boxes. We are finalizing our inventory of the remains and will soon officially hand over the collection to the National Museum.

The archaeologists who filled some of the pages of this book are generally doing well. Aida Blanco still works at the National University and lives in the area. Francisco Corrales got his Ph.D. at the University of Kansas and is, as of this writing, acting director of the National Museum. Miguel Espinosa has been working for a private archaeology firm in Wisconsin. Bill Doonan received his Ph.D. and got a job at Sacramento City College, where he recently won tenure. Larry Conyers also got his doctorate, then a job and tenure at Denver University. Chris Raymond is in Hawaii. Andrew Gordon was in Washington, D.C., but recently went to South Africa to work for a program of community development that sets up local basketball teams for troubled youths. Jeff Frost is a graduate student and Ph.D. candidate at the University of Wisconsin, Madison. This summer, he is digging in the back dirt of looter holes on the Panteón de La Reina as his dissertation project and is now learning about the ridge-top cemeteries in detail. I visited him on my most recent trip to the area.

I am still at Dumbarton Oaks and have spent a lot of my spare time at home, writing this book. In 1999, I went back to Peru after an eleven-year absence. I have gotten involved in a wonderful project there working with fine colleagues. Although I plan to continue my research in Peru, I have to admit that when I was up on the Panteón this summer I recognized something magical about the place. It wasn't the sad-looking, pockmarked landscape of looter holes that enchanted me but instead the view of that beautiful country— with the mists sweeping off the mountain slopes and the broad vista down the valley with the coastal hills in the far distance. No matter where I may go, I have a feeling I'll be returning to this place for many years to come.

APPENDIX

TABLE A1. Radiocarbon Assays

Chart	Beta #	Locale	Conv (B.P.)	Intcpt (A.D.)	2 Sigma (A.D.)	1 Sigma (A.D.)	Analysis
A1	54745	S44/E14 (42–53)	900±80	1160	990–1280	1030–1230	St.
A3	54747	S40–41/E30.5–31.5 (30–40)	660±70	1300	1250–1420	1280–1400	St.
C1	146200	W11.8/S8.7 (20–40)ᵃ	1080±40	980	890–1020	910–920 & 960–1000	AMS
C2	146201	S7.7/W8.9/A11 (130)	560±40	1410	1300–1430	1320–1340 & 1390–1420	AMS
C3	54748	S9.5/W7.7 (125)ᵇ	710±70	1290	1200–1400	1260–1300	St.
D1	54742	N34–35/W25–26 (40–50)	970±60	1030	980–1200	1010–1160	St.
D2	54743	N50–51/E6–7 (65–75)	870±80	1180	1010–1290	1040–1260	St.
D3	54744	N38–39/W31–32 (100–110)	920±110	*	900–1290	1010–1240	St.
E1	65944	S6–7/E36–37 (40–50)	980±70	1025	910–920 & 955–1210	1000–1155	Ext.
E2	65943	N0/E17 (40–50)	820±50	1225	1055–1085 & 1150–1285	1185–1265	St.
E3	65947	N2/E14 (10–24)	690±70	1290	1220–1410	1270–1310 & 1360–1385	Ext.
E4	65946	N2/E14 (24–51)	1250±70	770	655–965	680–875	Ext.
E5	65945	N0/E14 (51–53)	900±110	1160	910–920 & 955–1295	1015–1255	Ext.
J1	146202	N295/W105 (20–30)	900±70	1160	1000–1270	1030–1220	Ext.
J3	146204	N294/W105 (20–30)	990±110	1020	790–1270	970–1180	Ext.
J4	103150	N295/W108 (30–40)ᶜ	1050±60	1170	1015–1265	1035–1220	St.
K1	103149	T4 S5.40/W20.70 (40–45)	990±60	1025	970–1195	1000–1055 & 1090–1150	St.
Questionable Dates							
A2	54746	N64–65/E18–19 (30–35)	3380±60	B.C. 1680	B.C. 1870–50 & 1780–1520	B.C. 1740–1610	Ext.
J2	146203	N295/W106 (20–30)	1690±220	380	B.C. 170–A.D. 770	90–610	St.
K2	103148	T2 (50)	5380±70	B.C. 4240	B.C. 4350–4015	B.C. 4330–4140	Ext.

ᵃC1 = T6/ Grp 1/A2; C3 = T5; ᵇD3 Intercepts = A.D. 1060, 1080, & 1150; ᶜJ4 = Hearth

Key: "Conv (B.P.)" = conventional date, B.P.; "Incpt (A.D.)" = intercept, A.D.; "Sigmas" = standard deviations;
"St." = standard radiometric analysis; "Ext." = radiometric analysis with extended counting time;
"AMS" = Accelerator Mass Spectography

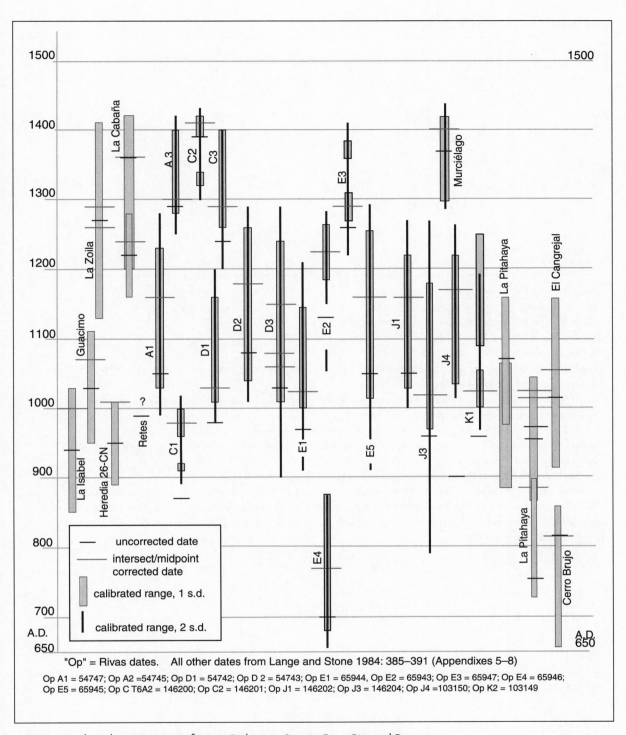

CHART A2. Radiocarbon Age Ranges for Late Prehistoric Sites in Costa Rica and Panama

TABLE A3. Artifacts from Looter Holes on the Panteón de La Reina

Looter Hole	BAP[1]	Papayal	Red Wares	Ceiba	No ID[2]	Body Sherds	Lithics	MNI[3]
A	-	-	-	4	-	28	-	1
B[4]	-	-	100	-	16	33	2	3
C	2	-	3	1	17	173	7	3
D[5]	-	-	3	3	-	48	3	2
E[6]	5	6	-	3	12	100	2	6
F[7]	34	-	34	66	-	305	1	3
I[8]	7	2	11	27	-	185	1	6
J[9]	9	21	1	4	-	136	3	4
K[10]	9	3	9	6	-	101	-	5
V[11]	50	-	69	97	3	286	4	25+

[1] BAP = Buenos Aires Polychrome.

[2] No ID = Unidentified ceramic types.

[3] MNI = Minimum Number of Individual ceramics.

[4] The 100 sherds in "Red Wares" appear to come from a single vessel.

[5] One solid tripod leg in collection.

[6] Looter Hole E was large and likely comprised more than one looting activity, possibly more than one burial. A sartén handle and part of the pan were included in this lot.

[7] Materials from this deposit consisted of eight bags containing 134 sherds, about half of them Ceiba, one quarter Buenos Aires Polychrome, and a quarter Red Wares.

[8] Two additional hollow tripod legs, possibly Buenos Aires Polychrome, found in this lot.

[9] One solid tripod leg, probably from a Papayal Engraved vessel, and three hollow tripod legs, one from a Fish Ware vessel, found in this lot.

[10] Eight hollow tripod legs and two miniature vessel fragments found in this lot.

[11] Estimates suggest there were 3 Buenos Aires Polychrome vessels, 10 Red Ware vessels, possibly 2 Ceiba vessels, 2 Ceiba-like miniature vessels, 1 Seúl Grabado vessel, 3 unusual sherds, and 1 plain vessel. In addition, the lot also included 1 spindle whorl, the figurine of the woman with a pot (see fig. 7.7), one stone flake, and 2 bags of fragments of a probable "jaguar" metate.

REFERENCES CITED

Aguilar Piedra, Carlos H.
1972   *Guayabo de Turrialba: Arqueología de un sitio indígena
       Prehispánico.* Editorial Costa Rica, San José.
1975   El Molino: Un sitio de la Fase Pavas en Cartago.
       Vínculos 1(1): 18–56.
1976   Relaciones de las culturas Precolombinas en el
       Intermontano Central de Costa Rica. *Vínculos*
       2(1): 75–77.

Balser, Carlos
1971   Una Extensión de la cultura de los Barriles de
       Panamá en Territorio Costarricense. *La Nación,*
       November 8. San José.

Baudez, Claude F., and Michael D. Coe
1962   Archaeological Sequences in Northwestern
       Costa Rica. *Actas, 34th International Congress of
       Americanists (Vienna 1960).* pp. 366–373.

Baudez, Claude F., Nathalie Borgnino, Sophie Laligant,
       and Valerie Lauthelin
1993   *Investigaciones arqueológicas en el Delta del Diquís.*
       Centro de Estudios Mexicanos y Centroaméri-
       canos (México) y La Delegación Regional de
       Cooperación Científica y Técnica en América
       Central, San José.

Benson, Elizabeth P.
1997   *Birds and Beasts of Ancient Latin America.* Univer-
       sity Press of Florida, Gainesville.
———, ed.
1981   *Between Continents/Between Seas: Precolumbian Art
       of Costa Rica.* Harry N. Abrams, New York.

Boas, Franz
1982 [1940] *Race, Language, and Culture.* University of
       Chicago Press, Chicago.

Bozzoli de Wille, María Eugenia
1966   *Observaciones arqueológicas en los valles del Parrita y del
       General Boletín de la Asociación de Amigos del Museo
       19* (mimeograph). Museo Nacional de Costa Rica,
       San José.

Bray, Warwick
1978   *The Gold of El Dorado.* Catalog of exhibition at
       the Royal Academy, Piccadilly, London, Novem-
       ber 21, 1978–March 18, 1979. Times Newspa-
       pers Limited, London.
1981   Gold Work. In *Between Continents/Between Seas:
       Precolumbian Art of Costa Rica,* E. Benson, ed., pp.
       153–158. Harry N. Abrams, New York.

Brook, Frederico, and Vittorio Minardi
1976   *Arte Precolombiana: Costa Rica/Panama.* Istituto
        italo-americano, Rome.

Brumfiel, Elizabeth M., and Timothy K. Earle
1987   Specialization, Exchange, and Complex Soci-
        eties: An Introduction. In *Specialization, Exchange,
        and Complex Societies*, E. M. Brumfiel and T. K.
        Earle, eds., pp. 1–9. Cambridge University Press,
        Cambridge.

Burger, Richard L.
1992   *Chavin and the Origins of Andean Civilization.*
        Thames and Hudson, New York.

Carneiro, Robert
1967   On the Relationship between Size of Population
        and Complexity of Social Organization. *South-
        western Journal of Anthropology* 23: 234–243.
1970   A Theory of the Origin of the State. *Science* 169:
        733–738.
1981   The Chiefdom: Precursor of the State. In *Transi-
        tion to Statehood in the New World*, G. Jones and R.
        Kautz, eds., pp. 37–79. Cambridge University
        Press, Cambridge.
1998   What Happened at the Flashpoint? Conjectures
        on Chiefdom Formation at the Very Moment of
        Conception. In *Chiefdoms and Chieftaincy in the
        Americas*, E. M. Redmond, ed., pp. 18–42. Uni-
        versity Press of Florida, Gainesville.

Carsten, Janet, and Stephen Hugh-Jones
1995   *About the House: Lévi-Strauss and Beyond.* Cam-
        bridge University Press, Cambridge.

Chávez Chávez, Sergio
1993   *Guayabo de Turrialba: Pasado y presente. 10° aniversario
        trabajo comunal Universitario Guayabo de Turrialba.*
        Universidad de Costa Rica, Vicerrectoria de Ac-
        ción Social, San José.

Clendinnen, Inga
1991   *Aztecs: An Interpretation.* Cambridge University
        Press, Cambridge.

Coggins, Clemency Chase, and Orrin C. Shane III, eds.
1984   *Cenote of Sacrifice: Maya Treasures from the Sacred
        Well at Chichén Itzá.* Exhibition Catalog. Univer-
        sity of Texas Press, Austin.

Cooke, Richard, Luis Alberto Sánchez Herrera, and Koichi
        Udagawa
2000   Contextualized Gold from "Gran Coclé,"
        Panama. In *Precolumbian Gold: Technology, Style and
        Iconography*, C. McEwan ed., pp. 154–176. Fitzroy
        Dearborn, Chicago.

Corrales, Francisco
1983   Prospección y excavaciones estratigráficas en el
        sitio Curré (P-62-Ce), Valle de Diquís, Costa
        Rica. *Vínculos* 11:1–15.
1986   Nota sobre la arqueología de Quebradas, Valle de
        General. *Boletín de la Asociación Costarricense de Ar-
        queólogos*, pp. 12–16. San José.

Corrales U., Francisco, Ifigénia Quintanilla J., and Orlando
        Barrantes C.
1988   *Historia Precolombina y de los siglos XVI y XVII del
        sureste de Costa Rica.* Proyecto Investigación y Pro-
        moción de La Cultura Popular y Tradicional Del
        Pacífico Sur, O.E.A./M.C.J.D., San José.

Corrales Ulloa, Francisco
2000   "An Evaluation of Long Term Cultural Change
        in Southern Central America: The Ceramic
        Record of the Diquís Archaeological Subregion,
        Southern Costa Rica." Ph.D. diss., University of
        Kansas.

Corrales Ulloa, Francisco, and Ifigénia Quintanilla Jiménez
1996   The Archaeology of the Central Pacific Coast of
        Costa Rica. In *Paths to Central American Prehistory*.
        F. W. Lange, ed., pp. 93–117. University Press of
        Colorado, Niwot.

Creamer, Winifred, and Johnathan Haas
1985   Tribe versus Chiefdom in Lower Central Amer-
        ica. *American Antiquity* 50: 738–754.

Descola, Phillipe
1993   *The Spears of Twilight: Life and Death in the Amazon
        Jungle.* Janet Lloyd, trans. New Press, New York.

Dietler, Michael, and Brian Hayden, eds.
2001   *Feasts: Archaeological and Ethnographic Perspectives on
        Food, Politics, and Power.* Smithsonian Institution
        Press, Washington, D.C.

Drolet, Robert

1983 Al otro lado de Chiriquí, el Diquís: Nuevos datos para la integración cultural de la región Gran Chiriquí. *Vínculos* 9 (1–2): 25–76.

1984a Community Life in a Late Phase Chiefdom Village, Southwestern Costa Rica. In *Recent Developments in Isthmian Archaeology: Advances in the Prehistory of Lower Central America*, F. W. Lange, ed., pp. 123–154. BAR International Series 212, Oxford.

1984b A Note on Southwestern Costa Rica. In *The Archaeology of Lower Central America*. F. W. Lange and D. Z. Stone, eds., pp. 254–262. University of New Mexico Press, Albuquerque.

1986 Social Grouping and Residential Activities within a Late Phase Polity Network: Diquís Valley, Southeastern Costa Rica. In *Prehistoric Settlement Patterns in Costa Rica*, F. W. Lange and L. Norr, eds. *Journal of the Steward Anthropological Society* 14(1–2): 325–338.

1988 The Emergence and Intensification of Complex Societies in Pacific Southern Costa Rica. In *Archaeology and Art in Costa Rican Prehistory*, F. W. Lange, ed., pp. 163–188. University of Colorado Press, Boulder.

1992 The House and the Territory: The Organizational Structure for Chiefdom Art in the Diquís Subregion of Greater Chiriquí. In *Wealth and Hierarchy in the Intermediate Area*. F. W. Lange, ed., pp. 207–242. Dumbarton Oaks, Washington, D.C.

n.d. Zonas funerárias del sítio Murciélago. Manuscript in possession of the author.

Earle, Timothy

1977 A Reappraisal of Redistribution: Complex Hawaiian Chiefdoms. In *Exchange Systems in Prehistory*. T. K. Earle and J. E. Ericson, eds., pp. 213–229. Academic Press, New York.

1978 Economic and Social Organization of a Complex Chiefdom: The Hidden District, Kaua'i, Hawaii. *Museum of Anthropology, Anthropological Papers* 63. University of Michigan, Ann Arbor.

1981 Chiefdoms in Archaeological and Ethnohistorical Perspective. *Annual Review of Anthropology* 16: 279–308.

1991 *Chiefdoms: Power, Economy, and Ideology.* School of American Research and Cambridge University Press, Santa Fe, N.M., and Cambridge.

1997 *How Chiefs Came to Power: The Political Economy in Prehistory.* Stanford University Press, Palo Alto, Calif.

Emmons, Louise H.

1999 *Mamíferos de los bosques humedos de América tropical. Una guia de campo.* Editorial F.A.N., Santa Cruz de la Sierra, Bolivia.

Feinman, Gary, and Jill Neitzel

1984 Too Many Types: An Overview of Sedentary Prestate Societies in the Americas. In *Advances in Archaeological Method and Theory*, Vol. 7, M. B. Schiffer, ed., pp. 39–102. Academic Press, New York.

Fernández Esquivel, Patrícia, and Ifigénia Quintanilla

2003 Metallurgy and Statuary in the Diquís Delta, Costa Rica: Local Production of Symbols of Power. In *Gold and Power in Ancient Costa Rica, Panama, and Colombia*, J. Quilter and J. Hoopes, eds. Dumbarton Oaks, Washington, D.C.

Fernández Guardia, Ricardo

1964 *Cartas de Juan Vásquez de Coronado.* Academia de Geografía e História de Costa Rica, San José.

Ferrero, Luis

1987 *Costa Rica Precolombina: Arqueología, etnohistória, tecnología y arte.* 5th ed. Biblioteca Patria No. 6. Editorial Costa Rica, San José.

Fonseca Zamora, Oscar Manuel

1979 Informe de la primera temporada de reexcavación de Guayabo de Turrialba. *Vínculos* 5(1–2): 35–52.

1981 Guayabo de Turrialba and Its Significance. In *Between Continents/Between Seas: Precolumbian Art of Costa Rica*, E. Benson, ed., pp. 104–109. Harry N. Abrams, New York.

1983 Historia de las investigaciones en la región de Guayabo. *Actas del IX Congreso Internacional para el Estudio de las Culturas Precolombinas de las Antillas Menores.* Centre de Rechèrches Caribes, Université de Montreal, Montreal.

1984 Reflexiones sobre la investigación arqueológica en Costa Rica: Una perspectiva histórica. In *Interregional Ties in Costa Rican Prehistory*, E. Skirboll and W. Creamer, eds., pp. 15–27. BAR International Series 226, Oxford.

Fragoso, J. M.

1991   The Effect of Selective Logging on Baird's Tapir. In *Latin American Mammalogy, History, Biodiversity, and Conservation*, M. A. Mares and D. J. Schmidly, eds., pp. 295–304. University of Oklahoma Press, Norman.

Fried, Morton

1967   *The Evolution of Political Society*. Random House, New York.

Gabb, Wm. M.

1875   On the Indian Tribes and Languages of Costa Rica. *American Philosophical Society* 14: 483–602.

Geertz, Clifford

1980   *Negara: The Theatre State in Nineteenth-Century Bali*. Princeton University Press, Princeton, N.J.

1988   *Works and Lives: The Anthropologist as Author*. Stanford University Press, Palo Alto, Calif.

Haberland, Wolfgang

1955   Preliminary Report on the Aguas Buenas Complex, Costa Rica. *Ethnos* 20(4): 224–230.

1959a   Chiriquían Pottery Types. *Panama Archaeologist* 2: 52–55.

1959b   Re-Appraisal of Chiriquían Pottery Types. *Actas, 33rd International Congress of Americanists, (San José)* 2: 339–346.

1961a   New Names for Chiriquían Pottery Types. *Panama Archaeologist* 4: 56–60.

1961b   Arqeuología del valle del Rio Ceiba, Buenos Aires. *Instituto Geográfico de Costa Rica, Informe Semesteral (January–June)*: 31–62.

1968   Las figuras líticas de barriles, en Panamá. *Boletín del Museo Chiricano* 6: 8–14.

1976   Gran Chiriquí. *Vínculos* 2(1): 115–121.

Harrison, Regina

1989   *Signs, Songs, and Memory in the Andes: Translating Quechua Language and Culture*. University of Texas Press, Austin.

Hartman, Carl V.

1901   *Archaeological Researches in Costa Rica*. Royal Ethnographical Museum, Stockholm.

1907   Archaeological Researches on the Pacific Coast of Costa Rica. *Memoirs, Carnegie Museum* 3(1). Pittsburgh.

Hearne, Pamela, and Robert J. Sharer, eds.

1992   *River of Gold: Precolumbian Treasures from Sitio Conte*. University Museum of Archaeology and Anthropology, University of Pennsylvania, Philadelphia.

Hegmon, Michelle

2003   Setting Theoretical Egos Aside: Issues and Theory in North American Archaeology. *American Antiquity* 68: 213–244.

Helms, Mary W.

1979   *Ancient Panama: Chiefs in Search of Power*. University of Texas Press, Austin.

1994   Chiefdom Rivalries, Control, and External Contacts in Lower Central America. In *Factional Competition and Political Development in the New World*, E. M. Brumfiel and J. W. Fox, eds., pp. 55–60. Cambridge University Press, Cambridge.

Holmes, William H.

1888   *Ancient Art of the Province of Chiriquí, Colombia*. Sixth Annual Report, Smithsonian Institution, Bureau of American Ethnology, Washington, D.C.

Hoopes, John W.

1996a   *In Search of Nature: Imagining the Precolumbian Landscapes of Ancient Central America*. Working paper for the Nature and Culture Colloquium, Joyce and Elizabeth Hall Center for the Humanities, University of Kansas, Lawrence. Published online at http://www.cc.ukans.edu/~hoopes/nature.html.

1996b   Settlement, Subsistence, and the Origins of Social Complexity in Greater Chiriquí: A Reappraisal of the Aguas Buenas Tradition. In *Paths to Central American Prehistory*. F. W. Lange, ed., pp. 15–47. University Press of Colorado, Niwot.

Iwaniec, Ursula

1986   La Pista Cemetery: Site Report. On file, Museo Nacional de Costa Rica, San José.

Jones, Julie, ed.

1998   *Jade in Ancient Costa Rica*. Metropolitan Museum of Art, New York.

Katz, Lois, ed.

1985   *Art of Costa Rica: Pre-Columbian Painted and Sculpted Ceramics from the Arthur M. Sackler Collections.* Arthur M. Sackler Foundation and the AMS Foundation for the Arts, Sciences, and Humanities, Washington, D.C.

Kirkpatrick, Sidney D.

1992   *Lords of Sipan: A True Story of Pre-Inca Tombs, Archaeology, and Crime.* William Morrow, New York.

Knight, Vernon James

2001   Feasting and the Emergence of Platform Mound Ceremonialism in Eastern North America. In *Feasts: Archaeological and Ethnographic Perspectives on Food, Politics, and Power,* M. Dietler and B. Hayden, eds., pp. 311–333. Smithsonian Institution Press, Washington, D.C.

Kudarauskas, M. O., Olga Linares, and I. Borgogno

1980   Ceramic Classes from Bocas del Toro Sites (CA-3 and CA-2). In *Adaptive Radiations in Prehistoric Panama,* O. F. Linares and A. J. Ranere, eds., pp. 385–393. Peabody Museum Monographs No. 5. Harvard University, Cambridge.

Lange, Frederick W., ed.

1992   *Wealth and Hierarchy in the Intermediate Area.* Dumbarton Oaks, Washington, D.C.

1993   *Precolumbian Jade: New Geological and Cultural Interpretations.* University of Utah Press, Salt Lake City.

Lange, Frederick W., and Doris Z. Stone, eds.

1984   *The Archaeology of Lower Central America.* University of New Mexico Press, Albuquerque.

Laurenchich de Minelli, Laura, and Luigi Minelli

1966   Informe preliminar sobre excavaciones alrededor de San Vito de Java. *Actas XXXVI Congreso Internacional de Americanistas (Roma-Geneva):* 1: 219–224.

Levi-Strauss, Claude

1969   *The Raw and the Cooked: Introduction to a Science of Mythology 1.* J. Weightman and D. Weightman, trans. Harper and Row, New York.

Linares, Olga F.

1980   The Ceramic Record: Time and Place. In *Adaptive Radiations in Prehistoric Panama,* O. F. Linares and A. J. Ranere, eds., pp. 81–117. Peabody Museum Monograph No. 5. Harvard University, Cambridge.

Linares, Olga F., and Anthony J. Ranere, eds.

1980   *Adaptive Radiations in Prehistoric Panama.* Peabody Museum Monograph No. 5. Harvard University, Cambridge.

Linares de Sapir, Olga F.

1968   Cultural Chronology of the Gulf of Chiriquí. *Smithsonian Contributions to Anthropology* 8. Washington, D.C.

Lothrop, Samuel K.

1926   *The Pottery of Costa Rica and Nicaragua.* 2 vols. Contribution 8. Museum of the American Indian, Heye Foundation, New York.

1937   Coclé: An Archaeological Study of Central Panama, Part 1. *Memoirs of the Peabody Museum of Archaeology and Ethnology,* Vol. 7. Harvard University, Cambridge.

1942   Coclé: An Archaeological Study of Central Panama, Part 2. *Memoirs of the Peabody Museum of Archaeology and Ethnology,* Vol. 7. Harvard University, Cambridge.

1963   Archaeology of the Diquís Delta, Costa Rica. *Papers of the Peabody Museum of Archaeology and Ethnology* 51. Harvard University, Cambridge.

1966   Archaeology of Lower Central America. In *Handbook of Middle American Indians* 4: 180–208. University of Texas Press, Austin.

MacCurdy, George Grant

1911   A Study of Chiriquian Antiquities. *Memoirs of the Connecticut Academy of Arts and Sciences* 3. New Haven, Conn.

Mason, J. Alden

1942   New Excavations at the Sitio Conte, Coclé, Panama. In *Proceedings of the Eighth American Scientific Congress,* Vol. 2, pp. 103–107. Department of State, Washington, D.C.

Mills, Barbara J., ed.

2000 *Alternative Leadership Strategies in the Prehispanic Southwest.* University of Arizona Press, Tucson.

Morgan, Lewis Henry

1877 *Ancient Society, or, Researches in the Lines of Human Savagery through Barbarism to Civilization.* H. Holt, New York.

Morison, Samuel Eliot

1963 *Journals and Other Documents on the Life and Voyages of Christopher Columbus.* Heritage Press, New York.

Oberg, Kalervo

1955 Types of Social Structure among the Lowland Tribes of South and Central America. *American Anthropologist* 57: 472–487.

Oviedo y Valdés, Gonzalo Fernández de

1959 *A Natural History of the West Indies.* A. Stoudemire, trans. and ed. *University of North Carolina Studies in the Romance Languages and Literatures* 32. University of North Carolina Press, Chapel Hill.

Patterson, Thomas C.

1994 *Towards a Social History of Archaeology in the United States.* Case Studies in Archaeology. Harcourt Brace, Fort Worth, Tex.

Pauketat, Timothy R.

1994 *The Ascent of Chiefs: Cahokia and Mississippian Politics in Native North America.* University of Alabama Press, Tuscaloosa.

Pérez Zeledón, Pedro

1907–08 *Las llanuras de Pirrís valle del Río General ó Grande de Térraba.* Informes Presentados a la Secretaria de Fomento. Tipografía Nacional, San José.

Pittier, H.

1892 Viaje de exploración al Río Grande de Térraba. Estudios Científicos X. *Annales del Instituto Físico-Geográfico y del Museo Nacional de Costa Rica. Tomo III, 1890.* Tipografía Nacional, San José.

Quilter, Jeffrey

1985 Architecture and Chronology at El Paraíso, Peru. *Journal of Field Archaeology* 12(3): 279–297.

1989 *Life and Death at Paloma, Society and Mortuary Practices in a Preceramic Peruvian Village.* University of Iowa Press, Iowa City.

1991 Late Preceramic Peru. *Journal of World Prehistory* 5(4): 387–438.

2000 The General and the Queen, Gold Objects from a Ceremonial and Mortuary Complex in Southern Costa Rica. In *Pre-Columbian Gold: Technology and Iconography,* C. McEwan, ed., pp. 177–195. British Museum Press; Fitzroy and Dearborn, Chicago.

Quilter, Jeffrey, and Aida Blanco

1995 Monumental Architecture and Social Organization at the Rivas Site, Costa Rica. *Journal of Field Archaeology* 22(2): 203–221.

Quilter, Jeffrey, and Terry Stocker

1985 Subsistence Economies and the Origins of Andean Complex Societies. *American Anthropologist* 85: 545–562.

Quintanilla Jiménez, Ifigénia

1943 Prospección arqueológica del Delta Sierpe-Térraba, sureste de Costa Rica: Proyecto hombre y ambiente en el Delta Sierpe-Térraba (Informe 1). MS., Depto. de Antropología e Historia, Museo Nacional de Costa Rica, San José.

Redmond, Elsa M., ed.

1998 *Chiefdoms and Chieftancy in the Americas.* University Press of Florida, Gainesville.

Reichel-Dolmatoff, Gerado

1976 Training for the Priesthood among the Kogi of Colombia. In *Enculturation in Latin America: An Anthology,* J. Wilbert, ed. *UCLA Latin American Studies* 37: 265–288. University of California, Los Angeles.

1985 *Los Kogi.* 2nd ed. Editorial Iqueima, Bogotá.

Roe, Peter G.

1982 *The Cosmic Zygote, Cosmology and the Amazon Basin.* Rutgers University Press. New Brunswick, N.J.

Roosevelt, Anna Curtenius

1991   *Moundbuilders of the Amazon: Geophysical Archaeology on Marajó Island, Brazil.* Academic Press, San Diego, Calif.

Rowe, John H.

1946   Inca Culture at the Time of the Spanish Conquest. In *Handbook of South American Indians*, Vol. 2. J. H. Steward, ed., pp. 183–330. Government Printing Office, Washington, D.C.

Sabloff, Jeremy A.

1990   *The New Archaeology and the Ancient Maya.* Scientific American Library, New York.

Saunders, Nicholas J.

1988   Stealers of Light, Traders in Brilliance: Amerindian Metaphysics in the Mirror of Conquest. *RES, Anthropology and Aesthetics* 33 (1): 225–252.

in press   Catching the Light: The Technologies of Power and Enchantment in Pre-Columbian Goldworking. In *Gold and Power in Ancient Costa Rica, Panama, and Colombia*, J. Quilter and J. Hoopes, eds. Dumbarton Oaks, Washington, D.C.

Schele, Linda, and Mary Ellen Miller

1986   *The Blood of Kings, Dynasty and Ritual in Maya Art.* George Braziller, New York, in association with the Kimbell Art Museum, Fort Worth, Tex.

Service, Elman R.

1962   *Primitive Social Organization*, 2nd ed. Random House, New York.

1993   *Origins of the State and Civilization: The Process of Cultural Evolution.* W. W. Norton, New York.

Sheets, Payson D., E. J. Rosenthal, and A. J. Ranere

1980   Stone Tools from Volcan Baru. In *Adaptive Radiations in Prehistoric Panama*, O. F. Linares and A. J. Ranere, eds., pp. 404–428. Peabody Museum Monographs, No. 5. Harvard University, Cambridge.

Skutch, Alexander F.

1991   *A Naturalist in Costa Rica.* University Press of Florida, Gainesville.

Snarskis, Michael J.

1979   Turrialba: A Paleoindian Quarry and Workshop Site in Eastern Costa Rica. *American Antiquity* 44: 125–138.

1982   *La Cerámica Precolombina en Costa Rica.* Instituto Nacionál de Seguros, San José.

1984   Central America: The Lower Caribbean. In *The Archaeology of Lower Central America*, F. W. Lange and D. Z. Stone eds., pp. 195–232. University of New Mexico Press, Albuquerque.

1992   Wealth and Hierarchy in the Archaeology of Eastern and Central Costa Rica. In *Wealth and Hierarchy in the Intermediate Area*, F. W. Lange, ed., pp. 141–164. Dumbarton Oaks, Washington, D. C.

2003   From Jade to Gold in Costa Rica: How, Why, and When. In *Gold and Power in Ancient Costa Rica, Panama, and Colombia*, J. Quilter and J. W. Hoopes, eds., pp. 159–204. Dumbarton Oaks, Washington, D.C.

Stone, Doris Z.

1943a   Una inspección ligera del llano del Río Grande de Térraba, Costa Rica. *Sociedad de Geografía e Historia de Costa Rica*, No. 4, pp. 41–54.

1943b   A Preliminary Investigation of the Flood Plain of the Río Grande de Térraba, Costa Rica. *American Antiquity* 9: 74–88.

1962   The Talamancan Tribes of Costa Rica. *Peabody Museum Papers* 48 (2). Harvard University, Cambridge.

1972   *Pre-Columbian Man Finds Central America.* Peabody Museum Press, Harvard University, Cambridge.

1977   *Pre-Columbian Man in Costa Rica.* Peabody Museum Press, Harvard University, Cambridge.

1986   Pre-Columbian Trade in Costa Rica. In *Pre-Columbian Painted and Sculpted Ceramics from the Arthur M. Sackler Collection*, L. Katz ed., pp. 15–39. Arthur M. Sackler Foundation and the AMS Foundation for the Arts, Sciences, and Humanities, Washington, D.C.

Wafer, L.

1956 [1699]
    A New Voyage and Description of the Isthmus of America. G. P. Winship, ed. Burrows Brothers, Cleveland.

Wilbert, Johannes, and Karin Simoneau

1992   *The Folk Literature of South American Indians.* General Index. UCLA Latin American Publications. University of California, Los Angeles.

Wittfogel, Karl August

1957   *Oriental Despotism; A Comparative Study of Total Power.* Yale University Press, New Haven, Conn.

Wright, Henry T.

1984   Prestate Political Formations. In *On the Evolution of Complex Societies: Essays in Honor of Harry Hoijer 1982*, T. K. Earle, ed., pp. 41–77. Undena Publications, Malibu, Calif.

Zilberg, John

1986   The Diquís Petroglyphs: Distribution, Archaeological Context and Iconographic Content. In *Prehistoric Settlement Patterns in Costa Rica*, F. W. Lange and L. Norr, eds. *Journal of the Steward Anthropological Society* 14(1–2): 339–360.

INDEX

San Isidro de El General, 1, 3, 4, 5, 11, 12, 14, 18, 19, 23, 62, 67, 79, 82, 92, 114, 115, 116, 131, 140, 146, 149, 163, 201

San José de Cabécar, 187, 192

Sangria Fine Red. *See* ceramics

Service, Elman R., 16, 198

shadow corpses. *See* graves

sherds, 13, 23, 24, 100, 157, 186; analyses, 155, 156–160, 158, 169–174; at Murciélago, 156; exotic at Rivas, 163, *165*; in Op A, 28, 32, 33, 34, 40–41; in Op B, 37, 39; in Op D, 52, 53; in Op D'94, 90, 91, 93, 95, 104; in Op E, 71; in Op K, 120, *121*, 123; in Plaza, 108, 110; on Panteón de La Reina, 135, 136, 140, 141; textile impressed, 179–180, *179*

Shovel Test Pit surveys: discover Op J, 125; in Op A, 34–35, 37, 95, 116; near Op C, 79, 112; near Op D'94, 90–91, 93–95, 101, 102; of site, 95–99, *98*, 131; STOps, 10, 35, 95–96, *98*

sites: Las Brisas, 6, 151; Caracol, 142; Cerro Juan Díaz (Panama), 134; Cola de Pato, 142; Conté (Panama), 185; Curré (Rey Curré), 142, 186;

Finca Remolino, 143; Grijalva II, 8; Guayabo de Turrialba, 7, 8, 57; Limón, 12; Macho Monte, 142; Las Mercedes, 7, 8; Murciélago, 12, 14, 18, 24 27, 35, 44, 54–55, 101, 152, 183, 190, 197; Pacuar, 84; Palmar Sur, 8, 14, 17, 114, 160; San Andres, 142; San Vito de Java, 143; El Zoncho, 143, 173. *See also* cemeteries

Skutch, Alexander F., 4, 151

Snarskis, Michael J., 14, 178

soil: backdirt, 80–81; colors, 33, 44, 87, 152; depths, 5, 48, 52–54, 112; nature of in Op C, 42; preservation qualities of, 57–58. *See also* graves; Piedra Muerta Fill

sonda, 64

Southern Zone (*Zona Sur*), 1, *2,* 4, 6, 7, *7*, 12, 13, 27, 146, 163

space: binary categories of, 41; crowds in, 7, 51, 54, 72, 75, 101, 106, 111; of funeral Bribri funeral feasts, 190; Op J reversal of, 126–127; sacred vs. profane, 39, 40–41. *See also* architecture

spindle whorls. *See* ceramics

stone: adzes/celts, 28, 45, *45*, 47, 136;

balls, 8, *8,* 11,13, 28, 114, 139–140, 142, 143, 150, 179, 194; barrels, 28; chipped artifacts, 21, 28, 37, 39, 174, *174;* freestanding sculpture, 7, 8, 117, 143, 178, 180; *lajas* (slabs), 44, 119, 120, 121, 123, 136, 143; manos, 21, 156, 157, 177; metates, 6, 21, 39, 40, 47, *175;* quartz crystals, 174; sources, 84, 139; tool production in Op B, 37; whetstone, 30–31. *See also* pillars

Talamanca Mountains, 4, 6, 9, 18

Tarragó Biscuit Ware. *See* ceramics

Tenedor Restaurant, 116

textiles, 169, 179–180, *179*

Tiahuanaco. *See* Huari and Tiahuanaco

tinkuy, 5

tropical forest. *See* forest

Turucaca province, 194, *195*

Turucaca White-on-Red. *See* ceramics

Tylor, Edward B., 16

Walker, William, 11

warfare, 7, 13

water sources at sites, 41

whistles. *See* musical instruments

Wittfogel, Karl A., 17